Employment, Trade Union Renewal and the Future of Work

The Future of Work Series

Series Editor: **Peter Nolan**, Director of the ESRC Future of Work
Programme and the Montague Burton Professor of Industrial Relations
at Leeds University Business School in the UK.

Few subjects could be judged more vital to current policy and academic debates
than the prospects for work and employment. *The Future of
Work* series provides the much needed evidence and theoretical
advances to enhance our understanding of the critical developments
most likely to impact on people's working lives.

Titles include:

Julia Brannen, Peter Moss and Ann Mooney
WORKING AND CARING OVER THE TWENTIETH CENTURY
Change and Continuity in Four Generation Families

Geraldine Healy, Edmund Heery, Phil Taylor and William Brown (*editors*)
THE FUTURE OF WORKER REPRESENTATION

Paul Stewart (*editor*)
EMPLOYMENT, TRADE UNION RENEWAL AND THE FUTURE OF WORK
The Experience of Work and Organisational Change

Michael White, Stephen Hill, Colin Mills and Deborah Smeaton
MANAGING TO CHANGE?
British Workplaces and the Future of Work

The Future of Work Series
Series Standing Order ISBN 1–4039–1477–X

You can receive future titles in this series as they are published by placing a standing order.
Please contact your bookseller or, in case of difficulty, write to us at the address below with
your name and address, the title of the series and one of the ISBNs quoted above.

Customer Services Department, Macmillan Distribution Ltd, Houndmills, Basingstoke,
Hampshire RG21 6XS, England

Employment, Trade Union Renewal and the Future of Work

The Experience of Work and Organisational Change

Edited by

Paul Stewart
University of the West of England
UK

First published 2005 by
PALGRAVE MACMILLAN
Houndmills, Basingstoke, Hampshire RG21 6XS and
175 Fifth Avenue, New York, N. Y. 10010
Companies and representatives throughout the world.

PALGRAVE MACMILLAN is the global academic imprint of the Palgrave Macmillan division of St. Martin's Press, LLC and of Palgrave Macmillan Ltd. Macmillan® is a registered trademark in the United States, United Kingdom and other countries. Palgrave is a registered trademark in the European Union and other countries.

ISBN 1–4039–1227–0 hardback

This book is printed on paper suitable for recycling and made from fully managed and sustained forest sources.

A catalogue record for this book is available from the British Library.

Library of Congress Cataloging-in-Publication Data

    Employment, trade union renewal, and the future of work : the experience of work and organisational change / edited by Paul Stewart.
      p. cm. – (The future of work)
    "This book arises out of a conference held at the Centre for Employment Studies Research at Bristol Business School in 2001 sponsored by the ESTC's Future of Work Programme"– Intord.
    Includes bibliographical references and index.
    ISBN 1–4039–1227–0 (cloth)
    1. Labor market – Great Britain – Congresses. 2. Foreign trade and employment – Great Britain – Congresses. 3. Labor unions – Great Britain – Congresses. 4. Industrial relations – Great Britain – Congresses. 5. Organizational change – Great Britain – Congresses. 6. Work environment – Great Britain – Congresses. 7. Globalization – Economic aspects – Great Britain – Congresses. I. Stewart, Paul, 1956 – II. Future of work (Series)

HD5765.A6G56 2005
331.1'0941—dc22   2004053035

10 9 8 7 6 5 4 3 2
14 13 12 11 10 09 08 07 06 05

Printed and bound in Great Britain by
Antony Rowe Ltd, Chippenham and Eastbourne.

Contents

v

Foreword

Globalisation and the wider application of new information and communication technologies are commonly cited as the key drivers of change in workplaces in both the advanced and newly developing economies. There is no doubt that the changes in the way that work is organised and managed are significant, but should we attribute all of the shifts to international market and technological forces? What role are employers and employees playing in shaping contemporary employment practices and the future of work? What are the new patterns of employment segmentation, subordination and inequality? And how are employees and their representative organisations responding to the challenges of the new management practices and the restructuring of organisations?

This important new book addresses these and other pressing questions. Reporting new research findings from the Economic and Social Research Council Future of Work Programme, the book scrutinises the nature and content of change management and the implications for the shape of organisations and the experience of paid work. It reveals that global tendencies do not necessarily dictate developments at national, sector and workplace levels. The interplay of forces is far more complex than some commentators claim.

The Future of Work Programme involved more than one hundred researchers at twenty-two UK universities. With a focus on changes in both paid and unpaid work in the UK, the research teams placed current developments and prospects in the UK in a wider international context. This is the fourth research monograph in the Palgrave Macmillan Future of Work Series. Bringing together the work of specialists in sociology, management, industrial relations, it represents a major contribution to the evidence base that is required by academics, policy-makers and practitioners with a stake in shaping the future of work.

PETER NOLAN
Programme Director

Director
ESRC Future of Work Programme

Notes on Contributors

Peter Bain is Senior Lecturer in the Department of HRM at the University of Strathclyde, Glasgow, and worked in the engineering and car industries before entering the groves of *academe*. Areas in which he has researched and published include occupational health and safety, workplace technological change, and contemporary developments in trade unionism. A lead applicant in a joint Scottish universities' project researching work in call centres and software development, funded under the ESRC's 'Future of Work' programme, he has also recently studied work and employment relations in call centres in the UK, as well as in the US, Netherlands and India.

Chris Baldry is Professor of Human Resource Management in the Department of Management and Organization at the University of Stirling. His research interests have included technological change in the workplace, occupational health, changes and continuities in the experience of work, and the social construction of workspace. He is also Editor of the journal *New Technology, Work and Employment*.

Irene Bruegel was director of the Local Economy Policy Unit at South Bank University while researching feminisation and the future of work. She is now working on a five-year programme of research into social capital, the family and the labour market at South Bank University, London.

Nickie Charles is Professor of Sociology in the School of Social Sciences and International Development at the University of Wales, Swansea. She is currently working on an ESRC–unded project, 'Social change, family formation and kin relations', and has recently published a book, *Gender in Modern Britain* (Oxford University Press, 2002).

Hazel Conley is a senior lecturer in HRM at Bristol Business School, University of the West of England. She completed her doctorate at Warwick University in 2000 and has published her research in *Work, Employment and Society* (2002) and *Gender, Work and Organisation* (2003).

Andy Danford is Reader in Employment Relations at the University of the West of England, Bristol. He has published widely in the areas of trade union renewal and critical studies of lean production in the aerospace and automotive sectors. He is the author of *Japanese Management Techniques and British Workers* and co-author of *New Unions, New Workplaces*.

Annette Davies PhD is Senior Lecturer in Organisational Behaviour at the Cardiff Business School, University of Wales. Her main research interests relate to issues of gender, change and managerial identities in public service organisations. She has a particular interest in the restructuring of the police service and the construction of new policing identities. She is currently involved in a number of research projects investigating gendered managerial and professional identities in a range of organizations in the UK, Sweden and Finland. She has published widely in, for example, *Journal of Management Studies, Sociological Review, Public Management and Cirtical Perspectives on Accounting.*

Ranji Devadason is currently working on a comparative study of young adults' working lives in Bristol and Gothenburg (Sweden) for her PhD. Prior to this she was Research Assistant of the 'Winners and Losers' project, investigating young adults' employment trajectories, based at the Department of Sociology, University of Bristol She has a masters in South Asian Studies and a masters in Social Science Research Methods. Her research interests include orientations to work, ethnicity and spatial inequalities in urban centres.

Steve Fenton is Professor of Sociology at Bristol and has published and researched principally in the field of ethnicity. His *Ethnicity* (Polity, 2003) was published last year. He is currently working on a study of class and national identify in Britain.

Dr Gregor Gall is Professor of Industrial Relations at the University of Stirling and author of *The Meaning of Militancy? Postal Workers and Industrial Relations* (Ashgate, 2003).

Irena Grugulis is Professor of Employment Studies at Bradford University School of Management. Her main research interests are in the area of skills and training. She has been funded by both the ESRC and the ERDF and has published in *Work, Employment and Society, British Journal of Industrial Relations, Human Relations* and *Journal of Management Studies.* Recent edited work includes *Customer Service* with Andrew Sturdy and Hugh Willmott (Palgrave, 2001) and *The Skills that Matter* with Chris Warhurst and Ewart Keep (Palgrave, 2004).

Will Guy is a Lecturer in Sociology at the University of Bristol, who teaches research methodology and about the period of 'transition' in Central and Eastern Europe. His main long-standing research has been on the situation of the Roma (Gypsy) minority in this region.

Jane Harrington is a principal lecturer at the University of the West of England. She completed her PhD in 2000 on Gender and Trade Unions. Her research interests include gender and the workplace, and research methodology.

Emma James is a Research Fellow in the National Centre for Public Policy, also at the University of Wales, Swansea, where she works in areas of public policy and health and pursues her interests in rural Welsh community studies. She has authored a chapter on Welsh rural communities in an edited book, *Welsh Communities: New Ethnographic Perspectives* (University of Wales Press, 2003).

Miguel Martínez-Lucio is Professor of Industrial Relations at the University of Bradford School of Management, UK. He has published on the subjects of trade union change, employment regulation, and European industrial relations in a number of articles and texts.

Theo Nichols is Distinguished Research Professor, School of Social Sciences, Cardiff University, UK.

Mike Richardson is a Senior Researcher in Industrial Relations at the University of the West of England. His research interests include labour history. Recently published articles include 'Leadership and Mobilization; SOGAT in the 1986–87 News International Dispute.'

Paul Stewart is Professor of the Sociology of Work and Employment at the University of the West of England. He has published widely in the areas of employment relations and labour processes in the automative industry and the new lean politics of partnership at work. He is currently editor of the British Sociological Association's journal *Work, Employment and Society*. He is also a member of the International Steering Committee of the French based *Gerpisa* network.

Mark Stuart is a senior lecturer at Leeds University Business School. He has published widely in the areas of social partnership and the industrial relations of training and development. He is currently leading an EU Framework 5 project looking at the restructuring of the European steel and metal sectors and also holds grants from the ESRC and DTI.

Nadir Sugur is Professor of Sociology, Faculty of Communication, Anadolu University, Eskisehir, Turkey and was formerly Research Fellow, School of Social Sciences, Cardiff University.

Stephanie Tailby is Principal Lecturer in Employment Relations at the Bristol Business School. Her recent research focuses on 'partnership at work' in the UK, and contingent employment in European healthcare and financial services.

Phil Taylor is Reader in Industrial Relations/HRM in the Department of Management and Organization at the University of Stirling. While call centre research has dominated his academic output, he has researched and published widely in many other areas including occupational health, trade unionism and human resource management, work organization, privatization and student part-time employment. He is a lead member of a major

Scottish-based project funded under the UK's ESRC 'Future of Work Programme.'

Robyn Thomas PhD is Senior Lecturer in Organisational Behaviour at Cardiff Business School, Cardiff University, UK. Her research interests centre on critical perspectives on management and organizations. Current research projects include: management of knowledge intensive organizations (in Finland, Sweden and the UK); theorising professional identities under New Public Management; policing identities, policing performance and change. She has published in a variety of journals and book chapters, including articles in *Organization Studies, Organization, Gender, Work and Organization, Critical Perspectives on Accounting, Culture and Organization, Public Administration* and *Public Management Review* and an edited book entitled *Identity Politics at Work* (with A. Mills and J. Helms Mills).

Dr. Martin Upchurch is Reader in International Employment Relations at the University of the West of England. His research interests include trade union strategies and comparative industrial relations. He is the co-author of *New Unions, New Workplaces*.

Introduction   The Changing Nature of Employment, Trade Union Renewal and the Future of Work

Paul Stewart

This book arises out of a conference held at the Centre for Employment Studies Research at Bristol Business School in 2001 sponsored by the ESRC's Future of Work Programme. The aim was to bring together participants from the programme and others researching the field of work and employment.

While considerable acres of newsprint and media air-time are given to encouraging academics to prognosticate on the future of work and labour markets generally, researchers of work and employment have usually been more circumspect in anticipating longer range outcomes from particular sectors. However, this does not deny the need to be able to respond, as occasion demands, and especially today when government spokespersons seem capable of painting a sanguine gloss on the difficult working conditions facing many people and especially those in, '...that time and that place who lose their jobs no matter how hard they work, however well-off the firm is'.[1] This bleak scenario can be the fate for many in Britain, however formalised the character of the partnership relationship between management and unions, if they are fortunate enough to have a union (never mind a partnership agreement) which of course is not as likely today as it once was. Perhaps it could be argued that the problem with too gloomy a view of work today is that it underplays any attempts however small, by employees, to respond positively to setbacks. Yet we cannot continue to approach the deterioration in men's and women's work and employment conditions as though these are somehow secondary to grand structural changes that lead inexorably to qualitatively better work and employment experiences in the UK and internationally. (For an assessment of the impact of new employment strategies on employees, including the consequences of absence-control regimes, see, *inter alia*, Brenner *et al.*, 1999; Burr *et al.*, 2003; Jones *et al.*, 2003; Watterson and LaDou, 2003; Stewart *et al.*, 2004.)

An alternative view of some happy optimists is to see any change, despite difficulties (inevitably interpreted as minor setbacks) as leading inexorably

1

towards greater benefits for all. One does not require analysis here, only hope and a little intellectual intransigence.[2] Yet the latter seems too frequently based on a perverse imbalance whereby the past is seen to be worse than it actually was in order to contrast more favourably with what are taken to be minor setbacks on the road to a bright and positive future for everyone in work. What we require rather are more realistic accounts of the relationship between managerial dominance and employee insubordination. While this is not the place to describe the myriad forms more critical accounts might take, recognition that things can be tough for people at work today, including many in management (Tailby, Stewart and Richardson, Future of Work Report, 2003) implies a more realistic grasp on the dynamics of persistent inequality at work. In their clinical treatment of the 'evocative' visions of the optimists and pessimists Nolan and Wood (2003: 173) counsel against 'stylised account[s] of the changing world of work [...] appealing to simple dualisms, such as the old (industrial) and new (knowledge-intensive) economies', to get a better understanding of actual change.

Perhaps then one of the signally important elements in a more realistic account of the changing nature of work and employment today is precisely to report that dissonant behaviour reflects employees' enduring inability to take bad deals at work quietly. (Ackroyd and Thompson, 1999; Stephenson and Stewart, 2001). So a greater degree of recognition of the way people resist can reasonably be expected from a social critique that, while far from offering pre-emptory pessimism, recognises that the persistence of inequalities of power in the employment relationship (Taylor, 2002: 8) not infrequently leads to resistance, in individual-collectivist ways.

One of the strengths of the chapters here is that whether they focus on sector, region, locality or international and global change, while they account for the specificity of particular employment relationships, despite differences in orientation, each seeks to unearth not just change, but also the reproduction of existing relationships. Yet, without reifying social relations they each can be read as hinting at where opportunities for change for the better might lie (Davies and Thomas and Conley) or, in unpacking the persistence of tradition and change in a local labour market, the tensions between ethnicity, gender and age (Bradley *et al.* and Charles *et al.* below). Taking account of changes at the level of political economy, Gall, Taylor, Baldry and Bain provide an account of the new ways in which existing social divisions and exclusions are being recast by what one could describe as a speeding up of the international capitalist political economy.

Since understanding social divisions, exclusions and political subordination are important in mapping the evolution of new spaces for innovative solidarities (Harrington's focus on the local) we need to look more closely at the context of actual subordination in defining the ways workers can respond to exploitation (Nichols and Sugur). While, of course, it is important to be able to make the point that while the chapters here do allow for a better grasp of the way political discourse directed at defending the excluded might be developed they have not in the main been written with this aim in mind. Moreover, as Davies and Thomas point out in Chapter 3, strategic choice for individuals involves a difficult calculation because one cannot be sure of outcomes since intervention is not easily controllable and is always contradictory.

One of the things we know about the political economy of neo-liberalism today is that while work in the UK has become more intensive people also are having to work longer hours (Green, 2001; Jones *et al.*, 2003; TUCworkSMART, 2004) and with increased levels of stress (White *et al.*, 2003). Neither is it the case that employees in Britain are satisfied with the balance between their working time and time spent away from work. Nor is it a source of comfort that, as Fagan and Warren (2001) demonstrate, workers in the UK are far from being alone in this respect. Finally, while the levels of satisfaction with the amount of time people are spending at work has declined, so too has the degree of commitment to their employer (Working in Britain in the year 2002, WIB, 2000).

This is important to emphasise since it necessarily defines the context in which discussion about trade union strategies can be understood. It is curious that it is against this background of the deterioration in employment conditions that notions of the decline of collectivism and the supposed rise of individualism have been advanced. Since in the public sector, including the commercialised utilities, from hospitals and local government, including social services, to the private sector, from aerospace to automotives, employees are working harder by working longer and under increasing duress, the concept of the 'individualised' workplace becomes problematical (Yates *et al.*, 2001; Danford *et al.*, 2004). Strategies for managing collective effort in the workplace through individualised performance appraisal mechanisms seem too easily to have been translated into the end of collectivism thesis. (O'Doherty and Willmott, 2001). For, individualised performance measurement, tied to workplace intensification and the diminution of employee control can also be understood as part and parcel of management's attempted composition of a new collectivism (Martinez Lucio and Stewart, 1997; Martinez Lucio and Stuart, 2004). A social democratic settlement would, of course, rather this were underwritten in some formalised manner by the state and preferably in the form of statutory workplace partnership strategies. If the latter is someway off as yet, management, where it considers partnership agendas, is, as Oxenbridge *et al.* (2003) have shown, quite clearly intent on securing advantage by reining in any possible union alternatives. For sure, while many employers might seek individualistic evaluation and reward systems (WIB, 2000), and while the pattern of workplace organisation has diminished worker autonomy and control, collectivism is far from finished. (See Taylor's 2002 response to the WIB Survey, 2000 and this of course depends upon what one means exactly by collectivism – see Martinez Lucio and Stewart, 1997; Stewart, 2005 forthcoming.)

One way to make sense of the 'problem of collectivism' might be to begin to focus more on what work organisations, employment relations and the labour process do to employees. We know for example from the WIB, 2000-survey that while there has been a trend towards greater involvement and employee participation in the form of Quality Circles many people report the fact that management seems nevertheless to have become increasingly dominant. Taylor, in his commentary on the WIB, 2000-survey states that, '...important evidence [...] suggest[s] that while a trend exists to greater freedom for the worker on the job, the degree of control and surveillance by management has also increased' (2000: 18).

Despite this one still hears the call for unions to civilise the employer and the best way to do this is to get them to accept a trade union presence. This is to be achieved by demonstrating that unions add value to the organisation. Is this the best way to reengage employees with trade unionism? Would this be the most appropriate means by which a refounded collectivism might emerge today? Is it really possible, let alone desirable to set a collectivist agenda around union and employee compliance in the context of a significant deterioration in working and employment conditions?

The Future of Work, UWE-Bristol team researching partnership at work in six organisations, has produced compelling evidence supporting a number of the findings of the WIB, 2000-survey on the deterioration of work while also identifying a possible link with the nature of employee and industrial relations more broadly. (See, Danford *et al.*, 2004; Richardson *et al.*, 2004.) One of the curious aspects to the debate about the changing nature of workplace relations is that it sometimes goes hand in hand with a description of the deterioration of the condition of labour as if there were no connection between the two. Moreover, it is odd that the link is rarely made between the increasing rise in the reported incidence of team and group working, continuous improvement meetings and increased monitoring (control) by management, even where many people perceive some improvement in their scope for day to day decision-making. (Notable exceptions both in the UK and elsewhere, include Nichols, 2001 and Brenner, *op cit.*, on the link between team work and other new management strategies and RSI (Repetitive Strain Inquiry) – Cumulative Trauma Disorder in the US. Also, see stewart, 2003.) It is rarer still for the link to be made between the deterioration in work, quality circles and group work and new forms of employee–management relations *qua* partnership, although it could arguably be included in the broader compass of Alan Dalton's critique in his controversial, *Consensus Kills* (2000). To the contrary, as was argued above, social democratic writers often promote partnership as a means to resolve what they see as the British Management problem. This is shorthand for the perceived intractability of British management when it comes to paying little more than lip-service to ideals of employee involvement and participation and notably where the agenda of partnership might be concerned. This view holds that as a result of the increasingly demanding nature of work today reform of the employment relationship is necessary if employees are to be brought along on the great journey of modernisation. While it has been noted that one of the roles for unions envisaged by social democratic writers in their promotion of partnership agreements is to civilise management through recognition agreements; another angle on 'modernisation' is to see it as a means for domesticating labour despite the continued incivilities of management.

There seems limited appetite for considering the possibility that work intensification, driven in the main by work reorganisation and increased surveillance linked to employer neo-liberal strategies, are closely bound together, not that trade unions as a consequence should be sceptical of management intent (Martinez Lucio and Stuart, Chapter 9). As the Bristol Partnership team found in their study of the process of partnership[3] in six organisations, employees themselves, while usually sanguine about the idea of partnership, remain less than convinced by management practice. Neither, in some cases were managers themselves won over to the verities of partnership, however formalised the partnership agreement (Danford *et al.*, 2004). Yet this increasing evidence that contemporary British management can be won to the idea of a pluralistic workplace agenda without some kind of already-existing, well-founded (alternative take on) collectivism is surely wishful thinking (Ackers and Payne, 1998). As Danford *et al.* discovered, a 'harsh reality' lies behind partnership deals. In a number of cases the study found that rationalisation strategies tended to undermine the gentle discourse of employee involvement and protection seen as central to partnership agreements. Added to this was the (almost) inevitable spectre of managerial resistance to the ethos of partnership – they just do not seem to like devolving real power. Nor is there any great degree of evidence to suggest they enjoy listening to employees in any meaningful sense when it comes to strategic orientations and decision-making. In a number of respects this compliments the perception of Oxenbridge *et al.* (2003) that where management may be fairly ready to engage with unions where they can be used to help with workplace reform they are somewhat less than happy to indulge them in traditional issues such as pay bargaining. Even where management may talk about inclusion it is nevertheless, arguably, focused on the pursuit of a fairly traditional unitarist agenda. This is assuming that unions can organise in the first place since there is evidence that management would probably prefer consultative forums as opposed to autonomous unions if they have to have any formalised employee relations processes. Furthermore, according to WERS 98, non-union companies are unlikely to experience any kind of formalisation.

Oxenbridge *et al.*'s conclusion is enlightening since it may be uncovering another dimension lying at the root of contemporary workplace politics of production. For, since we know that work presents employees with many difficulties, and in view of the fact that discussion around harsh working conditions are devoid of real participation, it is here that a new politics of work and production might be advanced by those dissenting unions rejecting partnership in favour of a new collectivism. This is developing specifically around concerns about the new workplace being driven by high work intensification, employee stress and increased management control.[4] These represent the other face; the reality as seen by many employees, of the High Performance Work Organisation (HPWO) so admired by social democratic reformers and modern management alike (Appelbaum, 2000).

Both in the UK and elsewhere, the HPWO makes the link between workplace reform embracing organisational change around, *inter alia*, team working and continuous improvement programmes (linked to forms of employee involvement) technological innovation and 'partnership' agenda. (Danford *et al.*, 2004 and Chapter 8 in this collection). In this case we need to see the nature of partnership agendas specifically as (employer) strategies developed in the context of the need to remake collectivism in a different form and especially one in which labour and labour organisations might be enlisted to the company's cause. And it is emphatically around issues of the quality of working life that new alternative agendas for organising might be forged. Moreover, this may provide the link to a robust collectivism that can address management–union agendas by shifting the (management) rhetoric of individual employee rights to a new union agenda of collective rights based upon vigorous union-monitoring of the employment relationship, including secure and controlled workplaces for all employees. The safe and secure workplace provides for employee and union organising agendas on collective workplace rights protecting women and men from sexual, racial and physical harm at work, taking into account the consequences of the deleterious conditions of HPWOs for employees' private and social lives (White *et al.*, 2003). As Keith *et al.* (2002) argue, 'Organising around work security provides workers with greater strength for bargaining to make changes and increase their level of security [...] they can: improve their basic socio-economic security; improve working conditions; increase their voice representation; gain power through organisation to also tackle income and employment issues' (p. 2).

Internationalisation/globalisation: management and labour strategies

The chapters comprise a number of themes; internationalisation/ globalisation, flexibility and the intensification of work, locality, identity, gender and trade union strategy. The first chapter by Phil Taylor, Gregor Gall, Peter Bain and Chris Baldry draws on their Future of Work research in Scotland. Their concern here is with employees' experience of call centre employment in the context of the evolution of globalisation. Their findings are salutary: 'Workers' experience of work in call centres has comprised, on the one hand, work intensification and extensification as well as immiseration of other material and psychological conditions like job satisfaction.'

The fieldwork focused on four call centres in Scotland. The data included interviews with shop floor workers (call handlers), team leaders, managers and trade union representatives and an employee questionnaire. They argue that the main cause of contemporary intensification of effort at work coupled to an extension to working time is the acceleration of market turbulence, a critical feature of all capitalist economies. In a notably visible way, call centres, embedded as they are in information and communication technologies, are of course being subject to rapid and continuous change. Very dramatically, globalisation has heightened the difficulties for capital by exacerbating tensions, whether at the level of the market or the firm, expressed as, '…unrestrained tendencies towards systematic instability'. This makes it both difficult for firms to anticipate change where they might want to respond in a measured way and at the same time troublesome in attempting to resolve the social and economic fallout from what Marx described as the 'full circuit of capital'.

What gives contemporary organisational churning its particular piquancy is that financialisation driving economic change and organisational development underlies the increasingly deleterious condition of labour in this sector and elsewhere. This macro-change is important to emphasise since it has the effect of disrupting employees' work experience, through 'social dislocation associated with staff turnover and organisational restructuring'. While market turbulence provided the structural context it was higher management who were responsible for the whole merry-go-round, though lower level managers supported them. 'Being "loyal lieutenants", they seek to make their charges "strive under chaos" to make the companies "thrive under chaos". The flux and churn which workers experience, notwithstanding worker resistance, … reflects attempts to "strive" under market turbulence.'

Nichols and Sugur are concerned with the character of trade unions in the Turkish metal working industry. They highlight the importance of a political economy of work that focuses on historically and sociologically specific employment relations and labour processes.

Examining the trajectory of labour management politics they explain how periods of apparent quietus tied to patronage and brokerage at the level of the plant, the firm and the locality have been created following military rule in 1980. This process, 'facilitat[ed] a trade union structure in the metal industry which frustrated the development of workers' democratic capacities', undermining earlier gains. Interestingly, while many in management increasingly extol the virtues of union democratisation, reflecting the influences and fashions of a metropolitan business class, they nevertheless preside over, and benefit from, autocratic paternalism at company level.

The existence of well-organised trade unions in this context presents a special case of union subordination and an apparently quiescent labour force – if judged simplistically by European standards that is. Yet this is a case study of a particular conundrum. If the union is so obviously subordinate why would workers join it especially since there is no legal obligation to do so and moreover, why retain their membership? At the heart of the analysis is the fate of one of Turkey's most important unions, Türk Metal, belonging to the largest union federation, TÜRK-IS.

Their argument is based on analysis of employee attitudes as expressed in survey data and interviews carried out in four firms (three white goods and one from automotives). The results highlighted the fact that workers felt the union was signally disinterested in their 'needs' and that there was an absence of democracy and dialogue. Nichols and Sugur consider the basis for the union's rise and pre-eminence and second, how it manages to reproduce an effective internal autocratic life. Eschewing simplistic notions of Islamic conservative culture and the ideological underdevelopment of countries such as Turkey, they reveal a more intricate (and of course contradictory) trade union trajectory where worker subordination, though obviously important, is nevertheless matched by autonomous and determined (and it has to be said, brave) shop floor responses. This can be seen at a number of levels. On the one hand, the survey indicates an extraordinary scepticism towards the union matched by an apparent commitment to a paternalistic management. On the other hand worker responses across the four companies bear witness to complex attempts to challenge the line of the union leadership on a range of issues including a critique of a lack of democracy and rejection of pay awards.

Annette Davies and Robyn Thomas take us into the turbulent world of the UK public sector 'professional/manager' as they describe them, in the police force, secondary education and social services. While clearly subject to the kinds of structural pressures created by global turbulence examined in the first chapter, Davies and Thomas focus on the implications of contemporary managerial workplace reforms, *qua*, New Public Management (NPM) on the identity formation of the professional/manager. Their research agenda is designed to get to the heart of the tensile character of the difficulties faced by those occupying this dual role. Following Foucault and Kondo, they see individual identities as socially and individually crafted. This is important to recognise when taking stock of the stresses NPM places upon individuals whose identity formation depends on both antecedents (professional training) and external ideational influences.

The tensions experienced by any professional/manager derive from a range of competing forms of reorganisation and discursive practices introduced since the 1980s and which are inevitably bound up with the increasing entrenchment of neo-liberal policies in the public sector. Since gender is to be understood not so much as, 'who you are', and rather more a constant iteration, '…what you do at particular times', the extraordinary political character of the impact of NPM strategies on an individual's identity formation will be ever present. The proscriptive and gendered discourse(s) of NPM cut across attempts by professional/managers to affirm who they thought themselves to be. As Davies and Thomas point out, it has to be remembered that these individuals bring to their working environment a range of dissonant, gendered conceptions of identity. Yet, far from imputing a kind of ideational merry-go-round on which individuals simply change horses at will, or lack control of micro-social processes, they challenge their subordination so that it becomes possible to view NPM as a 'resource' from which people seek to create anything but subordinate identities.

This space for opposition occurs for women constrained by masculinist discourses since they nevertheless find that some 'soft' HRM rhetoric allows them to find, 'voice, legitimacy and a positive sense of self'. Although, as the authors point out, recognition of this can hardly be used to deny the fact that women (professional managers) do find it tough in problematical and ambiguous ways. While for Davies and Thomas, gendered discourses are crucially part of identity formation in the context of what this editor might describe as the increasing torpor of NPM, what are we to make of the increasing participation of women in management when it comes to improving things for women at work generally?

Gender at work, trade unions and flexibility

Using data from her Future of Work research, Irene Bruegel examines the relationship between the growth in women's participation in management and the impact this might have for family-friendly policies. She argues that despite the increasing 'quantitative feminisation' of management in the UK, there is still someway to go before we can anticipate management's 'qualitative feminisation'. In contrast to those who might argue that this quantitative feminisation would lead to distinct sociological improvements in workplace opportunities and outcomes for all women, Bruegel argues persuasively that we need to examine the 'quality' of their management practice and the 'opportunities offered to other women in [...] enterprises'. Furthermore, with respect to increased participation, to what extent can one argue that these managers drive forward progressive (vital) agenda on working time and other policies? She shows how the percentage of women managers with children has remained fairly stable for the last 10 years despite the fact that much family-friendly provision accrues to them. What is more, women managers have not to any obvious extent been terribly successful at 'growing' additional women to work with. Yet perhaps the more arresting conclusion is that while there is a relationship between the availability of family friendly policies for others (non managers) and the participation of women this would seem to be more likely attributable to an 'equal opportunities culture' than the proportion of higher women management cadre. One reason for this might be that, 'women managers continue to operate largely as individuals in a man's world; they remain gendered in the types of management jobs they have access to, but unlike men, they do not act on their gender interests to create powerful mutual support structures'. Bruegel notes finally, that we need to be clear about the implicit relationships between what she terms a 'more caring' management orientation and the preponderance of women managers in the public sector together with the importance of union recognition and family-friendly policies.[5]

The difficulties faced by women in the labour market raises the question as to what leads women to participate in trade union activities. Chapter 5 by Jane Harrington directly addresses this concern arguing that part of the answer can be found by understanding the local context within which activism takes place. She reflects on two case studies of women activists, one of the cases is from BIFUs South and West of England region and the other from USDAW's South Wales and Western division. Complementing the long history of work on the obstacles to women's participation in trade unions this chapter focuses on the rationale women present for their activism at local level.

While some research has assumed an unwarranted degree of homogeneity of consciousness, Harrington argues that unpacking two themes, those forces impacting on women's participation and the critical influence of gender, can allow a more realistic picture of reasons for participation. She makes the necessary point that a specifically gendered notion of 'protection' informs the way women respond to questions about their rationale for union participation. 'Protection and support are two terms that the women in BIFU continuously refer to in accounting for their decision to join and to become active trade unionists.' While this often reflects the commonplace notion of 'protection' as job insurance in an individualistic sense, nevertheless it equally conveys a collectivist idea of common struggle by and for all. Collectivism too, of course, can be ambivalent, expressing a fairly conventional union response but the argument made here is that we need to go beyond this to recognise the impact of a specifically gendered set of identities.

Thus, the idiom of 'protector' may mean, '... the "carer" of the workforce, an extension of the notion of the secretary reproducing her domestic role in the workplace, the trade union women activist reproducing her domestic role in the union'. Individualist and collectivist notions then can be said to be at the centre of the way these women perceive their union involvement. Furthermore, when family background was considered, the complexities between individualistic attitudes and more orthodox collectivist beliefs came to the fore with the women from BIFU presenting a more heterogeneous range of responses than those in USDAW who strongly associated family background and union participation.

Finally, Harrington argues that notwithstanding the gendered dimension of individualist and collectivist attitudes and ideological orientations, locale and sense of place are critical in the 'how' and 'why' of women's activism.

While the BIFU women suggested a more heterogeneous set of causes, no less bounded by class and sector restructuring, by contrast the USDAW women working in south Wales appeared to be more firmly committed to the idea that employment and union participation were inextricably tied, such that joining unions was seen as the, ' "natural" thing to do when you go to work'.

For the last twenty-five years Conservative and Labour governments have been hammering on about the imperatives of flexibility for economic and social success in the new globalised world. In her chapter on contingent workers in the state sector – teachers and residential social workers (RSW) in two local authorities – Hazel Conley highlights the negative consequences for those without secure, full-time employment contracts. She illustrates how their experiences belie government rhetoric about the supposedly obvious benefits enjoyed by contingent employees in the state sector. This is hardly surprising when one considers that flexible work in the sector has become synonymous with 'modernisation', one of neo-liberalism's glib but highly effective linguistic responses to any kind of resistance which thus can be easily rendered recalcitrant and backward-looking. Conley argues that the experience of temporary teachers and temporary RSWs reflects increasing job intensification amplified by job cuts. As she puts it, 'job insecurity in one form or another is now a visible feature of public sector employment, bringing a perverse meaning to the concept of the state as a "model" employer'.

In her study this serves as a prelude to challenging another stereotype of the privileged, professional status of state employees. Her interviewees describe labour market and labour process conditions that are multidimensional in terms of the tensions between personal, career and financial insecurity. This was perceived as leading to significant vulnerability as highlighted by incidents of, '[d]epression, marital tensions and fatalism'. Nevertheless, irrespective of their unfavourable conditions the temporary employees, 'were committed to their jobs but were concerned about the quality of the service they were able to provide'. In the end, their various insecurities inhibited expression of grievances to either union or employer and discontent was more typically reflected in high exit rates for sets of workers. The unions in turn had a problem mobilising workers faced by these conditions of insecurity with the various attendant consequences for the quality of life at work and in the community.

Nickie Charles, Emma James and Paul Ransome, examine a range of dimensions of job insecurity in the retail sector ('Big Shop') in south Wales. This drives from their three sector Future of Work study that includes manufacturing and the public sector. Their major concern is whether, 'globalisation and non-standard employment are associated with a newly emerging Total Social Organisation of Labour' (TSOL, see Glucksman, 2000). While the Working in Britain survey highlighted the extent to which increasing flexibility may be exaggerated, as Charles *et al.*, argue here, it is nevertheless a persistent assumption. Another aspect to this belief is that increasing flexibility and non-standard employment are contemporary phenomena. An additional to this has non-standard work inevitably linked to job insecurity. Outlining an appropriately sceptical view they point out first that for many workers, for much of the time, permanent, full-time work, was an unknown labour market experience. Second, while the period since 1945 has seen an expansion of women's employment this has mostly been part-time. Crucially then, '... the division between "standard employment" – full-time, permanent "jobs for life" – and other forms of employment, in addition to being a class and racialised division, has historically been gendered: standard employment being associated with men and non-standard employment with women'.

Retail is an especially apposite sector to choose since because it employs large numbers of women and since it has pioneered non-standard employment it can be seen as a test of part of the insecurity discourse. These links are important to assess since the evidence associating job insecurity and non-standard employment 'is inconclusive'. As Charles *et al.*, point out, 'these findings suggest that there is no essential connection between flexibility, non-standard forms of employment ... and job insecurity and that much depends on employer policies.' Furthermore, feelings of security were not unambiguous as was reflected by the responses of the older, least skilled women in the sample who felt less sure about the prospects for other work.

If overall, there is no unambiguous connection between non-standard employment and perceptions of insecurity and since much 'depends upon employer policies', how are we to explain employee perceptions of insecurity? James *et al.*, argue that the concept of the TSOL allows us to adjust our understanding to focus on the complex links between insecurity and paid and unpaid labour. In so doing we can see how at different moments, according to occupation, class and gender, 'women and men continue to organise their labour differently at different stages of their lives and that the demands of paid work and unpaid care and domestic labour have gendered effects'.

The problems with partnership and the future of work

While much has now been written about partnership in the employment relationship perhaps too frequently the scope of research has been somewhat limited by the assumptions of lead officials in trade unions. Sometimes accounts may be even more restricted to extrapolating outcome from ideological or political intent of policy documents.

Andy Danford, Mike Richardson, Paul Stewart, Stephanie Tailby and Martin Upchurch argue that discussion of partnership has been insufficiently grounded in the sociology and political economy of work and employment relations. In analysing High Performance Work Systems (HPWS) in the UK aerospace sector they problematise institutionalist approaches to partnership by underscoring the centrality of history and social conflict in labour–management agreements. (See Godard, 2004, for a discussion of different forms of HPWS.) Specifically, Chapter 8 addresses employee elements in the TUC's 'win-win' partnership code in the context of changing employment relations at 'Jetco' and 'Airframes' based in the south west of England. If firms were to provide 'real joint decision making and problem solving' for employees leading to 'greater control over their immediate working environment', then one would expect to see evidence of these in HPWS. Yet, ironically, the contrast with the past when a high degree of trust was crucial to labour and capital relations could hardly be starker. As Danford *et al.*, argue, 'The introduction of HPWS in such an environment, involving managerial decentralization, teamworking and multifarious problem-solving techniques, might be expected to foster employee autonomy and mobilize worker discretion for the benefit of the organization and workforce alike […] The reality, however, was quite different [leading to] feelings that continuous improvement campaigns ignored independent worker agendas for improving the quality of working life.'

They argue that while some of this could well be anticipated in other employment environments this remains unlikely where worker resistance is underplayed in favour of portrayals of the passive employee, 'acquiescent labour'. It is crucial we bring back labour as an active presence, a forceful participant the better to understand the dynamics of work place change. 'In some areas of the plant the sustained collective defence of a set of ethical practices and norms marked out an alternative "employee autonomy" that exposed the superficial empowerment claims of partnership and high performance management.'

Chapter 9 by Miguel Martinez Lucio and Mark Stuart focuses on local union officers and their experiences of Partnership. They derive their arguments from a large-scale survey of workplace representatives of the white-collar union, the Manufacturing, Science and Finance Union (MSF) and two qualitative case studies (a food ingredients manufacturer and a hospital Trust). Their assessment of the fate of Partnership is drawn from the views of union representatives in a range of sectors including those without Partnership agreements. Without compromising a critical view of Partnership, they argue that it would be better to begin by viewing unions in the Partnership context as undertaking what they term 'strategic ventures'. These should be seen as inevitably bounded by the, 'politics of employment relations and the realities of strategic calculations within trade unions, as organisations with a variety of levels and spheres of decision making'. Thus despite national union commitment to sustaining a Partnership agenda, they found that, 'even "supportive" views amongst trade unionists of partnership are paralleled by very strong sets of concerns in terms of the risk of institutional engagement and the nature of management commitment'.

Far from reflecting an ideological predilection against Partnership, in practice, union representatives' understanding and reactions to Partnership highlighted the tension between national union preference, local union orientation and shop floor experience of management strategies. Martinez Lucio and Stuart argue that a more complex framework for judging Partnership could focus on the interactions between 'intra-union', 'management-union' and 'inter union' engagements. For the MSF, this approach can be used to reveal tensions that, while not undermining a favourable predisposition to the idea of partnership, and notably as expressed in conference resolutions, nevertheless sat uncomfortably with the circumstances (and a questionable trust in management intent) and experience of Partnership. As the authors point out, commitment to more radical positions that emerged from the union conferences seemed to be reinforced by workplace experiences that in turn led to, 'a general unease with the *context* and *deliverables* of partnership and not necessarily the *process*'.

Support, in other words, was conditional – which was hardly surprising since, according to workplace representatives, while they were frequently given space to comment on business issues, 'at a more practical level, low levels of involvement were visible in relation to the development of business issues'. If conditionality is vital in defining the response by workplace representatives to Partnership, what are we to make of Partnership 'accords' set in the context of new contractual arrangements following outsourcing? Partnership, in this case is taken broadly to include formal company level accords (private–public partnership PPP) together with the management–trade union agreement covering union rights after outsourcing. Moreover, how do employees experience the change process, and especially in terms of the quality of working life? Steve Vincent and Irena Grugulis consider these themes in the context of their Future of Work research into the changing nature of contractual relationships between a government department and a private IT company.

Govco, contracted a dominant market operator, FutureTech, to deliver IT services under the auspices of a PPP. They discovered evidence of, '...poorly performing new IT systems, increased control of IT workers at various levels and a question mark over the organisation's ability to reproduce its skill base'. Vincent and Grugulis deem many of the problems to have derived principally from the way in which contracts were made. They compare the new dispensation with the way previous IT services were provided internally, reminding us of Friedman's injunction that, 'The way that organisations control employees is central to understanding organisational choices and strategies.' The belief was that cost efficiencies would be accompanied by 'a new contractual discipline brought in to control the work of managers' ensuring a fitter, leaner service of benefit to all. A union bargaining agreement supposedly exemplified the inclusiveness of the new arrangements.

Outsourcing impacted in a profound way on the control of the programmers' labour process. Whereas under the previous regime they had been allowed considerable latitude, in part due to recruitment difficulties that exacerbated skill shortages, the new partnership set-up eliminated much of their scope for control as well as overseeing a perceptible increase in workload. While a minority of IT specialists certainly benefited, the deterioration in the quality of working life could nevertheless be linked to individualisation of contracts which included performance monitoring.

They conclude that programmers' difficulties were extraneous to the evaluation of success. It was simply imperative that the outsourcing succeeded. As they point out, 'Management is a political, rather than a neutral process, and managerial actions will be influenced by expectations of performance.' All in all, this conclusion creates a less than rosy prospectus for PPPs. Too many decisions were driven by what Vincent and Grugulis describe as 'opportunistic behaviour' that far from encouraging transparency actually discouraged it.

All of which raises the question as to employee perceptions of changing status of employment. With the ever-increasing intensification and extensification of labour noted earlier, together with the consequent negative impact on an individual's ability to 'plan' their time away from work, one might reasonably wonder at the extent of an employee's perspective regarding their job prospects. The question of employee perceptions of their job trajectory – the future of their work – is critical for Michael Rose in considering how the employment relationship is evolving in contemporary capitalism. To try to make sense of the crucial changes in employee perceptions of job status he examines the period 1986–2002 using the 1985–86 Social Change and Economic Life Initiative (SCELI) Work Attitudes/Histories survey together with the 2001 Office for National Statistics Omnibus survey (Rose, 2003).

He begins by noting the increased perception of 'career' holding by both 'employment professionals' and employees over the last 2 decades of the twentieth century. Rose builds upon the convention which came to define 'career' in terms of jobs characterised by '... success in achieving a number of significant promotions, either in an organisational hierarchy or in a series of well-judged moves between employers'. The concept of 'career' can be seen to comprise three aspects: 'self-concept', 'prospective rationale' and 'constructive action'. While we might anticipate the persistence of a perception of career holding by class and education (skill hierarchy and pay) one of the intriguing findings is the increased perception of career holding amongst assembly-line workers, bus and coach drivers and packers. More compelling still is the extraordinary decline for postal workers (down from 35 to 0!) – 'catastrophic', according to Rose. 'The virtual disappearance of the "career postman" surely reflects changes in organisation, market position, and ethos in this industry. The postal service has also suffered a drastic erosion of job satisfaction since the 1980s ... .'

While the latter may be a dramatic exemplar of declining perception of career status, his (tentative) assessment of the complexities of employee perceptions is that while 'perception of having a career' rose sharply during the latter part of the 1990s there was a fall in perceptions of 'promotion opportunities'. Even accepting the 'paradoxical' nature of results, from a negative standpoint these might be seen to 'tarnish key' arguments advanced by the advocates of the new world of employment in their assumption that the future of work will allow for steady personal progress. Finally, Rose suggests we may soon need to revisit the implications for employees as they seek to make sense of what he describes as 'disappointed aspirations'.

Disappointed aspirations for the increasing number of employees perceiving themselves to have careers can be set against the experiences of young adults for whom, according to Harriet Bradley, Ranji Devadason, Steve Fenton, Will Guy and Jackie West, 'transitions into employment stability and adult independence are...now more complex and problematic....' Recent globalisation processes have had the effect at the local level of establishing 'new cohorts of "winners and losers"...[and those] "in between"'. The authors draw on Phase 1 of their ESRC project centred on the City of Bristol, taken as an example of a 'globalising urban labour market'. Using rich ethnographic research of young adults' (aged 20–34) employment trajectories they argue that complex, interacting spatial features in the city's local labour market frame the context and character of young adults' relationship to employment. In fact, the city comprises, '...three interlocking sets of labour markets with different spatial configurations' which in their distinctive ways constrain labour market participation according to, *inter alia*, qualifications, discrimination and also 'choice'.

Against this labour market backdrop, Bradley *et al.* identify two broad ideal types of 'self-development' trajectories. The first, 'shifters', comprises those with mobile labour market experience which can be subdivided into a group whom they describe as 'settlers', those who, '...may make a decision that the time has come to settle down'. The second ideal type by contrast is made up of those – 'stickers' – who remain in the same job and it too contains a sub category comprising those who, hitherto ostensibly settled, apparently decided somewhere along the line to undertake an 'abrupt change' of career.

Overall, a picture is painted of young adults with a robust orientation to work whose expectations 'are not perhaps markedly different from previous generations (good job, marriage, nice house and car) but they may have to be mobile and flexible to achieve them'; not only more flexible but also experiencing a somewhat longer transition to adulthood and independence than was the case for previous generations. For Bradley *et al.*, this reinforced the centrality of family support and thus inevitably the crucial perpetuation and significance of class divisions.

Notes

1. Delegate speaking in favour of a resolution in support of the campaign to repeal anti-trade union legislation at the TGWU Biannual delegate conference, Brighton, 2003.

2. For those keen as ever to imagine the possibility of a more interventionist labour government, Tony Blair recently restated his belief in the eternal beneficence of market-globalisation. In a speech to the US investment bank, Goldman Sachs, he argued that market reform, including flexibility and outsourcing are critical for business survival and workers' jobs. 'Globalisation presents us with a choice … ' Without hesitation we believe in embracing globalisation and making it work (*Guardian*, 23 March 2004). The not so hidden subtext could be, 'And unions, this means you too. Listen, change, modernise.' Which is the not so social democratic version of the old Thatcher mantra, 'market and labour reforms shall make you free'.

3. The idea of 'partnership as process' contrasts with the usual distinction made between partnership and non partnership organisations where the formal, institutional characteristics of management–union agreements are priviledged over the historical, sociological and political dynamics of tension and contradiction between labour and capital in the employment relationship. (See Kelly's, 2001, critique of partnership as subordination)

4. Over the last eighteen months, a number of unions have come out in opposition to workplace partnership, most significant among them perhaps being the TGWU. Prior to taking over the position of General Secretary, Tony Woodley stated in his address to the union's Biannual Delegate Conference, 'This union is opposed to partnership agreements.' (Brighton, June, 2003). This sentiment was echoed by Billy Hayes of the CWU at a fringe meeting in support of the campaign, 'United for a Charter for Workers' Rights.'

5. For an interesting assessment of the gap between policy espousal and outcome regarding equal opportunities see Hoque and Noon, 2004.

References

Ackers, P. and Payne, J. (1998) 'British trade unions and social partnership: rhetoric, reality and strategy'. *International Journal of Human Resource Management*, 9 (3): 529–50.

Ackroyd, S. and Thompson, P. (1999) *Organisational Misbehaviour*, London: Sage.

Appelbaum, E., Bailey, T., Berg, P. and Kallenberg, A. L. (2000) *Manufacturing Advantage: Why High-performance Work Systems Pay Off*, Ithaca, NY: Cornell University Press.

Brenner, M. D., Fairris, D. and Ruser, J. (1999) ' "Flexible" work practices and occupational safety and health: Exploring the relationship between cumulative trauma disorders and workplace transformation', mimeo, UC Riverside.

Burr, H., Bjorner, J. B., Kristensen, T. S., Tuchsen, F. and Bach, E. (2003) 'Trends in the Swedish work environment 1990–2000 and their association with labor force changes.' *Scandinavian Journal of Work, Environment and Health*, 29: 270–9.

Dalton, A. J. P. (2000) *Consensus Kills*, London: A. J. P. Dalton.

Danford, A., Richardson, M., Stewart, P., Tailby, S. and Upchurch, M. (2004) 'High performance work systems and workplace partnership'. *New Technology, Work and Employment*, 19: 14–29.

European Foundation for the Improvement of Living and Working Conditions (2002) *Quality of Work and Employment in Europe Issues and Challenges*, Foundation Paper, No. 1, February.

Fagan, C. and Warren, T. (2001) *Gender, Employment and Working Time Preferences in Europe*, Luxembourg: Office for Official Publications of the European Communities.

Glucksman, M. (2000) *Cottons and Casuals: The Gendered Organisation of Labour in Time and Space*, Durham: Sociology Press.

Godard, J. (2004) 'A critical assessment of the high performance paradigm'. *British Journal of Industrial Relations*, 42: 349–78.

Green, F. (2001) ' "It's been a hard day's night": the concentration and intensification of work in late twentieth century Britain'. *British Journal of Industrial Relations*, 39: 53–80.

Hoque, K. and Noon, M. (2004) 'Equal opportunities policy and practice in the UK: evaluating the "Empty Shell" hypothesis'. *Work, Employment and Society*, 18 (3): 481–506.

Jones, J. R., Huxtable, C. S. and Price, M. J. (2003) 'Self-reported work related illness in 2001/2002: results from a household survey'. Bootle, Merseyside: Health and Safety Executive.

Keith, M., Brophy, J., Kirby, P. and Rosskam, E. (2002) *Barefoot Research. A Workers' Manual for Organising on Work Security*, Geneva: International Labour Organisation.

Kelly, J. (2001) 'Social partnership agreements in Britain: union revitalisation or employer counter-mobilisation?' Paper delivered to Assessing Partnership: the prospects and challenges of 'modernisation'. Leeds, 24–25 May.

Martinez Lucio, M. and Stewart, P. (1997) 'The paradox of contemporary labour process theory: the rediscovery of labour and the disappearance of collectivism', *Capital and Class*, 62: 49–77.

Martinez Lucio, M. and Stuart, M. (2004) 'Swimming against the tide: social partnership, mutual gains and the revival of "tired" HRM'. *International Journal of Human Resource Management*, 15 (2): 404–18.

Nichols, T. (2001) 'The condition of labour – a retrospective', *Capital and Class*, 75, 185–98.

Nolan, P. and Wood, S. (2003) 'Mapping the future of work'. *British Journal of Industrial Relations*, 41: 165–74.

O'Doherty, D. and Willmott, H. (2001) 'Debating labour process theory: the issue of subjectivity and the relevance of post-structuralism'. *Sociology*, 35: 457–76.

Oxenbridge, S., Brown, W., Deakin, S. and Pratten, C. (2003) 'Initial responses to the statutory recognition provision of the employment relations act 1999'. *British Journal of Industrial Relations*, 41: 315–34.

Richardson, M., Stewart, P., Danford, D., Tailby, S. and Upchurch, M. (2004) 'Employees' experiences of workplace partnership in the private and public sectpr', in Martinez Lucio, M. and Stuart, M. (eds) *Partnership and the Modernisation of Employee Relations*. London: Routledge.

Rose, M. (2003) Labour Market Trajectories and Rationales of Work: End of Award Report, ESRC award no. 21230200251.

Stephenson, C. and Stewart, P. (2001) 'The whispering shadow: collectivism and individualism at Ikeda-Hoover and Nissan UK', *Sociological Research Online*, 6 (3) <http://www.socresonline.org.uk/6/3/stephenson.html>

Stewart, F., Ricci, J. A., Chee, E., Morganstein, D. and Lipton, R. (2003) 'Lost productive time and cost due to common pain conditions in the US workforce', *Journal of the American Medical Association*, 290: 2443–54.

Stewart, P., Lewchuk, W., Yates, C., Saruta, M. and Danford, A. (2004) 'Patterns of labour control and the erosion of labour standards: towards an international study of the quality of working life in the automobile industry (Canada, Japan and the UK)', in Charron, E. and Stewart, P. (eds) *Work and Employment Relations in the Automobile Industry*. London: Palgrave Macmillan.

Stewart, P. (2005 forthcoming) 'Individualism and collectivism in British sociology', in Martinez Lucio, M. and Alonso, L. E. (eds) *Labour Regulation and Labour Processes in Europe*. London: Palgrave Macmillan.

Tailby, S., Stewart, P. and Richardson, M. (2003) NHS Future of Work Report. Britsol UWE: ESRU.

Taylor, R. (2002). Britain's world of work – myths and realities. Economic and Social Research Council: Swindon.

TUCworkSMART sickness absence guide (2004) www.worksmart.org.uk.

Watterson, A. and LaDou, J. (2003) 'Health and safety executive inspections of UK semiconductor plants', *International Journal of Occupational and Environmental Health*, 9: 392–5, October–December.

White, M., Hill, S., McGovern, P. and Mills, C. *Working in Britain in the Year 2002* (WIB) ESRC Essex.

White, M., Hill, S., McGovern, P., Mills, C. and Smeaton, D. (2003) ' "High Performance" management practices, working hours and work-life balance'. *British Journal of Industrial Relations*, 41: 175–95.

Yates, C., Lewchuk, W. and Stewart, P. (2001) 'Empowerment as a Trojan horse: new systems of work organisation in the North American automobile industry', *Economic and Industrial Democracy*, 22: 517–41, November.

1

'Striving under Chaos': The Effects of Market Turbulence and Organisational Flux on Call Centre Work

Phil Taylor, Gregor Gall, Peter Bain and Chris Baldry

Introduction

The Marxist concept of the 'full circuit of capital' (see, for example, Kelly (1985: 32)) is seldom used to understand the processes and outcomes of workplace change. However, movements in the capitalist economy, such as market turbulence, and relations between units of capital often have a direct influence on work organisation and the employment relationship. The 'full circuit' comprises both downward vertical relationships between market–workplace and capital–labour and horizontal relationships between units of capital, involving production and realisation of surplus value. This perspective allows for contextualised analysis of articulation and disarticulation between market and workplace consequent upon the capitalist imperative to accumulate. But mindful of replacing one error, the narrow horizons of workplace studies on control, for another, mechanically imputing workplace change from market change, such environmental forces are seen to *shape* rather than *determine* work, and employment relations (Hyman, 1987; Blyton and Turnbull, 1998: 66), thereby allowing for the role of agency while at the same time recognising the compulsion to accumulate.

This chapter examines how workers experience the effects of market turbulence on their work and employment through organisational churn and flux. Turbulence is conceived of as continual disorder, disruption and disturbance in levels and nature of economic activity in general as well as in specific product markets, leading to agitation which produces change in courses of action, that is, organisational churn and flux. Churn and flux are conceived as continual intra-company change and disruption in structures, workforce composition, work design, work organisation and process, work rates and attendant regulations. The salience of turbulence lies in the widespread belief that not only has market turbulence been a constant feature of capitalism, but it has increased since the early 1980s as a result of economic and social deregulation. There seems plentiful evidence for this: shorter and more accentuated cycles of growth and recession, increasing rates of company births and deaths, ever greater mergers and acquisitions, never ending organisational restructuring, and more 'new' management techniques. Concomitantly, there have been widespread job cuts, increasing employment insecurity, rising work intensification, and growing incidence of atypical work. This chapter investigates the extent and nature of these links and their effects.

Methodology

The research draws on findings from a 3-year study of call centres in central Scotland, funded by the ESRC 'Future of Work' programme. In each centre, four to six members of the research team spent 6 months examining the content and organisation of work and the employment relationship, as well as assessing the links between workplace, community and household. Given the diversity within, and spread of, call centres, the concept of a 'typical' call centre is unsustainable, notwithstanding commonalities *vis-à-vis* integration of computers and telephony. The four call centres – referred to here as M, E, T and H – were selected to represent not only some of the most important sectoral concentrations (finance, media/telecoms, outsourcing and travel), but also because they carried out a range of services requiring differing employee abilities and skill levels. Informal and semi-structured discussions were conducted with call-handlers, team leaders, union reps and managers. In addition, a detailed staff questionnaire was carried out with response rates from 45 per cent to 85 per cent and a range of each company's policy documents, reports and statistical data examined.

Global capitalism

Central to understanding the processes and outcomes of the globalised economy is that it comprises the main component of capitalist society. Accordingly, the central dynamic of both economy and society is the compulsion to accumulate surplus, whereby production, distribution and exchange heavily influence and structure human activity in private and public spheres (Harman, 1986). Capitalism is characterised by an interlinked cycle of booms and slumps, of varying magnitudes, where the conditions of one provide the basis for the other. The unplanned, uncoordinated and relatively decentralised nature of capitalist economic activity at the supra- and inter-firm level creates sharp and unrestrained tendencies towards systemic instability, whether of growth or contraction (Harman, 1986).

Our research was undertaken during the period (late-1999 to 2001) in which the US economy's boom reached its zenith and, following the bursting of the speculative boom which had characterised it, gave way to recession. The causes, nature and consequences of boom and crisis in the world capitalist system during the 1990s have been the subject of recent debate, stimulated by Brenner (1998, 2002) and responses of Marxist and critical thinkers (*Historical Materialism,* 1999a,b). Agreement exists on the significance of features of the real, but exaggerated, boom and the transition to crisis. The boom was made possible by recovery in levels of profitability resulting from large-scale restructuring that eliminated inefficient capital, historically unprecedented repression of real wages and the devaluation of the dollar relative to other major currencies (Callinicos, 2003: 41). Yet, by the late 1990s, these effects had ceased to create dynamism as the Clinton administration reverted to a high dollar and the rate of return in manufacturing fell. But, following Federal government intervention in 1998 as a response to the profound fears generated by the Russian economic collapse, the greatest financial bubble in history developed. Equity prices exploded and there occurred, 'the absurd disconnection between the rise of paper wealth and the growth of actual output, and particularly of profits, in the underlying economy' (Brenner, 2002: 182). Despite this obvious divergence, the Federal Reserve Bank continued to fuel the hype surrounding the 'new economy', asserting that the dynamism of this sector had ushered in a new era in which the boom–slump cycle had been overcome.

However, 'the economy could defy the gravitational pull of actual relations for only so long' (Brenner, 2002: 188) and when the rate of profit began to fall, the end of the boom was inevitable. From this perspective, the role of the financial markets is: 'less an autonomous source of instability, more as one dimension of a set of interconnected processes driving capitalist economies towards crisis' (Callinicos, 2003: 13). From 2000, e-commerce firms saw their share values collapse first and then the broader markets began their precipitous drop. In both the US and UK, over-investment and overcapacity became widespread, particularly in the 'new economy', most notably technology, media and telecommunications. The 'new economy' has suffered particularly severely as a result of asset price inflation, the dominance of shareholder value, chronic indebtedness and the 'financialisation' of the economy (Froud *et al.*, 2002). The profound effects generated in the course of the rapid transformation from superheated boom to supercooled contraction could not but act as a general source of uncertainty and instability at sector, company and workplace levels.

While, from the late 1970s, leading western governments had publicly vilified the state's role in the economy, in reality, they had played an active role in social and economic developments. First, privatising state-owned industries or removing sector regulation, has allowed companies access to new, profitable opportunities. Second, this was achieved by targeting 'supply-side' factors, for example, deregulating labour markets to facilitate 'flexibility', and/or imposing tighter legal restrictions on workers' rights.

Organisational turbulence

Reflecting tensions emanating from the systemic 'chaos' was the stance of the UK government, described as 'more wary of the European Social Model' than of US 'hyper-individualism and social authoritarianism' (Marquand, 1998: 19). Moreover, dissolution of the post-war settlement's socio-economic regulation, has meant that management and employers have been in uncharted territory. When combined with increased competition, delayering and downsizing, and rapid technological change made possible by ICT, this has resulted, at the organisational level, in an urgent search for new panaceas and paradigms. One of the dominant themes of the academic 'post-ism' literatures is that post-modern/bureaucratic/Fordist social organisation is characterised by fluidity and an absence of stasis, making previous organisational paradigms redundant. Thus, it is argued that bureaucracy embodies too rigid a set of organisational principles to be effective in responding to change and that hierarchies have been replaced by networks, with the concept of flexibility being given iconic status as both a goal and *post hoc* justification for change (Peters, 1987, 1997). For those of a managerial perspective, this could only be a 'good thing', and companies could stay ahead only if they constantly embrace change and 'thrive on chaos' (Peters, 1987). Such exhortations ignored the shop floor experience. Even if companies survive and 'thrive', what have been the effects of constant change (downsizing, mergers, takeovers, just-in time, TQM, HRM, BPR, 'customer care' and 'zero defect' programmes, and teamworking) on workers?

Contextualised workplace relations

Following Kelly (1985) and Hyman (1987), Thompson (2003) argued that current trends in capitalism should serve to emphasise that there are periods when work relations are not the principal drivers of change and that focussing solely on the workplace is likely to neglect the underlying machinery of (capitalist) markets. In one sense these are truisms, but in the context of recent trends in the sociology of work, post-Foucauldian labour process theory and organisational analysis, these observations valuably refocus attention on the system-wide dynamics which structure and shape the contemporary workplace. According to Thompson, a period has been entered in which financial markets are now the dominant drivers whose impact on labour is experienced through processes of organisational restructuring. Sturdy and Morgan (2001) argued that the consequence of the 'financialisation' of change in response to the new dynamics of capital markets is a 'continuous churning inside the companies'. These insights need to be taken on board when analysing workplace and intra-firm change in order to broaden the analytical framework to consider the impact of political economy on the workplace. Just as market operations shape but do not determine managerial action, so changes in work organisation and labour process at the workplace are not solely explicable by reference to managerial control strategies *per se.* They are understandable only when the wider connections with capital and product markets are explored, and the workplaces are situated in the dynamics of their respective industrial sectors.

Call centres

In the above context, call centres have become an organisational imperative in customer interactions. Their rapid establishment and position of dominance in service delivery has been created by being able to remain competitive by using the speed and data-integrative capacity of ICTs to offer quicker, more complete and, critically, more cost-effective, customer services (Marshall and Richardson, 1996; Taylor and Bain, 1999: 102). With origins in centralisation of bank customer servicing and back-office operations, the cost advantage gained in the UK by Direct Line and First Direct's lead in integrating telecoms and computerising telebanking and insurance stimulated others in financial services to follow (Bain and Taylor, 2002). This established a model for sale and delivery of services that was quickly taken up by the travel industry, telecommunications, public utilities and by any company wishing to expand into direct selling and marketing.

The advantages were obvious – closure of small, relatively high-overhead high street branches, banks and travel agents, and creation of large customer databases, housed in a few centres serving the whole country, increasingly operated on a '24/7' basis, with the ability to respond to customer enquiries and to offer a 'one-stop shop' for sale of ancillary products. The consequences, however, have been those usually associated with innovative work systems. While those who first adopt such models potentially gain windfall profits, imitation by others sees the 'competitive advantage' disappear. The only way to continue to compete is to use the, now established, work system more intensively. Here, although similar trends are evident in telecommunications, travel and utilities, and are additionally found in the growing outsourced sub-sector (Taylor *et al.*, 2002), financial services provides the clearest illustration (Bain and Taylor, 2002). Continual internal restructuring, the translation downwards of performance criteria, ultimately in the form of enlarged targets for call-handlers, and the transformation of customer service roles through the requirement to sell, have all been evident. Therefore, as the product of increased competition and market turbulence, it is not surprising that call centre work displays a schizophrenia of alternating priorities between customer service quality and cost reduction, with concomitant inherent tensions, change and uncertainty.

Four sectors of economic activity

Before examining the experience of work in the call centres, accounts are presented of the market turbulence affecting the companies and the sectors in which they operate.

Finance

Although retail banking has been subject to continuous change in products and processes of delivery since the 1970s, the dominant firms were protected by industry regulation and their ownership of the central clearing system (Morris *et al.*, 2001: 241). However, by the late 1980s, several factors brought sweeping changes to banking, insurance and financial services. Deregulatory reforms, particularly measures contained in the 1986 financial services and building society legislation, facilitated 'rapid change and inter-penetration of the hitherto discrete markets' (Marshall and Richardson, 1996: 1848). The combined effects of tighter market conditions and new ICTs 'irredeemably shattered a post-war honeymoon period in the clearing banks of almost uninterrupted staffing expansion' (Cressey and Scott, 1992: 84). Recession and debt crises led to cost containment strategies, with employment in English banks falling by 80 000 to 220 000 between 1989 and 1999 (while part-timers rose from 45 000 to 72 300), and compulsory redundancies enforced for the first time in 1993 (Morris *et al.*, 2001: 241–2).

The growing sophistication and integration of ICTs saw 'home-banking' develop, pre-dating Midland Bank's launch of First Direct in 1989 (BIFU, 1996: 5). Customers could phone any time, day or night, to conduct transactions normally performed in Midland branches, thus offering: 'a new identity at a time when customer dissatisfaction with traditional banks was generally high, with perceptions of poor service and high charges' (BIFU, 1996: 6). Similarly, Direct Line, established by Royal Bank of Scotland in 1988 to sell car insurance, soon expanded into household insurance, personal loans and mortgages (Marshall and Richardson, 1996: 1852). Although closure of high street branches began in the 1980s, the rapid take up of the call centre medium for delivery of financial services contributed to one in seven closing between 1990 and 1994 (BIFU, 1996: 9). By the late-1990s 'all the main players [were] now vying for a share of the same market [amid] readjustment and rationalisation of existing facilities' (IDS, 1998: 7).

In 1989, M abandoned mutual building society status and became the UK's fifth largest bank (with a market capitalisation of £1.7), offering an expanded range of financial products and services. In its first year, profits and the share price rose from £501 m to £582 m, and £1.30 to £1.81 respectively (M, 2002). Thus, 'With more money available to build the business, and fewer restrictions on its activities, M's conversion to a bank meant it could expand quickly, both organically and by acquisition' (M, 2002).

Table 1.1   M's acquisitions and mergers in the 1990s

Year	Nature of acquired business	Value (£)
1992	Life assurance company	288 m
1995	Point-of-sale finance house	285 m
1996	Car-leasing and used-car finance companies	128 m
1996	Merger with another building society	assets increased by 11.6bn
1997	Wholesale money market and offshore banking company	195 m
1998	Point-of-sale finance operations	347 m

Source: M (2002).

Throughout the 1990s, M pursued an extremely aggressive acquisition strategy (Table 1.1). The company was to later summarise its development during this period as representing 'the transformation of the Group from a newly converted mortgage bank into a diversified, international provider of financial services' (M, 2001).

Like its competitors, M closed many high street branches, expanding services in four new call centres in the UK in the mid-1990s. However, as the business environment became stormier and more competitive, heralded by the dot.com companies' collapse, M continued seeking ways to gain competitive advantage and cut costs. It launched the first interactive computer bank in the UK, expanded its branch-franchising scheme and outsourced its general insurance business. However, due to a flagging share price and perceived lack of strategy, after 2000 M came under heavy pressure and itself became the subject of take-over bids (*Herald*, 2001).

Telecommunications

The last two decades have witnessed a transformation in virtually every aspect of the telecommunications industry (Cave *et al.*, 2002). Technological innovation and application, including increases in capacity through optical-fibre technology, digitilisation and connectionless architecture based on Internet protocols which enable integration of voice, data and video, have been powerful engines of change. Yet, arguably of greater salience, and facilitating technological diffusion in the sector, have been the effects of liberalisation, market developments and growth of financial markets. Since the mid-1980s, neo-liberal governments subjected state-controlled telecom monopolies to competition with the process accelerating in the 1990s following the *Telecommunications Act 1996* in the USA, and the EU's decision in 1998 to liberalise the sector. Consequently, incumbents were challenged by new entrants. At a more fundamental level, the structure of vertical specialisation in telecommunications allowed new entrants to 'buy in' the most recent technology, thereby significantly lowering barriers to market entry (Fransman, 2002). But this emerging structure of 'easy and rapid entry (made possible in the first place by regulatory change) brought about an increase in the intensity of competition in parts of the Infocommunications Industry' (Fransman, 2002: 21), constituting both precondition for the boom of 1996 onwards and the subsequent bust of 2001–02.

The role of financial markets proved equally decisive, facilitating the entry and initial growth of new companies (Fransman, 2002: 55) and then mergers and acquisitions (e.g. WorldCom's takeover of MCI) which characterised the sector in the mid- to late 1990s (Trillas, 2002). While the scale of investment in telecoms was staggering, estimated at $1805bn between 1996 and 2001 (Fransman, 2002), share prices of these dynamic new entrants increased disproportionately. Over-optimistic expectations regarding profitability were universally held by investors, telecom operators, equipment suppliers and even regulatory bodies, inducing a gold-rush mania of speculation and over-expansion. Fransman (2002: 25) consequently argued, 'once these exuberant expectations changed to become pessimistic (a reflection of general changing stock market sentiment), the emperor's clothes quickly fell away'. Share prices, inflated far beyond the real level of profitability in the sector, or indeed the economy, started to fall as prices fell and profit margins failed to materialise. The subsequent crash was as spectacular as the boom that preceded it. At its height in early 2000, the total stock market value of all telecom operators and equipment suppliers was $6300bn. Before '9/11', $2500bn was wiped off (*Financial Times*, 2001). Since then, the sector has been characterised by universal revenue and profit crises and wide-scale bankruptcies amongst the successful new entrants, such as WorldCom (*Financial Times*, 2002).

This analysis is essential to understanding E's activities and performance, and for contextualising work organisation and the experience of work in its call centres. E, as a large transnational company providing a range of cable-delivered telecommunications and entertainment services in both analogue and digital modes, was a direct beneficiary of deregulation, acquiring in the early 1990s the UK terrestrial television transmission system. Following acquisition by a smaller competing cable company, it grew rapidly through aggressive takeovers, including in 1998 the major player in this market segment, which resulted in the acquisition of its four UK call centres. E exemplifies the generic weakness of the new entrants – exaggerated expectations of customer demand, revenues and profits; massive indebtedness; 'merge to grow' strategies; and inflated share price. Even during the sector's boom period of late 2000, its pre-tax losses of $630 m almost outstripped revenue of $666 m[1] (*Financial Times*, 2000a). These problems have been compounded by issues specific to the cable sub-sector and the difficulties caused by attempting to integrate acquired operations. With corporate debt of $17.5bn by late 2000 (*Financial Times*, 2000b), E attempted to overcome its problems through continuous capital and operational restructuring. Through the 'Planning for Growth' (PFG) strategy, 2300 redundancies were planned for 2000 and a further 5000 for 2001. With severe internal financial constraints, the intractability of its difficulties in unfavourable telecoms and financial markets, allied to continued competitive pressure from its remaining UK competitor, E was forced to seek Chapter 11 bankruptcy protection in 2002.

Outsourcing

Outsourcing is a relatively new development in the organisation of production, distribution and exchange under late capitalism. Previously, the *modus operandi* was agglomeration via direct ownership to obtain economies of scale, although significant sub-contracting existed in manufacturing. Outsourcing is now one of the main methods by which the organisation of capital is being reconfigured to meet the present challenges of accumulation. Others include de-mergers, selling off 'non-core' businesses and joint-ventures. Outsourcing, it is argued, reduces exposure to economic risk in uncertain environments as well as facilitating market sensitisation of intra-firm activity, leading to reductions in basic costs associated with full in-house provision. Wage rates can be 20–40 per cent less in outsourced operations compared to in-house. Furthermore, it is argued economies of scale with regard to quality and productivity can be created by dedicated and specialised operations. Outsourcing may suggest, via de-agglomeration, support for the 'disorganisation of capitalism' thesis (Lash and Urry, 1987). In practice, outsourcing is not without problems: control can be weakened not strengthened through creation of dependency, 'quality' of good or service can be reduced and costs can spiral, in spite of contractual terms.

Outsourcing represents a departure whereby sub-contracting now concerns contracting out of key functions (e.g. IT, accountancy, personnel) within service parts of the economy (business services, public sector). Outsourcing has, thus, moved from production to distribution and exchange, and covers back-office functions and interface with customers. However, outsourcing can also involve service sector firms becoming mere 'shell' companies that conduct their core activities through deploying services of others.

Consequently, firms have specifically emerged to provide these services, while existing companies have moved from servicing in-house operations to providing these services *in toto* such as TCS and Vertex. Call centres are a prime mechanism in outsourcing by virtue of their geographical mobility and functional separation from production/delivery of products/services as a result of ICTs. They offer the ability to concentrate sales and customer service functions into a small number of operations at a distance from outsourcees with considerable cost reductions.

In terms of call centre activity, outsourcing represents a dramatically growing specialism within a dramatically growing 'sector'. In Scotland, for example, the number of outsourced call centres grew from 18 (with 2905 employed) to 42 (9010 staff) between 1997 and 2000, representing a growth in its proportion of call centres from 18.2 per cent to 20.4 per cent (Taylor and Bain, 2001: 12). Originating as an in-house operation of a utility provider and following expansion of its customer services call centre activity (sales, billing, after-sales service) in the early 1990s, T now provides customer services on behalf of about 20 clients operating in Britain and Europe. It sells 'competitive advantage' through selling its expertise, being able to provide tailored services with short lead-in times and lower labour costs. According to T (1998: 3),

> Rather than ascend the steep learning and investment curve [of establishing call centres], many companies choose to outsource [which]... reduces the bureaucracy and overheads associated with in-house call centres [and] can raise service levels and increase revenue as well as providing the latest technology at no added expense.

Thus, T provides design, organisation and implementation services for establishing, running and expanding an (outsourced) call centre. Customers have a Service Level Agreement (SLA) with T to establish and maintain the qualitative and quantitative dimensions of performance.

T was launched in 1999 with a share price of about £3 that climbed to approximately £8 within six months on anticipated profits. But although an expanding sector, the process of matching supply to demand in a competitive environment is a fragile and indeterminate one. Demand is not real until it is made tangible through a contract or viewed retrospectively and it can be created as well as found. T planned for growth speculatively [sic] by creating capacity to operate more accounts but this was not always forthcoming and, that which did was not always the high-value, quality business sought. This created financial performance problems, and continual refinancing from the parent group which was not repaid through profits. In turn, these created pressures at a lower level on costs and performance. Turnover targets were attained but costs were higher and losses greater than anticipated. This, and growing market instability, created delay in T's floatation from the parent company, flotation that was intended to fund further expansion in internet and interactive services. This culminated in a 30 per cent then 90 per cent slump in share price (*Sunday Herald*, 2000; *Times*, 2000) on news of both worse than anticipated growth and losses, reflecting the bursting of the dot.com bubble. Over-valuation, then corrective action, led to a further collapse in business confidence in this sector.

Holidays

The structure of the lead organisations in the sector follows the vertically integrated model established in the 1980s by UK market leader Thomsons, consisting of a three-tiered sandwich of holiday company/travel agency/ charter airline. Although in 1997, the EU Competition Commission had declared itself satisfied that this structure was 'broadly competitive' (*Financial Times*, 1999), the sector was *de facto* an oligopoly, the UK market being dominated by four companies (Figure 1.1).

This concentration had been stimulated by increasing pressure on profits. This arose, first, from movement in customer demand away from all-inclusive packages (on which the profits of the big four had been based) and the rise of budget airlines which removed much of the price difference between standard and chartered flights and allowed holiday makers to construct their own holidays. Package holidays fell from 70 per cent of all trips abroad by UK citizens in the mid-1980s to barely 50 per cent by 2000 (*Marketing Week*, 2000). Second, profit margins in UK holiday companies were already slender because heavy discounting of holidays in the 1980s had led many British holiday-makers to reject any full-priced holiday that did not seem like a bargain. Since 1995, the average inclusive holiday price had stuck at about £400, with a corresponding depreciation in real income for the companies over this period and steeply falling profit margins.

These pressures led to three main responses: an increase in 'self-focus', merger and acquisition, and use of telephony and e-sales. Originally, the travel agency arms of the big companies acted as general agencies who, for a commission, would sell their rivals' products. By 1999, this was becoming less likely; Thomsons had used its market leadership to impose a smaller commission on sales of its holidays by rivals and, as profits tightened, they in turn retaliated by largely cutting out Thomsons and promoting their own brands. Thomsons was forced to push sales of its own holidays via Lunn Poly which, paradoxically, reduced the commission Lunn Poly earned from selling rivals' packages.

Pressure of increased competition, post-1992 EU market re-positioning and EU endorsement of the vertical integration model, encouraged successive waves of acquisitions: the value of mergers in the sector rose from £200 m (1997) to £900 m (1998) (*Financial Times*, 1999). The process had been set in train earlier when, in 1992, Midland Bank sold Thomas Cook to the WestDeutsche Landesbank (WDL) and the German LTU group. In 1994,

Figure 1.1 Structure of UK holiday sector market leaders in 1998

Holiday company	Thomsons/ Skytours	Thomas Cook /Sunworld/ Club18-20	Airtours	First Choice
Travel agency	Lunn Poly	Thomas Cook	Going Places	Sovereign travel
Airline operator	Britannia	Flying Colours	Airtours international	Air 2000

Airtours purchased the Scandinavian Leisure Group and in 1997, Thomsons bought the Swedish company, Fritidsresor. In 1998, cross-border acquisitions accelerated, involving airline rationalisation in response to the challenge of budget carriers. First Choice bought Leisure International and their airline Unijet (to be integrated with Air 2000) and Carlson Leisure (owners of Caledonian Airlines) bought a 22 per cent stake in Thomas Cook: the other 78 per cent was now owned by WDL through subsidiary Preussag. Caledonian Airlines and Flying Colours were merged and rebadged as JMC. By 1999, bids and counter-bids were being continually announced. Swiss Kuoni bid for First Choice, prompting a rival bid by Airtours that was disallowed by the EU Competition Commission. Preussag then bid for Kuoni to stop the latter's bid for First Choice, which would have created a rival company with similar European coverage. The following year saw Preussag (or rather its subsidiary TUI) successfully purchase Thomsons for £1.8bn, forcing through competition regulation, Preussag to sell its Thomas Cook holding. This was bought, together with Carlson's holding, by German C&N Touristic (formed from Condor Airlines and Neckerman Touristic and owned by Lufthansa and retail group Karstadt Quelle). C&N Touristic was previously outbid by Thomsons for Airtours (now renamed MyTravel). In mid-2002, the European Court of Justice's overturning of the block on Airtours' First Choice bid was widely seen presaging further consolidation. However, paucity of surplus capital, the big players having exhausted their reserves in the first round of merger mania, and the shock to long-haul sales of '9/11' further squeezing profit margins, called a temporary halt to the process.

As a third response, companies sought to increase the flexibility of means of purchasing a holiday, primarily through call centre and internet access for customers, later augmented by digital TV channels. By early 1999, call centres were handling 4000 holiday enquiries a day and the telesales share of the market had risen to 28 per cent. As part of this trend, our holiday company 'H' established and acquired four UK call centres between 1996 and 1999, including the one examined here.

Experience of work

We are now in a position to examine the experience of work in the four call centres. Following this, we analyse the connections between market turbulence and organisation flux and churn.

The finance company: 'M'

The call centre had commenced operations in 1995 and, at the time of our research (1999–2000), employed 170 people. Two-thirds of the workforce was engaged in routinised, low-value loan operations, and the other third in providing higher-value mortgage and personal financial advice. Overhead electronic boards showed the number of calls received, handled and lost, longest call time waiting, and number of customers queuing. Individual and team performances and targets were displayed in each team area, alongside league tables. Increasingly, by 1999, concerns were being expressed about how work content and organisation was being moulded by a seemingly never-ending process of change and, in the light of their aggressive strategy, about the sort of company M was becoming. Issues such as the hugely increased utilisation of temporal flexibility and outsourcing, and the con-tinuous re-structuring and re-composition of work teams, contributed to feelings of unease amongst employees.

However, a central and recurring feature of company policy was the drive to increase profitability by raising employees' targets. In December 1999, this strategy was made explicit at a special conference of UK call centre managers when, under 'Year 2000 Challenge', the Board revealed new sales targets for all products. While there was one projected increase of 5 per cent, eight between 32 per cent and 176 per cent, one of 400 per cent and one of 1015 per cent, only one product's sales were expected to fall (by 4 per cent). Furthermore, to remove any dubiety about how these targets were to be achieved, the managers were informed 'income must grow two or three times more than costs; therefore, productivity must increase'. The implica-tions of this for the workforce are discussed later, but some managers anticipated problems when employees heard the news. Questions were asked concerning the rationale and analysis used in setting the new targets, and if there were any guarantee they would not be increased again during 2000 (as had happened in 1999). When the corporate plan was cascaded down to the call centre workforce, although there was heavy emphasis on the need to improve performance, management did not mention the new sales targets.

The reality of how these changes were perceived by, and affected, the work-force was graphically illustrated in employee interviews. It had only been a few months since targets had last been increased and a new bonus scheme introduced, and one customer advisor (CA) spelled out what all this meant:

> The last two years my targets have practically doubled ... When I started I took £5 million worth of loans. [T]his year ... it's rumoured to be £9.5 million in Loans.

The issue of how these policies would affect the quality of customer service was also addressed by another CA:

> ... if a customer had a problem ... with their branch or something, we took it on board and we used to follow it through. Now it's like they don't care ... 'get them on the phone – get them off the phone – next'. It's a production line.

As for the new bonus scheme, a team manager was clear concerning the limitations of its efficacy and allure: 'the targets are too high – I wouldn't use it to attract new workers'. However, the pressure from the company took other forms and brought other problems in its wake. Under a revised employment contract introduced in 1999, new starts had to be available to work between 7.00 to 23.00 hrs. (instead of 8.00–21.00 hrs.), Monday to Saturday, and some were on annualised hours (M, 1999). Consequently:

> I hate ... com[ing] to work ... because ... you're coming in and you're going to get hit with something else that's changed ... : 'next week on Monday we're doing an 8–5 shift, and we're getting our lunch at eleven o clock in the morning' [but] ... the canteen isn't even open. ... They want you to take half an hour for your lunch and stay and do a couple of hours overtime. That would be a 12-hour day.
>
> [I] feel as though I'm working for IBM, you know, a little robot. Whereas they always took take time out and said how are you getting on, now you're just a number ... it got so bad at one stage in here you had to put your hand up to go to the toilet ... Changes kind of started about eighteen months ago ... it just snowballed from there. We have to do mortgages, car insurance, bank accounts, health checks and you're like 'I don't know anything about this, how can I try and sell it?' But they weren't giving you any briefs to read, so you would put your customer on hold and go and ask, then get shouted at 'You're on that call too long.'

It was also clear the revised targets meant that the 'bottom-up' method by which the high-grade FPA (financial planning advisor) schedule of four customer appointments per day had been organised, was to end. Instead, it would be a 'top-down' exercise in which the company centrally set targets for each call centre, and these would be dis-aggregated to team level and then allocated to individual advisors. This FPA seemed to speak for colleagues in all areas of the call centre:

> I've got concerns about the targets that we have been given this year because they have gone quite a bit higher than they were last year, and 95 per cent of the centre struggled to hit them last year. So that tends to make you think, God, here's another struggle again. Every year it's another struggle.

The telecommunications company: 'E'

The prolonged crisis of E described earlier generated uncertainty, insecurity and a reorganisation and intensification of work for call centre staff. First, a merger with its erstwhile principal rival was the source of two issues causing concern amongst operators. Non-integrated customer databases whose effects managers 'had not thought through' proved to be a nightmare for call-han-dling. Second, and at the same time, in its drive to reduce costs, E embarked on a strategy to erode the superior terms and conditions of those operators who remained on their original contracts, harmonising downwards to the new E contracts. Third, the effects of E's precarious position were directly felt through the constant fear of redundancy. One manager stated: 'all staff were feeling vulnerable and demotivated', and predictions of impending closure periodically circulated: 'There are actually some rumours that E aren't going to stay here all that long and they are going to sell to Sky or whoever for a better price.' Several operators reported that the implementation of the PFG strategy had caused many of their fellow workers to leave in pursuit of more secure employment. That the high annual turnover rate of 37 per cent for 2000 was caused in no small measure by such fears of insecurity was confirmed by a manager. An integral part of PFG was reduction of adminis-trative resources and support leading to the identification of vulnerable groups – quality, service performance and retention teams – where unneces-sary tasks were to be stripped out. One operator reflected a cynicism that ran through much of the workforce: '[PFG] is a pretty unfortunate name, I think Planning for Pay Offs would be more accurate.'

For those operators who remained, PFG also brought about work intensi-fication which was acknowledged by a manager: 'It means we are trying to squeeze out extra performance from each area: customer analogue, digital customer services, moves and transfers.' Operators commented on how targets had been revised upwards as part of the drive to increase productivity, for example,

> I feel as though the goal posts were moved. When we came to retentions we were told the bonus would be based on the save rate, average handling times (AHT), call shape and call accreditation.[2] Then … we were told your bonus will be based on your save rate, and your AHT target has to come down 30 seconds every month since January. It was 520 seconds.

Bain *et al.* (2002: 167) argued that targets lie at the heart of call centre management strategy. Upward target revision, a contemporary expression of speed-up, became the principal means by which E attempted to raise the productivity of its workforce in the circumstances of general crisis of uncer-tainty and profitability that bedevilled its operations. Intensification of labour was a direct consequence of the collapse of E's grand strategy of expansion, which itself was a symptom of the crash of the briefly exuberant new economy of telecommunications.

The outsourcing company: 'T'

The call centre at T, employing between 320 and 400 staff, has been subject to general and specific churn but less than might be expected as a result of particular internal organisational configuration and relations of capital. The inherent nature of rapidly establishing new 'live' accounts for external customers creates its own problems despite economies of scale. Pressure on costs reduces lead-in time, creating hurried preparation. Unfamiliarity with new set-ups and products is revealed. In turn, these are magnified by a high degree of account turnover, either through many short-term and/or loss of accounts. These processes lead to intra-organisational instability and shop floor disharmony that impacts deleteriously on performance quality and quantity. To this are added various factors: the differing nature of accounts and client demands, reflecting, in part the pressures clients respond to by virtue of the sectors they operate in. A countervailing factor is that SLAs stipulate, *inter alia*, response times and quality benchmarks. This exists not because of SLAs *per se* but because they have been initially set with staffing levels for projected demand which can fail to materialise, often substantially so. Although staffing can be reduced through turnover, some staff are agency staff, some contracts are short-term and internal staff move to new start-up accounts, 90 per cent of contracts are permanent, creating 'rigidity' in numbers employed. Furthermore, T's parent, a highly profitable 'old economy' company, has been able and willing to support and fund refinancing, creating some distance between T and the impact of poor accumulation rates. *In toto*, this means that, other than in a couple of high-volume, low-quality accounts of established products and established clients, the volume of calls has not materialised, producing a relatively slack pace of work.

That said, staff turnover, created by processes resulting from rapid business expansion and staff 'exit' strategies, comprises a major source of flux. Expansion has created vacancies that constitute promoted posts for many aspirant staff belying the usual impact of flat managerial structures. Owing to the specialised nature of outsourcing and in order to maintain organisational affiliation, an internal labour market has been the most efficient and effective way to fill these posts. Concomitant, the heavy graduate bent of the workforce tends towards staff movement by dint of aspiration towards upward mobility. Further vertical flux is created, where new staffs are needed to fill incumbents' posts, with knock-on effects further down. Notwithstanding the ensuing general dislocation, the training and experience of promoted staff are often insufficiently developed because of short tenure and training needs succumbing to performance demands, so adding to dislocation. There has also been horizontal flux, where owing to the creation of new accounts and the monotony of work in others, staff chose to transfer to other similar posts. Others have left T altogether due to the monotony of work and to gain better remuneration elsewhere.

The internalised labour market for middle and senior-level call centre staff is such that there is a turnover of staff within the call centre sector, again accentuated by rapid growth. This feeds through to a total turnover of about 29 per cent (officially 12 per cent (T, 1998: 8)) with substantial account variation, a 15 per cent drop-out rate in training, 4 per cent sickness-absence rate, only 34 per cent of staff having worked for T for 18+ months, only 14 per cent are 35+ years with 42 per cent being between 17 to 25 years old and the absence of espoused team meetings. In turn, these are manifested in lowered productivity and service provision leading to various cultural initiatives to create commitment, motivation and loyalty as routes to enhanced performance, such as 'Building windmills: inspiring motivation' in 2000, and 'Winning Team Restructure' in 1999, where supervisors and managers had to reapply for jobs under competencies-skills matching. However, there has been no reorganisation of work as operations continue on standardised model of layout and process. While quantitative targets and subsequent monitoring exist, cumulatively increasing targets, enforced rigidly, have not featured widely at T. There is, though, use of normative and qualitative targets. Working time and shifts were reorganised to some extent to provide longer hours of opening.

The holiday company: 'H'

The consequences of restructuring and enhanced levels of competition were felt in H initially through employment levels. After one merger in 1999, H announced 325 job cuts (190 in Scotland) resultant largely from closing agency shops as the company's call centres expanded. In late 2001, a further 1500 jobs cuts followed. Although attributed to the '9/11' demand downturn, many staff believed this had been planned beforehand by the new German owners in response to an inherited surplus capacity and duplication of provision.

Less direct consequences were experienced through a series of incremental changes to work organisation and control that cumulatively intensified the labour process and generated high levels of insecurity over targets and earnings. Workflows at H were divided between customer help and sales, with sales having four distinct product groups. The trend away from acting as a general travel agency and towards promotion of own brands was evidenced in the pecking order of products suggested to customers who did not have a fixed idea of what package they wanted, starting with H products and ending with Thomson. Sales Consultants (SCs) were also left in no doubt that the competitive environment included not only other companies in the sector but also other H call centres and, particularly, H's high street agencies.

The impact of external sectoral changes was felt through marked monthly fluctuations in target levels, in addition to the normal marked seasonal sales fluctuations, and in an increasing complexity in the number of target dimensions to be met before bonuses were gained. The monthly sales target was set by head office, often only sent to the centres at the very end of the preceding month, and according to the union rep, determined by what market share H wanted to aim for. Managers then divided it up among the sales groups and these were used to establish team and mostly importantly individual targets (see Bain *et al.*, 2002). The available bonus therefore not only varied from month to month depending on the projected volume of sales but also from individual to individual. Added to this there was also a 20 per cent shift allowance, all of which meant that SC take-home pay could vary month on month by about £400.

Targets had been originally set in terms of calls per hour and sales volume, including the sale of additional products such as holiday insurance which the SCs were under increasing pressure to promote. In mid-2000, call conversion rates (CCR) were included in target make-up and, by late 2001, as sales still had not picked up, the further ingredient of call-handling time was added. Compared to the start of our observation period, bonuses were getting smaller and harder to reach: as the sales were not forthcoming and few were reaching their targets, the company did not need to cut bonuses, it just did not revise targets downwards.

The effect of the increasing complexity of targets was certainly a decrease in the 'porosity' of working time, as all calls counted towards either volume targets and/or CCR:

Q: Does call conversion mean that you put more effort into persuading a customer to buy a holiday?

A: I think you've always had that pressure to sell ... what call conversion means is that you don't now have a breather time in the month.

In addition to target complexity, the result of mergers and acquisitions was by now being reflected in an increase in the number of different types of call which workers had to remember how to process: one SC estimated she handled eleven different types of product.

Labour intensification was compounded by other developments including a draconian new sickness-absence policy and, most significantly, the introduction in early 2000 of 'Blue Pumpkin', a software system that allocated shifts and break-times automatically, thus eliminating what little control workers had over working time. Previously, although start times could vary, it was usual and expected for a given start time to be kept for the week. Under Blue Pumpkin, start times could vary by 15 minutes on a random daily basis and Saturday was treated as a normal working day. The ability of SCs to take lunch breaks in pairs and at times that allowed breaks to be fitted around call patterns now ended and the loss of Saturdays was resented by the young workforce. Complaints abounded that, because hours were allocated to individuals regardless of team membership, team spirit was being undermined as team members might not be working the same days together. This increasing disjuncture between the official ethos of teams and workers' experience was further heightened by frequent changes in team management, and the decision to shuffle team membership in the main reservation area. Finally, the pressure of the shake-out of surplus capacity and the '9/11' effect on already meagre profit margins was made apparent in November 2001 when H requested salary cuts; after a union campaign these were rescinded in 2003.

Discussion

Workers' experience in the call centres has comprised, on the one hand, work intensification and extensification as well as immiseration of other material and psychological conditions like job satisfaction, although not uniformly so. On the other hand, workers have also experienced the social dislocation associated with staff turnover and organisational restructuring. The latter resulted in lowered productivity, occasioning corrective action by employers, suggesting something of a vicious circle. As with the dominant findings in the growing research on call centre labour processes, there is little evidence of 'shiny happy' workplaces and workers. The immediate source of this churn and flux was not market turbulence *per se* (general, sectoral) but senior management's *assessment* of the meaning and consequences of it for cost bases, revenue, profitability and share price as well as assessments of responses by their competitors, shareholders, investors and financial analysts. Following company assessments, courses of action were taken to deliver set objectives under prevailing conditions. Senior management has choices here but within fairly tight parameters, explicitly and implicitly set by the nostrums of the aforementioned third parties rather than an impersonal 'market'. Their responses invariably include raising labour performance and reducing unit labour costs as the hegemonic *modus operandi*, although launching of new products and mergers and acquisitions to gain market share also feature but in more minor and supporting roles. Notably, responses seldom involve innovative and fundamental redesigns or reorganisations of work such as Volvo's Kalmar experiment. But the prevailing conditions are seldom static because of the dynamism of capitalism, the growth in availability of finance and the recent deregulation leaving the market more unfettered. The degree of turbulence is arguably higher in the four sectors than in some others because of the rapidity of technological change unlocking new productive capacities (Morgan and Sawyer, 1988: 264). This leads to continual reassessments and changes or developments in courses of action.

Courses of action are then translated into initiatives and implemented by lower-level management creating organisational flux and churn. Being 'loyal lieutenants', they seek to make their charges 'strive under chaos' to make the companies 'thrive under chaos'. The flux and churn which workers experience, notwithstanding worker resistance that may dilute this, reflect attempts to 'strive' under market turbulence. Added to this is the impact of their responses to flux and churn, for example, exiting that creates staff turnover, that in turn increases the degree of flux and churn. In this way, we can follow the 'full circuit' of capital downwards from the global economy to regional and national economies and then to industry and firm, prior to reaching the workplace. This means developing a tapestry of levels of analysis with intersecting processes and dynamics that avoid uni-dimensional sequences and causation while not losing sight of the totality of the imperative to accumulate under capitalism. Consequently, the general and particular can be accounted for and explained; on the one hand, the drive to expand or cope with crisis bearing down on labour costs, and on the other, T's dual but idiosyncratic specificity of SLAs and capital structure. So too can we account for the vicious circle created by the mantra of 'staying the same isn't an option'. The call centres were created in order to reduce labour costs but, as market turbulence ensued, they too were subject to flux and churn as employers sought to respond to crises. Indeed, the forces that create churn and flux continually undermine stability such that further churn and flux are then instituted.

Acknowledgement

The research was conducted under the ESRC 'Future of Work' programme (award no. L212252006), and the other researchers involved in the project were Nick Bozienelos, Kay Gilbert, Cliff Lockyer, Gareth Mulvey, Dora Scholarios, Aileen Watson and the late Harvie Ramsay (Strathclyde), Dirk Bunzel (Keele), Jeff Hyman (Aberdeen) and Abigail Marks (Heriot-Watt).

Notes

1. Although E's core operations were located in the UK, it was listed on the New York stock exchange.
2. The preceding four terms are mechanisms for measuring different aspects of individual call centre workers' productivity in E.

References

Bain, P. and Taylor, P. (2002) ' "Ringing the changes?" Union recognition and organisation in call centres in the UK finance sector'. *Industrial Relations Journal*, 33 (3): 246–61.
Bain, P., Watson, A., Mulvey, G., Taylor, P. and Gall, G. (2002) 'Taylorism, targets and the pursuit of quantity and quality by call centre management'. *New Technology, Work and Employment*, 17 (3): 154–69.
BIFU (1996) *Dialling the Future? Phone Banking and Insurance*, London: BIFU.
Blyton, P. and Turnbull, P. (1998) *The Dynamics of Employee Relations*, ed. London: Macmillan.
Brenner, R. (1998) 'The economics of global turbulence'. *New Left Review*, 229: 1–265.
Brenner, R. (2002) *The Boom and the Bubble: the US in the world economy*, London: Verso.
Callinicos, A. (2003) *An Anti-Capitalist Manifesto*, London: Polity.
Cave, M., Majumdar, S. and Vogelsang, I. (eds) (2002) *Handbook of Telecommunications Economics*, vol. 1, Amsterdam: Elsevier.
Cressey, P. and Scott, P. (1992) 'Employment, technology and industrial relations in the UK clearing banks: is the honeymoon over?' *New Technology, Work and Employment*, 7 (2): 83–96.

Financial Times, The (1999) 9 May, London.

Financial Times, The (2000a) 10 August, London.

Financial Times, The (2000b) 8 December, London.

Financial Times, The (2001) 5 September, London.

Financial Times, The (2002) 19 December, London.

Fransman, M. (2002) *Telecoms in the Internet Age*, Oxford: Oxford University Press.

Froud, J., Johal, S. and Williams, K. (2002) 'Financialisation and the coupon pool'. *Capital and Class*, 78: 119–52.

Harman, C. (1986) *Explaining the Crisis*, London: Bookmarks.

Herald, The (2001) 17 February, Glasgow.

Historical Materialism (1999a, 1999b) special editions on the world economy, 4 and 5.

Hyman, R. (1987) 'Strategy or structure? Capital, labour and control'. *Work, Employment and Society*, 1(1): 25–55.

IDS (1998) *Pay and Conditions in Call Centres 1998*, London: Incomes Data Services.

Kelly, J. (1985) 'Management's redesign of work: labour process, labour markets and product markets' in Knights, D., Willmott, H. and Collinson, D. (eds) *Job Redesign – Critical Perspectives on the Labour Process*, Aldershot: Gower. 30–51.

Lash, S. and Urry, J. (1987) *The End of Organised Capitalism*, Cambridge: Polity.

'M' (2001) *Directors' Report and Accounts*, London.

'M' (2002) website information.

Marketing Week (2000) 3 August, London.

Marquand, D. (1998) 'The Blair paradox'. *Prospect*, May: 18–20.

Marshall, J. and Richardson, R. (1996) 'The impact of 'telemediated' services on corporate structures: the examples of "branchless" retailing in Britain'. *Environment and Planning*, (28): 1843–58.

Morgan, K. and Sawyer, A. (1988) *Microcircuits of Capital: 'Sunrise' Industry and Uneven Development*, London: Routledge.

Morris, T., Storey, J., Wilkinson, A. and Cressey, P. (2001) 'Industry change and union mergers in British retail finance'. *British Journal of Industrial Relations*, 39 (2): 237–56.

Peters, T. (1987) *Thriving on Chaos: Handbook for a Management Revolution*, London: Macmillan.

Peters, T. (1997) *The Circle of Innovation: You Can't Shrink Your Way To Greatness*, London: Coronet.

Sturdy, A. and Morgan, G. (2001) 'From transformation to financialisation? Towards a discursive approach to organisational change and a structural approach to discourse'. Critical Management Studies Conference, UMIST, July. Manchester School of Management.

Sunday Herald, The (2000) 6 August, Glasgow.

'T' (1998) *Corporate Profile*, Glasgow: 'T'.

Taylor, P., Mulvey, G., Hyman, J. and Bain, P. (2002) 'Work organisation, control and the experience of work in call centres'. *Work Employment and Society*, 16(1): 133–50.

Taylor, P. and Bain, P. (1999) ' "An assembly line in the head": work and employee relations in the call centre'. *Industrial Relations Journal*, 30(2): 101–17.

Taylor, P. and Bain, P. (2001) *Call Centres in Scotland in 2000*, Glasgow: Rowan Tree Press.

Thompson, P. (2003) 'Disconnected capitalism: or why employers can't keep their side of the bargain'. *Work, Employment and Society*, 17(2): 359–78.

Times, The (2000) 9 November, London.

Trillas, F. (2002) 'Mergers, acquisitions and control of telecommunications firms in Europe'. *Telecommunications Policy*, 26: 269–86.

2

The Production and Reproduction of Trade Union Autocracy in the Turkish Metalworking Industry

Theo Nichols and Nadir Sugur

The idea that less developed countries will one day inevitably catch up with those that are presently more developed, or that increases in GDP in those countries will necessarily trickle down to the poor are rightly disputed. By contrast, few would take issue with the idea that cheap labour is likely to be an important advantage to those developing countries which seek to export to more developed ones. Seen in this light, however, the role of trade unions in those societies becomes a particularly interesting one. Strong and effective trade unions might be thought to undermine cheap wages and increase labour costs. On the other hand, to suppose that such trade unions can only exist in these countries in so far as they are ineffectual is only to raise further questions: how, then, is such trade unionism brought into existence? Why do workers tolerate it? Why do workers join such unions? Why don't they quit them? These are the essentially sociological questions that concern us in this paper. Our aim is to address them by examining one important trade union in Turkey, Türk Metal, which is the major trade union in the metal industry in the Izmit triangle, itself the major centre of Turkey's export industry.[1]

This paper necessarily begins by explaining how trade unions in Turkey are organised into several different federations. Then the position of Türk Metal, which belongs to the largest of these federations, Türk-İş, is described, as is its operation in that part of the metal industry which is situated in the Izmit triangle, a key location of Turkey's current industrialisation. Case study evidence from four firms in the white goods and car industries is then introduced and it is seen that criticism of the union by workers focuses on its lack of responsiveness to their needs, lack of internal democracy and dialogue. This provokes the questions that are systematically addressed in the body of the paper: how did the union come to its present prominence? And how is its autocracy reproduced? The answer to the first question is seen to be inseparable from the policy and practice of the military regime which came to power in 1980 and which paved the way for Turkey's shift to export-oriented industrialisation and the opening to the free market economy. The answer to the second question is seen to be found – apart from the role that management plays in this process – in a mesh of legal and illegal practices that constrain workers with respect to how they can influence the union, whether they can choose not to join the union in the first place, or indeed even leave it.

Trade unions in Turkey

There are four main union federations in Turkey – Türk-İş, DİSK, MISK and HAK-İŞ – and in addition some independent unions, which have relatively few members.

Türk-İş is the biggest federation. Founded in 1952, it spans 32 member unions and has 2.2 million individual members. All other federations have been formed by splits from it in the 1960s and 1970s (Sakallioglu, 1991). It is sometimes regarded as an American form of union. This is not without reason: between 1960 and 1970 US financial aid constituted a sum equal to the income that came to Türk-İş from its membership dues. There were frequent visits to the States by the leadership and other training activists (Isikli, 1987: 319). Politically Türk-İş claimed a centre and centre-left position in the 1970s with sympathies toward the CHP (Cumhuriyet Halk Partisi or Republican People's Party). Today it occupies a centre-right position. Its formally declared aims include a commitment to 'a high level of national democratic secular and social and state structure based on Ataturk's principles and the Constitution' (Article 3, Türk-İş Regulations). It is mainly composed of right wing unions but its constituent unions include also some which are left wing, notably the petrol workers' union, Petrol-İş. Türk Metal is part of Türk-İş and is the union, which is at the centre of this paper.

DİSK (the Revolutionary Workers' Trade Union Confederation) was founded in 1967 when several unions left Türk-İş, including those representing mineworkers, tyre workers, press workers, workers in food stuffs and metal workers. It now has 28 affiliated unions, covering around a third of a million individual members. During the 1970s DİSK was close to the Turkish Workers' Party (Türkiye İşçi Partisi) and at the centre of a militant socialist trade unionism. Today it adopts a rather less radical stance but it is still regarded as left wing among the federations.

MİSK (the Federation of Nationalist Workers' Union) is the smallest of the federations. Founded in 1970, it is a federation of far right wing trade unions covering less than one per cent of those unionised. The independent unions cover a similar proportion.

HAK-İŞ (the Confederation of Justice Seekers' Trade Unions) was formed in 1976. There are seven unions affiliated to the federation. Before the 1980 coup it covered over half a million members and currently has around one third of a million. It is a federation of Islamic unions. It was sympathetic to the FP (Fazilet Partisi or Virtue Party, which embodied rightist Islamic values) and its successor the AK or Justice and Development Party which came to power in 2002. It has its main base amongst companies which belong to MUSIAD, the Moslem industrialists' federation. Its constitution pledges to 'respect national and moral values; to abide by the rule of social order and rights; to create peace and harmony between workers and employers; to upgrade the living conditions of workers and to enable them to fully utilise human rights and freedoms and to create a prosperous and developed Turkey based on national unity' (Article 3, Hak-İş Regulations).

The metal industry and Türk metal

The Izmit triangle is an area that runs from Istanbul at its apex to Izmit and Bursa. It is the site of extensive industrialisation, which expanded in the 1980s as industry spilled out of Istanbul in a second phase of development. In 1999 and 2000 research was conducted in four plants in or adjacent to the Izmit triangle as part of a larger project. Three of these plants were in the whitegoods industry; one was a major car plant. All of them were unionised by Türk Metal. All are subject to the same collective agreement, with average wages for a worker with five years service of about £300 a month, including bonuses, in 2000.

GebzeWG is a washing machine factory that is owned by a large Turkish conglomerate. This is one of the biggest whitegoods manufacturers in Europe. The plant produces about one and a half million washing machines annually, of which 25 per cent were exported in 1999 and over 40 per cent by 2003. It has over 50 per cent of the home market. The plant is situated at Gebze, near Izmit. Just under 1000 are employed in the factory. The plant is a well-laid out modern one, which has the status of a show plant within the company. The plant has invested heavily in new technology since the end of a partnership with a German multinational in 1986. Metal cutting and bending units are highly automated. There are robotic devices and numerically controlled machines throughout the production process. In the paint unit where metal frames are painted automatically, workers are largely reduced to pressing buttons when necessary. In the pre-assembly unit, most work tasks are highly automated through the use of CNC machines. However, in the final assembly unit, most of the work is carried out manually with a minority of women working side by side with the men. In the final quality control, the work tasks are again highly automated. At the time of the fieldwork the plant had undergone considerable reorganisation of its management, lean management having made for fewer managers in a flatter structure.

BoluWG produces ovens. Situated at Bolu, it is also owned by the same Turkish conglomerate. BoluWG produces over half a million ovens annually.

It has just over 50 per cent of the home market and in 1999, 25 per cent of sales were for export, this having risen to over 40 per cent by 2003, mostly to the UK market. The plant is situated to the east of the Izmit triangle proper and is again a product of the spill-over of industry from Istanbul that occurred in the 1980s. Just under 1000 are employed. BoluWG was scheduled for management reorganisation, but at the time of the fieldwork this had not yet occurred. There are more long-service managers and workers here than elsewhere. Of the four factories BoluWG is one of the most labour intensive. Although the company began to upgrade its technology in the mid-1990s as it bid to concentrate more on the international market, most work has not been highly automated with the exception of the metal cutting and bending unit where there are a few computer controlled machines and CNC lathes and the paint unit where work tasks are highly automated. There are no women in the production process. Part of the shop floor is set up for cellular production but this makes only a minor contribution.

The third plant, ÇerkWG, produces fridges. It is part of a three-handed German-Turkish joint venture company, which dates from 1996/97. The plant has over a third of the home market, producing around a million fridges annually and exporting 40 per cent of them. One of the two German partners is one of the biggest whitegoods manufacturers in the world. Situated to the west of Istanbul in Trakya (Thrace, the European part of Turkey), this plant was again a product of the industrial overflow that stemmed from Istanbul in the 1980s. Nearly 2000 are employed in the refrigerator plant at peak season, which is itself part of a much larger whitegoods manufacturing complex which employs over 3000. The plant has recently undergone a major management reorganisation which had stripped out the management levels of deputies and assistant managers and in which the bottom level of management consists of teamleaders appointed by management and in charge of teams between 9 and 45. Since the arrival of the German partner, who appointed a German managing director, the plant, which hitherto had been starved of investment, has benefited considerably from upgrades to its technology. Most pre-assembly line work in the paint section, in metal cutting and bending, in plastic cutting and in moulding has been highly automated. German managers claim the equipment used is the same as that at the corporation's factories in other countries. Final assembly and some sub-assembly (where some women are employed) are labour intensive, but with some final quality control again being highly automated.

The fourth plant, BursaCar, is a car factory. The car company is a joint venture in which the two partners are European and Turkish. The company started production at Bursa in 1969. It has 5000 employees, including about 4000 manual workers. It currently produces about 100 000 cars per year. In the past production has been mainly for the home market, though the plant's new model is aimed predominately at Europe. It has six main production units: press shop, engine, under-body, welding, paint and assembly, which includes pre- and final assembly lines. Some new machinery and lathes have been introduced in all units and in the press shop and paint units in particular. Most of the work in the paint unit is highly automated. Generally, though, the production process is labour intensive. Fifteen kilometers of conveyors run from the press shop to final assembly where there is a marked absence of highly developed electronic devices and even relatively few powered hand tools.

Workers in all four plants were asked how good managers and their union were at keeping them up to date about proposed changes; providing them with the chance to comment on proposed changes; responding to suggestions; dealing with work problems; and treating employees fairly. As can be seen from Table 2.1 (bottom row), on average workers in each of the plants

Table 2.1 Evaluation of managers and union

How good managers and union are at	BoluWG	GebzeWG	ÇerkWG	BursaCar	All
keeping everyone up to date about proposed changes (% very good + good)					
managers	78	54	32	50	54
union	60	51	22	38	43
providing everyone with the chance to comment on proposed changes (% very good + good)					
managers	63	35	36	48	46
union	46	30	18	32	32
responding to suggestions from employees (% very good + good)					
managers	76	72	60	60	67
union	56	53	20	30	40
dealing with work problems you or others may have (% very good + good)					
managers	94	77	76	72	80
union	70	68	26	40	51
treating employees fairly (% very good + good)					
managers	82	53	52	56	61
union	66	62	28	38	49
average management score	79	58	51	58	62
average TU score	60	53	23	36	43
percentage difference in favour of management	+19	+5	+28	+22	+19

rated their management better than their trade union. On closer inspection it can be seen that they did so with respect to nearly every item in nearly every plant, so that whichever way Table 2.1 is read management comes out more highly rated than the trade union. Management's own attempts to consult workers and to involve them have not gone very far. The TQM that has been implemented is of the hard rather than soft variety (Nichols, Sugur and Demir, 2002b).

Further evidence of the union's relative failure compared to management comes from a question we asked workers about what they would do if they had a grievance. Actually, our intention in asking this question had been to assess the possible effect of relations with hemsehri (fellow townspeople), since research conducted in earlier years had shown this to play an important part in the lives of people in the expanding cities (Ayata, 1987). Interestingly, as can be seen from Table 2.2, the question revealed little role for hemsehri – but equally evidently, little role for the trade union. Those saying they would take their grievance to the trade union were a small, sometimes very small minority. In all plants the great majority of workers said that if they had a grievance they would take it to management. In no plant did more than one in five say they would go to the union and the proportion was sometimes very considerably less than this: at BoluWG 20 per cent favoured the union (76 per cent management); at GebzeWG 15 per cent (64 per cent); at ÇerkWG 14 per cent (64 per cent); at BursaCar only 4 per cent (92 per cent).

The reliance on management is such that managers themselves sometimes complain that workers come to them for help with personal disputes, for example, about getting fellow workers to pay back debts. This might imply a considerable deference to authority on the part of some workers and stands in contrast to that form of working class consciousness according to which 'you don't take your problems upstairs'. However, to talk to workers about their union and to consider their criticism of it is to find that this centres very often on complaints about its lack of responsiveness to workers' needs and sometimes too its failure to act independently of management. It is not that these workers are uncritically pro-management and anti-union. Rather it is that they find their own union so unresponsive to their needs that the management consults them more than their union does, and acts, as several

Table 2.2   Who would you go to if you had a grievance?

Per cent	BoluWG n = 50	GebzeWG n = 53	ÇerkWG n = 50	BursaCar n = 50	All n = 203
Manager	76	64	64	92	74
Trade union	20	15	14	4	13
Relatives /friends /other	4	21	22	4	13

of them put it, like 'an employer's union'. Below are some of the workers' perceptions of the union in the four companies investigated.

BoluWG:

> The trade union is inadequate. They should conduct a survey related to the problems of workers, but they don't do this.

> There is no communication with workers. They aren't interested in our problems. I haven't seen the face of the union president.

> They don't deal fairly in the elections. There is not enough notice to become a delegate candidate. They have their list of candidates in the elections. They are not successful in improving social rights.

> I have no relationship to the union except for my membership.

> Our trade union is an employer's trade union and does what the employer says.

ÇerkWG:

> I see the union here as a puppet of the employer. They don't have any dialogue with the workers. A union must develop a dialogue with the workers and defend the worker's right.

> A union should defend the worker's right. The union here is finished. They make agreements in their own way. They support the employer. They don't do anything about dismissals. There was a decrease in dismissals after the German company came here. This firm appreciates the workers, but the union doesn't.

> They just take the membership fee. Workers themselves must elect their representatives, not have them come from the top. The elections are showpieces because the representatives' list is made from the top and this list is accepted. Most workers don't know when the election is.

> There's no difference if there is a trade union here or not. It's an employer's union.

> I have been here for 6 months. I haven't had any contact with the union.

GebzeWG:

> Trade unions are very important organisations for workers. But union officials can make mistakes. The big mistake in this plant is that the representatives are appointed not elected.

> Our trade union isn't good. They don't deal with worker's problems. They don't treat everyone the same. They are politically biased. They are not open to criticism.

They don't tell us about elections for representatives. We don't know when or how they are appointed.

For me there is no trade union here.

They don't do anything. But they celebrate birthday and marriage anniversaries with the company. The manager comes and congratulates them. The union must renew itself. We can't elect our own representatives.

The union isn't democratic. The representatives are appointed. The union must integrate with the worker. The representatives must be elected by the workers.

BursaCar:

It's useless. I don't think it has any function in here. It doesn't really matter to me whether this union exists or doesn't exist. It should respond to workers' demands.

I see this union as a parasite. A union should always keep in touch with workers.

I don't find this union successful. A trade union should be transparent, and all decisions should be taken together with the workers.

They don't know anything about trade unionism. They have become union officials through someone's help. A union should always be on the side of workers when they discuss things with the management, because we pay their salaries.

I think nothing about this union. Does it really exist? Where is it? What is it? I can't see it.

The above criticism of the union is often focused on its lack of responsiveness to workers' needs, lack of internal democracy and dialogue. The question therefore arises of how the union has come to be the biggest union in the metal industry and how its position in relation to its members is reproduced. Part of the answer to this second question is already suggested by some of the above quotations that refer to internal union organisation and election procedures. First, however, we will consider how the union came to its present prominence. To answer this, it is necessary to shift our attention from plant level to that of the state.

The coming to its current prominence of Türk Metal

In 1964, Bulent Ecevit, then Minister of Labour, had spoken as follows upon presenting new trade union laws to Parliament:

In almost all the Western democracies, the rights we are about to grant the Turkish worker with this law were only acquired after long and bloody struggles. ... There can be no doubt that by granting the Turkish worker these rights without necessitating such struggles, you will have rendered history and society a great service. ... In the countries of the West, application preceded the laws ... with us, the laws will come first and the application will follow. (cited in Isikli, 1987: 317–18)

Ecevit had been correct. These laws had been a real step forward. This is pertinent here, for it has been argued that it was especially workers such as those considered in this paper who benefited from such changes in the 1960s and 1970s – namely, those who worked in large scale manufacturing firms that produced *inter alia* consumer durables and cars with modern technology, often with foreign investment (Keyder, 1987: 160–1). These benefits had derived from a process of top-down bureaucratic reform however; and what the state gives, the state can take away.

At the end of the 1970s Turkey was in crisis. For a variety of reasons the import substituting industrialisation that had been based on the selective protection of the domestic manufacturing sector had run into trouble. The balance of payments effects of adverse terms of trade, the shrinking world market for exports, rising oil prices and reduced remittances from Turkish workers in Europe all pushed toward a reduction in the imported inputs and technology without which higher levels of profitability and economic growth could not be sustained (Keyder, 1987). Turkey was driven into the hands of the IMF in 1978 and into a major stabilisation and structural adjustment programme in January 1980. In the midst of political turmoil, a military coup ensued on 12 September 1980. Turkey was then ruled by the National Security Council. This marked a decisive moment in the modern history of trade unionism in Turkey, and for Türk-İş and its affiliate Türk Metal.

In 1982 a new constitution placed major restrictions on the political activities of trade unions and further weakening of trade unions ensued through the 1983 Trade Unions Act. Unions were forbidden to pursue political objectives – in particular they were forbidden to engage in political activities, to establish relations with political parties, or to use the name or symbols of political parties. Politically motivated strikes, general strikes and sympathy strikes were all made illegal; so too were slow-downs, sit-ins, and similar forms of concerted action. Strikes and lockouts were not permitted during a state of war or full or partial mobilisation, and they could be prohibited in the event of major disasters adversely affecting daily life and temporarily restricted in the case of martial law or 'extraordinary emergency law' circumstances.

Furthermore, a lawful strike likely to endanger public health or national security could be suspended for 60 days by order of the government and be taken to compulsory arbitration at the end of that period, if the parties to the dispute failed to reach an agreement. Strikes were prohibited over

grievances arising from the interpretation or application of collective agreements. In addition the new legislation denied the right to unionise and to
bargain collectively to civil servants and certain public employee groups,
including the newly created contract worker category in the state economic
enterprises. During the first half of the 1980s wage settlements were taken
over by the Government controlled High Board of Arbitration, which systematically awarded increases below inflation. In a catch-all move against
free collective bargaining, and in particular of the right to strike, the 1982
Constitution had stipulated that the right to strike 'shall not be exercised in
a manner contrary to the principle of goodwill, to the detriment of society,
and in a manner damaging national wealth', the violation of these conditions inviting a court injunction to halt the strike.

The 1970s had seen the unions, and most especially DİSK, manifest a new
militancy. Strikes increased as did days lost. Legislation protected workers
from being fired at will and imposed heavy costs on companies in the form
of severance payments awarded on the basis of seniority (Keyder, 1987: 191)
and in some larger factories employers complained that it was not possible
to sack workers. The 1980 coup reversed the gains made in the previous
decade. Boratav has rightly stressed that the new measures were intended to
cause a significant decline in the value of labour power (1990: 209). Nor is
there any doubt about the short-run success of this policy. Between 1970 and
1979 overall union density had risen from 16 per cent to 27 per cent. By
1985 it was down to 9.5 per cent and by 1990 it was still only 10 per cent
(Cam, 2002). Whereas strikes and days lost had increased in the decade up
to 1980, they fell in the subsequent period. Wages followed a similar course.
Between 1970–79 real non agricultural wages in Turkey had risen over 50 per
cent, the largest gains being made in the second half of the decade. In 1980
they fell by 30 per cent. By 1984 they were back below the level they had
been in 1975 a whole decade earlier (compare Figures 2.1a and 2.1b).

The political background to the coup is that in the 1970s the position of
Türk-İş had been challenged from the left by the more militant federation
DİSK. When the coup came, Türk-İş publicly welcomed the advent of the
military government, and its Secretary General took office as its Minister of
Social Security. This led Türk-İş to be suspended by the International
Confederation of Free Trade Unions (ICFTU). But the new legislation was
such that Türk-İş also came to enjoy a significant longer-term advantage
compared to other unions, and especially DİSK. The law conferred the right
on individuals to freely choose the union to which they should belong. But
what is crucial is that in 1980 the National Security Council closed down all
the trade union federations – except for Türk-İş. Although the right to strike
was not restored until 1983, this one union federation was allowed to operate again within months of the coup. The Islamic federation HAK-İŞ was
treated only a little more harshly. Favoured by the Generals for its conservative nature, it was allowed to operate without collective bargaining or the

(a) (b)

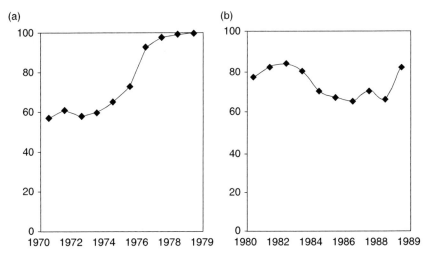

Figure 2.1 Real non-agricultural wages in Turkey (a) 1970–1979 (1979=100),
(b) 1970–1979 (1979=100).

right to strike in 1981 and began to operate fully as a confederation in 1983.
The nationalist federation MİSK was reinstated in 1984. But DİSK was treated
very differently. It remained banned until 1991. In the meantime most of its
top union officials had been imprisoned and its property seized by the state.
In 1981 the Military Court had prosecuted 1477 DİSK trade unionists, 78 of
them being charged with offences punishable by death. Part of the Generals'
attempt to curb the power of the left, the case went on for five years, at the
end of which 264 trade unionists were given prison sentences ranging from
five to fifteen years (Pekin, 1996: 220).

Following the 1980 coup, a further component in the disadvantage suffered by DİSK (and an advantage for Türk-İş) derived from the requirement
that trade unions must qualify as national unions with a presence throughout one of a number of specified industry groups – for example, mining, textiles, metals. In Turkey, trade unions cannot take the form of craft unions or
enterprise or plant unions and the new legislation decreed that in order for
a trade union to be entitled to bargain with a plant or company, it had to
represent at least 10 per cent of the workers in the industry and more than
half the workers in the plant or company. These rules made it yet more difficult for those unions previously affiliated to DİSK to regain a foothold. In
fact, it gave those unions which got established first a great advantage –
generally those of the centre and right and especially Türk-İş.

Each of the trade union federations has constituent unions in the metal
industry. Leaving aside here the HAK-İŞ union, Öz-Çelik, which has just
under 100 000 members and the small MİSK union, Türk Çelik Sen, which
fails to reach the 10 per cent bargaining threshold, the effects of the coup

can be readily seen at the level of the individual trade unions by reference to the history of the DİSK and Türk-İş unions in the industry.

The DİSK union in the metal industry is Birleşik Metal-İş. The union has over 56 000 members. It is the product of a 1993 merger between two unions, Maden-İş and Otomobil-İş. Maden-İş was founded after the first trade union act came into force in 1947. The union affiliated to Türk-İş when the confederation came into existence in 1952. In 1967 Maden-İş withdrew from Türk-İş and formed DİSK with four other unions. Kemal Türkler, who had been the chairman of the union since 1964 then served as chairman of DİSK until 1977 (he was murdered by rightists in an armed attack in 1980). So what happened to Maden-İş? The military regime suspended Maden-İş as a part of DİSK and it was not reopened until 1991.[2]

The Türk-İş union in the metal industry is Türk Metal. The union was founded in 1973 in Ankara and immediately affiliated to Türk-İş. The union grew considerably in the second half of the 1970s when it gained control of a few plants in big companies in the industry. But then, after the military coup the union gained recognition in workplaces formerly unionised by the still banned Maden-İş. In 1979 Türk Metal had over 60 000 members. As a result of the coup and its aftermath it had reached 200 000 by 1987 and now has 240 000.

In each and every one of the four plants the uneven nature of the banning of the different union federations gave an advantage to Türk-İş and its constituent union Türk Metal.[3] The military coup and its aftermath therefore go a considerable way to account for the coming to prominence of Türk Metal in these plants – a union which espoused a very different ideology to DİSK, which was the union to which those of the plants which existed in the 1970s had been affiliated. Mustafa Özbek became chairman of Türk Metal in 1975 and still holds this position. He comes from Kirikkale as do some of the union's other leading officials. Once a district of Ankara, and now a city in its own right, Kirikkale is renowned in Turkey for its right wing politics and support for the MHP (Milliyetçi Haraket Partisi or Nationalist Movement Party). In 1980 Özbek made a speech welcoming the coup, declaring that it had 'torn away the masks of those speaking of a confrontation between capital and labour' and that it had 'initiated a period of national unity and harmony' (*Türkiye Sendikacilik Ansiklopedisi*, 1996: 361). In this he neatly paralleled the contribution made by the body with which his union negotiates, the Turkish Metal Industrialists Union (MESS, Metal Sanayicileri Sendikasi). MESS welcomed the coup as 'establishing an atmosphere of peace and security in the country'. (In December 1979 Turgut Özal the previous head of MESS, was appointed Under Secretary of the Prime Ministry. The key architect of Turkey's journey into the free market economy in the 1980s, he was to become Prime Minister in 1983 and serve as President of Turkey from 1991 until his death in 1993.)

The above events go a considerable way to account for the coming to prominence of Türk Metal. They cannot however explain how Türk Metal has reproduced its position. It is to this matter that we now turn.

The reproduction of union autocracy

Turkey has experienced huge migratory flows from East to West over the last half century and a more general shift of population from the countryside to the growing urban areas (Peker, 1996: 11). Many of the workers in these plants therefore have fathers or grandfathers who were peasants. The vast majority are Moslem; a considerable proportion of them pray. Attributes such as these are often considered a recipe for conservatism by promoting reliance on authority and unthinking acceptance. Whatever the plausibility of such general assumptions, it is important to note that these workers have not blindly accepted their fate as far as Türk Metal is concerned. In each of the four plants, there have been attempts to leave the union.

GebzeWG: In 1994 workers complained that when the company sacked around 200 of them the union did nothing. In 1998 following the results of the collective bargaining of that year workers began to resign from Türk Metal and attempted to join Birleşik-Metal İş. With inflation running at about 70 per cent, the union had promised a 90 per cent pay rise and gained only an initial 43 per cent. Hundreds of workers resigned from the union and walked out protesting at the union's failure. Hundreds of gendarme and police were drafted in to preserve order. Following this about 40 to 50 were sacked by management.

BoluWG: In 1986 some workers tried to leave the union and join an independent union Otomobil-İş (a breakaway from Türk-İş, which later, in 1993, became a constituent part of DİSK). The management sacked those active in this move. From memory workers put the number involved between 60 and 100. In 1989 and 1990 another attempt at a breakaway from Türk Metal occurred, again with the intention of joining the same independent union. Again management sacked those active in this attempt. Again workers put the figure at between 60 and 100. Up till this date there had been no local union branch but only a branch office about 100 km away at Sakarya. The union set up a local branch. At the same time however new workers were recruited through the union from its stronghold in Kirikkale, Ankara. Since then Türk Metal has escaped further challenge.

ÇerkWG: The top branch officials again come from Kirikkale, Ankara. In the second half of the 1980s Otomobil-İş started to make inroads into the factory but could not legally displace Türk Metal. In this plant, too, the results of the 1998 collective bargaining unleashed profound dissatisfaction with

Türk Metal and workers left the plant, thousands marching 3 km from the company's various plants to town centre where the office is located of the Public Notary (who is charged with the registration and de-registration of union membership). Management did nothing for a few days when union officials and the local Governor attempted to quieten things down and coax workers back to work. It then issued an ultimatum: either workers had to re-register their membership of Türk Metal or lose their job. Around a hundred lost their job.

BursaCar: In 1994 the company sacked thousands, the number employed reducing from about 9000 in 1993 to around 3000 by 1996. Failure of the union to intervene led to widespread disaffection. In 1998 workers played a prominent part in the wider reaction to the deal struck by Türk Metal. There was a massive walkout. Thousands marched the 5 km to the Public Notary's office in Bursa to resign and join the DİSK affiliated Birleşik-Metal İş (United Metal Workers' Union). Management followed the same course pursued at ÇerkWG. Putting its weight behind the union, it threatened workers with the sack if they did not stay with Türk Metal. After workers had re-joined the union between 200 and 300 were sacked – according to management because of the world crisis of that year and, according to some workers to clear out the activists. According to Türk Metal, at national level, 8000 workers switched to Birleşik-Metal İş in 1998 and then switched back. According to Birleşik-Metal İş, 40 000 did so.

Apart from anything else the above account serves to warn us that in interpreting the results in Table 2.1 it is necessary to keep in mind that the workers interviewed were not an unbiased cross section. First, those who had been active in seeking to switch unions were almost certainly under-represented by virtue of past dismissals. Second, and probably to the same effect, management sought to screen out potential militants when selecting new workers (and when offering permanent jobs following an initial probationary period). As one of the managers put it to us: 'Of course we have to consider "political issues" as well.' Third, pro-Türk Metal workers had been deliberately recruited through the union from its ideological strongholds.

It remains to be considered why workers join the union in the first place. Why, if they are disaffected, as some of them certainly are, have they not reformed the union from within? And why have they not left it?

Why did workers join this trade union? In Turkey the Trade Unions Act of 1983 stipulates that the hiring of workers must not be made subject to any condition as to their membership of a union, individuals having the right to become a member of a trade union or not. These rights imply that there can be no 'closed shop'. On the face of it, then, the question of why these workers joined the union is something of a puzzle. But it isn't. In practice, there is a closed shop. In all the four plants there is 100 per cent membership of

Türk Metal for permanent workers who form the great majority of all workers.[4] This is effected by recruits being sent to the union office to sign on as part of the process of being taken on by the company. The procedure is part of standard practice. It is as unproblematic as going to the hospital to register for social security purposes: in fact it occurs as part of the same routine. Why do workers put up with this? A metal industry manager put it like this: 'There is much unemployment. These are good jobs. Of course workers join. They dare not refuse.'

Why is it that workers themselves do not fight more to change the union from the inside? One part of the answer is that the union President, Özbek, rules Türk Metal with an iron hand and union officials are Özbek's men. They are tied to the union, and to him, by a mixture of personal loyalty and nationalist ideology. Photographs of him striking powerful poses dominate Union offices. The grey wolf symbol of the MHP, the party closely associated with the street violence of the 1970s and attacks on the left, is part of the union emblem (despite the illegality of this). The union publishes books about the emergence of the Turks from central Asia and about the Turkic grey wolf myth (Caglar, 1990). Özbek is also President of the Federation of Eurasian Metal Workers; an entity based on the Turkic republics in Central Asia. Union officials talk in terms of, 'Our great President says ...'

There are also material interests at stake. There are visits abroad for officials on union business. The chairs of branches can be invited to union meetings usually held in five star hotels at holiday resorts. At rank and file level, Türk Metal organises holidays in the union education resort in Northern Cyprus and on the Aegean and Mediterranean coast of Turkey for workers and their families, all expenses paid. There is a large education and training centre in Ankara. All these are mechanisms whereby loyalty can be bought and retained. These rewards are not for everyone – indeed they are part of what makes many resent the union and the way it operates. These feelings are particularly strong at ÇerkWG:

> It pretends to be active when collective bargaining comes round. Apart from that they do nothing. Strangers came to work here from places like Kirikkale and Yozgat. They [union officials] protect their own men and *hemsehries* (fellow townsmen) from the cities of Kirikkale and Yozgat. They get them to come and settle here and show favouritism toward them.

> I wish this union would leave here. Our union sends around 50 or 60 people to its holiday resorts in Antalya and North Cyprus. But they're all from Ankara – what a coincidence! I resent having to pay my membership fee.

The potential for favouritism and an ability to ride roughshod over the membership inheres in the union's internal structure, as a consideration of its various levels makes plain.

Shop stewards: According to 1995 trade union law, workplaces with 1–50 employees can have no more than one shop steward; those with 51–100 two; those with 101–500 three; those with 501–1000 four; those with 1001–2000 six; and those with over 2000 no more than eight. They are formally appointed by the head of the union branch. However, officials in Türk Metal try to hoodwink workers with their apparently superior legal knowledge and claim that the law actually requires shop stewards to be appointed by the union. What they do not point out is that it is perfectly in order to have an election first and that other unions do just this. When asked why representatives weren't elected prior to being formally appointed, a head union official explained:

> The shop stewards and the head of a union branch should work in harmony. If they do not work in harmony, it will adversely affect workers anyway. I mean if a steward, who is elected, has a problem with me; he may not bring the workers' problems to me. In other words, if there is a disagreement between the head of a union branch and a shop steward, he could create problems in the enterprise, and the branch would not even hear about it … I mean if I don't appoint a steward who works in harmony with me, I may not hear anything about the problems over there. He can even misinform the people who work there, make it as if the union is not interested in workers' problems. A successful labour unionism is based on teamwork. In a metaphorical sense, you can only be successful if the goalkeeper keeps goal well, the one in the middle field plays well and if the forward scores the goal, otherwise it's very difficult to be successful.

Typically the stewards who do get appointed are right wing people who can provide an upward chain of communication to the local branch.

Delegates: Local union officials are elected by delegates (a separate position from that of shop steward) who are also supposed to monitor the activities of the local union branch. Delegates are directly elected by workers for three years – one to every forty workers. However, the local union office provides a slate of approved candidates and it is an uphill struggle for workers to elect delegates who have not been approved. Workers report that when delegates on an opposition list were actually elected in Istanbul, the union closed down the branch. In any case, workers in all four plants are not well informed about elections and have no faith in their ability to elect non-listed delegates.

Branch union officials: These inhabit a separate world to workers; and they act as the delegates of their branch to elect the head office union officials. Suffice to say that to make in-roads into this structure is extremely difficult. But if it is very difficult to fight from inside to change things, then what of flight?

Why don't workers leave the union and join one that is more responsive to their needs? As we have seen, this has been tried. So far though such moves have not met with success and they are difficult to achieve (in some respects even more difficult than the predominantly European and North American literature would suggest: Lerner, 1961; Hemingway, 1978). In order to join a new union each individual member has to visit the office of the Public Notary and complete a formal procedure. This requires that 3 million TL be paid to leave the current trade union and a further 11 million TL be paid to join the new one. This cost is itself a disincentive. At 2000 prices 14 million TL was the equivalent of 5 days' pay for a probationary worker and approximately 2 days' pay for an average permanent worker. In addition of course the new union has to demonstrate it has 50 per cent plus one of the plant and 10 percent of the industry. Moreover, once an agreement has been made it remains in force for 2 years even if the workers leave the union and join another one. To this has to be added that if workers do leave they fear they will face the sack. And, according to other unions, if workers do join another union surreptitiously, and Türk Metal finds out, it has been known to pass the word to management and get them sacked.

As already reported, managements have supported the Türk-İş union against DİSK and this support, according to credible reports from workers, included removing active trade unionists from the labour force. For management, Türk Metal has its positive side. Union officials regard the new management methods such as TQM, which have been introduced in all these plants, as a means toward producing a bigger cake. As one trade union official put it:

> We should base our relationship on dialogue. The factory is ours including unions, employees and employers regardless of differences between them. Our principle is: 'We should make the cake bigger and then take our share'.

In line with this is the union's practice of leaving management to manage on the shop floor. In this respect, managers at all the plants refer to Türk Metal being 'no problem'. Indeed, it is said that 'they understand our problems'. Türk Metal is therefore favoured in preference to a union that might threaten something worse in terms of militancy. In the eyes of management, support for Türk Metal is not unequivocal however and the union is seen to have a negative side, an aspect that in the long run might prove a mixed blessing.

Managers are critical of the union's lack of internal democratic procedures. 'The unions need to change themselves radically', says one:

> In fact, we [the company] have already talked about that issue: we ourselves did some work about what the unions need to do, what the union management needs to do, then we tried to pass the decisions of some of

our meetings to them in order to make them more effective, more participatory, to make the people feel their need for a union.

That managers sometimes express concern at the lack of participation in the union is at one level pragmatic; they want to contain any trouble that might otherwise well up from below and they need a union that can deliver the membership. In some cases, though, the concern clearly goes beyond this and stems from a social democratic regard to the need to strengthen the institutions of civil society. Either way, such concern amply underlines the absence of internal democracy. But this point about the need to develop the institutions of civil society has wider implications for Turkey and for other social formations that share similar characteristics and is returned to in the following section.

Discussion

We hope it is clear from this chapter that these workers' relations to their union cannot be understood in terms only of some general orientation (e.g. passivity/Asiatic obedience) or in terms of the operation of some general sociological law (Michel's 'iron law of oligarchy' being a classic example of this).

As far as the first possibility is concerned, these workers are Turkish and it is tempting for Westerners to find ready-made explanations for behaviour in generalities about Islamic culture. It has long been argued for example that Islam is likely to promote a static way of looking at the world which in turn discourages departures from orthodoxy and thereby promotes reliance on authority so that employees themselves put up with a high degree of centralisation of authority, this neither disturbing them nor resulting in major organisational conflict (Lauter, 1968: 98). Even to the extent that it might be thought that such assumptions have some validity they really do make it difficult to account for the very different character of labour relations in different periods (as we saw there was a pronounced change in Turkey between the 1970s and 1980s). This is why rather than follow this general line of interpretation consideration was directed above to the specific constraints and difficulties to which these workers are subjected.

Concerning the second possibility, there is a very long established literature on trade unions that can be traced back at least as far as the Webbs at the end of the nineteenth century (Webb, 1897: 161) and which has come to occupy an important place in modern Weberian-influenced social thought via the idea of an 'iron law of oligarchy' (Michels, 1915). Thankfully, attempts to counter the unqualified pessimism of such thinking continue to the present day (Voss and Sherman, 2000). This paper is located in this counter tradition in so far as it rejects any unqualified law of sociological tendency towards union autocracy. It has been seen of course that the leadership of Türk Metal most certainly attempts to reproduce itself and that thus far it has been successful in this. But it has been argued that there is a specific historical explanation for its present prominence which stems from history of the Turkish state, most especially from the consequences of the 1980 coup, and from the interests of the capitalist firms that recognise the union. And it has also been seen that workers' continued membership of a union that effectively denies them a voice has not been for lack of attempts to quit it, attempts that have been frustrated amongst other things by the actions of the employers and legal requirements.

In short, the intention throughout is to get behind the generalities – whether these relate to the reduction of the position of labour in developing countries to cheap labour alone, to generalisation about universal tendencies to oligarchy in trade unions or the invocation of conservative notions about an Islamic mentality – and to examine, in the case of this one important trade union in Turkey, the specific practices and regulations that conspire to reproduce both the position of the union hierarchy within the union and of the union within the industry. A series of specific obstacles existed which tended to frustrate workers' attempts to change the union. The 1980 coup had had the effect of reversing the gains made in the previous decade and, in the longer term, of facilitating a trade union structure in the metal industry which frustrated the development of workers' democratic capacities. Despite this, workers have attempted to bring about change in all of the plants, so that there is no justification here to resort to what Gouldner nicely summed up as 'metaphysical pathos' (1955: 496–507). There is also some evidence that external leverage, applied by trade unions outside Turkey, has had some success.[5]

If the voices of workers in these plants have been largely rendered ineffective there is no reason to depict them as inherently apathetic and no reason either to assume that they have always accepted their lot in the past or that they always will do so in the future. This said, however, it is undeniable that these workers are presently subject to the power of a trade union autocracy. In relation to this, some further issues arise that have a wider significance both for developing countries such as Turkey and for comparative political economy.

With respect to the development of Turkish society, whereas it is perfectly evident that the sort of trade unionism described in this chapter does not lend itself at all readily to a politics of worker mass mobilisation, it is also deficient when judged against another sort of politics – one indeed that is publicly favoured by certain elements of big capital in Turkey. In 1980 Turkey shifted from a policy of import substitution to one of export orientation and the opening of domestic markets. Subsequently there has been increasing exposure to international competition. The employers' federation TUSIAD, which is essentially an organ of big capital, now sees advances in the liberalisation of society as a necessary complement to the economic liberalisation, which it urged upon the Turkish state in the 1980s. The signing of a Customs Union Agreement with the EU in 1995 has done much to stimulate such thinking and to lead to renewed advocacy of western democratic forms. As TUSIAD's Board of Directors put it in their Foreword to the organisation's *Perspectives on Democratisation in Turkey* (TUSIAD 1997) 'to become fully integrated in Europe, a broader application of democracy in economics and politics is required, and this is a pre-condition'. Such advances, even as seen by the employers' organisation, include *inter alia* the need for improvement in the position of trade unions. For instance, TUSIAD noted critically that in Turkey 'it is [too] easily possible for a meeting or demonstration to be deemed illegal' and 'in most cases of decisions to postpone or ban, no need is even felt to indicate a reason'; it also endorsed moves in the 1990s to permit trade unions to hold meetings outside their own purposes and aims and thus to contribute to the democratic purpose more fully. Such liberalisation with respect to trade unions (and of course with respect to other aspects of life) is sorely needed. Yet if there has been a need to strengthen the rights that trade unions have in terms of their relation to the state, there has also been a need in some cases to strengthen their internal democratic processes, which is the issue upon which this chapter has concentrated.

Following the calamitous earthquake that shook Turkey in 1999, commentators inside and outside the country frequently expressed regret at the lack of developed institutions in civil society. The enhancement of internal union democracy is itself a potentially important contribution to the development of such institutions. For to the extent that workers can engage in a collective democratic practice at their place of work the chances for the emergence of a more fully developed civil society might be thought less bleak. It is on just this point, however, that the progressive line of big capital in Turkey on workers' rights presently meets its limit. For it is in fact some of the very same employers who give public assent at national level to increased freedom for trade unions who simultaneously tolerate the autocratic mode of operation of Türk Metal in their own factories. It remains to be seen if and when these same employers who give public assent to the view that a broader application of democracy is required in economics and politics will extend an unequivocal welcome to such changes on their own shop floors.

With respect to the wider significance for comparative political economy, it is not possible to understand the development of the part of the metal industry in Turkey that is dominated by big capital only in terms of low wages. The wages paid are certainly low by the standards of advanced capitalist societies and this is of course a very important factor that induces foreign companies to set up joint ventures. But the actual configuration of production relations entails more than this; it also entails an autocratic trade unionism, and to explain how this has come about requires an historical account of the restructuring of Turkish trade unions by the military regime, which in turn paved the way for a shift from import substitution to export orientation. In other words, what we have here is a specific example of how production in a developing country is effected by political means and cannot be understood only in terms of economic relations.

Acknowledgements

This chapter arises from the ESRC financed project R000237766 'Change in Management Strategy and Employee Relations in Turkish Manufacturing'.

Notes

1. This chapter draws on Nichols, Sugur and Demir, 2002a. A much more extensive account of trade unionism in the Turkish car, white goods and textiles industries is provided in Nichols and Sugur 2004: Part IV.
2. The other trade union, Otomobil-İş, with which Maden-İş merged in 1993 to form the new union, Birleşik Metal-İş, had been founded in 1963 and had been a member of Türk-İş from 1965 to 1974, after which it withdrew from Türk-İş and became an independent union. In 1979 Otomobil-İş signed an agreement with Maden-İş for joint action on various issues. The union was closed down by the 1980 coup and reinstated in 1983 as an independent union, in which capacity it increased its membership. It merged with Maden-İş and was affiliated to DİSK in 1993.
3. The pattern of advantage for Türk Metal can be seen at work in each of the four plants. GebzeWG: The plant moved to the district from Istanbul in 1968. It was unionised by Maden-İş, a constituent union of DİSK, which had been formed the previous year. The plant remained organised by Maden-İş until the 1980 military coup. This union was then closed down. In 1983–84, DİSK still being banned, the plant was unionised by Türk Metal.

    BoluWG: in 1993 the relatively new plant was unionised by Türk Metal which at this time was of course part of the only major union federation in existence.

    ÇerkWG: in the 1970s the plant had been unionised by the DİSK union Maden-İş. After the military coup the union was closed. In 1983–84 the plant was unionised by Türk Metal.

    BursaCar: initially, the plant was organised by Maden-İş. In the 1970s in the context of the strengthening of the left and of violent clashes between left and right on the streets, there were serious clashes between the Maden-İş and Türk Metal. Two union members lost their lives. Others suffered serious injury. At one point rightists entered the factory to intimidate Maden-İş members. The management preferred to recruit those with right wing connections and helped Türk Metal. The police intervened on a daily basis, also favouring Türk Metal. Türk Metal began to displace Maden-İş and gained control in 1978. As we have seen, come the 1980 coup Türk-İş was not closed down, although there was no collective bargaining or right to strike. But, with its funds and organisation intact, it began to operate again in 1983, as did Türk Metal as its constituent union within the company.
4. All permanent direct production workers are members of the trade union. Workers serve a probationary period usually of six months to a year prior to becoming permanent. At ÇerkWG the seasonal nature of fridge production means that around

200 people are recruited on a temporary basis. These are often students from local colleges working on placement in the summer months. In all four plants indirect production activities such as packing, security, catering and cleaning also make use of tacheron labour. In Turkey a tacheron is a subcontractor and a tacheron worker one who works for such a subcontractor. Tacheron workers represent between 10 and 15 per cent of the workforce of the three plants. They are employed for less than 11 months to avoid the employer's obligation to pay compensation on dismissal; they lack legal contracts, receive only the minimum wage, are not trade union members and have no holiday entitlement (further accounts of tacheron labour are provided in Nichols and Sugur, 2004: 106; Cam, 1999; Sugur *et al.*, 1999).

5. During the 1970s, and in the 1998 struggles, DİSK had sought the help of unions in Italy in connection with the Bursa car company and of those in France in connection with another car firm, Renault. In the 1970s the French unions were successful in putting pressure on Renault, which was a contributory factor that helped Maden-İs keep its position until the military coup in 1980. At Bursa, the Italian unions did not prove as helpful as the French unions had been at Renault, so the position of Maden-İs was relatively weaker. In 1998 even though the plants were now both organised by Türk Metal, DİSK again looked to French and Italian unions for help. The same pattern repeated itself. The French unions were successful in exerting pressure and Renault sacked less than a dozen workers. At the Bursa factory in our survey no comparable support was forthcoming.

References

Aricanli T. and Rodrik D. (1990) (eds), *The Political Economy of Modern Turkey: Debt, Adjustment and Sustainability*, Basingstoke: Macmillan.

Ayata, A. G. (1987) 'Migrants and natives: urban bases of social conflict' in Eades, J. (ed.) *Migrants, Workers and Social Orders*, London: Tavistock.

Boratav, K. (1990) 'Inter-class and intra-class relations of distribution under "structural adjustment": Turkey during the 1980s' in Aricanli, T. and Rodrik, D. (eds) *The Political Economy of Modern Turkey: Debt, Adjustment and Sustainability*, Basingstoke: Macmillan.

Caglar, A. N. (1990) 'The greywolves as metaphor', in Finkel, A. and Sirman, N. (eds) *Turkish State, Turkish Society*, London: Routledge.

Cam, S. (1999) 'Job security, unionisation, wages and privatisation: a case study in the Turkish cement industry. *The Sociological Review*, 47 (4): 695–715.

Cam, S. (2002) 'Neo liberalism and labour within the context of an emerging market economy'. *Capital and Class*, 77.

Gouldner, A. (1955) 'Metaphysical pathos and the theory of bureaucracy'. *American Political Science Review*, (49): 496–507.

Hemingway, J. (1978) *Conflict and Democracy: Studies in Trade Union Government*, Oxford: Clarendon Press.

Heper M. (1991) *Strong State and Economic Interest Groups: The post-1980 Turkish Experience*, Berlin: Walter de Gruyter.

Isikli, A. (1987) 'Wage labour and unionisation', in Schick, I. C. and Tonak, E. A. (eds) *Turkey in Transition*, New York: Oxford University Press.

Keyder, C. (1987) *State and Class in Turkey: A Study in Capitalist Development*, London: Verso.

Lauter, G. P. (1968). *An Investigation of the Applicability of Modern Management Processes by Industrial Managers in Turkey*. Los Angeles, University of California (unpublished PhD thesis).

Lerner, S. W. (1961) *Breakaway Unions and the Small trade Union*, London: George Allen and Unwin.

Michels, R. (1959) *Political Parties: A Sociological Study of the Oligarchical Tendencies of Modern Democracy*, New York: Dover Publications (first published in 1915).

Nichols, T. and Sugur, N. (2004) *Global Management, Local Labour: Turkish Workers and Modern Industry*, Houndmills, Basingstoke: Palgrave Macmillan.

Nichols, T., Sugur, N. and Demir, E. (2002a) 'Beyond cheap labour: trade unions and development in the turkish metal industry'. *The Sociological Review*, 50 (1) February.

Nichols, T., Sugur, N. and Demir, E. (2002b) 'Globalised management and local labour: the case of the whitegoods industry in Turkey'. *Industrial Relations Journal*, 33 (1) March.

Pekin, F. (1996) 'DİSK Davasi', *Türkiye Sendikacilik Ansiklopedisi*, cilt1, Istanbul: Tarih Vakfi Yayinlari.

Peker, M. (1996) 'Internal migration and the marginal sector', in Kahveci, E., Sugur, N. and Nichols, T. (eds) *Work and Occupation in Modern Turkey*, London: Mansell.

Sakallioglu, U., C. (1991) 'Labour: the battered community', in Heper, M. (ed.) *Strong State and Economic Interest Groups: The post-1980 Turkish Experience*, Berlin: Walter de Gruyter.

Schick, I. C. and Tonak, E. A. (1987) (eds) *Turkey in Transition: New Perspectives*, Oxford: Oxford University Press.

Sugur, N., Demir, E., Kasapoglu, A. and Nichols, T. (1999) 'Özelleştirme ve Çalişanlar: Türkiye'de Çimento Sektörü Çalişanlarinin Tutumlari Üzerine Sosyolojik Bir Araştirma', [Privatisation and employees: a sociological inquiry into the attitudes of employees in the turkish cement industry], *Sosyoloji Arastirmalari Dergisi [Journal of Sociological Research]*, 2, (1–2): 1–32.

TUSIAD (1997) *Perspectives on Democratisation in Turkey*, Istanbul: Turkish Industrialists' and Businessmen's Association.

Voss, K. and Sherman, R. (2000) 'Breaking the iron law of oligarchy: union revitalisation in the American labour movement'. *American Journal of Sociology*, 106 (2).

Webb, S. and B. (1897) *Industrial Democracy*, London: Longmans Green.

3

Changing Professional Identities under New Public Management: A Gendered Perspective

Annette Davies and Robyn Thomas

Introduction

What does it mean to be a public service professional/manager[1] at the start of the twenty-first century? How do individuals, occupying managerial roles within the UK public services define themselves as professionals and also managers? And what tensions do these constructions of the self present with other elements competing for identity make-up? These questions are pertinent given that much of the focus of reform within the public services over the past two decades has been aimed at reconstructing the identities of professional workers (Pollitt, 1993; du Gay, 1996; Halford and Leonard, 1999). This chapter offers an empirically informed exploration of the impli- cations of managerial reforms, often referred to as New Public Management (NPM) in the UK public services for the lived experiences of individual professional/managers. Whilst acknowledging the contribution of recent research that has explored the impact of NPM on professional workers, this chapter aims to provide a more nuanced understanding of the enactment of NPM and professional identities to explore the meanings that individuals ascribe to NPM and how they locate their 'selves' within these meanings. The research aims to address two specific limitations in existing knowledge. First, to offer an understanding of NPM and professional identities that can accommodate difference and diversity, avoiding the tendency to treat pub- lic service professionals as a homogenous, univocal and gender neutral entity. Second, it explores the gendered meanings of NPM and considers the implications for female and male professionals/managers.

The research is based on a two-year study of middle and senior ranking professionals/managers in three public services, the police, social services and secondary education. The empirical material is based on in-depth semi- structured interviews with male and female professionals/managers. The chapter starts by detailing the context of change within the public services. This is followed by an account of the epistemological and methodological approach taken, leading on to an overview of the changes that have taken place within each of the sectors studied. The main empirical section presents a number of texts that illustrate how the enactment and character of NPM has been received at the localised level. Finally, we conclude by considering the contribution of the research for male and female public service professionals/managers.

Restructuring the public services: organisations and professionals

The language of change and discontinuity has over the past two decades dominated organisational and managerial discourse. For some commentators, developments in organisations have merely been piecemeal and pragmatic responses to a more competitive, cost conscious and deregulated environment, masked by the rhetoric of 'new wave management' (Ezzamel *et al.*, 1996). For others, not necessarily opposing this position *per se*, these developments represent a much more significant 'paradigm shift' in the nature of organisations, to that of the postmodern organisation (Clegg, 1992). Regardless of position, however, organisational change seems to have been relentless over the past few decades, especially in the public services in the UK. Under the banner of NPM, the public services in the UK (as well as a number of other Anglophone and Northern European countries), have witnessed a period of major change in ideology, structures and management (Pollitt and Bouckaert, 1999; Hood *et al.*, 1999). It is difficult to encapsulate NPM as one concept (indeed to attempt to do so would be flawed empirically and theoretically, given its incremental, organic and fluid nature). The changes sweeping through the public services in the 1980s have been driven by a continual need to curb 'excessive' demands on government spending, accompanied by the promotion of an ideologically driven agenda of neoliberal economics, aimed at extending market forces (Kirkpatrick and Martinez Lucio, 1995). Developments have largely centred on the three areas of the market, the customer and the manager (Hasselbladh and Selander, 2003). A broad overview of the developments taking place includes: privatisation, deregulation, competitive tendering of services, the creation of internal markets and the devolving of management. Accompanying these structural changes a range of new management practices can be noted, including the use of profit centre management, performance management, quality management, business planning and 'culture management' (Pollitt, 1995; Hoggett, 1996). More recently, under the Blair administration, the emphasis has been on 'modernising' the public services whilst keeping to strict public spending targets and a commitment not to raise taxes (Holloway *et al.*, 1999). The distinct flavour of NPM under 'New Labour' has been the emphasis on 'joined up government' with greater inter-agency cooperation and collaboration. With New Labour's 'mantra of partnership' (Horton and Farnham, 1999: 255), there has been pressure to break down organisational boundaries and promote greater vertical and horizontal integration between government bodies, voluntary bodies and private business.

Therefore, the last two decades of the twentieth century have marked a coming together of two dominant discourses – the New Right ideology (free market, customer sovereignty, individualism) and 'post-modernism' emphasising change, discontinuity and flexibility in organisations (Davies and Thomas, 2002). Both discourses can be seen to place their disciplinary gaze on professional workers, especially those occupying the middle layers of the hierarchy. The focus of much of the change has been on 'recrafting' of these layers, not just in terms of organisational structures but also professional identities (Thomas and Dunkerley, 1999; Davies and Thomas, 2002). During the 1980s public sector professionals came in for considerable criticism from the New Right, for showing allegiance to their own professional body rather than to senior management or the customer (Crompton, 1990). Lambasted as unaccountable monopolies, professionals were seen at best to be inhibiting the government from bringing in its desired reforms and, at worst, being no better than closed-shop trade unions 'out to feather their own nests' (Ackroyd and Soothill, 1994). A strong focus then of NPM has been the desire to introduce new disciplinary technologies (Townley, 1994) designed to inculcate professionals with new attitudes, values, priorities and self-understandings (du Gay, 1996; Clarke and Newman, 1997).

The implication for public service professional identities of the enactment of NPM has only been a focus of study in recent years (du Gay, 1996; Clarke and Newman, 1997; Exworthy and Halford, 1999; Whitehead and Moodley, 1999; Barry *et al.*, 2003). These studies have suggested that the ideological motives underpinning much of the restructuring strategies have promoted new professional/management subjectivities around innovation and entrepreneurialism as opposed to the benign and knowledgeable expert (Pollitt, 1995; du Gay, 1996; Clarke and Newman, 1997; Halford *et al.*, 1997). Cost consciousness and a culture of performativity has meant that professional activities have come under closer scrutiny (Crompton, 1990). Increasingly, belief in the ideals of professional discretion and trust has been replaced by sets of measurable performance indicators and efficiency measures (Dent and Whitehead, 2002). These studies suggest that not only has there been a reduction in professional autonomy by the imposition of managerial controls, but also that professionals are being expected to adopt managerial values and to align themselves with managerial concerns. However, with much of the existing research there has been a tendency to focus on the *impact* of NPM on professional identities in a rather deterministic manner and consequently presenting an image of a largely passive and homogenous professional body responding to NPM. Neither NPM nor professional identities are fixed essences. The enactment of NPM can be understood more as a contested terrain (Goode and Bagilhole, 1998; Barry *et al.*, 2001), recognising the fluidity of meanings ascribed to NPM, organisation and professional identities.

Gendering NPM and professional identities

Despite a burgeoning literature over recent years on gender and organisations (see for example, Mills and Tancred, 1992; Alvesson and Due Billing, 1997); and more specifically on women in management (Cooper and Davidson, 1984; Rosener, 1990; Marshall, 1995; Fondas, 1997; Maddock, 1999) and on men and masculinities and management (Connell, 1987; Collinson and Hearn, 1994), the arguments for taking a gender perspective, or even acknowledging that gender matters has, by and large, not spilled over into research on public sector organisations and NPM (Barry *et al.*, 2003). Research on public sector professionals/managers and NPM is almost exclusively from a gender-neutral position (Halford *et al.*, 1997). Criticisms of the gender-blind nature of management and organisation research are not new. Since the early 1980s feminist researchers have challenged the so-called gender neutrality of management and organisational theory, arguing that what is understood about organisations, organisational processes and management has been derived from theory that is gender-blind, based on masculine assumptions. Feminist and pro-feminist writers have drawn attention to the gendered nature of the research process itself, recognising that the knowledge creators are gendered and so too is the knowledge generated (Acker, 1990; Jacobson and Jacques, 1990; Calas and Smircich, 1996). With the gendering of organisational theory, there has been increased attention given to the masculine discourses making up the organisation and management.

Taking an ontological realist position, there are a few pieces of research that explore women's marginalized positions within the public sector and how NPM might affect this (Coyle, 1988; Lovenduski, 1988; Escott and Whitfield, 1995; Margetts, 1996; Cunningham *et al.*, 1999). This research has explored the impact of changing structures and management processes on the career opportunities of female professionals. The research paints a largely negative picture, with the championing of the market and the diminution of bureaucratic controls resulting in an erosion of equal opportunities policies and practices as well as reducing promotion opportunities in a slimmed down organisational structures and resource constraints (Margetts, 1996). There have also been a small number of studies taking a poststructuralist feminist position focusing on the privileging of managerial masculinities embodied within the NPM discourse (see Whitehead and Moodley, 1999 and Barry *et al.*, 2003 edited collections; Halford *et al.*, 1997; Leonard, 1998; Maddock, 1999; Davies and Thomas, 2000, 2002). Here it is suggested that the new professional/managerial subjectivities promoted under NPM privilege certain understandings of masculinities, and identities that correspond with the macho, workaholic and aggressive (Maddock and Parkin, 1993; Thomas, 1996; Halford *et al.*, 1997).

In sum, this chapter aims to provide greater complexity and nuance than is currently offered in the literature, emphasising the socially constructed and contested nature of both NPM and identity. In doing so, it provides a richer insight into the manifold ways in which individuals and groups respond to the discourses of change and the material outcomes on their daily lives.

Researching professional identities and NPM

The research examines how the discourse of NPM has affected, and is affected by, professional identities. Influenced by Foucault's conception of power and the subject, 'discourse' refers to bodies of power/knowledge that set the pattern for demarcating what is true and not true, right and wrong, normal and abnormal etc. Discourses are thus normalising. However, they are also creative in that they provide the resource by which identities can be constructed and thus discourses form a 'multiplicity of discursive strategies' (Foucault, 1982: 100) that are both constraining and enabling to the discursive subject. Through discourse, individual subjectivities, social institutions and social processes are defined, constituted and contested. Rather than seeing identities as being fixed, biologically determined or essential, an inner core unique to each individual, we view identity as self and socially 'crafted' (Kondo, 1990). This 'crafting of the self' takes place within 'discursive arenas', in particular situations, and particular cultural and historical settings. An individual's identity therefore, can be understood as a transitory and mobile site where various discourses temporarily intersect in particular ways in the ongoing act of identity makeup (Kondo, 1990). This fluidity of identity also means that gender is a daily achievement. Gender is what you do at particular times, rather than being a universal *who you are*: 'There is no gender identity behind the expressions of gender – identity is performatively constituted by the very "expressions" that are said to be its results' (Butler, 1990: 25). However, whilst gender is not wholly determined, neither is it wholly arbitrary. It is not only a construct, it constructs us. Thus the self is regulated but not determined. Symbolically sets of meanings ascribed to male and female influence our identities. Gender differences are constituted in discourse and disciplinary practices, and as individuals (whether knowingly or not) we contribute to this process by turning ourselves into particular (gendered) subjects. So we come to think of ourselves, and interact with others, in ways that reflect dominant understandings of what it means to be *either* a man *or* a woman.

NPM can be understood as one of a matrix of discourses vying for attention in the process of identity makeup. This is not to suggest that an individual's identity is *determined* by discourse; s/he is not merely 'subjectivised'. Individuals may challenge the subject positions offered by dominant discourses in a constant process of adaptation, subversion and re-inscription of the meanings these discourses offer. This takes place as individuals reflect on their own identity performances and in doing so, subtly shift meanings and understandings. Tensions, contradictions and internal flaws are revealed as the individual reflects on her or his 'self' in conjunction with the subjectivizing forces of NPM.

Research methods

The sectors studied (Police, Secondary Education and Social Services) were selected not only on the basis that each have faced significant restructuring and redefining, and comprise of professional workers, but also because they have not been the focus of extensive in-depth research, unlike for example, the health service. Case study selection was also influenced by sectors that would be of particular interest in gender terms. In two of the sectors, education and social services, a large number of women are employed, albeit at the lower levels of the hierarchy. In the third sector, the police service, the level of female employment is lower, and there is a strong tradition of a highly masculine occupational culture (Ianni and Ianni, 1983; Fielding, 1994; Brown and Heidensohn, 2000).

The empirical material is derived from a two-year project, split into two phases. Following a pilot study, emerging themes were incorporated in a questionnaire survey, distributed to a sample of 1950 male and female managers/professionals in October 1999. The questionnaire sample was drawn from 21 police constabularies, 11 social services departments and secondary schools from 12 local education authorities (46 per cent response rate). While a questionnaire research design may be regarded as wholly inappropriate within a social constructionist-influenced methodology (Alvesson and Deetz, 2000), it contributed to the research in two ways. First, it provided us with an appreciation of the extent and nature of restructuring and a general overview for the way professional roles are being reconstructed under NPM. Furthermore, the questionnaire gave an indication of the strength of individual positioning with their understandings of NPM. Second, it provided us with a sample of male and female managers within each of these services who were eager to talk with us in depth about their lived experiences of NPM (see Davies and Thomas, 2002).

The third phase of the project, upon which this chapter is based, took place during 2000/2001. This involved semi-structured interviews with male and female professional managers in seven case organisations drawn from the three case sectors (three police constabularies; two social services departments and secondary schools from two local education authorities). One hundred and five interviews have been conducted with approximately 15 individuals from each case organisation. In addition, information was also collected from senior managers within these organisations relating to the context of restructuring and to equal opportunity initiatives.

Context of professional change

At a macro level, the three public services have all undergone similar patterns of restructuring. They typify developments taking place in the public services in the UK over the past two decades.

The police service

In the decades from 1980, police services around the world have faced an increased climate of restructuring and change in response to governmental, public and media scrutiny over performance. In the UK, the police service has had to respond to a rising barrage of criticism over its effectiveness, in relation to its 'value for money' (Nash and Savage, 1994), the quality of its leaders, and, in particular, over issues of ethics, professional integrity and the relationship with the communities it serves (Holdaway, 1997; Holdaway and Barron, 1997; Macpherson, 1999). In terms of efficiency, a range of performance indicators have been developed which cover almost every aspect of police activity with the costing and value of such activity being set out in Local Policing Plans. The Audit Commission's 1991 review of police internal structures also recommended the reorganisation of police forces and the removal of the two-tiered division and subdivisional structure. This meant a move towards single policing units which would have responsibility for all policing and financial matters. The trend with the development of these single policing units or basic command units (BCUs) has been towards more devolution and decentralisation. A further development also affecting the management style and culture of the police is that of increased 'civilanisation' within the service. At the same time as the structural changes in the police service, new policing professional subjectivities can be noted, reconstituted as business leaders and are now accountable for the performance of decentralised 'business units' within the force (Davies, 2000). In addition, a 're-branding' of the police can be noted, from 'force' to 'service', emphasising a reorientation to a service ethos, and a different policing style (Edwards and Robinson, 1999; Davies and Thomas, 2003).

Social services

A number of commentators have suggested that social services have faced a 'crisis' over the decades of the 1970s and 1980s, with rising critique from both the Right and the Left over the lack of choice and control of services, as well as epistemological challenges posed by postmodernism's challenge to its core values of social justice, human rights and professional ethics (Yeatman, 1994; Camilleri, 1999; Ife, 1999). Over the past two decades, the social services have witnessed dramatic changes, marking a move from a professionally regulated service to one increasingly subject to external regulation and forms of managerialism (Lawler and Hearn, 1995; Shardlow, 1998; Jones, 1999). The period has been marked then by increased legislation and major restructuring of Social Service Departments (SSDs) through the introduction of market principles following the 1990 National Health Service and Community Care Act. Restructuring has meant that the social worker is increasingly taking on a quasi-managerial role, with the 'care manager' being responsible for purchasing services within a defined budget. Day-to-day activities are configured around line management duties, budget management and contract negotiation (Causer and Exworthy, 1999). Significantly, underlying all these changes has been the need to cut the public spending budget and to make the service more economically efficient. For the social work professional this has meant a sidelining of professional power (Aldridge, 1996), with values of trust and professional ethics being replaced with 'customer rights' (Smith, 2001). Materially, social work has witnessed several high-profile tribunal cases of ill health from stress and a survey by the professional journal, *Professional Social Worker* (1996) reported that half the profession had considered leaving the profession during the period 1993–1996 because of stress and frustration over conflicting and unachievable demands.

Secondary education

Finally, again in secondary education the period marks a significant discursive shift in the management of education (Gewirtz, 2002). There has been a dramatic redefinition in the way in which the head teacher's role and identity is constructed. Marketisation, schools league tables, the parent as consumer, and the Head as a quasi-business leader has led some commentators to observe that education is now treated as a commodity in contemporary society (Grace, 1995; Parker and Jary, 1995). The period from the early 1980s onwards marked the development of a quasi-market in education reflecting the belief by successive Conservative governments that better efficiency and effectiveness is schools would be achieved through exposure to the disciplines of the market (Farnham and Giles, 1996). The 1988 Education Reform Act (ERA) brought in the decentralisation of management structures. Structural changes included the instigation of Local Management of Schools (LMS), 'opting out' (the move to Grant Maintained status), marketisation and competition for pupils, increased accountability and inspection, and greater parental choice and power (Bartlett *et al.*, 1994). However, this went hand in hand with greater centralisation and bureaucratisation of the teaching process with greater government control and the introduction of a National Curriculum and national testing (Healy, 1999). Schools are now responsible for their own budgets and staff (including compulsory performance appraisal and performance related pay), with powers to recruit and dismiss staff. Head teachers now are required to take on much more of a managerial and leadership role, with the education leader now redefined as the 'chief executive' or 'managing director' (Grace, 1995; Levacic, 1995; Harris, 2003). The changes taking place in the profession over the past two decades have been associated with work intensification, greater stress, reduced autonomy and greater insecurity (Sinclair *et al.*, 1996; Healy, 1999; Thom, 1999).

Managerial and professional identity work

In the interviews, we sought to understand how the enactment of NPM was received at the localised level. Focusing on the normalising discourse of NPM, we sought to understand its strength and unity, and the promotion of particular new professional/managerial subjectivities. From the social texts generated in the research engagement, we do not see this linear relationship of NPM impacting on, and resisted by, these public services professionals, with the enactment of NPM being far from clear cut and cohesive. We present here four subject positions derived from the texts of the interviewees, as they reflect on the changes taking place in their organisation and profession. These are: the managerial self, the competitive masculine self, the disciplined and docile self, and the feminised managerial self. These work in the texts, sometimes in collusion, sometimes complementary, sometimes contradictory. As individuals construct different meanings of NPM in the construction of their self-identity, they pitch their 'self' against their understanding of NPM in a dynamic presentation of meanings of the self and NPM. We present here the texts generated from this act of critical reflection. When facing the subjectivising effects of NPM, individuals here may choose to draw on some aspects, as a 'discursive resource' (Parker, 1997) in asserting an identity, whilst attempting to subvert and 'wriggle out' of the other ways that NPM attempts to classify, determine and categorise them. Thus both NPM and the self work in a matrix of power relations (Foucault, 1982) where meanings are highly contradictory and dynamic.

The new public service leaders

A strong message within the texts is the requirement for individuals to behave and think as leaders. Within the police we can see the promotion of new managerial police subjectivity, with the setting down of core managerial and leadership competencies. These emphasise the codifying of a set of 'leadership' attributes; being strategic and having 'leadership skills'. Steve, for example, a police superintendent comments that it is the strategic and managerial qualities that are now valued over and above the operational work. In the texts generated from the interviews with deputy and head teachers, we see the promotion of a new managerial subjectivity centred on the small business entrepreneurial leader. The effective head and deputy head teacher is reconstituted as the financially astute, strategic, market-oriented leader. Head teachers are urged to take on a more commercial entrepreneurial identity, to *'sell your school, to deliver a commodity and to meet demands'*. Jenny, a deputy head teacher commenting on her Head's new role observed: *'[he's] just a manager of, it could be anything, Oxo cubes or something, for all that person cares, for all that person is allowed to care'*. Added to this we see a far stronger focus on performance and a particular conception of performance, based on quantifiable results. Susan, a female Head of a small community college, comments: *'every head teacher knows that in the end unless they manage to move the exam results along they're regarded as a poor head teacher'*. Jenny, talks of the headship training she is currently undergoing as being like a *'military exercise'*, drawing on private sector, guru style leadership knowledge:

> ...you will think about this, you will do it like this...[the message] is to be what they want you to be. They want to clone you, all right? And occasionally they will use an entrepreneurial term or concept.

Bound up with images of leadership is the notion of the charismatic figurehead, as Max, a head teacher comments:

> Yeah it's a bit like people talk about, you know, Richard Branson's Virgin empire, you know, like Alex Ferguson's Manchester United. It's not his club but he's the persona that seems to represent that club, you know. And you get that with schools...You know, so there is a kind of persona, a personality, a charisma that is attached to headship.

Within the texts we see individuals drawing on the language of NPM to locate their selves within this new leadership subject position. These were ones that coincided with an individual's understandings of doing the best for the service. For example, Joe, a team leader in Townville Social Services comments:

> I don't know whether it's public service ethos, or whatever, but there is, you know, a commitment, I think, with the wanting to do a good job. And I think that there's been a lot of extra demands placed on us, and, how can I put it, it's hard to argue against them because they have improved things quite a lot, in terms of what we do, compared with how we did things 10 years ago.

Furthermore, many texts reveal the 'buzz' that individuals find from being involved in demanding and interesting work. For example Sam, a female Head teacher spoke of the importance of focusing on a wider agenda and of being strategic:

> I think it's good for you to do that because otherwise your brain cells get atrophied into the managerial side of keeping the school running – which, you know, is your comfort zone really.

Despite this, however, we also see within the texts individuals drawing on an alternative subject position to assert an alternative identity to that offered in the NPM discourse. Here, we see how NPM is seen as a distraction from what was viewed as the more importantprofessional work within these services. Within the police service, for example, both uniformed and civilian managers voiced these tensions. Many uniformed officers constructed their identities on the basis of their 'operational' experience. The emphasis on management, budgets and strategic planning was thought to be in conflict with the 'real' police work of 'going out and fighting crime'. As Steve, a Superintendent, comments: *'We have lost our way with trying to be all things to all people. We are not focused anymore, we are not actually delivering what people want.'* Jim, who has been a civilian manager for the past 30 years, takes issue with the language of management and, in particular, with being called a 'manager': *'it is a particularly technical role, it's not a management role'.* He tells how his job title has recently changed from supervisor to 'manager' and he voices resentment towards the managerial tasks that he now has to perform and what he sees as name changing for the sake of 'corporate identity':

> There are more and more meetings that you are having to attend to in your management role so there are all sorts of meetings, seminar projects, lord knows what … And all of them, from my own personal point of view, are distractions from the main issue which is getting the job done.

Jim continues his criticisms, commenting: *'they want individuals who have expertise in their field learned over a period of time to become company directors and corporate image producers'.* Positioning himself as other, Jim is highly critical of attempts to get him to identify with an entrepreneurial leader subjectivity: *'It's like the organisation can call me what they like, but I know what I am'.*

Within secondary education, head teachers and deputies can also be seen to voice a tension between how they saw themselves as an 'educational leader' and what they saw as the expectations from the Local Education Authority (LEA) and the government to be a 'business manager'. According to John, a secondary school head teacher:

> There's a conflicting message, which is to do with running a business. You know we think you should be taking on all these additional delegated powers, you should run the school meals service, you should run your own grounds maintenance. We're going to give you all the money and you don't need support services around. And that seems to me to be saying that the head shouldn't be the educational leader …

Janet, a female head teacher of a large community college, states that there are often disagreements between her and the LEA over her own personal targets. Drawing on an alternative subject position, as a pedagogue, Janet comments: *'I expect I'll be told that I've got to firm these up and make sure they're smart targets'*. Her reply to being told that her targets are *'too large'* or *'beyond your control'* is *'don't ask me to choose silly little targets that are not actually my major priorities for the coming academic year'*. Again, we see in the text of Janet this refusal to take on the new subject position and the assertion of an alternative professional identity: *'you need to work to your own style and stand up for your school and your own professional judgement'*.

Other research has illustrated how NPM has worked to promote a managerial subject position and the attempts to 'convert' professionals into managers (du Gay, 1996; Exworthy and Halford, 1999). As Hoggett (1996: 254) argues, 'rather than attempt to strengthen "management" in order to control "professionals" the strategy shifts towards creating managers out of professionals'. However, we see from the texts presented here that the operation of NPM at the micro level is far less clear-cut than this. The indeterminacy and contradictions in the meanings of NPM is manifest in the promotion of other subject positions, sometimes contradictory and sometimes complimentary with the managerial subject position. In the research engagement we see individuals drawing on these different meanings at different times and in different ways in their identity construction such that a more dynamic picture of the self and NPM is presented than suggested in the literature. We see this, for example, with the promotion of the competitive self.

Competitive individuals

Within the police case, the competitive subject is underpinned by a particular understanding of commitment. The need to demonstrate commitment has always been fundamental to the police ethic (Metcalf and Dick, 2001). This is evidenced by visibility on the job, 'being available', working long hours as a 'badge of pride', and 'living on the job'. Commitment underscores a police officer's reputation. Jim, specialist civilian manager comments: *'You are made to feel guilty [if you don't work these hours] and there are no "militants" at this level'*. In education too we can see this emphasis on competition and the expectation that professionals within this service will work longer hours, take less time off work, and work evenings, weekends, and during holidays. Again, the pressure of the performance culture was seen to promote 'excessive commitment' to the job. For example, Susan, a head teacher, comments on the 'repackaging' of education as part of the market economy, and an effective head teacher will be one who gets the best results, and engages in ruthless competition for resources, pupils and the best public profile. Susan reflects on how, despite her reservations, she also takes on this competitive subjectivity. She states:

> This is not about providing a service for the district, it's not about the children and their educational needs, this is a market economy and they're the commodity...and you want to grow bigger sunflowers than the man next door to you.

The difficulties in not taking on this competitive subjectivity are illustrated in the text of Jenny, explaining why she had decided to delay having children because of work pressures: *'how can I have a family when we're a failing school? So I put it on hold again for a year and a half'*. Here we see the internalising of the new competitive subject position and the expression of tensions derived from the feelings of no longer performing their role as they would have liked. We see in some texts a psychological withdrawal from the holy grail of high performance. Some point to anxieties over increased stress and ill health, particularly in the social services, where increases in stress-related illness amongst colleagues has led to increased questioning over commitment and its costs. Work intensification is particularly acute in Social Services due to resource constraints from a low-spend Authority and staff shortages from high turnover, recruitment problems, and a critically high number of staff on long-term sick leave. Restructuring, new legislation, and heightened media attention over social work activities (especially in Child Protection) add further pressures, anxiety and stress for the individuals interviewed in the case organisation.

The texts suggest tensions and challenges surrounding the promotion of a more competitive and individualised subject position. We can see expressions of concern about the intensification of roles, about long working hours and the pressures to display competitive 'presenteeism'. We see in the texts a conscious effort of putting boundaries around understandings of effective performance, and a refusal to rake on excessive commitment located within the 'ideal professional' self embedded in a discourse of competitive masculinity (Acker, 1990; Meriläinen and Tienari, 2001). For example, in the text of Phil, a senior police superintendent, we see recognition of the need to operate within certain parameters. Phil argues: *'You need to get pragmatic and say we can't do that … not feel guilty for not achieving it'*. Similarly, Kate, a civilian personnel manager from Central Constabulary challenges this demand for excessive commitment. We see her presenting her 'self as Other' – as a personnel professional, a woman and a civilian. Here we see her reflecting on her refusal to let work encroach into her private life:

> I think it's part of my job to break this perception, you know, I see myself as a bit of a, leading the way on some of these things, which is how I persuade myself to feel good about it rather than guilty about it, I suppose … and I'll forgo the career, you know, I don't give a damn about promotion and money if I can, if I can keep that balance and get a better balance and stay in this job with the satisfaction I get from it and the sense of achievement I get from it … .

This insistence at not being made to feel guilty about any failure to perform also came through strongly in the texts of both teachers and social workers. Janet, our head teacher, for example, spoke of her refusal to be *'overstressed'* and her refusal *'to blame yourself for everything that goes wrong ... we're doing the best job we can'*. Francis, a team manager in Social Service, was also asserting an 'adequate self', one that meets a preferred position for living with self and others:

> There's a limit to what I can do, that's the only way I can deal with it, by being clear about what I can and can't do. I regularly write memos up the line and keep copies to say that because we haven't got enough clerical support this work hasn't been done.

Francis spoke at length of her refusal to take on the blame for the state of the service she was offering. She talked of the successive cuts from the budget by the Authority and the loss of any public service ethic.

> When you first start you've got this idea about going out and helping and you realise that you just provide services and you had a romantic view. You know you've got to go through all these changes haven't you and now I feel that they voted for this lot [Conservative run Council]. If they don't like what they're getting that's their tough luck. It's a low spend authority – that's what you voted for.

Many of these individuals stated that they simply refuse to perform certain tasks. The phrase 'I just don't do it' appears frequently in the texts, referring to tasks that they were 'expected' to perform.

Similarly, in social services, for example, we can see the promotion of a strong performance culture with the texts peppered with comments such as *'it is seen to be very ruthless'*, *'you have to comply with the bottom line'*, *'sink or swim'*, *'it's everyone for themselves'*, *'dog eat dog'*, *'zero defects'*, *'they will crucify you if something goes wrong'*. The promotion of a competitive subjectivity was singled out by some female professionals in the research as offering a particularly masculine subject position against which these individuals placed themselves in understanding their preferred position. Sue, a superintendent illustrates this by challenging the belief in her constabulary that *'the white male way is the only way'*. Helen, a female inspector in South Constabulary pointed out that *'as a policewoman, there isn't 100 per cent comfortableness ... it is very isolating and it is quite lonely'*. Catherine, a police civilian manager also spoke of how she and other senior civilian and uniform managers, both male and female, were struggling with what they saw as an organisational bullying regime within the force. The 'cult of masculinity' (Young, 1991) in the police is well documented in the literature, where the emphasis on 'being a real man' and on fighting crime is fundamental to policing identity. New forms of competitive masculinity, and the promotion of masculine images of the aggressive and 'pushy' individual, based on competition, ruthlessness and being target oriented, overlays rather than replaces more traditional images of police that emphasise militaristic forms of virility. As Sue comments,

> I operate a very different level to the majority of my male colleagues...it's like going into testosterone city. Bang! Bang! Bang! Bang!, 'we do it like this', and the blokes all puffing their chests out, and...there is no doubt about it had I not changed my style and actually upped the little bits of testosterone and been a bit more 'in yer face', and a bit more against my tendency if you will, I don't think I would have survived it.

This critique of highly masculinist and aggressive ways of working was also offered in the texts of female head teachers who drew on a discourse of femininity and embodied notions of womanhood, in offering a being more compromising, caring and student-focused self. So, for example, Susan asserts that:

> Male heads are much more hard headed. They have less emotion than I do. They are probably less caught up with the children than I am. And I doubt if there are many heads that teach as much as I do. And I doubt that there are as many heads who know their children as well as I do...They don't see it as part of their role.

Disciplined organisational members

So far, we have presented two subject positions we have drawn from the texts. A third subject position can be seen, that of the disciplined and docile self. Here we see that presentation of NPM as a highly normalising discourse where an understanding of the professional subjectivity is tied up with notions of unquestioning and loyal acceptance to the new regime. Again, we can see tensions surrounding the offering of a subject position that is disempowered and docile. The police service has traditionally had a strong reputation as a highly disciplined organisation, based on a quasi-military structure (Johnston, 1988). The committed police officer is a disciplined and obedient subject where challenging behaviour, criticism or questioning is neither welcome nor encouraged. We see the continuation of this with some individuals seemingly resigned to accepting what is expected of them. For example, Brian, a chief inspector, who described himself as *'too interesting, too outspoken and too friendly for the organisation'* spoke of the selection of 'clones' into senior management: *'I think what they want is an android who is totally and utterly without voice, without any potential to go into anything...somebody who is not really human'*. To question or criticise is viewed as lacking commitment and such behaviour can result in individuals being sidelined or marginalised within the organisation. Steve, a police Superintendent refers to the 'dopes', that is, those who do not recognise that *'saying bad things ain't going to win you any favours'*. He recalls how he was once duped into believing he had a 'voice', which would be listened to, but *'later discovered that the decision had already been made'*. Steve's text illustrates that while to some extent he is resigned to this subject position, he also feels frustration over what it offers, or fails to offer:

> When I signed up that's what I signed up to do, no point in taking your bat home, you know, but it doesn't make me any happier with it, its just the way it is. That's showbiz and this ain't Hollywood.

In education, while recent changes have been seen as offering greater autonomy and responsibility, we can also see, as in the text of Jenny, that 'what a head teacher is' or 'what that person is expected to do' is very clearly specified. However, we see in the texts of many of these teachers a clear professional vision and strength of purpose and how they draw on this professional discourse to create a less constrained subjectivity which challenges and ignores requests or edicts from the LEA or government. We can see this in the text of Susan, the Head teacher of a small community college:

> As an intelligent and caring person you make your decision on how far or not you are going to, how much lip service you're going to give to it and whether you're going to go in to it wholeheartedly … I understand the context within which my school works and therefore I understand the context in which I apply all the things that come down from above. I'm quite a good girl really but I am naughty at times.

Janet, another head teacher of a larger community college, also spoke of being prepared to challenge and be critical. Here we see an awareness of re-inscribing of meanings to cynically subvert the normalising discourse. She refers to her: '… *infinitely interpreting what comes down so being prepared to say 'yes' … when you know perfectly well it is not what the government intended'*.

This promotion of the disempowered subject, was seen as a strong normalising discourse within social services. As Joe, a team leader in child protection argues: *'The perfect manager is one who eliminates all risk from within the functions of the department. It's almost like one is judged on a set of 100% perfection'*. Here NPM is portrayed more as the operation of a range of disciplinary technologies. NPM is seen as deskilling and deprofessionalising social work managers/professionals, through the exertion of external bureaucratic procedures. As Bob, a team manager in child protection observes:

> I think it is a lot more procedure based, a lot more … yes … um, 'make sure that this is done and that's done', and therefore almost by process you end up with good practice at the end of it.

NPM is portrayed as a loosely configured set of autocratic and 'faceless' management practices, operating in a climate of severe resource constraint and an increased legislative framework. A great emphasis is placed on quantitative measures and performance through circumscribed procedures. This renders professionals/managers highly accountable to these set rules, guidelines and procedures. The texts here tell us of the huge pressures to adhere to a range of compliance standards, which stifle professional judgement and serve to disempower. David, a senior social worker, believes that *'the professionalism has become second to the ticking of boxes'*. Another social worker manager, Tom, also raises similar concerns: *'We're becoming obsessed by that quantitative stuff. You get this scenario where you don't get good practice, you get good procedures compliance'*. Here, we see the drawing on professional discourses to critique what they saw as a reduction in their discretion and creativity as a result of increased compliance requirements and legislation. According to Tom, a team leader in child protection:

> We have a lot less professional autonomy because of all these compliance tasks ... It's almost like you need less and less bright people doing social work because actually what you don't want them to do is kind of really think too much about the wider issues, the wider aspects of what they're doing, what you want them to do, really, is to do what they're told.

A colleague of Tom, Bob, also highlights this loss of professional discretion. In particular, he is highly critical of the bureaucratising of social work and the privileging of quantitative performance indicators over a more flexible and intuitive approach: *'I feel a lot more disempowered ... there's far less creative thinking 'cos I don't have time, and I think it's not actually encouraged much either'*.

Feminised managers

The final subject position that we wish to present here is that of the feminised management self. Again, standing in contradiction with other understandings, we can see the assertion and legitimisation of a soft HRM discourse, the promotion and valuing of diversity and so-called feminine leadership skills, such as counselling, coaching and support (Fondas, 1997; Maddock, 1999). Within the police, the promotion of a more 'professional' police officer incorporates an emphasis on Equal Opportunities and a more 'tolerant' organisation, together with the emphasis on less hierarchical, authoritarian, command and control approach. We see the promotion of a 'soft' HR discourse, emphasising mutual respect, and a more relaxed, informal, caring and supportive organisation. Some individuals drew on this new feminised management subject position to claim voice, legitimacy and a positive sense of self. For example, for Sue, a female Superintendent, this has meant feeling much more included within the organisation and being able to assert a positive identity. As a woman in a highly masculinist occupational culture (Graef, 1989; Brown and Heidensohn, 2000) and as a lesbian in a highly homophobic occupational culture (Burke, 1993; Praat and Tuffin, 1996), the promotion of a feminised management subjectivity offers Sue a 'discursive resource' (Parker, 1997) to assert a legitimate and positive self. Thus we see Sue here drawing on cultural scripts of femininity (Fine and McPherson, 1994) to critically reflect on and critique the masculinist subject position offered to her. In presenting this feminised management self, Sue comments:

> My skills are networking, using different, softer skills to try and get things done…that is not necessarily the norm for the way in which a lot of senior men get things done, and by opening that debate with the men it's been really good in trying to recognise that people do operate in different ways, and they do have something extra to offer.

Sally, a female superintendent from South Constabulary also draws on a feminised management subject position, which she feels corresponds with her own work ethic. For Sally, '… *it's a much more feeling organisation than perhaps it was'*. Again, we see a drawing on this subject position to offer a feeling of inclusion within the organisation.

In the same way that we saw tensions created by the construction of subject positions that valorised competitive masculinity, we can also see resistance to promotion of this feminised management subject position. For example, we can see in South Constabulary talk of frustration and cynicism over 'soft' HRM and the weakening of the managerial prerogative and authority. Ted, the civilian middle manager, who had worked in private industry for many years before joining the police service, was 'appalled' at his lack of influence and control, and felt strongly that he has lost his right to manage. He resents being offered a subject position in which, as a manager, he is expected '*to hold their [subordinates] hands'*. He goes on to say:

> We are quite weak with the way that we are able to manage our staff and I know that goes into the police staff as well. We have got similar issues whereby the police officer tells somebody what to do and they are able to raise a grievance and not do what they are being told to do.

Ted talks at length about his inability to influence his workforce and discipline individuals who are not performing or who are misbehaving: '*I want to know that I can deal with it. It's not going to be swept under the carpet and say well I'm sorry it's too hard to do or you can't really do that'*. Sally, the female superintendent at South Constabulary, also referred to the cynical reactions to soft 'HR' practices, which she says is referred to by many as '*the goody two-shoes stuff that is laid down by the Chief Constable on valuing diversity, leading by example ...'.*

The tensions surrounding the feminised management subject position were also evident in the social services. Jonathan, a social work manager with a background in industry, voiced his frustration over the lack of opportunity to be enterprising. Here we see the assertion of the competitive subject position to negate a feminised management one. He presents highly critical talk over the managerial subject position offered him, drawing frequently on an enterprising, innovative managerial identity during the interview:

> They don't want someone who wants to get ahead, who's quite ruthless, because they are going to cause problems, be too dynamic ... I can produce a hell of a service but I can make it better if I'm allowed to shape it myself and not be constantly stifled from above.

Discussion

The aims of this chapter have been two-fold. First, by focusing on the lived experiences of individual public service professionals, we offer an empirically grounded understanding of NPM with greater nuance than that currently offered in the literature. Second, we empirically illustrate a more contradictory and complex understanding of NPM and professional identities, focusing on how individuals exploit the looseness around meanings in a constant process of re-inscription of NPM and identity.

In focusing on the gendered meanings of NPM, the research suggests that a new form of entrepreneurial masculinity has entered these organisations, overlaying and to some extent replacing traditional bureau-patriarchal masculinities. This entrepreneurial masculinity can be seen to be made up of two elements. First, the championing of rational, calculative, ruthless, hard-nosed and target-oriented behaviours. Second, the promotion of competitive presenteeism, with the privileging of the public over the private, and the construction of the selflessly dedicated organisational member. The creation of high-pressure managerial jobs, linked to long working hours, greater individualism and competition sustains and promotes strong images of masculinity within these organisations. Within the sectors studied in the research, particularly the cases of the police and secondary education, it can be seen how these discourses appeal to images of being a man, positioning 'woman' as 'the other'. However, in contrast, for many other men and women, conceptions of being positioned as 'the other', of not fitting in to the 'masculinist ideal', were evident in the responses. For women who emulate more masculine styles of management, however, this can raise difficulties in denial of sexuality, tensions in identity management and for their life experiences and relations (Collinson *et al.*, 1990). This would suggest that whilst NPM, restructuring and change may heighten problems of identity and 'fit' for all managers, for women the promotion of particular forms of competitive masculinity creates further tensions.

However, such a conclusion is too broad and limiting. Our empirical work also suggests a more paradoxical and multiple conception of NPM and professional identity than is suggested in these more generalised portrayals. The portrayal of NPM as a hegemonic discourse, sweeping across the public services, deprofessionalising all in its wake would be questioned by the texts generated in this research. We have seen in the texts that there is no single uniform and coherent meaning to NPM. Rather, NPM is highly dynamic, with individuals appropriating different meanings of this in their reflections on their self. From the texts we can see how individuals have an understanding of the NPM discourse as a 'package' of changes aimed at getting them to think, feel and act differently. As the individual is confronted with the NPM discourse, choices are made through the contradictions, weaknesses and gaps revealed between alternative subject positions offered. Taking a micro-politics approach, we see NPM more as an arena of contest, with individuals exploiting the contradictions within and between the NPM discourse and other discourses making up the organisation and professional identities. While acknowledging the strength of new disciplinary technologies (Townley, 1994) and the campaign throughout the 1990s to inculcate public sector professionals with new attitudes, values and identities, we emphasise that individuals are not merely passive recipients of these discourses. Identities are constituted and reconstituted through the interplay of multiple discourses. In this research we have presented both male and female professionals who are active in their engagement with the discourses of NPM and exercise power in the way they position themselves and find their own location (Kerfoot and Knights, 1993). We therefore move far away from any simplistic notions of what it is to be a woman, or a man, or a public sector professional and manager, emphasising the importance of multiple voices and representing the multiplicity and complexity of individuals. This means that there are many possibilities for alternative identities to be played against conventional ways in which we are constituted.

In conclusion, this paper argues that existing portrayals of NPM are often overly deterministic and illustrates how the enactment of NPM is neither coherent nor unified at the localized level. While on the one hand the paper provides evidence of the promotion of a more entrepreneurial masculinist managerial subjectivity, this is only part of the story. NPM is a far from cohesive project and individuals exploit the looseness and contradiction within it and between competing discourses in their identity construction. Therefore, we do not see NPM here as a single coherent project, impacted on individuals, against which the response is either to comply with or resist. Rather NPM can be understood as a resource through which individuals construct their identities, offering new opportunities for new subject positions and challenging existing power relations.

Note

1. We are interested in public sector workers who have professional backgrounds but who are clearly performing managerial roles in the organisation. For simplicity, we refer to these as professionals/managers. A large body of knowledge has been devoted to the differences between professional workers and managers and, more specifically on the changing professional/managerial dynamics in the public sector. For details on these debates, see Exworthy and Halford (1999).

References

Acker, J. (1990) 'Hierarchies, jobs, bodies: a theory of gendered organizations'. *Gender and Society*, 4: 139–58.

Ackroyd, S. and Soothill, K. (1994) 'The new management and the professionals'. Paper presented at the ERU Annual Conference 'The Contract State? The Future of Public Management', Cardiff: Cardiff Business School.

Aldridge, M. (1996) 'Dragged to market: being a profession in the postmodern world'. *British Journal of Social Work*, 26(2): 177–94.

Alvesson, M. and Billing, Y. D. (1997) *Understanding Gender and Organisations*, London: Sage.

Alvesson, M. and Deetz, S. (2000) *Doing Critical Management Research*, London: Sage.

Bartlett, W. Propper, C., Wilson, D. and Le Grand, J. (eds) (1994). *Quasi-Markets in the Welfare State*, Bristol: School of Advanced Urban Studies.

Barry, J., Dent, M. and O'Neill, M. (eds) (2003) *Gender and the Public Sector: Professionals and Managerial Change*, London: Routledge.

Barry, J., Chandler, J. and Clark, H. (eds) (2001) Between the ivory tower and the academic assembly line. *Journal of Management Studies*, 38 (1): 87–102.

Brown, J. M. and Heidensohn, F. (2000) *Gender and Policing*, Hampshire: Macmillan.

Burke, M. (1993) *Coming Out of the Blue*, London: Cassell.

Butler, J. (1990) *Gender Trouble*, London: Routledge.

Calas, M. and Smircich, L. (1996) 'From the "Woman's point of view": feminist approaches to organization studies', in Clegg, S. R., Hardy, C. and Nord, W. R. (eds) *Handbook of Organisational Studies*, London: Sage.

Camilleri, P. (1999) 'Social work and its search for meaning: theories, narratives and practices', in Pease, B. and Fook, J. (eds) *Transforming Social Work Practice: Postmodern Critical Perspectives*, London: Routledge.

Causer, G. and Exworthy, M. (1999) 'Professionals as managers across the public sector', in Exworthy, M. and Halford, S. (eds) *Professionals and the New Managerialism in the Public Sector*, London: Sage.

Clarke, J. and Newman, J. (1997) *The Managerial State*, London: Sage.

Clegg, S. (1992) Modernist and postmodernist organization, in Salaman, G. (ed.) *Human Resource Strategies*, London: Sage.

Collinson, D. and Hearn, J. (1994) 'Naming men as men: implications for work, organization and management', in Ely, R. (ed.) *Gender, Work and Organization*, 1 (1): 2–22.

Collinson, D. L., Knights, D. and Collinson, M. (1990) *Managing to Discriminate*, London: Routledge.

Connell, R. W. (1987) *Gender and Power*, Oxford: Polity Press.

Cooper, C. and Davidson, M. J. (eds) (1984) *Women in Management*, London: Heinemann.

Coyle, A. (1988) 'The limits of change: local government and equal opportunities for women'. *Public Administration*, 67: 39–50.

Crompton, R. (1990) 'Professions in the current context'. *Work, Employment and Society*, Special Issue: 'A Decade of Change?': 147–66.

Cunningham, R., Lord, A. and Delaney, L. (1999) 'Next Steps for equality? The Impact of organizational change on opportunities for women in the civil service'. *Gender, Work and Organization*, 6 (2): 67–78.

Davies, A. (2000) 'Change in the UK police service: the costs and dilemmas of restructured managerial roles and identities'. *Journal of Change Management*, 1 (1): 41–58.

Davies, A. and Thomas, R. 'Talking COP: Discourses of change and policing identities'. *Public Administration*, 81 (4): 681–699.

Davies, A. and Thomas, R. (2002) 'Gendering and gender in public service organisations'. *Public Management Review*, 4 (4): 461–84.

Davies, A. and Thomas, R. (2000) 'Researching public sector change: the argument for a gender inclusive framework'. *Public Management*, 2 (4): 548–54.

Dent, M. and Whitehead, S. (2002) (eds) *Managing Professional Identities*, London: Routledge.

du Gay, P. (1996) *Consumption and Identity at Work*, London: Sage.

Edwards, C. and Robinson, O. (1999) 'Managing part-timers in the police service: a study in inflexibility'. *Human Resource Management Journal*, 9 (4): 5–18.

Escott, K. and Whitfield, D. (1995) *The Gender Impact of CCT in Local Government*. Equal Opportunities Commission.

Exworthy, M. and Halford, S. (1999) *Professionals and the new managerialism in the public sector*. Buckingham: Open University Press.

Ezzamel, M., Lilley, S. and Willmott, H. (1996) 'The view from the top: senior executives' perceptions of changing management practices in UK companies'. *British Journal of Management*, 7 (2): 169–81.

Farnham, D. and Giles, L. (1996) 'Education', in Farnham, D. and Horton, S. (eds) *Managing People in the Public Services*, Hampshire: Macmillan.

Fielding, N. (1994) 'Cop canteen culture', in Newburn, T. and Stanko, B. (eds) *Just Boys Doing Business*, London: Routledge.

Fine, M. and Macpherson P. (1994) 'Over dinner: feminism and adolescent female bodies', in Radtke, H. L. and Stam, H. J. (eds) *Power/Gender: Social Relations in Theory in Practice*, London: Sage.

Fondas, N. (1997) 'Feminisation unveiled: management qualities in contemporary writings'. *Academy of Management Review*, 22 (1): 257–82.

Foucault, Michel. (1982) 'The subject and power', in Hubert Drefus and Paul Rabinow (eds) *Michel Foucault: Beyond Structuralism and Hermeneutics*, 208–26, New York: Harvester.

Gewirtz, S. (2002) *The Managerial School: Post-welfarism and Social Justice in Education*, London: Routledge.

Goode, J. and Bagilhole, B. (1998) 'Gendering the management of change in higher education: a case study'. *Gender, Work and Organization*, 5 (3): 148–64.

Grace, G. (1995) *School Leadership*, London: Falmer.

Graef, R. (1989) *Talking Blues*, London: Fontana.

Halford, S. and Leonard, P. (1999) 'New identities? professionalism, managerialism and the construction of self', in Exworthy, M. and Halford, S. (eds) *Professionals and the New Managerialism in the Public Sector*, Buckingham: Open University Press.

Halford, S., Savage, M. and Witz, A. (1997) *Gender, Careers and Organisations*. London: Macmillan.

Harris, A. (2003) 'The changing context of leadership', in Harris, A., Day, C., Hadfield, M., Hopkins, D., Hargreaves A. and Chapman, C. (eds) *Effective Leadership for School Improvement*, London: Routledge.

Hasselbladh, H. and Selander, M. (2003) 'Plural frames of work in public sector organisations', in Barry, J., Dent, M. and O'Neill, M. (eds) *Gender and the Public Sector: Professionals and Managerial Change*, London: Routledge.

Healy, G. (1999) 'Structuring commitment in interrupted careers: career breaks, commitment and life cycles in teaching'. *Gender, Work and Organization*, 6 (4): 185–201.

Hoggett, P. (1996) 'New modes of control in the public service', *Public Administration*, 74 (Spring): 9–32.

Holdaway, S. (1997) 'Responding to racialized divisions within the workforce – the experience of black and Asian officers in England', *Ethnic and Racial Studies*, 20 (1): 69–90.

Holdaway, S. and Barron, A. (1997) *Resigners? The Experience of Black and Asian Police Officers*, London: Macmillan.

Holloway, D., Horton, S. and Farnham, S. (1999) 'Education', in Horton, S. and Farnham, D. (eds) *Public Management in Britain*, London: Macmillan.

Hood, C., Scott, C., James, O., Jones, G. and Travers, T. (1999) *Regulation Inside Government: Waste-Watchers, Quality-Police and Sleaze-Busters*, Oxford: Oxford University Press.

Horton, S. and Farnham, D. (1999) New labour and the management of public services: legacies, impact and prospects, in Horton, S. and Farnham, D. (eds) *Public Management in Britain*, London: Macmillan.

Ianni, E. and Ianni, F. (1983) Street cops and management cops: the two cultures of policing, in Punch, M. (ed) *Control in the Police Organization*. Cambridge, MA: MIT Press.

Ife, J. (1999) Postmodernism, critical theory and social work, in Pease, B. and Fook, J. (eds) *Transforming Social Work Practice: Postmodern Critical Perspectives*, London: Routledge.

Jacobson, S. W. and Jacques, R. (1990) 'Of knowers, knowing, and the known: a gender framework for revisioning organisational and management scholarship'. Paper given at the Academy of Management Annual Meeting: Women in Management Division, San Francisco, 10–12 August.

Johnston, L. (1988) 'Controlling police work: problems of organisational reform in large public bureaucracies'. *Work, Employment and Society*, 2 (1): 51–70.

Jones, C. (1999) 'Social work: regulation and managerialism', in Exworthy, M. and Halford, S. (eds) *Professionals and the New Managerialism in the Public Sector*, London: Sage.

Kerfoot, D. and Knights, D. (1993) 'Management, masculinity and manipulation: from paternalism to corporate strategy in the financial services in Britain'. *Journal of Management Studies*, 30 (4): 659–79.

Kirkpatrick, I. and Martinez-Lucio, M. (eds) (1995) *The Politics of Quality in the Public Sector*, London: Routledge.

Kondo, D. (1990) *Crafting Selves: Power, Gender and Discourses of Identity in a Japanese Workplace*, Chicago: University of Chicago Press.

Lawler, J. and Hearn, J. (1995) 'UK public service organizations: the rise of managerialism and the impact of change on social services departments'. *International Journal of Public Sector Management*, 8 (4): 7–16.

Levacic, R. (1995) *Local Management of Schools: Analysis and Practice*, Buckingham: Oxford University Press.

Leonard, P. (1998) 'Gendering change? management, masculinity and the dynamics of incorporation'. *Gender and Education*, 10 (1): 71–84.

Lovenduski, J. (1988) 'Implementing equal opportunities in the 1980s: an overview'. *Public Administration*, 67.

Macpherson, Sir W. (1999) *Stephen Lawrence Inquiry*. CM 4262–I.

Maddock, S. (1999) *Challenging Women: Gender, Culture and Organization*, London: Sage.

Maddock, S. and Parkin, D. (1993) Gender cultures: women's choices and strategies at work. *Women in Management Review*, 8 (2): 3–9.

Margetts, H. (1996) 'Public management change and sex equality within the state'. *Parliamentary Affairs*, 49: 130–43.

Marshall, J. (1995) *Women Managers Moving On: Exploring Career and Life Choices*, London: Routledge.

Meriläinen, S. and Tienari, J. (2001) 'Managment consultant talk: a cross-cultural comparison of normalising discourse and resistance'. Paper presented at the EGOS Colloquium, Lyon.

Metcalf, B. and Dick, G. (2001) 'Exploring organisation commitment in the police: implications for human resource strategy', *Policing: An International Journal of Police Strategies and Management*, 24 (3): 399–419.

Mills, A. and Tancred, P. (1992) (eds) *Gendering Organisational Analysis*, Newbury Park, CA: Sage.

Nash, M. and Savage, S. P. (1994) 'A criminal record? law, order and conservative policy' in Savage, S. P., Atkinson, R. and Robins, L. (eds) *Public Policy in Britain*, London: Macmillan.

Parker, M. (1997) 'Dividing organizations and multiplying identities', in Hetherington, K. and Munro, R. (eds) *Ideas of difference*, Oxford: Blackwell/ The Sociological Review.

Parker, M. and Jary, D. (1995) The McUniversity: Organization, Management and Academic Subjectivity. *Organization*, 2 (2): 319–38.

Pollitt, C. (1993) *Managerialism and the Public Services*, Oxford: Blackwell.

Pollitt, C. (1995) 'Justification by works or by faith?', *Evaluation*, 1 (2): 133–54.

Pollit, C. and Bouckaert, G. (1999) *Public Management Reform: A Comparative Analysis*, Oxford: Oxford University Press.

Praat, A. and Tuffin, K. (1996) 'Police discourse of homosexual men in New Zealand'. *Journal of Homosexuality*, 31 (4): 57–73.

Professional Social Worker (1996) 'Parliamentary concern about social work stress'. *Professional Social Work*, August: 1–2.

Rosener, J. B. (1990) 'Ways women lead'. *Harvard Business Review*, November–December, 119–25.

Shardlow, S. (1998) 'Values, ethics and social work', in Adams, R., Dominelli, L. and Payne, M. (eds) *Social Work: Themes, Issues and Critical Debates*, London: Macmillan.

Sinclair, J., Ironside, M. and Seifert, R. (1996) 'Classroom struggle? market orientated education reforms and their impact on the teacher labour process'. *Work, Employment and Society*, 10 (4): 664–74.

Smith, C. (2001) 'Trust and confidence: possibilities for social work in "high modernity"'. *British Journal of Social Work*, 31: 287–305.

Thom, L. (1999) 'Rhetoric versus reality: why women tend not to apply for senior positions in secondary education', in Whitehead, S. and Moodley, R. (eds) *Transforming Managers: Gendering Change in the Public Sector*, London: UCL Press.

Thomas, R. (1996) 'Gendered cultures and performance appraisal: the experience of women academics'. *Gender, Work and Organization*, 3 (3): 143–55.

Thomas, R. and Dunkerley, D. (1999) 'Janus and the bureaucrats: middle management in the public sector', *Public Policy and Administration*, 14 (1): 28–41.

Townley, B. (1994) *Reframing Human Resource Management: Power, Ethics and the Subject at Work*, London: Sage.

Whitehead, S. and Moodley, R. (eds) (1999) *Transforming Managers: Gendering Change in the Public Sector*, London: UCL Press.

Yeatman, A. (1994) *Postmodern Revisionings of the Political*, New York: Routledge.

Young, M. (1991) *An Inside Job: Policing and Police Culture in Britain*, Oxford: Clarendon Press.

4
Seeking the Critical Mass: Quantitative and Qualitative Aspects of the Feminisation of Management in Britain in the 1990s

Irene Bruegel

By the turn of the twenty-first century nearly two in every five managerial posts in the US and the UK were held by women, a steep rise from the position 25 years before. The scale of growth suggests to some writers that we are witnessing a revolution in gender relations (Faludi, 1999; Freeman, 2000) or at least in dominant management styles (Colgan & Ledwith, 1996a; Maddock, 1999), much as Kanter predicted from her early research on women in management (Kanter, 1977). Drawing on Simmel's classic analysis of 'the significance of numbers for social life: the way numerical shifts transform social interaction', Kanter argued that women managers were forced into stereotypical behaviour so long as they remained tokens in an environment of male (numerical) domination. Her prediction was that 'forms of relationships and peer culture should change' as the ratio of women to men begins to shift (1977: 209). In a similar vein Etzkowitz (1994: 51) argues that 'as the (minority group's) presence and level of participation grows, at a particular point the perspective of the minority group and the character of relations between minority and majority group changes qualitatively'. More generally, a social relational approach to organisations would suggest that the social and demographic context of any work-group influences a range of individual decisions, including the take-up of family-friendly provision (Blair-Loy and Wharton, 2002).

Some deny it is a question of numbers. For example Wacjman (1998) argues that women managers act like men in relation to the workforce as a whole as a result of their position in the management structure. But women managers can also be seen to have interests in conflict with their male colleagues. In their own interests ambitious women might seek to foster female dominated informal networks as a counterpoint to the male buddy networks which restrict their career advancement (Roper, 1994; Davidson and Cooper, 1992). While the networks would be female, the women could be said to behave like men in seeking degree of 'homosociability' (Kanter, 1977). To do this female managers are likely to be drawn into promoting more rigorous and more explicit equal opportunity policies and more flexible organisation of working time. In this way the proportion of female managers could increase cumulatively where a core group had been established, without necessarily entailing any broader feminisation of the managerial culture.

This chapter arises from research on feminisation for the ESRC Future of Work programme, which looks at a range of potential cumulative processes of feminisation. Whatever the original (external) reason for an increase in female employment in any given occupation/ enterprise, once some initial threshold level has been reached, female employment can be expected to expand faster than male, as the job becomes less attractive to men as a direct, or indirect, result of the increasing numerical presence of women. Feminists have proposed that such a mechanism may work through changes in male self-esteem, in relative pay and in promotion prospects (Cockburn, 1983; Reskin and Roos, 1990). In principle, too, a feminisation of trade union membership and power could raise the profile of women in a labour force (Colgan and Ledwith, 1996b).

This chapter concentrates on identifying the links between the feminisation of management of enterprises included in the Workplace Employment Relations Survey (WERS) and changes in the opportunities offered to other women in such enterprises. While it is to be expected that enterprises which adopt equal opportunity policies and which employ women in their core activities will employ more women as managers, what is at issue is whether these female managers can be seen to exert an independent influence on working time and related policies. To do so they need both to have achieved positions of power and influence and to identify common interests with women as a whole.

Existing research on family-friendly policies in the WERS sample has established that large, public sector, unionised establishments are more likely to be 'family-friendly' (Dex and Smith, 2002; Cully *et al.*, 1999; Wood, 1999), and that women have more access to provisions than men, but the possible impact of a more female management on these policies, and particularly on provision for staff on lower grades has not yet been explored, though it is clear that within any given establishment there are important differences in access to provision between different people (Dex and Smith, 2001).

The chapter proceeds by discussing the usefulness and difficulties in using WERS for such a study; and moves on to consider the pattern of employment of women in management and the pattern of change in the period from 1990–98, partly to throw some light on the ability of women managers to hold on to their jobs when managements themselves faced cutbacks. The relationship between the gender composition of management teams at establishment level and the locus of decision-making is then discussed.

The WERS data-set

WERS is a survey of establishments across the range of industries and occupations in the UK.[1] This paper considers two recent WERS data sources: the 1998 survey of over 2000 establishments and the separate panel survey, linking data from 1990 and 1998 for over 800 establishments.

The 1998 WERS provides information on issues of equal opportunity and family-friendly working, in contrast to earlier versions of the survey and to the panel data (Dex and Smith, 2002). Amongst the data-sets making up the 1998 survey is a survey of some 28 000 employees across the occupational hierarchy, with up to 25 in each establishment. In 1998 for the first time in the history of (Workplace Industrial Relations Survey) WIRS/WERS respondents were asked about their children and their family status and whether they worked in the same job only with other people of the same sex, mainly with people of the same sex or equally with both sexes. Thus the information on gender segregation is much richer than is generally available. Information on family-friendly working is available for the 1998 survey both from the survey of 28 000 employees over 2000 establishments (employee data-set) and from the responses of managerial representatives in each enterprise (management survey).

The panel data helps to unpick some of the interactions between personnel policies and the gender profile of management of different establishments. In particular it is possible to explore some effects of a more female management team in 1990 on policies and outcomes in 1998, at least for the surviving enterprises.[2] Unfortunately no questions relating to family-friendly provision were asked of the establishments in the panel survey, so that the direct effect of a more female management team on such policies cannot be established. Moreover enterprises employing fewer than 25 people were excluded from the panel survey , but not the 1998 cross sectional WERS survey. This means that the two datasets are not strictly comparable (Airey, 1999).

Using the employee data-set it is possible to identify which people had access to a range of family-friendly provisions by their gender and family situation, their job type and the degree to which they worked alongside men or women. These included flexi-time, job sharing, parental leave, a workplace nursery or childcare subsidy and working at home during normal office hours. The employee survey also asked whether respondents found managers to be responsive and understanding of their needs as parents or others with care responsibilities.

There is some ambiguity in the questions about provision. People appeared to interpret the terms flexi-time and parental leave differently.

Employees were asked whether the various provisions would be available, '*if they needed them*'. Some people may have responded negatively because they felt they had no need of the facilities rather than because there were not generally available. This does not appear to be a very serious problem with the data because questions to employees on the availability of family-friendly provision were augmented by more straightforward questions to Human Resource Managers about such provision. In general the match was good – where employees said facilities were not available, so did managers; though it is also clear that facilities were only selectively available to different groups of employees.

The WERS data-set provides limited information on the *uptake* of family-friendly policies. Managers were asked a general question about usage, but not in a way that can be tracked back to the occupation or gender of the workers concerned. Earlier research in the USA and the UK (Fried, 1999; Hogarth *et al.*, 2000; Blair-Loy and Wharton, 2002) shows that such benefits are taken up selectively. Those with access may feel that competitive pressures at work are too great to allow them to take them up; others may have no need of them. There may be a critical mass effect: if enough people take up the provisions, it becomes the norm. Equally there may be threshold effects: so long as only a very few people take up provision, it is allowed beyond that pressure will be exerted not to employ people likely to seek such benefits. From the Work Life Balance Survey 2000 an interesting pattern emerges; whereas eligibility for work solidus life balance provision is weighted towards the top, take-up is not (Hogarth *et al.*, 2001).

It is possible to get some sense of the degree of autonomy of managers in different enterprises from WERS, though it is clearly not designed to contrast the relative autonomy of men and women managers. People responsible for human resource management in the establishment – that is the respondents in the management questionnaire – were asked a series of questions about their jobs, their gender and their qualifications. It was therefore possible to draw out gender contrasts in decision-making for this group of 1382 men and 810 women. They were asked about which areas of human resource management were subject to protocols established by managers elsewhere. In addition, the employee questionnaire, which included 979 female and 1599 male managers, asked about aspects of the autonomy offered by their jobs. We look at this issue next because the argument that the gender composition of management might influence the local establishment policies rests on the assumption that female managers have some degree of discretion.

Patterns of female management

Women managers in the 1998 cross sectional survey were found disproportionately in female dominated enterprises, generally within female dominated industrial sectors (Table 4.1). Some 37 per cent of the variation between establishments in the gender composition of management is explained by

Table 4.1 Female share of management 1998 by characteristics of establishment

	%	se
Total	36.58	0.83
Industry		
Manufacturing	13.91	1.20
Construction	3.00	1.09
Wholesale and retail	36.92	1.72
Hotels and restaurants	45.05	2.46
Transport and communication	8.40	1.58
Financial services	41.01	4.50
Other business services	33.03	2.19
Public administration	27.75	3.66
Education	47.39	2.66
Health	70.92	2.03
Other community services	35.55	3.79
Head Office	24.44	2.23
Employees at establishment		
10–24	38.13	1.27
25–49	40.46	1.63
over 500	29.10	4.47
Public sector	45.12	1.88
Southern England	39.37	1.95
Female share of workforce		
10% and less than	5.70	0.73
11–20%	13.06	1.51
21–35%	15.28	1.35
36–50%	22.09	1.87
51–70%	36.99	1.67
71–80%	44.21	2.19
81–90%	42.55	2.63
91–100%	57.66	2.21

Source: WERS 98 (Management Questionnaire).

the gender composition of the rest of the workforce. The upshot is that female managers rarely manage men; they tend, however, to work in mixed sex teams and relatively rarely in female dominated management teams.

There are indicators in the WERS sample that women are the junior managers: they are less likely to be working at head office, implying that they wield less influence over corporate decision-making, particularly since the enterprises in which women managers are working at head office are generally smaller.

While there is little difference in the perks they get, average hourly pay for female managers as a whole is 33 per cent less than for male managers in the WERS employee sample (Table 4.2). Amongst graduate managers the gender

Table 4.2 Characteristics of male and female managers 1998

	Male n = 748	Female n = 413
% under 30 years	11.2	18.8
% parent of		
child 0–4	17.4	11.4
child 5–11	26.1	12.5
child 12–19	26.5	11.4
hourly pay	£11.40	£8.60
graduate hourly pay	£12.60	£9.60
job content		
% never constrained to external protocols	34	24
% constrained in relation to		
Equal Opportunity Implementation	48	52
% rating autonomy high for		
way do job	74	72
range of job	60	53
pace of work	55	53

Source: WERS 98 Manager Survey and Employee Questionnaire.

wage gap was 25 per cent. Some of this is associated with generalised low pay in the sectors women manage, particularly in retail and catering, but this is not the whole story. New Earnings Survey data shows that *within* individual sectors women manager's earnings are generally between two-thirds and four-fifths of men's.

Consistent with their lower pay and more junior status, female human resource managers appear to be more constrained in the policies they can pursue than their male equivalents. One-third of male establishment-level human resource managers had considerable autonomy with no external protocols on any of the policy issues investigated, compared to fewer than 25 per cent of the female equivalents (Table 4.2). Moreover the more female the management team, the more limited the local managers' discretion. All but 18 per cent of female managers who worked in wholly female management teams were constrained to protocols established at a higher level. This compares to all but 42 per cent of the female managers who were working in a largely male management team. Thus there is no evidence of any breakthrough beyond a critical point: the more female the management team, in general, the more centralised the policies of the companies/institutions.

Against this there were no gender differences in managers' assessments of their autonomy with regard to how they did their jobs, the scope and pace of their jobs, nor in their satisfaction with the autonomy offered by their jobs (77 per cent of both male and female managers were satisfied on that score). By 1998, too, there was no difference in the size of establishments managed by men and women who were the sole managers of their establishments. In relation to the specialised area of equal opportunities, gender differences in management responsibilities were relatively small, with 48 per cent of male human resource managers and 52 per cent of female simply implementing an externally determined policy. In over half of all establishments equal opportunities policies are operated locally; where they are, women form over a third of the management team responsible.

There is then considerable scope for individual managers to adopt more 'family-friendly' policies, and relatively little structural difference in the potential influence of individual women in this area compared to individual men, even if the broader evidence from WERS suggests that male managers retain more power and influence over corporate policy.

The rise of the female manager: findings from the WERS panel survey 1990–99

Kanter's critical mass model of feminisation would imply an S shape relationship between the *level* of feminisation of an establishment in the first period (1990) and the rate of increase in feminisation in the subsequent period (1990–98); feminisation being defined here as the proportion of managerial posts in the establishment which are held by women. From the evidence of the establishments included in the WERS panel survey it is clear from Table 4.3 that the feminisation of management proceeded quite quickly in Britain between 1990 and 1998, but more detailed analysis of the pattern of change (Table 4.4), does not support Kanter's model.

Table 4.3 shows how overall proportion of managers who were female increased from 24 per cent to 31 per cent between 1990 and 1998, but much of the expansion of women in managerial posts came in establishments that had had no women in management in 1990. While 40 per cent of establishments had no female manager in 1990, 70 per cent of establishments had at least one female manager by the end of the decade. The increase in establishments that were wholly managed by women – from 6.5 per cent to nearly 10 per cent – is associated with an increase in the proportion of establishments with only one manager. Overall in those establishments the proportion of women managers increased fast, from 17 per cent to 42 per cent. But there were importance differences between single-establishment organisations, that is in small firms owned by women, and multi-establishment organisations especially those in finance and health care where the feminisation of management was particularly dramatic.

Overall in the period the panel data showed that nearly two-fifths (38.7 per cent) of establishments increased their management posts by over 50 per cent while 'de-feminising' lower level white-collar, semi-skilled and unskilled manual work. Thus the expansion of women in management was associated with a general shift of the labour force towards jobs defined as managerial

Table 4.3   Proportion of jobs held by women in WERS Panel establishments

	1990		1998		index
	n	%	n	%	1990 = 100
Occupation					
managers (overall)	729	23.6	679	30.7	130
supervisors	526	38.5	453	53.3	138
senior professional/technicians	493	35.7	450	36.8	108
junior professional/technicians	478	46.7	406	45.6	98
clerical	750	85.6	679	83.4	97
skilled manual	417	17.5	383	19.8	113
semi-skilled manual	418	29.1	338	28.6	98
unskilled manual	584	51.9	504	47.3	91
Proportion of establishments with manager present with					
any female managers	730	60.3	730	69.6	115
only female managers	730	6.5	730	9.8	138
Establishments with a sole manager % of sole managers who were female	128	17	100	42	247
Independent establishments/ partnerships % of sole managers who were female	93	14.6	271	22.5	154

Note: n = number of establishments with at least 1 person in that job category in that year.
Source: WERS Panel Survey 1990–98.

and a general upgrading of the status of women in work, associated with the expansion of women completing higher education. At the same time, on evidence from the Labour Force Survey, the proportion of all managers who were mothers remained at around 10 per cent throughout the 1990s. As Table 4.2 shows, the 'gender gap' in parenthood amongst managers was stark, particularly for those with children over five years old: male managers were twice as likely to have children over the age of five as female managers.

Table 4.4 looks at the pattern of *increase* in women managers between 1990 and 1998 between establishments according to the density of female managers in 1990 in those establishments.[3] It shows that 12 per cent of the gross increase in numbers of women in management in the panel establishments was in establishments with no female managers in 1990 and that over two-fifths (43 per cent) of the gross increase in women managers in the WERS survey occurred in establishments where fewer than 10 per cent of the managers had been women in 1990.[4] Over a third of women managers (35.8 per cent) were working in establishments with over 40 per cent of women in management in 1990; but barely a quarter of the total net increase in female managers between 1990 and 1998 (26.6 per cent) occurred in these

Table 4.4 Distribution of establishments and of women managers in 1990 and change in numbers of female managers 1990–98 by gender composition of managements in 1990

Gender composition	Numbers in 1990			Change in female managers 1990–98: (not weighted) Establishments which			
	Establishments	Female managers		Increased female managers		Reduced female managers	
Female share of management in 1990	N	Number of females	Distribution of female managers	N females	Distribution of female managers	N females	Distribution of female managers
0	277	0	0	307	11.8	0	0
1–10%	121	461	12	816	31.3	−107	8.0
11–20%	83	751	20	273	10.5	−259	19.5
21–30%	47	783	20	226	8.7	−254	19.1
31–40%	49	516	13	283	10.9	−89	6.7
41–100%	116	1377	36	697	26.6	−589	44.0
Total	703	1139	100	2602	100	−1330	100

Source: WERS Panel Survey 1990–98.

establishments. this group experienced less than proportionate growth in female managers (27 per cent) and a higher than proportionate loss of female managers (44 per cent). In the sense of providing a protection from job loss, a 40 per cent level of females in management appears not to provide a critical mass.

Rather than being S shaped, the relationship between the gender composition of management of an establishment in 1990 and the feminisation of management within that establishment between 1990 and 1998 is essentially negative; the less female the management composition in 1990, the more likely women were to enter management. Given that over 40 per cent of establishments in the survey had no women managers in 1990, there was plenty of scope for such a change. It suggests, nevertheless, a spreading out of female managers across enterprises. It was in the main a spreading out across enterprises within the areas of the economy where women are concentrated: the public services, retailing, catering and finance. Nevertheless the strong correlation between the gender composition of an establishment's management team and the gender composition of its non-managerial workforce fell from 0.687 in 1990 to 0.539 in 1998, suggesting that women managers are, increasingly, managing men.

Table 4.5 looks at the distribution of gross increases and decreases in female manager numbers across sectors for the 443 establishments for which data is available from the Panel Survey. The third column shows that exclusively male management teams are found disproportionately in manufacturing and transport, but not in construction, probably reflecting the involvement of wives in the management of small construction firms. The extremely fast overall growth of female management in finance is evident: whereas finance accounted for 9 per cent of all female management personnel, 13 per cent of the growth in female management was in that sector. The relative decline in women's share of retail management suggests that restructuring and de-layering may indeed have had particularly adverse effects on women.

Our analysis from WERS suggests that feminisation of management is associated with changes in work methods, but probably not in a direct causal relation. Organisational change, on the other hand, tends to be in association with lower rates of feminisation of management; it could be that in the scrabble for positions in the wake of mergers and ownership changes, female managers lose out, though we found no consistent effect of managerial retrenchment on the gender composition of managements. The data suggests that the more successful establishments – those that increased the total number of managers and generally, employees – were more likely to have increased the share of women in their managements. But we cannot infer from this that an increase in the presence of women in management induced such success.

De-feminisation of management occurred disproportionately in areas of high female employment in management, retail, catering and government

Table 4.5 Establishments by share and change in female share of management 1990–98 by organisation type 1998 (weighted by size of establishment)

(excludes establishments with no change in female share of management)	Establishments with no female managers 1990	Establishments with female managers 1990		
	Distribution of managers	Distribution of female managers between		All establishments
		Establishments in which female share of management		
		Increased	Decreased	
Industry/Organisation type:				
Extraction and utilities	11.8	4.5	3.7	6.2
Engineering and related	13.7	8.1	5.9	8.4
Other manufacturing	15.5	6.3	5.9	8.4
Construction	2.5	3.2	3.7	2.7
Distribution, hotels and catering etc	17.4	24.0	29.6	21.8
Transport and communications	11.2	3.2	1.5	4.6
Banking, finance, insurance, bus services and leasing	9.3	12.7	2.2	9.1
Other services	18.6	38.0	47.4	38.8
	100.0	100.0	100.0	100.0
Of Other services				
Local and central government	10.6	22.4	31.1	20.9
Public service agency	7.5	4.9	2.3	6.9
Other	0.5	10.7	14.0	11.0

Source: WERS Panel Survey 1990–98.

in particular. In these fields large differences between establishments are evident, since disproportionate *increases* in the share of women in management were also experienced in these fields. Thus nearly a third of establishments (31 per cent) that de-feminised their managerial workforce were in local and central government, yet 22 per cent of those that increased the female share of the workforce were also in public administration.

This complicated pattern of growth and decline across establishments suggests that cumulative processes at establishment level are weak. While the growth of female management is still concentrated in typically female industries, growth is not particularly concentrated between establishments within those sectors; rather than women going from strength to strength in numerical terms, the evidence is of some plateau effect. The evidence WERS suggests that gender segregation of management operates *within* larger enterprises; that is both men and women describe themselves as working exclusively with men or women in establishments which overall appear to have quite a mixed management team. Although 7 per cent of female managers say they work exclusively with women, 44 per cent of managers in those very establishments were found to be men. In practice there were islands of female management in a sea of predominantly male management. Indeed amongst establishment with 2 or more managers in 1998, only 1.7 per cent actually had a totally female management team.

The presence of women managers in any given place of work does not then appear to increase the likelihood that women will be more successful in getting managerial jobs than would otherwise be the case, at least on the evidence of WERS between 1990 and 1998. This may well be because management jobs remain highly gender defined and segregated within establishments, but this cannot be examined further here. Instead we move from considering quantitative effects of a high density of female managers to an examination of the possible qualitative effects.

Assessing the impact of female managers on equal opportunities and family-friendly policies

Firms that operate more 'family-friendly' policies should, other things being equal, enable more women to compete successfully for management jobs. Indeed the low proportion of mothers working in managerial jobs testifies to the continuing barriers to gender equality. However, the association between equal opportunity/family-friendly policies and higher shares of women in management can be theorised to operate in both directions. It may arise because women managers chose (or are constrained to choose) establishments which offer such support, or because women managers have been in a position to promote such policies. In practice it is likely to reflect three processes: the direct impact of equal opportunity policies on access to managerial jobs; the influence of women managers on policy stances and the indirect relationship through the gender composition of the workforce as a whole. Women managers are found more often in more female domi-nated establishments, where some form of family-friendly working, if only the provision of jobs on a part-time basis, is also likely to be more common. It is therefore difficult to tease out what the independent effect of a high density of female managers on the provision of family-friendly policies might be. Before trying to assess the direction of causation, we first review the relationship between equal opportunity, and most especially family-friendly policies, and the gender composition of different workforces.

The relationship depends on how family-friendly policies are defined. While the ability to switch between full-and part-time working is a marker for flexible working, it is not at all clear that part-time work as such offers the flexibility of flexi-time. Yet a number of part-time workers in the employee study saw themselves as having flexi-time. The problem is compounded because 'true' family-friendly policies can be taken to be those that enable women to move out of the ghetto of female part-time work, whether through job share, nurseries, parental leave or other policies. Unfortunately, the term 'parental leave' is also employed ambiguously by WERS respondents, some-times relating only to paternity leave and other times to paternity, maternity and special leave relating to a child's sickness (Dex and Smith, 2002). It is for this reason that individual family-friendly policies are considered as well as access to provision as a whole in what follows. We concentrate on the more common policies: job sharing, flexibility and working from home where numbers are large enough to provide reliable estimates of variation across establishments.

Table 4.6 shows that amongst the array of family-friendly policies, aware-ness is far more gendered for some policies than others – job sharing, for example, is more readily seen to be available to women than men and work-ing from home is generally more available to men than women (see also Hogarth *et al.*, 2001) – and some are far more linked to the proportion of parents in employment than others (as shown also by Callender *et al.*, 1997). The possibility of working from home is generally something that parents – of both sexes – across an array of occupations, are more aware of than other men and women, in contrast to flexible working, where parenthood does not influence responses, except for mothers working in sales and as opera-tives for whom it appears particularly important. In general, awareness of provision amongst the 28 000 employees questioned in WERS reflects occu-pational status as well as gender and parental status, with clerical workers, both male and female generally reporting the greatest access.

Though family-friendly policies might be expected to be available to all employees within an establishment or at least within an occupational group within an establishment, they generally remain subject to management dis-cretion and are not always widely publicised. In Table 4.7, therefore, differ-ences in apparent access to job sharing and flexible working amongst

Table 4.6 Access to family-friendly provision by gender, occupation and parenthood

% with					Occupation group					
	all	1.0 managers	2.0 profess	3.0 assoc prof	4.0 clerical	5.0 skilled	6.0 personal	7.0 sales	8.0 operatives	9.0 other
No provision										
all men	53	38	39	40	35	70	51	43	66	63
fathers	51	37	37	39	36	68	48	43	60	64
all women	39	27	32	32	33	40	40	44	55	55
mothers	35	25	32	31	29	44	38	38	38	48
Flexible working										
all men	28	37	33	42	53	18	21	34	17	23
fathers	26	35	31	40	53	20	19	21	16	15
all women	38	46	31	38	47	43	34	38	23	30
mothers	39	50	28	36	50	39	32	45	36	31
Job sharing										
all men	10	15	17	12	26	2	15	8	3	8
fathers	10	15	18	11	27	3	19	3	3	6
all women	24	29	33	29	32	10	19	11	8	10
mothers	26	33	36	34	36	10	23	11	16	10
Work from home										
all men	11	32	26	18	9	2	5	15	0	1
fathers	13	35	26	18	9	3	6	28	0	3
all women	7	37	17	8	6	7	1	2	1	1
mothers	7	37	17	6	7	2	1	1	2	1

Source: Employee questionnaire.

Table 4.7 Patterns of access to flexible work and job share within establishments

Unweighted	Women in the WERS employee survey				Two surveys compared all non-managers (M & F)	
	Managers	Professional	Associate	Manual	Employee survey	Management survey
Flexible working available to						
some respondent	50	55	60	56	89	84
all respondents	35	18	33	11	3	n.a.
job share available to						
some respondent	31	47	45	33	66	64
all respondents	20	14	18	4	0	n.a.
n establishments =	599	654	528	1022	1783	2191

Sources: WERS Employee Survey 1998.
WERS Management Survey 1998.

women in the same occupation working for the same establishment are considered. Here the individual responses are aggregated to describe the pattern of access within each establishment for all respondents of a given grade. While *some* professional women in nearly half of the establishments (47 per cent) with professional grade female respondents said they could job share, in only 14 per cent did *all* professional women say that. Very few establishments – 4 per cent – are said to provide comprehensive access to job sharing to all manual women workers. This may reflect a lack of knowledge but could also signal that access is discretionary. It certainly suggests that where some of the non-managerial workforce has access to various measures, these are not universally known to be available. Table 4.7 shows a good fit between the aggregated answers of employees about facilities and the response of managers as to what was available for non-managerial workers. On both counts over 80 per cent of establishments provided some access to flexible working and 65–66 per cent to job sharing.

Family-friendly conditions for managers and non-managers

The employee survey enables us to look at the relationship between the characteristics of establishments and the provision of family-friendly measures for different groups of employees. We start with provision for managers and then look at provision for all non-managerial workers, followed by consideration of white and blue-collar workers as a subset of the non-managerial workforce.

Table 4.8 looks at how the gender composition of management in an enterprise relates, first, to provision of family-friendly working conditions for women in management, and second how it relates to provision for

Table 4.8 Family-friendly policies for female managers and all non-managers by share of women in labour force

	(a) Female managers			(b) Non-managerial staff					
Policy	FSMG	se	sig	FSMG	se	sig	FSNMG	se	sig
Management understanding									
well	66	2.9	***	45.5	1.3	***	70.7	0.9	***
not well	45.3	2.3	F = 17.4	28.7	1.6	F = 34.6	41.9	1.4	F = 158.5
Family-friendly provisions									
none	52.7	2.4	*	27	1.2	***	45.9	1.1	***
some	57.3	1.7	F = 2.48	42.1	1	F = 82	62.9	0.7	F = 156
Flexible hours									
yes	57.9	1.9	*	37	1.7	ns	61.6	1.4	**
no	53.5	2.1	F = 2.5	36.4	0.9		50.4	0.7	F = 11.7
Job share									
yes	67.8	2.5	***	45.5	1.9	***	72.2	1.2	***
no	51.2	1.7	F = 27.3	34.5	0.9	F = 28.1	53.1	0.7	F = 123
Parental leave									
yes	61.3	2	***	41.2	1.5	***	61.2	1.1	***
no	50.3	1.9	F = 15.4	34	0.9	F = 18.0	54.1	0.8	F = 23.7
Work from home									
yes	54.1	2.1	nsig	33.5	1.9	nsig	61.2	1.5	*
no	56.2	1.8		36.9	0.9		55.8	0.7	F = 6.7
Nursery									
yes	62.5	5.4	nsig	53.6	3.7	***	70	2.3	***
no	55.1	1.5		35.4	0.8	F = 27.9	55.6	0.7	F = 25.0

Notes:
* just significant (p<.01)
** significant (p<.005)
*** highly significant (p<.001)

Sources: Employee Survey with establishment level variables added.
FSMG = Female Share of Management/ FSNMG = Female share of non-management.

non-managerial women. In the first case the relationship is assumed to go very largely from the provision of facilities to the composition of the management team, while in the second, differences can be hypothesised to reflect the impact of a more female management team. Though as we discussed above, the link will also reflect the association between the gender composition of the workforce as a whole (as given in column 3) and more general equal opportunity stances of the enterprises.

The establishments included in the analysis in Table 4.8 are those in which there were at least some female managers; the exclusion of the 30 per cent of establishments in which there was no female manager raises the female share of management from 31 per cent to 55 per cent in the establishments included. The figures in column 1 contrast the female share of management (FMSG) in establishments where managers said they themselves had access to the various facilities to those where they thought that they did not, for each of six types of family-friendly provision. We also look at how managers rated the management team as a whole in their understanding of parental needs.

Management was significantly more female (66 per cent, compared to 45 per cent) in establishments in which female managers saw 'the management as understanding the needs of parents well' than those where they did not, even though relatively few managers were parents themselves. The proportion of female managers was significantly higher – at 68 per cent and 61 per cent respectively – in those establishments in which women managers said that job share and parental leave were available, compared to 50/51 per cent where no such provision was available. Differences were much smaller for flexible hours and the ability to work from home, where the 'family-friendly' policies are used by quite large numbers of men without children.

The second column of Table 4.8 shows how the responses of non-managerial staff to the same questions related to the gender composition of the management team. Where non-managerial staff thought managers related well to the needs of parents, management teams were more female – 45 per cent female compared to 29 per cent – even though male managers were more likely than female to have children themselves. That would appear to be a pure gender effect; though column 3 also suggests a learning effect; the 'more responsive' managements are in more female dominated establishments (they have a 71 per cent female workforce compared to 42 per cent for those not rated responsive).

We also see from column 2 that the more female the management, the more likely some family-friendly provision would have been identified – (only 27 per cent of managers were female where no provision was identified, compared to an average of 42 per cent for those were the non-managerial workforce said that some facilities were available to them). There is a significant relationship between the gender composition of management and the apparent provision of job share and parental leave for non-managerial staff. Where women have access to a nursery, or support towards childcare costs, over 50 per cent of the management is female on average, compared to 35 per cent where no nursery is available. Almost half of the 132 establishments offering a nursery or help towards childcare are educational or health facilities, but they are those with especially female managements (and staffs) within the overall category of health and education service. As ever, the direction of causation remains unclear.

The third column of Table 4.8 looks at the way provision of family-friendly arrangements reported by the non-managerial workforce relates to the gender composition of the overall workforce. Comparing those establishments which were said to allow non-managers to job share with those where respondents denied they could job share, 72 per cent of the former non-managerial workforce (FSNMG) were female, compared to 53 per cent of the latter. Similarly, 70 per cent of the workforce in the few establishments that provided childcare were female, compared to 56 per cent of those that didn't. Hence we can't assume that improved provision is a response to the gender composition of *management*. As noted above, both the provision and the gender composition of management could reflect the gender composition of the workforce as a whole.

Disentangling the distinct effect of more female management

To tease this out a series of logistic regressions (Table 4.9 and Table 4.10) were undertaken. These take as the dependent variables in turn: overall provision (Table 4.9a and 4.10a); access to flexible working time (Table 4.9c and Table 4.10b); access to job share (Table 4.9d and Table 4.10c); access to parental leave (Table 4.9e and Table 4.10d); access to help with childcare (Table 4.9f and Table 4.10e) and ability to work from home (Table 4.9g and Table 4.10f). The first set (Table 4.9) uses the management survey and considers the provision of family-friendly measures to the entire non-managerial workforce. It is possible therefore to look at managers view of the take-up of provisions as a whole (Table 4.9b). Table 4.10 derives from the individual employee questionnaires, with the addition of some data on the characteristics of the establishment and considers only the responses of blue- and white-collar (clerical, sales and personal service workers) to the question of whether they thought given facilities were available. The dependent variables in Table 4.10 relate to the pattern of availability reported by these groups of respondents in each enterprise. The numbers of blue-and white-collar workers in each establishment varied between 1 and 23. The dependent variables are weighted by the size of establishment and by the sampling fraction at establishment level. In Table 4.10 two sets of dependent variables are considered to take account of the uneven distribution of access: whether or not *any* blue- or white-collar respondents said they had access to the facility (Tables 4.10a1; b1; c1; d1; e1; and f1) and whether more than half the blue-and white-collar respondents said they had access (Tables 4.10 a2; b2; c2; d2; e2; and f2).

In the absence of panel data, we differentiated between establishments with a long-standing female share of management and those in which women had only recently entered management in some numbers. Where the female share of management had not increased recently (STABLEFEMGR = 1), we took the level of family-friendly provision to reflect the gender composition of management. Where the increase was recent (STABLEFEMGR = 0), the gender composition of management was interpreted to be more an *effect* of policy, rather than a contributor. In many instances a recent increase in women in management was associated with the provision of family-friendly facilities.

All the variables listed in Appendix 1 were included as far as possible in both sets of regressions, though only those variables that proved to have a

Table 4.9 Logistic regressions: access to family friendly provision for non-managerial staff as a whole

	B	S.E.	Wald	Sig.	Exp(B)
(a) No Provision					
FSNMG	−0.01	0.15	54.2	***	0.99
PUBLICSC(1)	−0.73	0.17	19.11	***	2.08
TUREC(1)	−0.44	0.13	11.21	***	1.55
STABLEFMGRS	0.63	0.1	39.5	***	0.53
GENDEQOP(1)	−0.9	0.11	72.45	***	2.47
Constant	−0.9	0.16	30.21	***	0.41
−2loglikelyhood =	2444				
(b) Take up (any provision taken up)					
Total Employ	0	0	30.44	***	1
PUBLICSC(1)	0.52	0.12	20.34	***	0.59
FSNMG	0.01	0	10.79	***	1.01
STABLEFMGRS	0.5	0.1	27.15	***	1.65
GENDEQOP(1)	−0.62	0.11	33.98	***	0.54
Constant	−0.53	0.16	11.49	***	0.59
−2loglikelyhood =	2611				
(c) Flexible working time					
Total Employment	0.00	0	3.54	**	1
PUBLICSC(1)	0.85	0.16	28.93	***	0.43
TUREC(1)	0.44	0.16	8.09	***	0.64
STABLEFMGRS	−0.49	0.12	17.46	***	1.63
Constant	−0.98	0.11	79.67	***	0.37
−2loglikelyhood =	1917				
(d) Job share					
FSNMG	0.02	0	46.32	***	1.02
Falling employment	0.01	0	11.34	***	1.01
Total Employ	0.00	0	3.49	**	1
PUBLICSC(1)	1.24	0.13	88.63	***	0.29
STABLEFMGRS	−0.50	0.12	16.01	***	1.65
GENDEQOP(1)	1.04	0.16	40.97	***	0.35
Constant	−1.62	0.2	63.01	***	0.2
−2loglikelyhood =	1698				
(e) Parental leave					
PUBLICSC(1)	0.67	0.14	24.09	***	0.51
TUREC(1)	−0.90	0.13	51.04	***	0.41
STABLEFMGRS	−0.45	0.1	20.21	***	1.57
GENDEQOP(1)	0.65	0.11	32.99	***	0.52
Constant	0.36	0.10	13.03	***	1.43
−2loglikelyhood =	2441				

Table 4.9   Continued

	B	S.E.	Wald	Sig.	Exp(B)
(f) Nursery					
FSMG	0.01	0.00	6.2	**	1.01
FSNMG	0.01	0.00	3.52	**	1.01
Total Employment	0.00	0.00	7.02	**	1
PUBLICSC(1)	0.48	0.20	5.92	**	0.62
GENDEREQOP(1)	1.42	0.29	24.05	***	0.24
Constant	−2.86	0.30	88.74	***	0.06
−2loglikleyhood =	892				
(g) Work from home					
TUREC(1)	−0.58	0.21	7.86	**	1.79
Total Employment	0.00	0.00	6.12	**	1
PUBLICSC(1)	0.95	0.22	19.14	***	0.39
POVR22K	0.02	0.00	56.93	***	1.02
FSNMG	0.01	0.00	17.58	***	1.01
FSMG	0.00	0.00	4.47	**	1
Constant	−2.83	0.28	104.51	***	0.06
−2loglikelyhood =	1479				

Source: WERS 1998 Management (Take up) and Employee surveys.

significant effect on the various outcomes reported in Tables 4.9 and 4.10 are included in the tables. Since both sets of regressions relate to the male and female workforces as a whole, it is not surprising to find that the gender composition of the non-managerial workforce (FSNMG) is often, but not always, a predictor of the availability of different family-friendly provisions. As discussed above, amongst non-managers as a whole, having flexible work and getting parental leave is not related to the gender composition of the bulk of the workforce. The latter may reflect the view that parental leave is about paternity as distinct from maternity leave. It is not surprising that the gender composition of the workforce has an effect, albeit small, on the take-up of facilities (Table 4.9b).

Managers were asked a range of questions about equal opportunity policies in their establishment. The inclusion of equal opportunities policy as an independent variable (GENDEQOP) shows that some elements of 'family-friendly' provision are more closely connected to such policies than others. Surprisingly establishments with written equal opportunities policies appear not to have a disproportionately high take-up of family-friendly policies (Table 4.9b). Non-managers are more likely to be able to work from home, the higher the overall level of pay in an organisation (POVR22K). This variable (the proportion earning over £22 000 in 1998) was included to tap the relationship between status and access to provision, but was only important in relation to working from home.

Table 4.10 Logistic regression: Access to family-friendly provision (blue- and white-collar workers)

(a) No provision

1. At least one respondent had access

	B	S.E.	Wald	sig
FSMG	-0.01	0.00	7.39	***
PUBLICSC(1)	-0.76	0.18	18.63	***
SOUTH(1)	-0.38	0.18	4.48	**
TUREC(1)	-0.40	0.19	4.34	**
Constant	1.23	0.20	37.06	***
-2loglikelyhood =	1254			

2. More than 50% had access

	B	S.E.	Wald	sig
GENDEQOP(1)	-0.47	0.13	14.16	***
STABLEFEMGR	0.30	0.10	8.37	***
FSNMG	-0.01	0.00	48.78	***
TUREC(1)	-0.45	0.11	16.41	***
Constant	0.71	0.13	31.46	***
-2loglikelyhood =	2223			

(b) Flexible working time

1. At least one respondent had access

	B	S.E.	Wald	sig
FSNMG	0.01	0.00	11.25	***
PUBLICSC(1)	-0.60	0.16	14.00	***
TUREC(1)	0.45	0.15	8.78	***
Constant	0.90	0.16	31.33	***
-2loglikelyhood =	1661			

2. More than 50% had access

	B	S.E.	Wald	sig
GENDEQOP(1)	0.33	0.15	4.93	**
STABLEFEMGR	-0.53	0.12	20.43	***
FSNMG	0.01	0.00	39.47	***
PUBLICSC(1)	0.43	0.12	12.74	***
Constant	-1.70	0.18	92.45	***
-2loglikelyhood =	1899			

(c) Jobshare

1. At least one respondent had access

	B	S.E.	Wald	sig
STABLEFEMGR	-0.28	0.10	7.55	**
FSNMG	0.01	0.00	70.78	***
PUBLICSC(1)	0.52	0.13	16.01	***
TUREC(1)	0.38	0.12	10.54	***
Constant	-0.25	0.15	2.94	**
-2loglikelyhood =	2235			

2. More than 50% had access

	B	S.E.	Wald	sig
GENDEQOP(1)	0.76	0.30	6.26	**
STABLEFEMGR	-0.40	0.18	5.06	**
FSNMG	0.01	0.00	15.82	***
PUBLICSC(1)	0.49	0.19	6.43	***
TUREC(1)	0.97	0.25	15.56	***
Constant	-2.50	0.26	89.83	***
-2loglikelyhood =	1003			

Table 4.10 Continued

(d) Parental leave

1. At least one respondent had access

GENDEQOP(1)	0.42	0.136	9.4785	***
PUBLICSC(1)	−0.37	0.156	5.6093	***
TUREC(1)	0.717	0.146	24.176	***
Constant	1.452	0.106	187.12	***
−2loglikelyhood =	1800			

2. More than 50% had access

GENDEQOP(1)	0.46	0.21	4.72	**
PUBLICSC(1)	0.48	0.17	7.99	***
SOUTH(1)	0.66	0.17	15.93	***
TUREC(1)	0.51	0.19	7.51	***
Constant	−1.17	0.24	23.27	**
−2loglikelyhood =	1335			

(e) Nursery

1. At least one respondent had access

TUREC(1)	−0.43	0.117	13.488	***
Constant	−0.99	0.071	193.16	***
−2loglikelyhood =	1893			

2. More than 50 per cent had access

GENDEQOP(1)	−1.14	0.61	3.481	**
Constant	−3.88	0.2	382.6	***
−2loglikelyhood =	290			

(f) Work from home

1. At least one respondent had access

GENDEQOP(1)	1.16	0.62	3.47	**
PUBLICSC(1)	0.68	0.34	3.86	**
Constant	−3.26	0.23	203.76	***
−2loglikelyhood =	346			

2. More than 50 per cent had access

GENDEQOP(1)	0.69	0.22	9.83	***
PUBLICSC(1)	0.75	0.15	24.79	***
Total employment	0.00	0.00	24.65	***
Constant	−1.44	0.11	159.3	***
−2loglikelyhood =	1295			

A measure of recent job loss (Falling Employment) was included in the regressions to see how far provision was associated with short-term labour supply considerations, but the scale of job loss rarely had any impact on provision. Nor was take-up significantly different in establishments that had experienced large job losses in the last year.

Three variables which other research showed to be important in determining enterprise level provision: size of enterprise (Total Employment), sector (PUBLICSC) and Trade Union recognition (TUREC) were included in the regressions to allow for association of these with the degree of female management. What stands out from the regressions is the frequent association between family-friendly policies and public sector organisation, and between family-friendly policies and whether or not any trade union is recognised. This is in line with earlier analyses of the data on family-friendly working (Forth *et al.*, 1997; Cully *et al.*, 1999, Dex and Smith, 2002) which also found the size of the overall workforce to be associated with good employment conditions (Forth *et al.*, 1997). When the size of establishments and the sector they operate in are held constant, it is clear that establishments where at least one union is recognised are more likely to have some family-friendly policies in place than similar establishments where no union is recognised. The same is true for a number of individual provisions, most especially for those engaged in 'routine' work. Sometimes trade union recognition appears to reduce the availability of family-friendly measures. In the case of non-managers working from home (Table 4.9g), this is probably because trade unions are still more often recognised in manufacturing where it is less feasible to allow working from home. In the case of parental leave trade union recognition is only negatively associated with parental leave for non-managerial staff (Table 4.9d); for blue- and white-collar workers the relationship with access to parental leave is positive (Table 4.10d).

Once these characteristics of establishments are allowed for and recent increases in female management (STABLEFEMGR = 0) are discounted – as being an effect, rather than a cause of 'family-friendly' policies – the impact of a more female management on facilities for the non-managerial workforce as a whole, is restricted to childcare provision (Table 4.9c) and the opportunity to work from home (Table 4.9g). In the case of blue-and white-collar workers, the result looks perverse: the more female the management, the less likely, if anything, the provision of any family-friendly facilities (Table 4.10a1), but the effect is tiny.

Once the Equal Opportunity stance of an enterprise/establishment is given, the effect of having a more female management team on the availability family-friendly provision is generally very small. We are not in a position to say whether more female management teams are responsible for the stronger equal opportunity stances of those employers that offer more family-friendly provision, or whether their numbers simply reflect that stronger equality stance, only that the three go together.

The provision of family-friendly working arrangements is then associated with organisations that have more formal and consensual decision-making processes (see Wood, 1999; Wood and Iasaosa, 2001; Dex and Smith 2001 for a further discussion of this point). Women are more likely to be found in the managements of such organisations, but given the organisational type, the gender composition of its workforce, and its stance towards equal opportunities, the proportion of women managers has no additional effect, once recent increases in female manager numbers are allowed for.

We included in the regressions the proportion of female managers who are themselves mothers, but found it to have no additional effect on the facilities open to blue- and white-collar workers. In general,[5] then, mothers who are employed as managers do not appear to have the clout to influence the range of provision. This is not really surprising when the pressures on women who seek to undertake managerial jobs on top of family responsibilities are considered.

Conclusion

This paper set out to explore iterative processes in the dynamics of feminisation, specifically the relationship between a feminisation of management and the investment in family-friendly measures for the workforce as a whole. The assumption being tested was that the implementation of such measures could fuel a further round of employment of women. In practice we are still far from a qualitative as against a quantitative feminisation of management in Britain. The pattern of growth of women in management in the last decade reflects the decentralisation of management responsibilities, or at least the decentralisation of management titles. As the number of managers grew in establishments with relatively few managers, so the proportion of women managers grew particularly fast, especially in the service sector and most particularly in the finance sector. A quarter of these women managers described their daily tasks as involving distinctly non-managerial work in routine administration and sales. They are not very different from most men in this, though the glass ceiling is still evident in the lower share of women in management at head office of larger undertakings. The limited hold women have in the managerial hierarchy is also evident in the pattern of retrenchment of management, despite the rhetoric of new, more female, management styles (Handy, 1994). Though there has been a very large rise in the numbers of women in management, nearly half was in establishments in which the numbers of managers as a whole increased by half as much again between 1990 and 1998.

This pattern could well imply a reduction in the possible influence of individual managers and raises doubts about the scale of the revolution in management implied by increasingly female managerial strata. When compared to women in the professions, the proportion of women able to hold down managerial jobs when they have childcare responsibilities has hardly changed over the last decade despite the apparent growth in family-friendly provision and the concentration of that provision on women in higher grade jobs. This difference may relate to more formal qualification based recruitment processes in professional jobs easing the re-entry of mothers (Crompton and Sanderson, 1990), but the differences in the culture of organisations, in the sense of security required to enable women in management to actually take advantage of family-friendly provisions may also be a factor.

From this analysis of WERS, women in management, appear neither to be in positions to 'grow' more female managers to work alongside them, nor to decisively influence the opportunities open to other women. While we can observe that the higher the proportion of women amongst managers of an establishment, the greater the availability of family-friendly measures for all those not in managerial jobs, the direction of causation would appear to go from an equal opportunities culture through to greater employment of women in higher grade positions, with relatively little evidence of any positive feedback from the composition of management. This may be because these 'survivors' in a male world (Gheradi, 1996) survive by suppressing any sense of themselves as gendered beings. While this may be true of some, qualitative research with women managers suggests that they continue to have an acute awareness of their own gender disadvantage and to recognise the value of having had a female mentor in their own career development (Davidson and Cooper, 1992). We might speculate from this analysis that women managers continue to operate largely as individuals in a man's world; they remain gendered in the types of management jobs they have access to, but unlike men, they do not act on their gender interests to create powerful mutual support structures. The disadvantages they face compared to their male colleagues are reflected in the large pay gap and in the fact that male manages are still far more likely to have children than female. But these disadvantages also suggest that to progress family-friendly working, the perspectives of male managers on the 'work–life balance' have to be addressed.

The link between more female and 'more caring' management operates to a great extent through the concentration of women in public sector management. This analysis shows the continued importance of public sector values and culture in providing working conditions that begin to recognise family care responsibilities, despite the enormous pressures on the public sector and indeed retrenchment in the feminisation of management in some areas. Behind this, perhaps surprisingly to some, is the association between trade union recognition and provision of family-friendly work conditions. The effect of the association between equal opportunity cultures and trade union organisation is that women are more often managers in enterprises in which trade unions are recognised, and that women managers are more often than male managers trade union members themselves. Though sex discrimination has been associated with high levels of trade union organi-sation both within neoclassical economics and feminist historical research, the feminisation of trade unions themselves as well as structural change within the economy, makes this a very largely a thing of the past (Colgan and Ledwith, 1996). Although Casey *et al.* (1997) argue that the increase in flexible working is a direct result of the decline in trade union power, a more positive interpretation is now possible, based on a link between the numer-ical feminisation of trade unions and the qualitative feminisation of trade union policy. This possibility requires much further research, but offers a potentially positive note: while family-friendly policies may not be open to all people when they need them, where trade union recognition has been maintained, so, too, has the principle of provision.

Appendix

Variables included in the logistical regressions

Total Employment	Employment in the enterprise as a whole
Falling Employment	Whether managers reported a reduction in employment in recent years in the establishment
FSNMG	Female share of non managerial posts in the establishment
FSMG	Female share of managerial posts in the establishment
STABLEFMGRS	Whether managers reported a recent increase in female managers
POV22K	Proportion of the total establishment workforce earning over £22,000
GENDEREQOP(1)	Managers reported a written Equal Opportunities Policy
TUREC(1)	Managers reported that at least one trade union was recognised
PUBLICSC(1)	Managers reported the establishment/enterprise was in the public sector in 1998
SOUTH(1)	Establishment was located in the Midlands and Southern England

Acknowledgement

This research was undertaken with the support of the ESRC Research Programme on the Future of Work L212252021.

Notes

1. The sample was biased across different industrial sectors and enterprise sizes but the results reported here allow for that in re-weighting the data as advised (Forth, 2001).
2. It is not possible to establish whether the non-surviving enterprises were more or less feminised than the survivors.
3. We look at the pattern of increase – the distribution of the total increase in female managers – rather than the percentage rate increase, to show that the negative

relationship found between the proportion of women in management and the rate of growth is not a statistical artefact based on small initial bases.

4. Table 4.4 gives information about the enterprises covered in the survey unweighted. It is not a representative sample of all enterprises in the UK, but identifies the relationships between the distribution of female managers and changes in numbers employed rather better than a weighted sample does. Gross increases in this context are the sum of all the increases in the enterprises experiencing a net increase in female managers, ignoring increases within enterprises where the overall total of female managers did not increase.

5. Although blue-and white-collar workers in the WERS employment survey rated managements which included at least one mother as significantly more understanding of their family needs than others. (Not reported in detail here.)

References

Airey, C., Hales, J., Hamilton, R., Korovessis, C., McKernana, A. and Purdon, S. (1999) *The Workplace Employee Relations Survey (WERS) 1997–98 Technical Report*, London: National Centre for Social Research.

Arnold, V. and Davidson, M. (1990) 'Adopt a mentor'. *Women in Management Review* 5 (1): 10–19.

Ashburner, L. (1994) 'Women in management careers: opportunities and outcomes', in Evetts, J. (ed.) *Women and Careers*. London: Longman.

Blair-Loy, M. and Wharton, A. S. (2002) 'Employees use of work-family policies and the workplace social context'. *Social Forces* 80 (3): 813–36.

Bond, S., Hyman, J., Summers, J. and Wise, S. (2002) *Family-friendly policies and organisational decision-making*, York: York Publishing Services.

Callender, C., Forth, J., Lissenburgh, S. and Millward, N. (1996) *Family Friendly Working Arrangements in Britain*, London: Policy Studies Institute, Research Report 16.

Casey, B., Metcalf, N. and Millward, N. (1997) *Employers use of Flexible Labour*, London: Policy Studies Institute.

Cockburn, C. (1983) *Brothers: Male Dominence and Technological Change*, London: Pluto.

Cockburn, C. (1991) *In the Way of Women*. London: Macmillan.

Colgan, F. and Ledwith, S. (1996a). 'Movers and Shakers-creating organisational change' in Colgan, F. and Ledwith, S. (eds) *Women in Organisations: challenging Gender Politics*, Basingstoke: Macmillan: 278–300.

Colgan, F. and Ledwith, S. (1996b). 'Sisters organising-women and their trade unions' in Colgan, F. and Ledwith, S. (eds) *Women in Organisations: challenging Gender Politics*. Basingstoke: Macmillan: 152–85.

Collinson, D. and Hearn, J. (eds) (1996) *Men as Managers: managers as men*, London: Sage.

Coyle, A. (1995) *Women and Organisational Change* Manchester: EOC.

Crompton, R. and Sanderson, K. (1990) *Gendered Jobs and Social Change*, London: Unwin.

Cully, M., Woodland, S., O'Reilly, A. *et al.* (1999) *Britain at Work as depicted by the 1998 Workplace Employee Relations Survey*, London: Routledge.

Davidson, M. and Cooper, C. (1992) *Shattering the Glass Ceiling: the Woman Manager*, London: Paul Chapman.

Dex, S. (ed.) (1999) *Families and the Labour Market*, Joseph Rowntree Foundation and London: Family Policy Studies Centre.

Dex, S. and Schiebl, F. (1999), 'Business performance and family friendly policies'. *Journal of General Management*, 24 (4): 22–37.

Dex, S. and Scheibl, F. (2001) 'Flexible and Family-Friendly Working Arrangements in UK-based SME's'. *British Journal of Industrial Relations*, 39 (3): 411–32.

Dex, S. and Smith, C. (2001) 'Which British employees have access to family-friendly policies? An analysis of the 1998 Workplace Employee Relations Survey' Judge Institute Research Paper No. WP 16/01, University of Cambridge.

Dex, S. and Smith, C. (2002) *The Nature and Pattern of Family-Friendly Employment Policy in Britain* York: York Publishing Services, Joseph Rowntree Foundation.

Etzkowitz, H. (1994) *Science*, 7 Oct.: 51–4.

Etzkowitz, H., Kemelgor, C., Neuschatz, M., Uzzi, B. and Alonzo, J. (2001) 'The paradox of critical mass for women in science'. *Science* 266: 51–4.

Faludi, S. (1999) *Stiffed: the betrayal of modern man*, London: Chatto.

Forth, J. (2000) '*Compositional versus Behavioural Change: combined analysis of WES98 Panel, Closures and New Workplaces*', WERS Technical papers 2.

Forth, J., Lissenburgh, S., Callender, C. *et al.* (1997) *Family Friendly Working Arrangements in Britain*, Sheffield: DfEE.

Freeman, R. (2000) 'The feminisation of work in the USA: a new era for mankind?' in Gustaffson, S. and Meudlers, D. (eds) *Gender and the Labour Market*, Macmillan.

Fried, M. (1999) *Taking Time: Parental Leave Policy and Corporate Culture*, Philadelphia: Temple University Press.

Gherardi, S. (1996) 'Gendered organisational cultures: narratives of women travellers in a male world'. *Gender, Work and Organisation*, 3 (4): 187–201.

Ginn, J. and Sandell, J. (1997) *Balancing Home and Employment*, WES 11 (3): 413–34.

Glover, J. 2000 *Women and Scientific Employment*, Basingstoke: Macmillan.

Green, E. and Cassell, C. (1996) 'Women managers, gendered cultural processes and organisational change' *Gender Work and Organisation*, 3 (3): 168–78.

Handy, C. (1994) *The Empty Raincoat*. London: Hutchinson.

Hogarth, T., Hasluck, C. and Pierre, C. (2001) *Work Life Balance 2000*, Sheffield: DfEE Report RR249.

Huffman, M. and Velasco, S. 'When more is less; sex composition, organisations and earnings in US firms'. *Work and Occupations*, 24 (2): 214–44.

Kanter, M. (1977) *Men and Women of the Corporation*, New York: Basic Books.

Lewis, S. (1997) 'Family-friendly employment policies: a route to changing organisational cultures?' *Gender, Work and Organisation*, 4 (1): 13–23.

Maddock, S. (1999) *Challenging Women: Gender, Culture and Organisation*, London: Sage.

Marshall, J. (1984) *Women managers, travellers in a male world*, London: J. Wiley.

Marshall, J. (1995) 'Gender and management a critical review of research'. *British Journal of Management*, 6 : 553–62.

Petersen, T. and Morgan, L. (1995) 'Separate and unequal: occupation-establishment sex segregation and the gender wage gap'. *American Journal of Sociology*, 101 (2): 329–65.

Reskin, B. and Roos, P. (1990) *Job Queues, Gender Queues: Explaining Women's Inroads into Male Occupations*, Philadelphia: Temple University.

Roper, M. (1994) *Masculinity and the British Organisation Men since 1945*, Oxford: OUP.

Rosener, J. (1990) 'Ways women lead'. *Harvard Business Review*, Nov.: 119–25.

Sheppard, D. L. (1989), 'Organisations, power and sexuality: the image and self image of women managers', in Hearn, J. *et al.* (ed.) *The Sexuality of Organisation*, London: Sage.

Tomaskovic-Devey, D. (1993) *Gender and race inequality at work: the sources and consequences of job segregation*, Ithaca, NY: ILR.

Tomlinson, F., Brockbank, A. and Traves J. (1997) 'The feminisation of management? Issues of sameness and difference in the roles and experiences of fem and male retail managers'. *Gender Work and Organisation*, 4 (4): 218–29.

Wacjman, J. (1998) *Managing like a man: women and men in corporate management*, Cambridge: Polity.

Wood, S. (1999) 'Family-friendly management: testing the various perspectives'. *National Institute Economic Review*, April 172 (2).

Wood, S. and lasaosa, A. (2001) *'Family Friendly Management in the UK: Testing various Perspectives using WERS 98' unpublished.*

5
Women's Employment and the Experience of Local Trade Union Activity

Jane Harrington

Introduction

The decline of trade union membership year on year since 1979 is well documented, as are explanations (e.g. Waddington and Whitston, 1995), which include the changing composition of employment, employers' policies, government policy and legislation and the business cycle and unemployment. Since the decline in trade union density has been most pronounced in some traditional union 'strongholds' – of male, manual workers in manufacturing – women's proportionate share of aggregate union membership has risen. Women are now a majority of the membership in five out of the ten largest TUC affiliated unions, and make up almost 39 per cent of total union membership (Equal Opportunities Review, 1999). Nevertheless, the growth in both female and part-time employment has prompted union leaderships to target recruitment strategies on these and other previously under-represented groups.

Studies of women's representation by trade unions (e.g. Drake, 1920; Rowbotham, 1975) have noted how women have been marginalised within union structures, rarely reaching high levels of trade union office. To a large extent this situation persists today. A number of writers have considered barriers to women's union participation. In particular, Wertheimer and Nelson's (1975) three stage model of socio-cultural, job-related and union-related barriers provides a useful framework for the analysis of women's under-representation in trade union hierarchies.

Other studies have attempted to understand the reasons for women's participation in trade unions. Recently there has been an increase in research publications that focus on senior women leaders and full time officers (e.g. Heery and Kelly, 1988, 1989; Cockburn, 1996; Kirton and Healy, 1999; Healy and Kirton, 2000). These studies consider the profile of the senior woman activist and question, for example, whether their style of bargaining prioritises different issues from those of male trade unionists. This has led writers such as Ledwith and Colgan (1996) to develop a typology of trade union women's consciousness.

Studies of senior women trade unionists, however, tell us little about women's local level trade union activity. Indeed, there remains a relative paucity of research conducted on women's participation at this level. The studies that do exist have tended to consider barriers to women's union participation. The study described here, whilst considering the barriers to women's local trade union activity, also addresses the reasons for women's participation. Where research has focused on women activists at local level the tendency of some studies has been to assume that they are a homogenous group, with a shared consciousness and set of interests as a consequence of either their sex or gender[1] (e.g. Charles, 1986; Cunnison and Stageman, 1993).

This paper draws on empirical data derived from Harrington (2000). The data focused on two broad issues: the factors shaping and influencing women's participation in unions; and second, the influence of gender in shaping women's union participation. The specific focus of this paper is on exploring the reasons for joining and becoming active in local level trade union activity.

Research design

The research reported is drawn from two qualitative case studies. The principal case is of women activists[2] in the South and West area of the Banking, Insurance and Finance Union (BIFU). The second case is of women activists in the South Wales and Western Division of the Union of Shop, Distributive and Allied Workers (USDAW).

The USDAW case[3] involved interviewing all women members of the South Wales and Western women's committee. In addition eight women activists were interviewed. The divisional officer, area organiser (she was also chair of the women's committee) and divisional training officer were also interviewed. Participant observation was the critical research method employed in order to gain further insight into women's local level activism. This included attending the division over a period of two years, spending a week with one of the Bristol area organisers visiting union sites, and attending three branch meetings in the South Wales and Western Division.[4]

Most of the women in USDAW worked in semi-skilled jobs, such as supermarket cashiers and machine cleaners in food processing factories. Their profile in terms of young children was more varied than the women in BIFU (see below). Some of the women had children at school, some worked night shifts to accommodate this, while others worked part-time. At the time of interviewing the Sunday trading laws were changing. This meant for most women a change in their contracts. One woman now found herself with a zero hours contract.

Access for the case study of the South and West area of BIFU was secured at both area and national level to try to ensure that all women who were potentially research participants could be interviewed. The initial access had been gained through the South and West area organiser who was interviewed on three occasions. The area organiser also provided access to the South and West area council and to two branch meetings. Forty-eight women, defined as active in BIFU were contacted and invited to interview. Twenty-seven agreed to be interviewed. The majority of the interviews were held in the women's homes. Where this was not possible they were held in their workplaces. Relevant national officers including the Deputy General Secretary (now joint General Secretary of UNIFI), the senior research officer and a research officer, and the equality officer were also interviewed. Participation at area council allowed for the research process to be explained and for direct observation at council meetings. Two branch meetings were attended to obtain further information on local level activism. The National Officers made documentary evidence available. This included BIFU research reports on part-time workers, maternity provision and employment and industrial relations in the 1990s.

The women in BIFU all held white-collar clerical posts and, with two exceptions, they were all employed in full-time jobs. Only two women had small children, one a single mother, the other married with step-children. The others were either single with no children, or married with no children or with grown-up children. A number of studies (e.g. Heery and Kelly, 1988,1989; Ledwith and Colgan, 1996) suggest that such a profile is the norm for trade union women activists. The age profile in the research described here was quite diverse, ranging from early twenties to late fifties. The majority, however, were women in their forties. Only one of these women worked in the recently established call centres. The rest held positions in the branch structure of banks or in insurance centres. However, some had been affected by the move towards 'clustering' and now worked in a devolved branch structure. Geographically they were dispersed across the South and West of England, from Oxford to St Ives.

This research has been concerned with exploring women's activism in context. Industry sector, union organisation and activity and geographical location bound the interviews. This chapter now turns to the context of the interviews. The critical argument being made is that women's local union activism is shaped and understood by them within the contexts in which they operate.

The industrial sectors (finance and retail)

Women's employment in the finance industry

Since the 1980s much has been written about the banking, insurance and finance industry (e.g. Morris, 1986; Cressey and Scott, 1992; O'Reilly, 1994; Storey, 1995). Specifically here, the focus is on the banking sector.

Until the 1990s the sector was generally regarded as offering a 'stable' career, or at least secure employment. As O'Reilly suggests (1994) the traditional stereotype of a bank employee. ... '*has been characterised by the bowler-hat, pin-striped suit and stiff collar of the male clerk, possessed with a certain sense of status and self importance*' ... (60). Certainly, working for a bank, and in many cases an insurance company, was seen as providing secure white-collar employment, frequently combined with internal career progression. There have been two key challenges to this notion. First, women have not experienced the same degree of stability and job security as men. Also, since the early 1990s jobs in this sector have no longer been regarded as stable and secure.

The proportion of women in banking increased, from 40 per cent of all employees in 1959 to 62 per cent in 1990 (Employment Gazette, 1995). By 1994 women's employment as a proportion of the total had decreased to 59 per cent, suggesting that women had been affected in slightly greater proportions than men by the downturn in employment. The number of part-time workers (predominately women) had also risen significantly during the 1980s. As a proportion of all women in banking, however, part-time female employment only rose modestly from 15 per cent to 16.5 per cent.

Many writers (Egan, 1982; Heritage, 1983; Crompton, 1989; Cressey and Scott, 1992) have noted that the image of bank work as a lifelong full-time career with set hours and conditions superior to much of the rest of financial services only held true for male workers. Women's employment has always been subject to discrimination both overt and indirect, in terms of promotion and location.

The feminisation of bank staff has also been documented by others (Lockwood, 1989; Crompton and Jones, 1984), emphasising that recruitment was gendered – women were recruited to 'women's jobs' and men to a 'career'. Egan's (1982) study in the 1970s demonstrated that women remained disadvantaged compared to men in banking employment, in terms of promotion, pay and conditions of work. Formally, by the 1990s women were treated equally. Cressey and Scott (1992) suggest that partly as a consequence of the number of equal value pay claims waged against them, the banks had been attempting to attract and retain women employees.

Whilst formal equality existed, informal discrimination and disadvantage remained evident. By 1990 women comprised 62 per cent of total employment. Yet, they remained over-represented in lower clerical and secretarial grades and under-represented among higher management positions. They made up almost 100 per cent of part-time clerical labour. Cressey and Scott (1992) suggest that domestic commitments, in particular child care, remain one of the key reasons for the lack of opportunity that women face. Indeed, Halford *et al.* (1997) suggest that women can now have a career in banking as long as they do not have children.

Cressey and Scott (1992) suggested that by the early 1990s it was more appropriate to view recruitment as a model of four distinct streams.[5] Halford *et al.* (1997) argue that a gendered work pattern in banks still exists today, where female labour is utilised for routine back office work, predominately data inputting. Studies conducted by Halford and Savage (1995) and Halford *et al.* (1997) indicate that whilst women in 1997 held 18 per cent of managerial posts, these posts may not be the same as their male counterparts. Their view is that the positions may be constructed as alternative 'career posts', and as such may not be an indication of women entering management in greater numbers.

In summary, women historically have been subjected to systematic discrimination in the banking sector. Whilst today they appear to have achieved formal equality, possibly precipitated by the fear from banks of equal value claims, they still remain disproportionally represented in the lower levels of employment in the sector. Even where they have achieved managerial status, this does not appear to be on a par with male management positions.

Jobs in banking and parts of the insurance sector until the end of the 1980s were viewed as stable, albeit boring, 'jobs for life'. Employment in banking in the 1980s was expanding, though within a context of intensifying competition and an accelerated pace of technological change. Tailby (1996:7) argues that competition was stimulated by maturing markets, the deregulation of the financial system (initiated from 1971 and pursued with gusto by the Thatcher administration), and technological innovation (lowering entry barriers into banking by lessening the dependence on an extensive branch network). However, in the 1990s, widespread changes across the financial services sector and in particular banking have resulted in substantial job losses. Analysis of why and how this has occurred is provided elsewhere (*inter alia* Cressey and Scott, 1992; Storey, 1995; Morgan and Sturdy, 2000).

The key shift in jobs for the clerical workforce appears to be in emphasis away from an administrative function to the more aggressive marketing of financial products. Related to this was the increase in performance-related payment systems introduced in most of the large banks. Morgan and Sturdy (2000) argue that there has been a shift from an administrative to a sales and/or marketing culture, and Halford *et al.* (1997) state that the shift is gendered. Employers utilise female labour for routine back-office work, predominately data inputting, and at the same time draw on the more competitive, sales and marketing ethos, associated with masculinity.

Where banks such as the Midland (now HSBC) have moved away from the branch structure in terms of back-office administration, the employment of female part-timers has increased. The work generally consists of repetitive data inputting tasks (Halford *et al.*, 1997). Work hours normally involve evening shifts to process the day's work. In some instances back-office functions are being removed and concentrated in district or regional centres. This offers the potential to reap economies of scale and use data processing equipment more intensively. The Midland bank provides an example of a bank that followed this route; since the early 1990s they have done all their processing in 8 district centres (*Financial Times*, 18 January 1993). This frees up space in the branches for staff to market financial services and notably bank products rather than dealing just with customer accounts and queries.

The importance for this piece of research is the effect that the changes have had on equality issues, for both employers and BIFU. Ed Sweeny (General Secretary, BIFU) in an interview in 1995 argued that such issues were often over-shadowed by concerns for job insecurity. At the time of the empirical study, the women in BIFU were experiencing the first wave of large-scale restructuring resulting in job losses. Their attitude towards issues for women trade unionists was examined within this context.

In summary women remain the subject of discrimination within this sector. Whilst they now have formal equality with men, there is evidence to support the notion that their jobs are gendered both at the lower levels, in back-office work, and also in managerial posts. The women in BIFU worked within a sector that in the 1990s still appeared to disadvantage them in terms of promotion and work location.

Women's employment in the retail sector

The retail sector ranges from small family-run shops to large multinational supermarkets, manufacturing and distribution operations. In 1993 it employed over 10 per cent of all employees in the UK.

Reynolds explored changes in the industry structure in the 1990s. He argued that the recession had squeezed consumer expenditure, which in turn had put pressure on firms to cut costs. Many small firms were forced out of business. The regulatory environment had altered, from a public policy emphasis on out-of-town development to one favouring investment in urban locations. For Reynolds, however, the key change impacting on this sector had been the deregulation of Sunday and extended trading hours. This had resulted in Sunday becoming the second most important trading day for grocery, DIY and other 'power' retailers. The effect of this has been a shift from full-time to part-time employees which USDAW had highlighted as a potential consequence of Sunday trading (USDAW, 1990).

Technological innovations have also played their part, with electronic point of sale, supply chain investments, electronic data interchange and efficient customer response. Reynolds argues here that contradictions emerge

... in retailers' attempts to invest in technology which results in greater levels of self-service, or remote marketing, whilst consumers increasingly seem to value investment in customer service. (Reynolds, 1996: 66)

Townsend *et al.* (1996: 218) suggest that changes in the forms and levels of retailing employment need to be understood as part of the restructuring of the overall production processes. They argue that we have seen radical changes in shop opening hours, increasing levels of part-time employees partly as a consequence of this and de-skilling of much retail employment. De-skilling has been a consequence of the trend towards self-service and the growth in electronic sales technologies.

The deregulation of Sunday and extended hours of trading has had a profound effect on working patterns, further exaggerating the increase of part-time workers (the labour market experience of most women in this sector) combined with technological changes in an attempt to reduce labour costs. Focusing on part-time work the Institute for Employment Studies predicts an increase in female part-time employment to the year 2006. In 1971 female part-time employment stood at 24 per cent and male part-time employment at 6 per cent. By 2006 Reynolds (IER,1999) suggests, this will have increased to 47 per cent and 15 per cent respectively. He argues:

> Retailer concerns over service levels and their need for mature, socially-skilled shop floor employees reinforces this trend into the next century.
>
> (1999: 43)

The unions (BIFU and USDAW)

BIFU and its women members

Until 1991 membership of BIFU had increased year on year since the 1950s. However, membership fell thereafter, from 162 429 to 134 352 in 1993. This reflected the changes occurring in the banking, insurance and finance sector in the early 1990s.

The South and West area has the third largest number of union branches (41 in 1990). This is reflected in membership – the South and West is the third largest area with 18 497 members in 1990. The only areas that exceeded this total are London and Scotland. This is no doubt in part due to the size of the South and West area, which stretches from Lands End to Uxbridge, taking in the Channel Islands. The South West has one of the lowest union densities of any region in the UK. Martin *et al.* (1996) argue that even though trade unions have experienced declines in membership numbers and density elsewhere, this is most pronounced in areas where labour organisation has been historically weak. BIFU does have a large union membership in the South West but this can be explained by the large number of financial organisations within this region. In Martin *et al.*'s (1996) terminology, union density remains peripheral.[6]

Women constituted 22 per cent of the union's membership in 1922. Egan (1982) notes that female membership grew at a faster rate than male membership between 1972 and 1979. This trend has continued throughout the 1980s and early 1990s to reach the level of 58 per cent in 1993.

As Egan (1982: 28) suggests, membership alone is not an adequate index of women's participation and influence in the union. In spite of women's attendance at meetings men predominated to a considerable extent in all 'official' positions. This remained the case in 1992. Whilst BIFU did have a female honorary vice-president, Edwina Hart, the first woman to hold this position, this did not reflect any degree of representation in 'official' positions. There were no women in senior roles, either in the executive structure (i.e. general and deputy general secretary for England and Scotland) or as assistant secretaries. Of the remaining 25 full-time officers, 12 were women. However this figure is slightly deceptive as many of the women with the exception of the three women negotiating officers and the two women research officers held 'feminine' roles. These were equality officer, administrative officer, administrative assistant, secretary to the general secretary, membership records officer, press and publicity officer and education officer. The composition of area organisers by gender also illustrates the under-representation of women; out of a total of twenty only six were women. The same point can be made in relation to seconded representatives; out of a total of thirty-two only ten were women (General Secretary's report to the annual delegate conference, 1992). Clearly women were not represented proportionately to their membership within the hierarchy of BIFU.

When interviewed in 1995, Ed Sweeny suggested that without targeting or quotas this would be difficult to alter. He felt that there would be significant membership opposition to the idea of quotas. He also argued that whilst the intellectual arguments of equality had been won, the union had been weaker in implementing the practicalities. For example, he felt that the structure was not 'female friendly'. In his view some basic changes could be made, such as acknowledging that meetings should not be held in pubs or in the evenings. Yet, his suggestion of union meetings on Saturday mornings with creche facilities for children would still place the burden of childcare with women.

In BIFU in the 1990s there remained no structure specifically for women although there was a national equality officer, Doris Henderson, and a national equal rights committee. The areas did not have such a structure. The national equality committee, a sub-committee of the national executive committee, reported to national conference and to area councils. Its membership is broader than the national executive committee. However, this is not to suggest that equal opportunities were only considered through the national equal rights committee. Many of the sections had sub-committees focusing on equal opportunities, as did some of the areas. The South and West area in 1994 did not have an equal opportunities sub-committee. There appeared to be a commitment to equal opportunities at national level, where Charles (1986) has suggested that an egalitarian ideology is evident in trade unions. Equally we could term the policies and practices that emanated from national level in BIFU as being informed predominately by a liberal feminist perspective. The policy direction appeared to be one of securing for women additional 'rights' such as enhanced maternity provision, workplace nurseries and creche facilities for meetings. As Cockburn (1989) suggests this is evidence of a 'short' agenda of equal opportunities and leaves the structures of discrimination and disadvantage in place. BIFU had started to address some of these structures. For example, from 1992 they had trained sexual harassment councillors. Ed Sweeny and Edwina Hart both admitted that BIFU still had a long way to go to address the inequalities evident within its own structure.

The impact restructuring of the finance sector has had on BIFU's policy direction at national level cannot be ignored. Ed Sweeny pointed out that between 1991 and 1995 110 000 jobs had been lost in the banking, insurance and finance industry, and that as a consequence the core issue had become security of employment. He felt that this had devalued much of the equality agenda. One of the key concerns, raised by the national officers in the 1990s, is whether equal opportunities and issues that are pertinent to women can remain a key issue, in a union which operates in an industry where job insecurity has become a dominant concern.

USDAW and its women members

During the period of the interviews USDAW was the seventh largest TUC affiliated British union. It had approximately 400 000 full-time and part-time members. Its membership is spread across workers in traditional food shops, modern supermarkets, department stores, dairies, bakeries, breweries, laundries, food manufacturing and processing factories, dental and optical technicians, research and laboratory assistants and dozens of other manufacturing or service operations. The women interviewed came from the sectors of modern supermarkets, department stores and food manufacturing and processing factories. They were therefore predominately located in the larger workplaces, where in general USDAW has had more success in recruiting members. However, USDAW has neither particularly high union membership nor density in South Wales, despite the higher than average union density overall in South Wales.

Women's membership levels have fluctuated. In 1912 there were 3014, or 9.2 per cent of total membership. By the end of the First World War this had increased to 42 per cent. However, many women's jobs were lost in retailing during the depression of the 1920s and by 1938 the percentage of female members was only 30 per cent. Richardson (1979) documents that women's membership had continued to grow since the Second World War both in absolute and percentage terms. By 1978 it had reached 61 per cent of total membership. The percentage of women in membership in 1997 was 59 per cent. In 1994 USDAW had the fourth largest female membership of any TUC affiliated union.

As with BIFU, the question remains, what part do these women play in union activity? Membership figures tell us little about participation and the hierarchical gender divisions in the union. In 1979 Richardson wrote,

Women do not yet play a part in the union that remotely measures their number. This is not a problem confined to USDAW; it is common to other unions that organise women workers. (321)

In 1985 USDAW created a women's committee structure with a national women's officer (Bernadette Hillon at the time of interviewing), and a national women's committee supported by eight divisional women's committees.[7] The agenda for 1992[8] stated USDAW's position in relation to women members. A number of women expressed discomfort with Bernadette Hillon's perspective on women in the union. She was felt to be interested in separatist politics. They found this of particular difficulty, especially as they felt it undermined their other roles as wives and mothers to sons. Nevertheless the USDAW women's committee structure has been instrumental in raising the profile of certain issues pertinent to their union. In particular they have focused on part-time workers. Currently one in four USDAW members work part-time and this figure continues to increase.

Employment turnover is highest amongst part-time workers, and as such, USDAW has to recruit 100 000 members a year just to remain static (USDAW, 1990). In addition, at the time of interviewing Sunday trading was starting to be imposed. USDAW resisted changes in contracts but were unable to directly oppose the legislation. This is not to suggest that they were unaware of the implications. They clearly recognised that the group most vulnerable to these changes were part-time workers. Their fear has been that offers of double pay and in some cases triple pay have meant that low-paid workers are placed in a position where they cannot afford to refuse the pecuniary attraction. They see it as further eroding the conditions of women workers.

At the time of interviewing, the South Wales and Western division had a female divisional officer, Pat Phillips (she was one of only two women divisional officers in the union). The chair of the women's committee, Pauline Russ, was the only female area organiser in the division. There were ten men. Nationally, the picture is even bleaker. There were no female national officers, other than the national women's officer. USDAW may have a developed women's structure but to date this has not substantially altered the balance away from men in the hierarchy. Women's union activism in USDAW is of interest for a number of reasons. These include the impact of the women's committee structure, the influence of the large proportion of women located in part-time low-paid work, and a national 'long'[9] agenda for equal opportunities.

In summary, it appears that both unions have high female membership rates, which are not reflected within their structures. They have both pursued equality for women, but tackled the issue in different ways. Employment restructuring and changes to work organisation have become key issues for both unions in the 1990s.

Women's local level trade union participation in BIFU and USDAW

The empirical focus of this chapter is to explore the reasons women gave for their union membership and activity. The aim was to establish the influences that shaped the women's participation and the relevance of family background. It was also to explain how union activism had been experienced by the women. Three themes are discussed here; why join a trade union, why become active in a trade union and, family background and trade union activism.

Why join a trade union?

The women union activists were asked why they had joined BIFU and why they had subsequently become active members. For the sake of anonymity levels of job responsibility are not delineated. It is worth recognising, however, that the women have a diversity of experiences. For some women, joint accredited office representative meant simply opening the mail and putting notices on the notice board. For others, their union activity had become virtually a full-time job in which they are expected to attend branch, area and national committees each month.

The women's responses when asked why they had joined BIFU fit into four broad categories: because they were the only person in their office willing to be the office representative or willing to be recruited as an office representative; to protect themselves in the workplace; a belief in trade unionism; and finally, because someone else they knew was involved. Clearly for some joining a trade union is synonymous with becoming active. They do not separate the actual joining from subsequently holding a union office.

Those suggesting that union membership and participation was 'by default', argued that it was not something that they had made an active decision about. A number of the women either joined BIFU or became a representative after being asked.

> ... the person who was dealing with it, the seconded rep approached me and said I think you'd be quite good at repping. (2:18:1)

Alternatively they felt that it was an accident, often due to circumstances that resulted in them joining BIFU. These women all imply that the decision to become active was one of limited engagement with unionism prior to becoming a union representative.

Nearly a third of the women reported that they felt a need for protection. For some women this meant protection for themselves, expressed as a fear for their own job security. For others this meant protection in a collective sense, the union acting as the 'protector of the workforce'. BIFU membership as an insurance policy to protect your job was an analogy that was used throughout all the interviews. BIFU has deployed the language of the banking, insurance and finance industry in their recruitment campaigns. This clearly had a resonance with the women interviewed, as without exception every woman interviewed in BIFU stated the slogan verbatim:

> You insure your house, you insure your car, you should insure your job.

It suggests that language is important when recruiting from different sectors of the union movement. No woman in USDAW expressed a rationale for joining in the same way.

Whilst the slogan can be argued to appeal to notions of individualism, whether this is how the women view their membership of BIFU remains unclear. It is plausible to argue that the term has different connotations for each woman. It does appear that the packaging of trade unionism in terms of accessible language, specific to their industry is the strength of the message. The women's comments illustrate this.

> … there needs to be an independent union to stand against the employer, the trade union is there for the worker. (2:3:1)

> When I joined the bank I got details through reading the literature, I joined straight away as an insurance policy. I joined [the staff association] at the same time. (2:4:1)

The 'insurance' analogy, however, does not necessarily mean allegiance to BIFU. The second quotation illustrates the point. It suggests that some employees join BIFU and the staff association as an insurance policy and then select the 'best' one at a later date, or in many cases remain in both never choosing between them. The quotation below illustrates this point further;

> In about two months I had swapped my subscriptions out of [staff association] because I saw it as weak. You can still join both and about three quarters of people belong to both unions for the sake of it, they never get involved, but people belonging to BIFU tend to have more views. (2:4:1)

The view here, reiterated by other women, suggests that BIFU is viewed as the more 'radical' alternative. The relative appeal for a radical or more moderate alternative has varied with the broader range of circumstances. In the early 1990s, the staff associations remained an alternative to BIFU for many staff. Since conducting these interviews, BIFU has amalgamated with two of these staff associations and is renamed UNIFI.

A group of six women acknowledged that joining BIFU was connected with a belief in trade unionism. This was expressed in terms of a political conviction, or in looser terms as something that 'they felt strongly about'.

> The first union I joined was BIFU and I joined the trade union because as an active member of the Labour party it was my political conviction that I should be a member of a trade union, and I worked in a bank, therefore I joined BIFU (2:23:1)

There is a diversity of views held by the women in BIFU. Many women were uncomfortable with the notion of trade unions as political organisations. One woman went as far as to state that she felt that Margaret Thatcher had been correct in curbing union power. For some, explicit political conviction is the key, for others collective notions of protection are important, and for a number, individual reasons remain influential.

> When I joined and decided to become active I was going out with a bloke who is now my husband and I thought well why not kind of thing, I started going to branch meetings. (2:26:1) [her husband when she met him was active in BIFU]

For some women in BIFU their joining and subsequent active participation was a consequence of locational circumstances; they joined a branch where BIFU membership was high. We could suggest that some women might not join where these factors are absent. Very few women were actually approached to join, yet Hartley (1992) argues that the main reason people join trade unions remains the fact that they have been asked to join. These data provide us with little indication of why as women they became active.

Among the women in USDAW the picture is rather different. Almost all reported joining a trade union as the 'natural thing' to do. You go to work and you join the appropriate union. It was part of their consciousness. There was only one exception to this prevailing view; this was a woman who argued that she joined USDAW by virtue of a specific grievance over an unfair warning.

Why become active in a trade union?

The next question tried to probe more deeply into the women's union activity. They were asked why they moved beyond trade union membership, to taking a position of office. For example, was there an actual event, reason or political conviction that contributed to this shift in activity?

The responses that the women gave to this question divide broadly into three themes; protection of their jobs and those of others, to have some influence, and to be able to articulate the views of the workforce. Only one woman in BIFU argued that it was the natural thing to do simply saying;

> It's the only thing to do. (24:25:21)

To protect themselves and others at one level can be seen as a traditional shop steward role. However, depending on how the women interpret that term it could also be perceived as a 'female' role, the notion of the 'carer' of the office – an analogy of the 'mother' protecting her children.

Eleven of the women talked about protection. For some this meant individual protection, returning to the earlier language of insurance, as expressed in reference to joining BIFU.

> Because I believe in it I suppose...but on the course they actually have training videos and they tell you that BIFU is an insurance policy – and you wouldn't not insure your house or your car – and I think that's how I see it now – so I can understand what they are saying – you would insure your house so why not insure your job. (24:20:18)

Many women moved beyond the 'corporate line' and argued that they wanted to protect other members from suffering or being in the position they had found themselves in. They saw themselves as the protectors and, 'carers' of others. They did not discuss their role in terms of negotiator or arbitrator. To some extent this reflects the formal bargaining structures.[10] The term protector was clearly the language that the women adopted. Their perceived skills lay in how they could support their colleagues. This could be viewed as feminine 'office' skills. Benet (1972) and McNally (1979) discuss the role of the secretary, arguing that the secretary reproduces the domestic role of mother and carer within the work place. It is possible to suggest that this analogy could be extended to women activists within BIFU, where they reproduce the domestic role of mother and carer through their union work, protecting and caring for the other workers. This is developed further in Harrington (2000). Charles (1986) argued that a familial role was evident in trade unions at local level. She used this term to suggest the paucity of equal opportunities practice evident at local level. This term, however, could be extended to suggest the dominance of a 'caring' role.

The women in BIFU discuss this protection frequently as support or, 'helping others'.

> Like I said I don't want anyone else to have the hard time that I had...– so yes, it's really just to help! to do whatever I can. (24:13:26)

> It's just something to do with helping people, it's just my small way of giving a little bit of myself to others who need my support and that just sums it up I suppose, I can only do small things but lots of small things added together can be a big thing. (24:21:19)

The other aspect of protection was the idea that women needed to ensure that others had a voice, that everyone was given a fair chance. Here we see the more traditional union role asserting itself, that of a common voice. This returns to the collective notions of joining and participating; a recognition that as part of a union they are not as one woman expressed it a 'lone voice'. The responses below illustrate the common feeling that was held by a number of women in BIFU;

> I believe that everyone should have an equal opportunity and a fair chance and the unions are there hopefully to make sure that we are not just a lone voice in a big company. (24:22:26)
>
> I want people to get what they are entitled to and have a voice for them. (24:12:3)

Three women explicitly saw the role as that of individual protection, a contrast to the quotations above. They argued that in becoming active in BIFU they were able to influence policy decisions and in turn protect themselves;

> I want a say in my future. (24:3:24)

This does not of course suggest that they do not protect others, or that they see that as negated by the desire to protect themselves. This simply tells us what the women's first thoughts on this subject were when questioned in an interview.

The final group of women in response to this question on becoming active saw it as a way of articulating their views. In many cases they felt that it gave them the freedom to express an unpopular viewpoint. In their workplace they would normally have had to remain silent. The quotations below reflect the views expressed.

> In the trade union you can say you disagree with something in the world of work. (24:7:5)
>
> I have very strong opinions on what I believe is right and wrong, whether it coincides with everyone else, of course it might not do. But yes I have very strong views on what I consider is the right way and the wrong way to treat people etc., and that is probably why I became involved. (24:16:13)

In summary the women cite a variety of reasons for becoming active, ranging from a political consciousness, ideas of protection and support, to the articulation of grievances which could not be expressed in the workplace. Protection here is worth highlighting as it pervaded many of their views. Protection of jobs in an unstable environment is an unsurprising concern. It can be suggested here that the term may be viewed in a number of different ways, from that of the collective response of trade unionism, to an individual concern with protecting their own positions and jobs, and to a stereotypical feminine notion of 'caring' for the workforce.

The women in USDAW responded rather differently. Many felt that they had already answered the question when they discussed their reasons for joining USDAW. Some referred directly to the role that their families, and in particular father and husbands, had played in influencing their decision to become active saying for example;

> I joined the union because Dad said it would be a good idea. (5:1)[11]

Others refer to an actual incident that propelled them into activity, but this is against the background of prior commitment to the union. For example, one woman discussed her anger on attending her first trade union meeting when the needs of part-time workers were ignored. Her anger at the injustice of her treatment by fellow trade unionists propelled her into activity. Hence the terminology of support and care or individual protection are not articulated in the same way as the women in BIFU.

Family background and trade union activism

As a subsidiary question the women interviewed were asked to comment on any family influences that had contributed to their joining. Whilst this might be viewed as a leading question, the intention, however, was to explore the perceptions that the women had of their prior attitudes to joining a trade union and where they had developed. Wertheimer and Nelson (1975) document socio-cultural barriers as impeding women's participation. Others argue, however, that socialisation can in turn encourage activity. Ledwith and Colgan (1996) suggest this to be the case in relation to 'senior' women trade unionists. They argue that most women who are active at senior level had parents who were either trade unionists or held positive attitudes towards trade unions. Hence, they suggest that there is a positive correlation between family background and trade union activity. It seemed appropriate to explore what role the women in BIFU and USDAW felt their families had played in influencing their decision to become active in the trade union movement.

Most of the women in BIFU argued that it had no effect or was irrelevant to their activity. They suggested that either trade unions were not discussed in their families or, where they were, one family member (usually a parent) held negative views. This view is not altogether surprising. BIFU itself has recognised that many of its members hold 'conservative' attitudes and have attempted to distance themselves from politics and perceptions of 'traditional' trade unionism. They have preferred to focus on notions of BIFU as an 'insurance policy', appealing to individual concerns of job protection.

Eight women did respond in more detail. These can be further subdivided. The first group argued that whilst there was a family member who had been an active trade unionist, or held pro-trade union views, this had no bearing on their own trade union activity. This does not mean that it was unimportant, but suggests that they wish to portray themselves in a particular way. The second group highlights the impact of family socialisation on their activity.

For two of the women who responded that their families had no bearing on their trade union activity they qualified this by saying;

> No. I say no … I suppose although I didn't realise until recently my father was actually in the police and he was representative for the police federation at

one point. But I didn't know that and certainly he wasn't particularly pro-trade union or anything like that. (7:16:1)

My father was a police man so they didn't have unions and my mother, well, up until I was quite grown up she didn't work and then she just went into a shop. (7:13:1).

The other woman in this group later reflected that whilst her father and mother may not have been influential, her grandfather had been.

My grandfather from my dad's side was quite involved with the union. He was a miner in South Wales for a while and that's probably where my interest in politics and unions came from originally. (7:14:4)

All the women responding negatively felt that their mothers had had no impact on their union activity. One woman explicitly stated that as her mother had not worked she could not have influenced her attitudes towards trade unions. This, of course, does not mean that she did not. Many of the women's mothers would not have had paid employment, or would not have been considered as the principal wage earner in the family. And this in itself may have propelled some women into activism. It is possible to suggest that there may exist for some of the women a feeling of unfairness in relation to their own mother's experiences.

The remaining women talk about how they were socialised into trade union activity.

One of my brothers was previously a BIFU member or whatever it was previous to being called BIFU, NUBE I think – he was always a NUBE member. So basically a family leaning towards union membership. (7:21:2)

Others felt that it was a way of life it was something that you did due to your upbringing.

It was just natural. My sister was a shop steward, my brother lectures in trade union policy. There was a history in the family, we were members of trade unions and I was brought up to be politically aware, quite a labour background really. (7:5:1)

I think again it's my background, the Labour party, family background. It's just the way things are, I couldn't see any other way of doing things. At one time I suppose it was my social life. [referring to her trade union activity] (7:25:8)

These findings suggest a plethora of attitudes towards trade unions and perceived family influence. For some women the idea that someone else may have played a part in their decision is an anathema. For others it is clearly of significance. The role that they actually play is rather ambiguous; have mothers outside paid employment influenced their activity indirectly? Family socialisation is not however perceived by the majority of women in BIFU to be a key factor influencing their trade union activism.

The data compiled on USDAW indicated a very different picture. With only two exceptions all the women discussed their family's influence. They discussed their backgrounds in terms of being 'traditional' labour supporters and both their mother and father's influence. Some of the women also discussed their husband's influence, for example,

> Always been in a union because father said it was for your own protection. Father was in a union, he was a shop steward. It was not talked about in our house, but you joined a union. (3:1)

> I was brought up in a socialist background, a very union background. USDAW was the first union I belonged to. Both my father and husband served as shop stewards. (4:1)

> I was always involved because of my mother's influence, she was a Labour supporter. (8:1)

This raises the importance of context. The women of BIFU work in white-collar occupations in an industry which until recently, and certainly in their view, was perceived as a stable and secure environment and one in which the banking employers cultivated commitment to the branch manager. Their attitudes towards trade unionism prior to joining BIFU reflect this. The USDAW women work in more varied jobs, many in semi-skilled manual occupations. Many of them also come from an area of traditionally high male unionism, South Wales, and this may have been an influence on their attitudes to trade unionism. A number of the women in USDAW when asked whether they felt that family background had influenced their joining simply replied 'of course'. For them it was taken for granted; it was not something worthy of discussion. Socialisation into union membership here suggests the various influences of gender relations, industry and geographical location. One woman in BIFU articulated this when she discussed her frustration on moving to the South and West area of BIFU from another area. She was 'shocked' by the lack of activity within this area.

Discussion

The intention of this section is to explore the rationale that the women presented for participating in trade unions and playing an active role. Two key issues emerge from the data; the notion of protection in relation to the women in BIFU and the importance of context to understand women's participation.

Protection and support are two terms that the women in BIFU continuously refer to in accounting for their decision to join and to become active trade unionists. The notion of protection is used in a variety of ways. One of the most common uses is its connection to the notion of insurance – '*You insure your house, you insure your car, you should insure your job*'. This both suggests that individualistic reasons for joining are relevant in the interviewees' explanations, 'protecting your own job', and also that BIFU has effectively deployed the language of the banking, insurance and finance industry to encourage membership. However, it is also used in a collectivist sense, as a form of protection for all members, enabling the women to support the members in the workplaces in which they operate. This in turn can be interpreted in two ways. First, it can be seen as a 'traditional' trade union role, the shop steward protecting and supporting his/her members. It may also have a gendered dimension. It could suggest the role of the 'carer' of the workforce, an extension of the notion of the secretary reproducing her domestic role in the workplace, the trade union woman activist reproducing her domestic role in the union. The use of the term remains both ambiguous and multifaceted.

Waddington and Whitston's (1997) influential study presented the argument that collective reasons for joining remain dominant. While this chapter does not refute these findings it nevertheless suggests that women's joining and active participation may in fact be more complex than it initially appears. The data provided here suggests (see Harrington, 2000) the notion that the terminology of protection and support can have both individual and collective connotations.

This was also apparent when the women were questioned about the role of family socialisation. Many women in BIFU wished to stress their own individual choices and therefore were uncomfortable with notions of others influencing their decision-making. They present a heterogeneous group with some women arguing that they came from a background of trade unionism and politics, others that they came from a background that was anti-trade union and for some women one where the issue was not discussed. The role of their mothers is of interest. Many women talked about the fact that their mothers either did not work outside the home, or else that they held 'secondary jobs' in their families. The influence this had on their subsequent participation is difficult to unravel. It may suggest that their mothers played a limited role in their decision-making. Equally, it may suggest that the perception that their mothers were disadvantaged in turn directly influenced their decision to join and become active in BIFU. Whilst studies of women full-time officers and 'senior' women trade unionists present the influence of family socialisation as being a crucial factor in encouraging activity (see Ledwith and Colgan, 1996), this appears less clear when we examine reasons for activism at local level. The women in USDAW, however, present a more unified picture. They suggested that it was through their families that they developed a prior commitment to trade unionism and that this in turn influenced their participation. This leads us to the second key issue, the importance of context.

The women in USDAW argue that joining a union is a 'natural' thing to do when you go to work. They stated that their families positively encouraged this attitude. They are located predominately in South Wales, an area traditionally associated with a 'strong' union identity centred around male employment in heavy industries. For them, joining a trade union is not a problematic issue, it is something you automatically do when you get a job. The responses of the women in BIFU are more complex. For some joining a trade union is the natural thing to do. However they appear to suggest that joining can be for many reasons. They do not present a unified argument of collective protection. Neither do they suggest a purely individualistic concern for their own jobs. They operate in an environment that has undergone rapid restructuring over the last ten years, where the perception of their jobs is that they are less secure than they were in the past. They work in white-collar occupations that have not traditionally been associated with militant trade unionism, and hence it is not surprising that many of the women appear uncomfortable with the perceived link between politics and trade unions. They are also located in the South and West, encompassing geographical areas that remain associated with low levels of trade union activity. Whilst this is as yet inconclusive, it does start to suggest that trade union renewal strategies need to be aware of both geographical and industrial locations. Studies of UNISON are frequently highlighted as exemplifying 'good practice' in reference to women's membership. This study suggests that 'good practice' may be context bound.

Conclusion

The increase in the numerical representation of women members in trade unions is well documented. However, it is also noted that women remain disproportionally under-represented within union hierarchies. The barriers to women's active participation have been well rehearsed in the literature, with Wertheimer and Nelson's (1975) seminal work providing a framework from which many subsequent studies have been developed. They propose a three stage model of socio-cultural barriers, job-related barriers and union-related barriers. Lawrence (1992) notes that while research on women trade unionists has tended to focus on barriers to participation, research on male trade unionists has tended to focus on reasons for participation. Studies that have departed from this and considered reasons for women's participation, have in the main considered senior women union leaders and full-time officers (e.g. Ledwith and Colgan, 1996; Kirton and Healy, 1999). The findings discussed in this chapter assessed women's explanations for joining and becoming active at local level in BIFU and USDAW.

A number of issues emerge:

- The importance of union membership seen in terms of the idea of 'protection' and the variety of meanings attached to this term
- The interaction of women's experiences outside and inside the workplace, and the influence of the industrial sector in which they are employed, the union in which they actively participate, and their geographical location
- The diversity of the women's interpretation of their activism.

These start to suggest that attaching one ideological position to women at local level is problematical. It can also be argued that a typology generated by a study of senior women leaders and full-time officers (Ledwith and Colgan, 1996) may be less appropriate for categorising women's local level activity and consciousness. The empirical study highlights the needs to move away from a homogeneous classification of women's activity, and recognise the diversity of attitudes held by women at local level. If trade unionism is to continue to have any meaning to the wage earners that it deems to serve, it needs to recognise that the treatment of women as a homogeneous group neglects the richness and diversity of attitudes and interests that women bring into the trade union movement.

Acknowledgements

This chapter is derived from my PhD 'Women's Local Level Trade Union Participation'. I would like to express particular thanks to Stephanie Tailby and Andrew Sturdy for their invaluable comments and support. I am also very grateful to Paul Stewart and Mike Richardson for reading and commenting on earlier drafts.

Notes

1. Cockburn (1996) suggests a useful distinction between union strategies which facilitate the representation of women as 'individuals in a sex category' and those which encourage the representation of women as 'an oppressed social group'. According to Cockburn (1996) women are treated as 'individuals in a sex category' when it is their biological (female) status which distinguished them from other members – such as the reservation of seats for women on union lay structures, the provision of creche facilities for union meetings. Women are treated as 'an oppressed social group' when their status within society distinguishes them from other members – such as the establishment of women only committees in which women consider and promote issues of specific concern to women members.
2. Activist is used in this paper to mean holding a position from Joint accredited office representative upwards. They can be described as formally participating (Barling *et al.*, 1992), as they were all office holders. Alternatively using Klandermans' definition (1986), they could be described as being both administrative and direct participants in decision-making. They were all active in the sense that they held office and all participated at local level. Some also held area and national positions.

This was a definition agreed by both USDAW and BIFU. It was also a definition that the women interviewed could relate to.

3. The case was originally intended to be used as a comparative case with BIFU. However, due to a complex set of political problems at local and national level the interviews could not be extended to all women activists in the South Wales and Western Division. An additional consequence was that access to national officers was not possible. As such, many of the findings discussed focus on BIFU. However, the USDAW data does highlight some interesting contrasts.

4. The interviews were conducted between 1990–94. Where possible the interviews were taped.

5. The first is female part-time clerical staff recruited to meet peak demands and undertake mundane branch processing tasks. The second is the main (though declining) service and retail staff working in a restructured branch network. The third stream includes technical specialist staff in head office and computing divisions. Finally, there is the set of managerial high fliers who may be able to expect promotion over the heads of the main clerical intake.

6. Martin *et al.* (1996) use the terms union heartlands and union periphery. Union heartlands is defined as a regional area if its membership share (in 1979) was above the share that each region would have if the union's membership was equally distributed across its region. The remaining regions with shares below the hypothetical value were then designated as the union's 'periphery' (67). The actual method yields vast differences in proportion of membership. For example unions, which are associated with economic sectors that are distributed fairly evenly across the country, such as retail and distribution (USDAW), are low (e.g. 28–30 per cent). Whereas unions associated with economic sectors that tend to be more localised, such as banking and finance (BIFU), and are concentrated in the more urbanised, metropolitan regions of the country are much higher (e.g. 50 per cent).

7. In the 1992 ADM Executive Council statement, the objectives for the women's committees were stated as: (1) To work within all levels of the union to ensure that the Union is welcoming, relevant and accessible to women members to ensure the continued recruitment of more women into the union and the retention and consolidation of that membership. (2) To assist with opening up the union to encourage and support the fullest involvement and participation of women members at every level of the Union. To organise to get a better deal for women at the workplace by aiming to inform and develop the collective bargaining agenda. (ADM Executive Council Statement, 1992.)

8. The agenda for 1992 USDAW women's committee states the following:

- To work with the other parts of the Union to ensure that the Union is welcoming, relevant and accessible to women members and potential recruits.
- To organise women get-togethers and workshops on issues of concern to women in USDAW.
- To combine Women's committee meetings with workplace visits to reach out to women members.
- To continue to encourage women, at every level, to become more involved in union activity.
- To work on union publications and materials and to develop, produce and update women on USDAW publications, as appropriate, and specifically in this coming year to finalise and publish the Equal Pay booklet.
- To work to ensure that the collective bargaining agenda continues to reflect the real needs and concerns of women in USDAW.

- To foster a climate within the union which is women-friendly and directly supportive of women. (ADM Executive Council Statement, 1992.)

9. This utilises Cockburn's (1989) terms the 'long' and 'short' agenda of equal opportunities. Cockburn characterised the 'short' agenda of equal opportunities as following a liberal approach towards equality, which focuses on treatment of the symptoms of discrimination and disadvantage, or pushing special policies to protect or enhance the positions of certain social groups. The 'long' agenda is suggested to encompass a radical approach by seeking to respect and respond to differences, rather than seeking to assist people to fit into existing organisations and cultures.
10. Seconded industry representatives and negotiating officers conduct formal pay bargaining. It is rare for women local activists to have any role within this process.
11. The referencing for the USDAW women is different to the BIFU. They have two references. The first refers to the woman speaking. The second refers to the page number. The reason for this is the fact that they were not taped. The only comments quoted were written verbatim at the time.

References

Barling, J., Fullagar, C. and Kelloway, E. K. (1992) *The Union and its Members: A Psychological Approach,* Oxford: Oxford University Press.
Benet, M. K. (1972) *Secretary,* London: Sidgwick and Jackson.
BIFU (1992) *General Secretary's Report to the Annual Delegate Conference,* London: Leif Mills.
Charles, N. (1986) 'Women and trade unions', in Feminist Review (ed.) *Waged work, a reader,* London: Virago Press Limited.
Cockburn, C. (1989) 'Equal opportunities: the long and short agenda'. *Industrial Relations Journal,* 20 (3): 213–25.
Cockburn, C. (1996) 'Strategies for gender democracy: strengthening the representation of trade union women in the European social dialogue'. *European Journal of Women's Studies,* 3 (1): 7–26.
Cressey, P. and Scott, P. (1992) 'Employment, technology and industrial relations in the UK clearing banks: is the honey moon over?'. *New Technology, Work and Employment,* 7 (2): 83–96.
Crompton, R. (1989) 'Women in Banking: Continuity and change since the 2nd World War'. *Work, Employment and Society,* 3 (2): 141–156.
Crompton, R. and Jones, G. (1984) 'White Collar Proletariat: Deskilling and gender in the Clerical Labour Process'. London: Macmillan.
Cunnison, S. and Stageman, J. (1993) *Feminizing the Unions: Challenging the Culture of Masculinity,* Aldershott: Avebury.
Drake, B. (1920) *Women in Trade Unions,* London: Virago Press Limited.
Egan, A. (1982) 'Women in banking: a study in equality'. *Industrial Relations Journal,* 13 (3): 20–31.
Employment Gazette (May 1995) 'Trade union membership and recognition: 1994 labour force survey data', 191–203, London: HMSO.
Equal Opportunities Review (January/February 1999) 'Women in the unions', No.83: 30, London: Eclipse Group Limited.
Financial Times (1993) 'Banks launch root and branch reform', 18 January.
Halford, S. and Savage, M. (1995) 'Restructuring organisations, changing people'. *Work, Employment and Society,* 9 (1): 97–122.

Halford, S., Savage, M. and Witz, A. (1997) *Gender, Careers and Organisations,* London: Macmillan Press Limited.

Harrington, J. (2000) Women's Local Level Trade Union Participation, PhD Thesis, University of the West of England, Bristol.

Hartley, J. F. (1992) 'Joining a trade union', in Hartley, J. F. and Stephenson, G. M. (eds) *Employment Relations: The Psychology of Influence and Control at Work,* Oxford: Basil Blackwell Limited.

Healy, G. and Kirton, G. (2000) 'Women, power and trade union government in the UK'. *British Journal of Industrial Relations,* 38 (3): 343–60.

Heery, E. and Kelly, J. (1988) 'Do female representatives make a difference? Women full time officials and trade union work'. *Work, Employment and Society,* 2 (4): 487–505.

Heery, E. and Kelly, J. (1989) ' "A cracking job for a woman" – a profile of women trade union officers'. *Industrial Relations Journal,* 20 (3): 192–202.

Heritage, J. (1983) Feminisation and Unionisation: A case study from Banking in Gamarnikow, E., Morgan, D., Purvis, J. and Taylorson, D. (eds) *Gender, Class and Work.* London: Heinman.

Kirton, G. and Healy, G. (1999) 'Transforming union women: The role of women trade union officials in union renewal'. *Industrial Relations Journal,* 30 (1): 31–45.

Klandermans, B. (1986) 'Psychology and trade union participation: joining, acting, quitting'. *Journal of Occupational Psychology,* 59: 189–204.

Lawrence, E. (1992) Shop stewards in Local Government – The influence of occupation, gender and department on union activism, PhD Thesis, CNAA.

Ledwith, S. and Colgan, F. (1996) 'Sisters organising – women and their trade unions', in Ledwith, S. and Colgan, F. (eds) *Women in Organisations: Challenging Gender Politics,* Macmillan Press Limited: 152–86.

Lockwood, D. (1989) *The Blackcoated Worker: A Study in Class Consciousness.* 2nd edition. London: Clarendon.

Martin, R., Sunley, P. and Wills, J. (1996) *Union Retreat and the Regions: The Shrinking Landscape of Organised Labour,* London: Jessica Kingsley Publishers Limited.

McNally, F. (1979) *Women for Hire,* London: Macmillan Press Limited.

Morgan, G. and Sturdy, A. J. (2000) *Beyond Organisational Change – Discourse, Structure and Power in UK Financial Services,* London: Macmillan Press Limited.

Morris, T. (1986) *Innovations in Banking: Business Strategies and Employee Relations,* London: Croom Helm Limited.

O'Reilly, J. (1994) *Banking on Flexibility,* Aldershott: Avebury.

Reynolds, J. (1996) *Retailing, Review of the Economy and Employment 1996/7: Labour Market Assessment,* Warwick: Institute for Employment Research.

Reynolds, J. (1999) *Retailing, Review of the Economy and Employment 1998/9: Labour Market Assessment,* Warwick: Institute for Employment Research.

Richardson, W. (1979) *A Union of Many Trades: the History of USDAW,* Newcastle-Upon-Tyne: Co-operative Press Limited.

Rowbotham, S. (1975) *Hidden from History: 300 years of Women's Oppression and the Fight Against It,* London: Pelican Books.

Storey, J. (1995) 'Employment policies and practices in UK clearing banks: an overview'. *Human Resource Management Journal,* 5 (4): 24–43

Tailby, S. (1996) 'The reorganisation of working time and employment in UK Banks', School of Personnel Research Papers, No. 2, October, Bristol: University of the West of England.

Townsend, A., Sadler, D. and Hudson, R. (1996) 'Geographical dimensions of UK retailing employment change', in Wrigley, N. and Lowe, M. (eds) *Retailing,*

Consumption and Capital: Towards the New Retail Geography, London: Longman Group Limited.

USDAW (1990) *Listening to Part-Time Workers*, Manchester: Women in USDAW, official publication, March 1990.

USDAW (1992). *The Agenda for 1992*, 1992 ADM Ex. Council Statement, Manchester: Women in USDAW, USDAW.

Waddington, J. and Whitston, C. (1995) 'Trade unions: growth, structure and policy', in Edwards, E. (ed.) *Industrial Relations: Theory and Practice in Britain*, Oxford: Basil Blackwell Limited.

Waddington, J. and Whitston, C. (1997) 'Why do people join unions in a period of membership decline?', *British Journal of Industrial Relations*, 35 (4): 515–46.

Wertheimer, B. M. and Nelson, A. H. (1975) *Trade Union Women: A Study of Their Participation in New York City Locals*, New York: Praeger.

6
What about the Workers? Bringing the Experience of Job Insecurity into the Flexibility Debate

Hazel Conley

> The 'things that really matter' have not changed much over the years. People still want a steady job, decent pay, a healthy environment, personal freedom and somebody to rely on if the going gets a bit tough. In short, they want security. But security is the one thing that the modern system cannot deliver. Indeed, it seems almost proud of the fact that it cannot offer security.
>
> (Elliott and Atkinson, 1998: 247)

In their book 'The Age of Insecurity' Elliot and Atkinson highlight the contradictions between the political rhetoric of labour market flexibility and the reality of its consequences on the day-to-day lives of the workers it affects. The purpose of rhetoric is often to mask the unpalatable realities from those who are likely to suffer the consequences. Flexibility is a concept that was conceived in rhetoric and it has become so stretched in its usage that it has become almost meaningless. However, unlike many fashionable managerial euphemisms, the language of flexibility continues to dominate political and managerial discourses.

How far the language of flexibility reflects actual changes in working practices has been the subject of much academic debate (Atkinson, 1984; Atkinson, 1985; Atkinson and Meager, 1986; Pollert, 1988a, b; Pollert, 1991; Proctor *et al.*, 1994). Empirical evidence of flexibility is limited in private sector workplaces (Casey, Metcalf and Millward, 1997). However flexibility has taken on a political mantle with successive governments, Conservative and Labour, hailing flexible labour markets as the way to national economic prosperity. It is therefore unsurprising that researchers have argued that, where flexibility does exist, it is more likely to be found in the public sector. Dex and McCulloch (1995) found that the sectors subject to government reorganisation tend to have the highest proportion of flexible jobs.

In relation to local government, Escott and Whitfield (1995) argued that numerical flexibility was an increasing aspect of employment policy and practice.

A new rhetoric of 'modernisation' has also come to signify government plans to make public sector employment more flexible. Bach (1999: 14) states that '*Modernisation* has become a ubiquitous term of discussion about public services reform and has been used loosely to signify a wide range of reforms ….' The use of modernisation as a managerial bargaining device is more latterly linked to work intensificaton and job cuts.[1] The reality is therefore that, contrary to traditional beliefs, job *in*security in one form or another is now a visible feature of public sector employment, bringing a perverse meaning to the concept of the state as a 'model employer' (Conley, 2002).

Allen and Henry (1997: 182) make the important point that, by allowing the flexibility debate to be dominated by a managerial agenda, the views of the workers it affects are ignored. Similarly Heery and Salmon (2000: 18) argue that refocusing the debate in terms of insecurity rather than flexibility is required to put workers' experience 'centre stage'. One explanation for the neglect of worker experience is methodological. The majority of research on this subject has been based on statistical data where legitimacy springs from the manipulation of numbers rather than an engagement with lived experience of workers coping with insecurity. Where attempts have been made to consider the motivations and life-style of the flexible workforce data has still been drawn almost entirely from large-scale surveys (Felstead and Jewson, 1999). The result has inevitably been abstract, generalist and an often-unsympathetic portrait. Perhaps the most controversial example is Hakim's (1991) conclusion that some women are satisfied with segregation into low paid and low status jobs that characterise much of the flexible labour market.

Focusing on temporary work Robinson (1999, 2000) uses aggregate data to argue that well-paid professionals in the public sector (1999: 89) undertake the majority of this form of work. In a later paper Robinson (2000: 37) concludes that, as such, insecurity is a price worth paying for any economic benefits obtained by a flexible workforce. Labour Force Survey data do quite clearly show that temporary work is largely to be found in the public sector. However, disaggregated analysis of public sector statistics highlight that, in local government, temporary employment is disproportionately prevalent amongst women, young workers and minority ethnic groups (LGMB, 1998). These are not the demographics normally associated with privileged professional status. On the contrary, these groups of workers are usually associated with a disadvantaged labour market position. Thus, public service workers may be amongst those least able to protect themselves from the inequality inherent in core–periphery models (Conley, 2003). Ironically these workers are also likely to be employed in areas of the public sector that are experiencing acute recruitment and retention difficulties (Conley, 2002) further indicating that any tenuous economic benefits of labour market flexibility must be weighed against pressing social costs.

What is striking about the conclusions of Hakim and Robinson is the palatable message they give to employers. Hakim's view of what motivates part-time workers coincides quite closely with what, in a classic qualitative study, Beechey and Perkins (1987) identified as the *employers'* perception of part-time workers. Furthermore, in contrast to Robinson, these authors also note that the state, often as employer, has reinforced the marginal position of disadvantaged groups of workers in their use of so-called flexible working practices. In arguing these points Beechey and Perkins (1987: 7) emphasise the importance of qualitative studies in researching the formation of worker consciousness and experience of work.

The aim of this chapter is to show how numerical flexibility, in the form of temporary work, has a huge and varied impact on the day-to-day lives of public sector workers that cannot be fully captured by statistical data alone. The qualitative data reported in this chapter show that, when viewed through the eyes of the workers it affects, temporary work is a multifaceted experience, which is beyond the reach of aggregated statistical data. The aim is therefore not to generalise the research findings to *all* temporary workers but to highlight the importance of context, both at work and home, when analysing the experience of temporary employment. In conclusion I argue that, although the views and experiences of workers are valid and important in their own right, public sector employers and trade unions have much to gain by an appreciation of the effects of job insecurity, stripped of the veil of flexibility, on the day-to-day lives of their employees and members.

The research

The evidence presented in this chapter stems from the experiences of teaching staff and residential social workers (RSWs) in two local authorities and their attendant local education authorities (LEAs). One authority, City, is a large metropolitan city council; the other, County, a rural county council. The majority of the data reported in this chapter was collected from 32 workers during 26 individual semi-structured interviews and two group interviews that took the form of a guided discussion. The data forms part of a larger research project that also examines employer and trade union responses to temporary work in public services (Conley, 2000). The names used in the chapter are pseudonyms but maintain the gender and ethnicity of the respondents.

As previous analysis has identified, many of the problems faced by temporary workers revolve, in some form or other, around their vulnerable contractual status and the insecurity this engenders (Conley, 2000). After speaking to temporary workers it became apparent that their feelings of insecurity had a number of elements. These ranged from the concrete and practical, such as the financial implications of their situation and an inability to plan for the future, through to the psychological states provoked by this sense of insecurity. These aspects are now considered in greater detail.

Financial insecurity

Despite their different experiences of temporary work, all of the workers interviewed said they would prefer a permanent contract and in the majority of cases the need for financial security was given as the main reason. Two of the teaching staff related how their career preferences had been subordinated to the need for financial security. Mr Dep, a Bengali language instructor in a school in City, said that, although he would like to stay in his current school because he felt he had built up good relationships with his pupils, his first priority had to be to secure a permanent contract and financial security. Karen, a newly qualified teacher (NQT) in City related how the need for financial security had driven her last career choice. She had been offered another temporary contract at a school that she considered would have been a wise career move, but had also been offered a permanent position at a school where she knew teaching conditions were much harder. However Karen wanted to buy a house and needed a mortgage – something she knew would be difficult when employed on a temporary contract. Karen opted for the difficult school and the permanent contract.

Marie, an NQT in County, had managed to get a mortgage whilst working as an agency teacher as the agency had arranged it for her. However, she considered that she had been given little choice and she felt the mortgage was probably not on the most advantageous terms. She also considered that, having secured the mortgage, the repayments were a constant source of worry and had kept her locked into agency and temporary work.[2] Marie also related how during the long summer break she had been forced to take work in a shoe shop because she had not received sufficient teaching work to secure a holiday payment.

For the most part working on a temporary contract meant that getting a mortgage was out of the question. Even shorter-term borrowing had proved daunting and financial arrangements, which would seem uncomplicated for most permanent workers, were considered to be a coup for them. As Katy noted:

> I have been very lucky with the bank. I was in the position where my car was past it – it had had it. But I just went into the bank, I was doing supply then, and I said 'you have got two choices. You can either have £285 a week coming in or you can have £40 coming in.' and they gave me the money to get a new car. But I was just lucky. (Katy, NQT, City)

Even Samantha, at 22 the youngest of the NQTs interviewed, who was quite happy to be free of mortgage commitments, expressed some concern over financial issues:

> I am renting at the moment and I don't want to buy because I don't know where I am going to be in five years time. But I have managed to get a car loan from the bank as a post-graduate. But I do know people who have struggled to get a loan from the bank because they have not had a permanent contract. But if I'd have had any difficulty then I wouldn't have been able to get a car and that would have been a real problem.
>
> (Samantha, NQT, County)

For Mr Dep even a car loan was out of the question:

> The amount of money that I am getting makes it difficult to fulfil my requirements. After you fulfil your requirements, then you can start thinking about luxuries... I can't think about holidays. My wife needs a car for work and every morning we have to worry about if it will start or if it is going to be stuck in the middle of the road. Every time I worry about it. If my job was permanent then I would be able to buy a better car than that. (Mr Dep, instructor. City)

Travelling relatively long distances to work was not an unusual feature in the daily routines of the workers interviewed. Most of them expressed that the temporary nature of their jobs meant it was not feasible or wise to relocate. Furthermore the RSW's complained that they were often given the unpopular early or late shifts, which meant public transport was often not a convenient option. Transport costs and the need for reliable personal transport were therefore a source of considerable stress for the majority of the temporary workers.

Fiona, a part-time temporary teacher in City, raised an important issue about the longer-term financial implications raised by the vagaries of temporary employment. Fiona had taken out a pension scheme during her earlier periods of temporary employment with a previous LEA, but in the constant switching of contracts the paperwork for the pension had been mislaid and it had now lapsed. Fiona also pointed out how the accessories of working life are designed around permanent employment and temporary workers are therefore thwarted even when they are attempting to be financially prudent:

> Somehow everything [pension details] just got lost so I never bothered chasing it again. Simply again, because I didn't fit the masses, I have fallen by the wayside. (Fiona, teacher, City)

Fiona's attempts to provide for her retirement were defeated because, at the time of the research, part-time teachers, unlike full-time teachers, had to make extra effort to opt in to the teachers' pension scheme. When this is accompanied by the constant changing of salary payment details associated with temporary work the amount of effort required eventually becomes overwhelming.

Pamela, a lone parent, took a positive and pragmatic view of the financial restrictions created by her temporary contractual status. She claimed that the uncertainty of her financial situation prevented her from entering into credit arrangements:

> I don't put any trust in the contract … it makes you more careful.
>
> (Pamela, RSW, City)

However, even Pamela considered that 'mortgages are different'. She said she had taken a permanent job, not in social services, to enable her to get a mortgage and that her current temporary work prevented her from moving house because she thought she would probably not get another mortgage. This was despite her good repayment record during her temporary work.

Part-time and temporary work, although conceptually different (Gallie *et al.*, 1998), are related by gendered perceptions of work and family commitments. Part-time teachers are particularly likely to be female and employed on temporary contracts (Conley, 2003). Fiona and Sally, whose part-time temporary work had originally been one wage in dual income families, were now facing changed situations as both of their partners had been made redundant. Fiona expressed this concern when saying:

> I was not the main breadwinner in the household so part-time suited. But my circumstances have changed. My kids have gone to university and that is a major expense for us. My husband's circumstances have changed. Whereas before, I didn't have to work, now I am looking at an income albeit part-time I am looking towards it because that income is used now.
>
> (Fiona, teacher, City)

The experiences of Fiona and Sally highlight that women's working lives are not static but change to accommodate the uncertainties of family life under wage labour in a capitalist economy. However gendered preconceptions remain stubbornly attached to women's employment (Halford *et al.*, 1997) and the view that women have a looser attachment to the labour market and therefore a greater ability to absorb job insecurity is one of them.

There are a variety of ways in which income insecurity becomes an issue for both men and women, particularly in relation to housing and transport. Financial arrangements, which would be seen as standard by most of their permanent colleagues, were complicated by uncertainty for the temporary workers interviewed. Teaching and social work are usually considered to be pensioned positions, thereby securing the future retirement of workers in these fields. However, as Fiona's experience indicates, the future of temporary workers, even in traditionally pensioned occupations, is far from certain. Insecurity about the short-term also featured extensively in the concerns of temporary workers and is considered in greater detail in the next section.

Insecure futures

A subject that frequently arose during conversations with temporary workers was their difficulty in seeing beyond the horizons of what were very often short-term contracts and a resultant inability to plan for the future. As Max stated:

> If you have a family you can't plan long term. You can't plan a holiday, you can't plan what is going to happen six months down the road. You can't plan whether you are going to have a job tomorrow. It is just a nightmare. (Max, RSW, City)

Katy had entered teaching as a mature student. She had given up many of the things that workers normally take for granted to enter higher education and gain a teaching qualification. Now qualified, her temporary status meant she was finding it difficult even to recoup the trappings of working life she had once taken for granted:

> I can't do anything. I am in a 'no win' situation. Now I can't get a mortgage, I can't really do much because I know that I could be out of work at the beginning of September. If the worst came to the worst, I could get supply [agency teaching work]. I still wouldn't be able to get a mortgage but I could pay rent. But it does put you in a very weak position.
> (Katy, NQT, City)

Similarly Pamela considered that even taking her eight-year-old son on holiday was an extravagant venture:

> It is a little bit of a risk, but we still go. (Pamela, RSW, City)

One of Fiona's main concerns was the planning that was necessitated by her work. As a dance instructor part of her job was to organise 'productions' for Christmas and Easter events at school. She felt this was difficult when her contract was renewed on a three-monthly basis and worried about the impact of this on her career:

> I think should I start this? Will I be able to see it through? So it is the case that I do what I can whilst I am here. I can't foresee next year. It does

really limit you and also your career prospects within the school. Regardless of how capable and efficient you can be at something, you just know that you may not be here tomorrow. So you hold back from working parties and things. (Fiona, teacher, City)

Fiona and some of the other temporary workers thought that much of the uncertainty could be avoided if they were kept informed of their contractual situation and had more warning about either the renewal or the termination of their contracts. Fiona stated that although she had been at her school for five years her contract had been renewed on a per term basis and, though the offer of a permanent contract would have been her preference, a twelve-month contract would have at least allowed her to plan her work more confidently. Fiona also felt that decisions about her contract were either taken at the last minute or not relayed to her until it would be difficult for her to get another post:

If you are left in limbo, if you are waiting to find out – I have at times had to go and say 'look am I coming back in September? Do you want me back in September?' When in actual fact I should have been told early enough so that I am then able to look out for a new post. (Fiona, teacher, City)

Pamela was in a similar situation in that her contract was renewed on a quarterly basis. However she had not worried unduly about her contract until it was about to reach twenty-four months – the point at which temporary workers, at that time, began to qualify for employment rights. She had noticed a distinct difference in the way the impending renewal date was being treated:

What they are supposed to do is tell you after three months, but they don't tell you anything. You just keep working and they might say 'oh your contract needs reviewing' but they don't do anything and you just keep working. But this time they are not saying to me 'your contract needs renewing' they are saying 'your contract is ending'. So I know that something must have been said ... but they prefer to keep you in the dark.
(Pamela, RSW, City)

In contrast Samantha had commented that her satisfaction with her contract had stemmed largely from the way it had been handled and the fact that she had been kept informed and been given prompt information that might affect her situation.

I know that my job is safe until this time next year ... as long as you are kept informed I don't think there is any problem with a temporary contract as long as you don't have huge financial commitments ... because I have been kept informed, I haven't had a problem with it.

(Samantha, NQT, County)

The lot of the temporary worker is often sealed by their reluctance to complain. Their dependence on often nothing more than the goodwill of their managers for the continuation of their contract, means that 'rocking the boat' is often not an option:

It [the renewal of his contract] is entirely dependent on the authorities – if they want to keep me in the job. If they want to kick me out then they can. I have no say. I feel powerless. They are really good people so it is all right. If they were bad people they can kick me out at any time. If I wanted to argue about anything, for example if I need more materials but the school authorities are not providing them. If they don't then I couldn't do my job properly so it could be a problem between me and the authorities. They could sack me even though it wasn't anything that was my fault. Now they are good people and they are providing me with the materials I want. But if they don't, I can't do anything.

(Mr Dep, instructor, City)

Mr Dep considered himself very fortunate to have found a job that allowed him to use his language skills. This was his first job in the UK since arriving from Bangladesh and he had anticipated that, like most of his friends and family, restaurant work was the most likely option. He was very grateful for what he considered to be the kind treatment he received from the managers of the school in which he worked and was therefore reluctant to say anything against them.

Conley (2003) highlights the incompatibility between the use of temporary contracts in the public sector and the implementation of equal opportunity policies. Moves towards decentralisation that devolve power for personnel decisions to local managers have weakened centralised equal opportunities policy by increasing the opportunities for personal preferences and prejudices to manifest themselves. This is particularly apparent when local managers have the power to offer or withhold the renewal of a temporary contract. In this respect it was clear that Mr Dep was aware of his vulnerable position and the necessity to keep on the good side of his employers. Karen's view of the situation was less opaque:

You don't question it [the reason the contract is temporary rather than permanent] because you want a job. You know there aren't enough jobs for everybody so you take the job and hope that it is made permanent.

(Karen, NQT, City)

This view quite clearly explains how the limited number of permanent jobs enhances the 'carrot' role of the temporary contract as an inducement to remain compliant. Ray also expressed these sentiments and noted how the vulnerability of temporary teachers compares with the more powerful position of their permanent counterparts.

> They [temporary teachers] have got a lot to lose, haven't they? I mean permanent teachers don't particularly want to address the head but they have got nothing to lose. They have got a permanent contract...But at the end of the day you are thinking 'I want to stay here and I don't want another temporary contract.' So you don't rock the boat do you.
>
> (Ray, NQT, City)

Katy, who felt badly used by her head teacher, had finally considered complaining when a personal comment was made about her appearance. The head teacher felt that Katy's appearance was not smart enough. Katy felt strongly that this was an inappropriate criticism based on personal taste and discussed the issue with her mentor. However Katy's mentor had advised her that 'it might not be a good idea' to confront the head teacher about it and eventually Katy decided to let the incident pass:

> When I calmed down enough, I thought it was probably best if I didn't complain. Especially in the position that I am in. You have to be so careful what you say. (Katy, NQT, City)

When discussing this incident the NQT group felt that Katy's actions had been wise. They considered that Katy's feelings of resentment about her contract had not gone unmissed by her head teacher. As such the group agreed that the remarks were possibly designed to provoke a response from Katy, which would provide the head teacher with grounds to refuse to renew her contract.

Psychological impact

The combination of insecurity and the lack of control over events understandably took a psychological toll on most of the temporary workers interviewed. Two workers said they had become depressed after worrying about their contracts and during particular periods of uncertainty their ability to do their job had been substantially reduced. One of these workers, Mr Dep, was recently married and he considered that the vulnerability of his position had put considerable strain on his marriage:

> I have been married for a year and you know married life is a 50:50 partnership. You have to share everything 50:50 – financial, social life, whatever. So now from this point of view, financial things, I am not able

to play my 50 per cent role. This is difficult in a new marriage. If I would like to buy a gift for my wife, I have to budget and think very carefully.

(Mr Dep, instructor, City)

A number of workers related how because they felt ill informed, they were constantly looking out for signs that might affect the renewal of their contract.

If there are any jobs coming up or if there are any changes in the department that I work in, then I am obviously the person that it really affects. Because I think if my timetable changes, if there is more time needed, then obviously I am a part-time person also, therefore I tend to feel that it indirectly affects me if there is a major change. (Fiona, teacher, City)

In a number of cases the temporary workers were optimistic, but this often led to even greater feelings of insecurity, passivity and fatalism if their contracts were not renewed. Marie saw her raised hopes as her own problem.

It does affect you but it is only yourself getting your hopes up. There is no one else to blame. (Marie, teacher, County)

Sandra saw her temporary state as ongoing and again her own individual problem:

I did hope that I would be taken on full-time... That's our situation. It's not anybody's fault. (Sandra, teacher, County)

Fiona saw insecurity in fatalistic terms:

I have got to be prepared at anytime to say 'well this is it'... no I feel no security in this school. (Fiona, teacher, City)

The most striking aspect of these comments is the self-blame that accompanies them. The failure to get a contract renewed was often experienced as rejection and a number of workers expressed the impact this had made on their confidence levels:

You have always got it hanging over your head. What am I going to tell my next employer – that I didn't get my contract renewed. What does that sound like? It sounds like you are no good at your job. (Katy, NQT, City)

Max noted the cumulative impact on his confidence:

... and it has a knock on effect because you can see your own managers covering their backs and using you, then your confidence has gone.

(Max, RSW, City)

Karen had considered the effects of temporary work in depth, and considered its impact was related to traits of character and individual confidence levels:

> It depends on the type of character you are and how strong you are. Because if I hadn't got a contract and they had said 'you weren't up to it' I would have just sat there and thought 'oh you are right'. Because if you are a strong character and you believe in yourself you might fight back. But if you aren't quite as strong or confident you would just believe what they say to you. (Karen, NQT, City)

Pamela had little faith in her ability to secure a permanent position and was additionally worried about the effect this would have on her confidence:

> If I have been doing the job for two years I don't see why I have to go and sit in an interview. Because if I was on a temporary contract and they didn't feel that I was good enough, why didn't they break the contract after three months or whatever? So now I am in a position where I have done two years and they want me to sit through an interview and, with all these things, they may not give it to you at that point. And then you think how do you move after that. (Pamela, RSW, City)

One paradoxical finding of this research is that temporary teachers often had their confidence boosted after going through a successful OFSTED (Office for Standards in Education) inspection. The temporary teachers who had gone through an OFSTED inspection had expressed how this had given them the confidence to challenge the implicit and sometimes explicit assumption that they were not worthy of permanent status and were in many respects still 'on approval'.

Training

The above analysis has identified a number of ways in which the nature of temporary work had affected not only the personal aspects of the lives of the workers involved, but also their work performance. One of the issues that concerned temporary workers considerably was the lack of or inequality in training provision. This is particularly interesting because government arguments in support of labour market flexibility stress the importance of a highly skilled workforce. The experience of temporary workers stands in stark contrast to the rhetoric. When managers were asked about access to training provision for temporary workers, the overwhelming response was positive. However all except one of the workers interviewed considered that their training was inferior compared to their permanent counterparts.

The NQTs were divided about training reflecting a disparity in the attitudes and practice of school managers. Two NQTs said that they had been given the statutorily required non-contact time for NQTs to allow some 'self-motivated' training. Another, Samantha, felt that she, as a NQT, had been given priority for training both in the provision of non-contact hours and also for external courses. However, Mr Dep who, up until this issue was raised had been very positive about his school managers, described his disappointment with the training which had been supplied:

> We have staff training. We meet at half term or full term and just talk about the normal things, not about what is happening in the classroom or anything like that. Just general – you couldn't discuss it in a training sense. It is a meeting, you can't say it is a training session. We meet and just share about very basic problems, which is helpful, everything is helpful, but it isn't enough to develop myself as a teacher. (Mr Dep, instructor, City)

Katy identified a similar situation in her school and also added that cost was the influencing factor behind poor training provision:

> We are supposed to have training as NQTs but because there are six of us out of twelve staff that work there, what she [head teacher] did is that we had a two and a half hour staff meeting after school that was classed as NQT training, for the simple reason that she didn't want to have to pay for supply and our wages. She just wasn't going to do it and that is how she got around it. So we had two and a half hours after school. (Katy, NQT, City)

The issue of costs and how this was now a prime concern for unit managers in social services and school managers in education were raised by a number of the workers interviewed. A few also raised the issue of how this had particularly influenced the reluctance of managers to provide training for what was seen as a transient and 'common' resource. Sandra had not had any training in her eight years of temporary work even though, paradoxically, her temporary work had been largely at the same school.

> I didn't do any courses because it wasn't looked upon as an investment because I was only temporary. (Sandra, teacher, County)

Similarly, in relation to social services in City, Max noted the elements of managerial control related to the issue of training:

> I suppose managers look at it as well you are a casual member of staff and you don't have an input into one particular unit so therefore money wise they don't want to have the expense of training casual members of staff when they know that that resource is going to be all over [City] ... You will find that the type of training that casuals get is very basic like instruction in restraint and basic first aid courses ... There is somebody up there, some 'fat controller' looking down and thinking 'why should we spend

x amount of pounds on training casuals when they don't stay in one particular place.' It saves money and everybody has got the idea that they have to save, save, save. (Max, RSW, City)

Pamela, who also worked for City social services, noted the same issues of arbitrary control and the inequality of training provision. As a result, Pamela felt that she had not even been provided with the basic form of training for her work:

> ...I think they say you have the same rights as other workers but you find that when they have got training or whatever because they say when the training comes up 'well you are only here for three months' and you don't seem to get the priority of the training like the permanent staff. And it is up to the managers whether you can go on this training. I have never been on training since I have been here. Not even first aid. I had to go and do first aid myself. (Pamela, RSW, City)

Two of the workers noted organisational problems in relation to training for temporary workers. The limited time horizons for planning experienced by temporary workers have already been noted and Marie felt that temporary staff missed out on many of the training courses because they had to be booked quite far in advance. Marie added that even if the courses were offered to temporary workers it might be impractical for them to commit themselves when they had very little confidence in what the future may hold.

Max noted that the nature of one form of training in social services, termed supervision, militated against genuine input by temporary workers. Supervision is a form of training that requires workers to discuss with their line manager any difficulties they have experienced in their work with a view to initiating some joint problem solving exercises. In practice, supervision sessions take on an almost confessional context. Max felt that the vulnerable position of temporary staff prevented them from adequately identifying any shortcomings for fear this may lead to the non-renewal of their contract:

> Ok, everyone makes mistakes but most minor problems and most minor mistakes that you make, you can discuss it in supervision. But when you are on a temporary contract you are not really given that opportunity.
> (Max, RSW, City)

Two of the temporary workers also expressed the view that the lack of training had impacted upon their work. Mr Dep complained that his classes were so short and fragmented that he was not given the opportunity to build up his skills through experience. Pamela also noted a lack of training and linked it to the way in which temporary workers were prevented from progressing:

> Without training we [temporary workers] will always be in this position. And then you get them [managers] saying 'such and such should have followed this and that procedure'. But my argument is that if we are not getting the training – they want us to function in certain ways, but if our minds are not opened to certain things, whatever, then we are not going to do it. And that means the kids [children in care] are not getting it are they. Its alright for the managers knowing all the stuff and coming out of the office and saying well you should have done this and that when nobody is giving us the training. So when the managers move out and do their thing in the office, they are still leaving us. And we can do it if we are given the skills to cope with the situation … but only certain people get the training. (Pamela, RSW, City)

Overall, the opportunity for training and related staff development was limited for temporary workers, which impacted on their ability to shift from temporary to permanent status. Temporary workers also raised major concerns about the quality of the service they were providing as a result of insufficient training.

Relationships between temporary and permanent workers

In social services the divisions between temporary and permanent workers seemed to manifest itself largely in the way duties and resources were allocated. Max thought this was particularly noticeable when he had worked on a casual contract and considered this was related to the continual 'new kid on the block' status of casual staff:

> I mean take for instance if you are a casual worker and you go to a building for the first time. It's a new, different group dynamic. Different kids, different atmosphere, different feel, different ethos. Because you don't know the place you have to seek somebody to go round with or you are going to have to link up with somebody for them to show you the ropes. Now some full-time staff look at it as a power thing and they look down at temporary staff and they get them to do the menial jobs and keep them suppressed. Whereas if I work anywhere in the city I want to find out the group dynamic and get on with the job and I don't see why people have to look down on me just because I am a casual member of staff. I have my part to play within the staff group and I have my part to play with the care of the young people. (Max, RSW, City)

Max also related how this had serious implications for certain aspects of his job:

> Some of the kids will know that you are on a temporary contract because members of staff have let it be known so that you become a target. The kids know that you are on a temporary contract so they will make allegations very, very easily. And then because they have made allegations and social services like to deal with it quickly, you will find that they will suspend you at the drop of a hat which doesn't do you any good because once you are suspended its on your record whether it is proven true or not. So you have got that for the rest of your life. (Ibid.)

Following a number of highly publicised cases of child abuse, residential child-care managers and staff were aware of the extremely sensitive nature of these issues. This is an issue that also has some resonance with the exclusion of temporary workers from grievance and disciplinary procedures (Conley, 2003). Max's comments raise the possibility that temporary contracts provide ease of dismissal with the minimum of investigation should allegations be made.

The teachers also noted clear divisions in day-to-day interactions between permanent staff and supply and agency teachers:

> In the staff room you were told not to sit in that chair and things like that. It was a bit pathetic really. (Marie, NQT, County)

Marie said that she disliked supply work because she had never had a chance to feel 'part of the team' and had very little contact with the permanent members of staff. In a similar way to Max, Marie particularly disliked the 'nerve wracking' experience of not knowing what the situation she was about to enter would be. She related this to a constant reliving of the horrible first day of a new job 'when you don't know anything or anybody'.

Resentment between temporary and permanent workers was also raised when temporary teachers were covering for maternity leave. This was partly related to the hope on the temporary teacher's behalf that the worker on maternity leave would choose not to return and therefore open the possibility of a permanent position. However it was also clear in relation to teaching staff that the allocation of holiday pay for the long summer break was a source of friction. Both Marie and Sandra were temporary teachers covering for maternity leave and both were facing a summer without holiday pay because the teachers they were replacing were returning from maternity leave early to ensure they continued to receive pay over the summer. This was not surprisingly the source of much indignation. First for Sandra:

> So she got her holiday money and I didn't, although I was coming back in September to do another temporary contract. But I got nothing for the holidays. (Sandra, teacher, County)

And also for Marie:

> It's not fair really – especially when you know they are coming back early.
>
> (Marie, NQT, County)

Strained relationships between permanent and temporary staff did not always occur and there were indications that some permanent workers were supportive of temporary staff and sympathetic to their situation. In a residential children's home in City the permanent member of staff who greeted me on arrival to interview Pamela about her temporary contract, told me in quite forceful terms that she thought it was about time Pamela's contract was sorted out and that she considered the way that Pamela had been treated by the council was disgraceful. This seemed particularly impressive when I later found out that she thought I was an official from the personnel department!

In County a newly recruited Unison shop steward said that she had taken up the post because temporary workers in her department had a number of questions about LGR (Local Government Reorganisation) and the future of their jobs. She said she was persuaded to become a shop steward because she considered that temporary workers obviously needed someone in a less vulnerable position to raise issues on their behalf. Similarly Karen, a NQT who had secured a permanent contract, arranged a number of interviews with temporary teachers for this research because she considered it was an issue that needed examination.

Competition between temporary workers

Competition between temporary workers seemed to be a particular issue for NQTs. All the NQTs interviewed expressed this view and considered head teachers had particularly fostered competition as a method of gaining extra work and to keep temporary teachers feeling insecure. One clear example occurred in relation to reception class teachers. In County there is an authority-wide policy of admitting infants in the term in which their fifth birthday falls. This is done essentially to save costs for the LEA as it means there are three 'reception' intakes each school year and money does not have to be allocated to the school until the term that children are admitted. As a result, a reception teacher is usually employed on a temporary basis at the beginning of each term to cover each new intake. Therefore, by the end of the year, there are three reception teachers but there will only be one reception class in the September of the new school year. A difficult situation ensues for head teachers and the teachers involved, as it is clear that only one of the three teachers will be taken on for the following year as the routine rolls over. Ray was a NQT in County and, because he taught reception children, had fallen foul of the multiple intake procedures:

> The problem with my job is that at the end of the academic year there is always going to be one extra teacher because of the way they stagger the reception classes … and I don't know how they are going to resolve that.
> (Ray, NQT, County)

Ray explained how this inevitably led to a great deal of competition between the teachers involved. However a forthcoming OFSTED inspection had again paradoxically provided Ray with a glimmer of hope. He explained how, to avoid OFSTED, three teachers from his school had left to take up positions in other schools. This exodus had created a number of vacant positions in the school, one of which he hoped to secure.[3] The threat of job loss for temporary teachers outweighed the dread of OFSTED bemoaned by their permanent colleagues. The rather perverse result was that the possibility of permanent jobs reduced the need for the temporary teachers to compete with each other.

Katy, on the other hand, described how her head teacher had replaced six out of twelve teachers in her school with temporary NQTs. Katy explained that the head had made it clear that only four of the six NQTs would be kept on:

> She [head teacher] has made us feel very insecure about our jobs. We were told just before Christmas that it would be a good idea to apply to the pool [LEA supply list] again because she didn't know if she could keep us on, and that some of us might have to go. Which obviously leads to competition between the teachers … my classroom has got to look better than [that of other temporary teachers]. My books have to look better than theirs, I have got to be in before them and go home after them.
> (Katy, NQT, City)

However one development was that the temporary teachers in Katy's school had now begun to talk amongst themselves about their situation and possible ways in which they could resist the pressure to compete. Katy felt the discussions had been tentative, but it was clear that anger was now at least building against school management rather than being directed at other teachers.

Conclusions

The above analysis has identified that temporary work and job insecurity in the public services is a multifaceted experience, which is not captured by generalisations drawn from aggregated statistical data. Experiences were wide-ranging but largely negative, characterised by financial and psychological insecurity, lack of training, under-utilised skills, damaged confidence and discrimination. Financial insecurity and an inability to plan for the future, both on a personal and professional level, arose as a major issue for temporary workers. The vulnerability created by insecurity and fostered by the management of temporary workers is identified as a powerful deterrent from confronting employers and managers. Similarly the powerlessness engendered by the inability to positively affect their circumstances had an adverse impact on the psychological well-being of temporary workers. Depression, marital tensions and fatalism were key complaints voiced by the workers interviewed. It was also clear that the 'carrot and stick' approach to managing temporary workers was instrumental in raising hopes only to severely damage confidence when these were dashed following the non-renewal of a contract. One important outcome of reduced confidence levels was the self-blame and passivity this elicited from temporary workers.

The experience of temporary work from the workers' qualitative perspective stands in stark contrast to Robinson's vision of the 'typical temporary worker' as 'much more likely to be a well-paid professional, employed on a fixed-term contract within the public sector' (1999: 89) gained from secondary analysis of statistical data. Instead the analysis in this chapter reflects what Rosenberg and Lapidus call the 'dark side of labour flexibility' (1999: 62). Temporary workers' experience of exclusion from training provision particularly belies the political rhetoric that links flexibility to a highly skilled labour force. Despite their inferior treatment temporary workers were committed to their jobs but were concerned about the quality of the service they were able to provide. Furthermore, the women interviewed were not content with the job insecurity they faced as a result of their temporary status but rather their vulnerability deterred them from voicing their discontent to their employers or union.

Amazingly the temporary workers in this study came from areas of public service facing acute skills shortages. Discontented workers who lack a voice are likely to 'exit' an organisation (Freeman, 1980) and considerable numbers of temporary NQTs and social care staff leave before the completion of their contract (Conley, 2000). Any benefits gained by numerical flexibility must therefore be offset against the costs of staff turnover facilitated by the use of temporary contracts.

Temporary workers clearly have a lot to be agitated about and they were vocal in their dissent when provided a 'safe' environment to unload their concerns. However what is missing from the above analysis are any indications of organised resistance. This chapter highlights that individually temporary workers are extremely vulnerable. The corollary is that more than most workers they need the collective support of their trade unions. Their un-organised discontent also offers opportunities for trade union renewal (Fairbrother, 1991, 1994a, b, 1996). How far this is converted into a collective voice depends on the ability of the public sector trade unions to recognise and grasp the opportunity.

Acknowledgements

The research was funded by the Economic and Social Research Council (Award Number R0042963455).

Notes

1. Kamal Ahmed and Oliver Morgan, 'Firefighters face severe job cuts', *Observer*, 15 December 2003. Niall Dickson, BBC News, 'Modernisation fans flames of dispute', 26 November 2002.
2. The provision of financial services by employment agencies raises serious issues concerning conflicts of interest. Marie's experience highlights some of these dangers for temporary workers. The NUT (National Union of Teachers) has noted similar concerns and is investigating related complaints by some of their members.
3. Ray had secured a permanent position when I followed up his case twelve months after our meeting. At that time he was the only worker I interviewed who had succeeded in securing a permanent position.

References

Allen, J. and Henry, N. (1997) 'Ulrich Beck's Risk Society at work: labour and employment in the contract service industries'. *Transactions of the Institute of British Geographers* (22): 180–96.

Atkinson, J. (1984) 'Manpower strategies for flexible organisations'. *Personnel Management* August: 26–9.

Atkinson, J. (1985) *Flexibility, Uncertainty and Manpower Management*, Brighton: Institute of Manpower Studies.

Atkinson, J. and Meager, N. (1986) *New Forms of Work Organisation*, Brighton: Institute of Manpower Studies.

Bach, S. (1999) 'Europe: Changing Public Service Employment Relations', in Bach, S., Bordogna, L., Della Rocca, G. and Winchest, D. (eds) *Public Service Employment Relations in Europe: Transformation, Modernisation or Inertia?*, London: Routledge.

Beechey, V. and Perkins, T. (1987) *A Matter of Hours: Women, Part-time Work and the Labour Market*, Cambridge: Polity Press.

Casey, B., Metcalf, H. and Millward, N. (1997) *Employers' Use of Flexible Labour*, London: Policy Studies Institute.

Conley, H. (2000) Temporary labour in the public sector: employers' policies and trades union responses in social services and schools, unpublished PhD thesis, Department of Sociology, Warwick University.

Conley, H. (2002) 'A state of insecurity: temporary work in the public services'. *Work, Employment and Society* 16 (4): 725–37.

Conley, H. (2003) 'Temporary work in the public services: implications for equal opportunities'. *Gender, Work and Organizations*, 10 (4): 455–77.

Dex, S. and McCulloch, A. (1995) *Flexible Employment in Britain: A Statistical Analysis*, Manchester: Equal Opportunities Commission.

Elliott, L. and Atkinson, D. (1998) *The Age of Insecurity*, London: Verso.

Escott, K. and Whitfield, D. (1995) *The Gender Impact of CCT in Local Government.* Manchester: Equal Opportunities Commission.

Fairbrother, P. (1991) 'In a state of change: Flexibility in the civil service', in Pollert, A. (ed.) *Farewell to Flexibility?*, Oxford: Blackwell.

Fairbrother, P. (1994a) *Politics and the State as Employer*, London: Mansell.

Fairbrother, P. (1994b) 'Privatisation and local trade unionism'. *Work, Employment and Society* 8 (3): 339–56.

Fairbrother, P. (1996) 'Workplace trade unionism in the state sector', in Ackers, P., Smith, C. and Smith, P. (eds) *The New Workplace and Trade Unionism. Critical Perspectives on Work and Organisation*, London: Routledge.

Felstead, A. and Jewson, N. (1999) 'Flexible labour and non-standard employment', in Felstead, A. and Jewson, N. *Global Trends in Flexible Labour*, Basingstoke: Macmillan.

Freeman, R. B. (1980) 'The exit voice trade-off in the labour market: unionism, job tenure, quits and separations. *Quarterly Journal of Economics* 94 (4): 643–73.

Gallie, D., White, M., Cheng, Y. and Tomlinson, M. (1998) *Restructuring The Employment Relationship*, Oxford: Clarendon Press.

Hakim, C. (1991) 'Grateful slaves and self-made women: fact and fantasy in women's work orientations', *European Sociological Review* 7 (2): 101–21.

Halford, S., Savage, M. and Witz, A. (1997) *Gender Careers and Organisations*, Basingstoke: Macmillan Press Ltd.

Heery, E. and Salmon, J. (eds) (2000) *The Insecure Workforce*. London: Routledge.

LGMB (1998) *Flexible Working: Working Patterns in Local Authorities and the Wider Economy*, London: Local Government Management Board.

Pollert, A. (1988a) 'Dismantling flexibility'. *Capital and Class*, 34 (Spring): 42–75.

Pollert, A. (1988b) 'The flexible firm: Fixation or fact?' *Work, Employment and Society* 2 (3): 281–316.

Pollert, A. (ed.) (1991) *Farewell to Flexibility?* Oxford: Blackwell.

Proctor, S. J., Rowlinson, M., McArdle, L., Hassard, J. and Forrester, P. (1994) 'Flexibility, politics and strategy: in defence of the flexible firm'. *Work, Employment and Society* 8 (2).

Robinson, P. (1999) 'Explaining the relationship between flexible employment and labour market regulation', in Felstead, A. and Jewson, N. (eds) *Global Trends in Flexible Labour*, London: Macmillan.

Robinson, P. (2000) 'Insecurity and the flexible workforce: measuring the ill-defined', in Heery, E. and Salmon, J. (ed) *The Insecure Workforce*, London: Routledge.

Rosenberg, S. and Lapidus, J. (1999) 'Contingent and non-standard work in the united States: towards a more poorly compensated, insecure workforce', in Felstead, A. and Jewson, N. (eds) *Global Trends in Flexible Labour*, London: Macmillan.

7

Perceptions of Job Insecurity in a Retail Sector Organisation

Nickie Charles, Emma James and Paul Ransome

The alleged increase in job insecurity in the last decades of the twentieth century has been associated with processes of globalisation, de-regulation of labour markets, increases in unemployment and inequalities, and the proliferation of variously termed – atypical, flexible, non-standard and contingent – forms of employment. This contrasts with the full-time, permanent, secure employment which was characteristic of western industrial societies in the aftermath of the Second World War: a period of expansion and stability which came to an end with the oil crisis of the early 1970s (Felstead and Jewson, 1999: 3). The growth of non-standard employment (to follow Felstead and Jewson's terminology) is significant globally, but in the British context there are three important points to make. The first is that full-time, permanent employment was never the experience of the whole workforce. In Felstead and Jewson's words it was typically 'white, male and middle-class' and associated also with certain sectors of the working class where trade union organisation was strong, such as skilled workers in the printing industry, and in manufacturing and heavy industry more generally (see for example Cockburn, 1983; Felstead and Jewson, 1999: 7). The second is that the increase in women's employment since the Second World War has, until relatively recently, largely been in part-time work (Hakim, 1995) – usually regarded as a non-standard form of employment (although see for example, Purcell, 2000: 120). And the third is that women with dependent children, young workers, workers approaching retirement, and ethnic minority workers are over-represented in non-standard employment with the exception of self-employment where men predominate (Felstead and Jewson, 1999: 6). Thus the division between 'standard employment' – full-time, permanent 'jobs for life' – and other forms of employment, in addition to being a class and racialised division, has historically been gendered: standard employment being associated with men and non-standard employment with women (Dex and McCulloch, 1995).

It is often assumed that job insecurity and non-standard employment are linked, both conceptually and empirically (see for example Rosenberg and

Lapidus, 1999). One of the sectors which has been a pioneer in experimenting with 'atypical' or non-standard forms of employment and which employs large numbers of women is the retail sector (Glucksmann, 1995; Felstead and Jewson, 1999). Indeed, it has been argued that, in retail, flexibility for employers has been bought at the expense of employees' job security and that it involves not only flexibility in working hours but also 'flexibility of function' or multi-skilling (Neathey and Hurstfield, 1996; Glucksmann, 1998). However the evidence linking job insecurity with non-standard forms of employment is inconclusive. Thus recent research into part-time employment in banking (Walsh, 1999), together with improvements in the rights of part-time workers in Britain, suggest that part-time employment and job insecurity are not necessarily linked. It is alleged that the retail sector has been under-researched and under-theorised by sociologists and this can partly be explained by its association with a largely female workforce (Glucksmann, 1995). However it is precisely this association, together with the widespread use of non-standard forms of employment in retail, that makes it important for any study of the association between gender, job insecurity and non-standard forms of employment.

It is also important to explore the link between the gendering of standard and non-standard forms of employment and gendered divisions of labour within the domestic sphere. Domestic divisions of labour were relatively stable in the inter- and immediate post-war years when the male breadwinner family had its heyday (Seccombe, 1993: 207) and full-time, permanent (male) employment was the norm. However the boundaries of paid and unpaid work and their gendering are subject to transformation and change (Glucksmann, 1995,[1] 2000; Brenner and Laslett, 1991). Miriam Glucksmann has developed the concept Total Social Organisation of Labour (TSOL) in an attempt to capture such change, arguing that it is a 'conceptual framework and an approach to analysis' which enables us to distinguish 'the differing connections between paid employment and household labour for particular people, occupational groups, and local labour markets' (Glucksmann, 2000: 20). Indeed, low pay and the extension of part-time hours, both of which are widespread in the retail sector, mean that many retail workers do not earn a living wage (Glucksmann, 1998). This distinguishes them from most (male) workers in manufacturing production and heavy industry in the years before and after the Second World War. This may have implications for the 'connections between paid employment and household labour' and raises the question of whether globalisation and the proliferation of non-standard forms of employment can be seen as a transformation of the gendered distribution of labour between paid and unpaid work in a way analogous to the transformations set in train by 'the mass production of goods for domestic consumption' (Glucksmann, 1990: 266, 1995).

In this chapter we present some findings from our research into the gender dimensions of job insecurity in a specific travel-to-work area in South

Wales. Although our study included three different sectors of employment, manufacturing, the public sector and the retail sector, our focus here is on the retail sector. We begin with a description of the study and the sample; we then look at the structure and culture of our retail organisation before exploring our interviewees' responses to a set of questions on the security, or otherwise, of their current employment. Finally we discuss whether or not our evidence lends support to the idea that globalisation and non-standard employment are associated with a newly emerging TSOL. Our aim is to contribute to the debate about the association of non-standard forms of employment with job insecurity and whether its proliferation is leading to changes in the gendered distribution of paid and unpaid work.

The study

Our research explored the extent to which gender affected women's and men's experiences of job insecurity. We wanted to investigate whether the assumption – apparent in policy statements (Social Justice, 1994) and in some sociological research – that job insecurity was more of a problem for men than for women actually reflected women's and men's experiences and, if so, how it fitted into the other dimensions of their lives, both in terms of domestic divisions of labour and their identities as workers, women/men, wives/husbands, mothers/fathers. We explored these connections through in-depth interviews with 111 employees in three large organisations. Once we had negotiated access, we sent out letters to all the employees in each organisation asking whether they would be willing to participate in research on the experience of work. In each organisation the sample was selected from those who responded so that it included women and men of different ages, working on different types of contract and with different hours of work and represented the range of jobs, occupations and positions in the hierarchy within each organisation. The interviews took place at the place of work (with one exception) and were tape-recorded and transcribed. The age and gender breakdown of the sample is shown in Table 7.1.

As we can see, we interviewed a roughly equal number of women and men in each organisation and, in the sample as a whole, they are evenly spread across the age range except for the youngest and the oldest (under 20 and over 60). In the retail organisation, however, hereinafter, BigShop, the age distribution is lopsided with more men than women being in the younger age groups and more women than men being in the older age groups. This means that age is likely to be as, if not more, important than gender in explaining any observable differences between women and men.

Table 7.2 shows the distribution of the sample between full and part-time employment and type of contract.

Table 7.1 Distribution of samples by gender and age

Age	Public sector BureauGen		Retail sector BigShop		Manufacturing sector Make-a-Lot		All
	Male	Female	Male	Female	Male	Female	
16–19	0	1	3	0	0	0	4
20–29	3	4	6	2	1	1	17
30–39	5	5	6	4	8	5	33
40–49	5	4	1	7	7	9	33
50–59	5	5	1	4	4	2	21
60–69	1	1	0	1	0	0	3
Subtotal	19	20	17	18	20	17	—
Total	39		35		37		111

Table 7.2 Distribution of samples by hours of work and type of contract

	Female				Male				Total
	Full-time		Part-time		Full-time		Part-time		
	Perm	Temp	Perm	Temp	Perm	Temp	Perm	Temp	
BureauGen	13	3	4	0	12	4	3	0	39
BigShop	8	0	10	0	9	0	8	0	35
Make-a-Lot	17	0	0	0	18	2	0	0	37
Total	38	3	14	0	39	6	11	0	111

In BigShop there was no one employed on a temporary contract (this was company policy) but 18 of the 35 interviewed were working part time. Six of the part-timers worked less than 16 hours a week (three men and three women); four of these were students and one was a pensioner. The male and female part-timers had different characteristics which reflects the age difference noted above. All but two of the male part-timers were either students and/or living in the parental home. In contrast only one of the female part-timers lived in the parental home, the others either lived with their partner and dependent children (seven) or their children had left home and they were now living with their partner (two). Only five of the men working at BigShop had dependent children compared with 13 of the women.

Many of our respondents had been working for BigShop for considerable lengths of time. Thus 21 (60 per cent) had been employed for five years or more and 14 (40 per cent) for ten or more years. This can be seen in Table 7.3.

Table 7.3   Length of service with BigShop

Length of service	Male	Female
< 1 year	1	2
1 to < 2 years	2	0
2 to < 5 years	5	4
5 to < 10 years	3	4
10 to < 20 years	3	8
20 years and over	3	0
Total	17	18

Workplace culture and practices

BigShop has several stores in the Swansea travel-to-work area and although we had hoped to carry out all our interviews at one of them this proved to be impossible. In Table 7.4 we show the gender distribution of staff in the three BigShop outlets where we interviewed. As we might expect, men out-number women at the senior levels – there are no women store managers for instance – while women outnumber men at the lower levels: women make up 74 per cent of the workforce overall. Significantly, there are no part-time employees at either manager or senior team level despite the preponderance of part-time employment overall (75 per cent of employees were working part time).

Whilst all three outlets were characterised by a dynamic atmosphere where the hustle and bustle of the retail trade was very much in evidence, they were also distinct, having undergone changes which had affected staff morale in different ways. Outlet one was undergoing restructuring, staff were tense and over-worked and communication was poor; this often led to fric-tion between managers and other workers. In the other two outlets, in con-trast, there was a 'feel good' working atmosphere. Outlet two was the most relaxed and friendly of the stores and there was a camaraderie between man-agers and other employees which was facilitated by its smaller size. This was despite the fact that a new competitor store had just opened nearby which had led to a fall in the number of customers and speculation about the impli-cations for jobs. Outlet three had recently opened, many of its staff had pre-viously worked in an old store and most had undergone interviews and retraining to start new posts.

BigShop deploys various means to instil a sense of commitment and loy-alty amongst its employees which is an important element when consider-ing perceptions of job insecurity. When an employee begins work at BigShop a 'Welcome' pack is issued which introduces new staff to the organisation's policies and working practices. It stresses the premier status of the organisation in relation to its competitors, documenting its pioneering working practices

Table 7.4 Distribution of BigShop employees by employment status*

Position in store	Males			Females			Total Males and Females
	Full-time	Part-time	Total	Full-time	Part-time	Total	
Manager	3	0	3	0	0	0	3
Senior team	11	0	11	6	0	6	17
Section manager	21	0	21	18	3	21	42
General assistants	98	111	209	75	577	652	861
Total	133	111	244	99	580	679	923

Note: * Includes staff from all three outlets.

and success stories. Confirming the place of the company as a market leader implies a secure future for both the company and its employees. A 'team' ethic is promoted and staff are encouraged to contribute to the overall success of the team, hence the organisation. Training and career development are crucial to the promotion of this ethic and are ostensibly available to workers at all levels of the organisation. Staff are given the opportunity to participate in training schemes and the achievements of each individual are taken into account as part of staff development. While training is presented as a positive achievement and as part of an individual's career development, it also serves as a means by which management can assess employees' performance thereby acting as a form of monitoring. These policies are seen as a means of fostering confidence in the security of employment with BigShop and this was reflected in the way our respondents talked about their work.

BigShop was reported as offering secure and highly flexible employment. Several of our respondents were students whose main priority was studying and their paid work had to fit in around this prior commitment, women who had young children to care for and who found BigShop provided the sort of flexibility that they needed, or older workers who had left more demanding jobs and were working part-time in order to supplement a pension and to keep active and involved. This flexibility on the part of the employer engendered high levels of loyalty amongst those who felt that BigShop enabled them to combine paid work with other responsibilities.

> Well I used to be ... on the shop floor filling shelves, enjoyed it. Hard work but I really enjoyed it. With me, because I've got the 2 children, I could only work so many days a week or in school hours.
>
> (022B,F,28yrs,PT)

There were also opportunities for those who wished to take them for training, or 'multi-skilling' and opportunities for promotion. Several of our respondents reported moving between part-time and full-time employment (in both directions) as their circumstances changed and some of the young men were being groomed for management. Part-time hours were seen as incompatible with higher levels of responsibility although some part-time workers had been given more demanding jobs, welcomed the greater responsibility and were hoping to go further.

> At the beginning I just didn't think, I thought I can't cope. It's too much responsibility for me, going home and worrying. Before I'd go home and forget about it. But, no, I am enjoying it now.... Obviously I don't just want to be part time for the rest of my life. I would like to work more hours. (022B,F,28yrs,PT)

In contrast, many were happy with the status quo. One woman told us she was 'quite happy as I am...I don't want more responsibility' (015B,F,52yrs, PT). Another said:

> I'm not looking for promotion. I've got a family. OK they're getting older and that but I'm still quite happy doing what I do. (006B,F,43yrs,PT)

Those in more senior positions were usually working full time, their hours were very long and their pay was not particularly high. However several mentioned that they had caught the 'retail bug' and were highly motivated and committed to their jobs, this was the case even for those who were only one up from the lowest level. One of the women said, 'I'm quite passionate about my work and my job...I'd die if I gave up work'. She went on,

> And I think retail, if you get a bug for retail, it's very hard to come out of it. It does get in your blood...and you just can't leave it.
>
> (021B,F,33yrs,FT)

High levels of commitment and motivation were found at all levels of the workforce, amongst part-time as well as full-time workers, particularly amongst the women. There were some respondents, however, who could not see any future in BigShop and felt alienated from their jobs and the culture of the workplace. For some the only reason they stayed was because they had experienced how difficult it was to find employment and preferred any job to no job. This was particularly the case for some of the young men. Others, again young men, found a mismatch between their gender-identity and the job but were tied into it because of the need for a regular and reliable pay packet.

> I think if I put the effort into it I could get promotion. I don't really want it...I don't really want a career here. I know I should because I've got the

responsibility of a family, I've got kids and need security in my life. But ... I think there's a certain type of person that works in a supermarket, a certain type of person that works in a butchers. Then there are certain types of people then who would rather go out and cut wood up, or smash bricks up, and that's me. (029B,M,25yrs,FT)

There was a clear gender division of labour operating in BigShop as described by one of our respondents.

I work primarily on the checkouts, dealing with customers. Also being male they'll put me out to work outside on trolleys ... [The checkouts are] very female orientated ... In the day I doubt you'll see a man on the check-outs. In the evenings you get the students like myself. In this store I think I know about 5 or 6 maybe men working on the checkouts ... Oh it's very much women, and you'll never be, you'll probably see it if one checkout manager is a male. (033B,M,22yrs,PT)

Moreover it seemed that several of the young men were being groomed for management and were almost expected to be interested in multi-skilling and possible promotion while this was not so obvious amongst the women, many of whom were 'stuck' on checkouts.

Likelihood of job loss

One of our central concerns was to investigate the experiences and perceptions of job insecurity. In order to facilitate comparison with earlier, quantitative, studies we included the questions used in the Social Change and Economic Life Initiative, 1986, and the Skills Survey, 1997 (see Burchell *et al.*, 1998). We asked how respondents perceived the risk of job loss in the next 12 months and how they assessed their prospects in the labour market. As Burchell *et al.*, note, this mobilises a conception of insecurity relating to the risk of unemployment and is a 'narrow conception' of job insecurity (Burchell *et al.*, 1998: 3). We asked the following questions regarding likelihood of job loss:

1. Do you think there is any chance of your losing your job and becoming unemployed in the next 12 months?
2. How would you rate the likelihood of this happening (very likely/ likely/ unlikely)?

The responses to these questions can be seen in Table 7.5 which shows that the majority of our respondents thought that they were unlikely to lose their job in the next 12 months.

These responses mirror the findings of the SCELI study and the Skills Survey (Burchell *et al.*, 1998). As with both the previous studies, the majority

Table 7.5   The job insecurity scale by sex 1986 vs 1997 vs 2000 (%)

Likelihood of job loss	All employed			Employed men			Employed women		
	1986	1997	2000 Retail Bigshop	1986	1997	2000 Retail Bigshop	1986	1997	2000 Retail Bigshop
No chance	80.0	77.1	71.4	77.1	73.7	70.6	84.0	81.4	72.2
Very unlikely	1.3	1.3	20.0	2.0	1.9	23.5	0.3	0.6	16.7
Quite unlikely	3.5	5.2	2.9	4.9	6.8	0	1.7	3.3	5.6
Evens	6.6	9.2	0*	7.3	10.9	0*	5.7	7.2	0*
Quite likely	4.0	3.5	0*	3.9	2.8	0*	4.0	4.2	0*
Very likely	4.6	3.6	5.7	4.8	3.9	5.9	4.3	3.3	5.6

Note: * '0' responses could reflect limited sample size.

N.B.: Only a loose comparison can be made between these results and those found in the Social Change and Economic Life Initiative (1986) and the Skills Survey (1997) due to methodological discrepancies and significantly reduced sample sizes within the Gender Dimensions (2000) sample.

Source: Social Change and Economic Life Initiative (1986) and Retail Bigshop (1997) (In *Burchell et al.*, 1998) and Gender Dimensions of Job Insecurity Interviews (2000) Retail Sector only.

of those interviewed felt confident that their job was *not* under threat. In contrast only two thought that they were likely to lose their jobs while eight were 'unsure' or 'could not say'. On further probing most of those who were unsure decided that they were 'very' or 'quite unlikely' to lose their job in the next 12 months. Thus very few in our sample felt that their job was insecure (in terms of this measure).

Most of our respondents felt secure because of working for this particular organisation where all contracts of employment are permanent and many had been employed for a considerable length of time. They thought that it would take a store closure or an indiscretion on their part to result in their losing their job. Some also said that the company was stable and this meant that there was very little chance that they would lose their job, either in the next 12 months or the foreseeable future. Security arose from the nature of retail and the position of this particular firm. One of the women said:

> As far as I'm concerned retail is a secure industry, people will always want food. Whether they come through the internet, which we've got running in this store, or whether they are actually coming through the door, they will always want food, there'll always be food retail. (021B,F,33yrs,FT)

And one of the men said,

> Within the next twelve months – no. ... I feel secure with this job at the moment. Because of the company. BigShop is a big company and they're

not going to close places down just for the sake of it. There'd have to be a good reason. And they'd probably try and place you somewhere else. No. I feel secure about this job at the moment. (002B,M,39yrs,FT)

Such confidence in the organisation's stability and therefore their own employment security results in part from the policies discussed above. The organisation has instilled in them a sense of security, which is associated with the success of the company in the market place. Potential job losses are therefore not an issue for the majority of the workforce.

However several respondents said that job loss/unemployment was something that they were unsure about and could not rule out. They were concerned about store closure as a result of company redevelopment in the local area and/or direct competition from other retail outlets within the same sector of the market, both of which were seen as a threat to the continuation of their employment. These sentiments were particularly evident amongst respondents in outlets one and two. The recent opening of outlet three in the area meant that respondents were acutely aware of developments, even those internal to the organisation, which could result in changes to their own employment. A respondent working at outlet two said:

Well we've gone really quiet here. Two other stores have said that they were closing. Two BigShop stores. They're building a megastore for a start. And the rumour's going round here that they might close this, amongst the staff. We haven't been told by the management mind. And they might move us up there. Because we've gone down hill since Newstore [direct competition]. (008B,M,38yrs,FT)

Both women and men voiced concerns about this and rumours were rife about possible closure. Others, however, perceived the organisation, and hence their employment, as stable even though individual stores may come and go.

I think they would have to have BigShop around here somewhere. You would get transferred and people would take redundancies people would take voluntary redundancies and you know I think it would, yeah I think it would be okay. (011B,M,22yrs,PT)

Individuals reassured themselves, commenting that only those who wished to go would have to and others would be transferred to other posts. For those who worked at the newest store this had actually been their experience, with many transferring there from an older one that closed down. The organisation had fulfilled its promise of continued employment. There were, however, fears that even though employment would probably continue, hours of work could change and this led to feelings of insecurity and fears that work would not fit so easily with other commitments.

For others insecurity arose from worries concerning personal performance levels. Employees are monitored regarding their development and progress and some of our respondents felt unsure of the tasks required of them and described feelings of inadequacy regarding training and skills. They described the feeling that what they do is under scrutiny.

> If anything goes wrong that something would be said to you … It affects it a lot really. Because of what goes on and if anything as I said about com- munication and all that, everyone would get on better. Then there'd be more security in the job. You'd feel a lot better in yourself. (007B,F,50yrs,PT)

This woman feels that the conduct of other staff has led to conflict between both full-time and part-time staff and also day and night staff, each blam- ing the other for tasks that are not completed. As a part-time member of staff she feels that she does not have everything at her finger tips and that full- time and night staff blame part-time staff for not doing things properly. She does not feel that section managers intervene sufficiently to rectify this sit- uation. These tensions add to her overall feeling of insecurity.

Two of the eight who said that they were unsure about their current posts were employed in management. For them uncertainty was tied to their spe- cific jobs rather than to the possibility of losing their employment. Both sug- gested that loss of their current job was a possibility (though 'unlikely') if they did not maintain targets and current performance levels:

> It's unlikely unless it's because I've failed in myself in delivering what I should be delivering. (013B,M,46yrs,FT)

For this respondent it was important to be seen to be 'achieving' and to build up a reputation so that he was both indispensable and highly valued in rela- tion to others employed in similar posts. This would ensure him a job in other outlets were he to lose his current post. His female counterpart expressed similar concerns:

> As I said it depends on my performance, so it depends on the succession plan. It depends on what my review will be like … Well I'm quite positive. As long as I can achieve my targets. (019B,F,42yrs,FT)

As the responsibilities of the job increase so do the demands for high per- formance and it seems that, for them, levels of insecurity had also increased although it was insecurity about their job or post rather than about their continued employment.

Indeed several of those we spoke to in managerial positions expressed con- cern relating to insecurity and the pressure of their current post even when they were 'sure' that they would not lose their jobs in the next 12 months.

For those in such posts the job is associated with considerable pressure since their own career development is related to the productivity of their department. Section managers monitor stock and sales whilst also maintaining staff development and morale and this increases the pressure of the job. They are also required to move around to gain experience. Many will be in posts for a short time before moving to a new one. They are often required to move not simply between outlets but between localities. It is frequently the case that whilst they have substantial years of service with the organisation they have only been in their current position for a short period of time. Indeed of our respondents in managerial roles, four had been in their current job for a year or less and one respondent had had eleven posts in the last ten years. Although all managerial staff had been employed by BigShop in excess of 12 years, only three had been in their current job for two years or more and this led to feelings of insecurity about whether they would remain in their current post; this type of insecurity, post insecurity, needs to be distinguished from feeling that they might be in danger of losing their employment (see Charles and James, 2003).

The overall picture from our respondents in BigShop is that levels of job and employment security are high which can be linked to the firm's position as a market leader and BigShop's attempts to create an ethos of valuing people. Where worries are expressed about insecurity it is due either to developments among competitors or to personal inadequacies and failings at work or is intrinsic to some of the more senior jobs. Thus while employment was perceived as secure, insecurity could arise from the possibility of being moved to other posts.

Difficulty of re-employment

When considering measures of insecurity, a key aspect is the cost of job loss. Following Burchell *et al.* (1998) we included the following question in relation to job loss:

- If you were looking for work today, how easy or difficult do you think it would be for you to find another job as good as your current one?

As we show in Table 7.6, responses from our respondents in BigShop were similar to those obtained in the SCELI and social skills surveys.

In explaining why they felt it would be easy or difficult to find alternative employment, women were concerned with issues such as age, the availability of part-time work and their family circumstances while men were more concerned with being able to match their current employment package.

Table 7.6   Difficulty of re-employment in 1986 vs 1997 vs 2000 (%)

How easy to get another job as good as current one	All employed			Employed men			Employed women		
	1986	1997	2000* (n = 32) Bigshop	1986	1997	2000 Bigshop	1986	1997	2000 Bigshop
Very easy	4.7	6.9	2 (5.7)	4.9	5.5	1 (5.9)	4.5	8.5	1 (5.6)
Quite easy	16.4	24.2	10 (28.6)	14.9	21.8	6 (35.3)	18.4	27.2	4 (22.2)
Quite difficult	39.1	40.6	12 (34.3)	37.2	39.7	3 (17.6)	41.8	41.8	9 (50.0)
Very difficult	39.8	28.3	8 (22.9)	43.0	33.0	4 (23.5)	35.3	22.6	4 (22.2)

Note: * Percentages do not total 100 as three responses are missing (n=32 but percentage calculated for whole sample of 35).

N.B.: Only a loose comparison can be made between these results and those found in the Social Change and Economic Life Initiative (1986) and the Skills Survey (1997) due to methodological discrepancies and significantly reduced sample sizes within the Gender Dimensions (2000) sample.

Source: Social Change and Economic Life Initiative (1986) and Retail Bigshop (In Burchell *et al.*, 1998) and Gender Dimensions of Job Insecurity Interviews (2000) Retail Sector only.

Thus several of the older women said that age would be a problem if they had to seek other employment.

> It would be more difficult now because of my age. I mean, I have to say that now because once you're past 40, you're classed as old … That's how you're made to feel. (007B,F,50yrs,PT)

These views were also expressed by older men who had experienced the ageism of the local labour market first hand.

> It's only when you are older when you realise you are not wanted, when you are not a commodity, when you are not a saleable asset, because you are 57 you can almost feel that you are on the scrap heap. In this country.
> (028B,M,57yrs,PT)

As well as the problem of age women also referred to their work experience, skills and qualifications as inadequate or inappropriate for the demands of the labour market.

> The way BigShop work here on the payroll, although my title is [name of job], I don't do anything with tax, I don't do any of those things. This store does it in head office. We're just set up here … We don't DO any of those things at the store … no I couldn't get a job in wages. I could get a job at my typing level, as I've just said, it isn't up to much. I would have a great problem. (004B,F,50yrs,FT)

Many of the women expressing these views were employed on part-time, permanent contracts and had worked for BigShop for five years or more. Their skills may have been acquired early on in their employment or even outside the labour market and are not perceived as marketable. This, coupled with the fact that they lack confidence in their own abilities and feel that age is against them, leads them to perceive the external labour market in a negative light.

Childcare responsibilities were also seen as making re-employment more difficult.

> Hopefully it would be easy, but there's like, me having young children. A lot of people, a lot of employers, it puts them off that you've got young children and you can only work certain days ... (022B,F,28yrs,PT)

As we have seen, the flexibility offered by BigShop was valued by women with children as was the convenience. One woman told us:

> I have to work around the children ... the baby suffers with asthma and they are really good here because I phone and say, 'Look the baby is really ill, can I take a couple of days off?' And they are really, really understanding, so I mean if I went for another job then maybe they wouldn't be.
> (020B,F,32yrs,PT)

And another told us:

> I have to work around the children ... the baby suffers with asthma and they are really good here because I phone and say, 'Look the baby is really ill, can I take a couple of days off?' And they are really, really understanding, so I mean if I went for another job then maybe they wouldn't be.
> (020B,F,32yrs,PT)

This flexibility was part of the 'package' offered by BigShop and the value of the package was the other main theme which emerged. The respondents who were students thought it would be difficult to find alternative employment because of the need to match the flexibility that they have in their present employment. One of the young men said that it would be 'very difficult' to get a job like the one he currently has because of,

> The sort of flexibility I get, if I need to come in an hour late or start an hour earlier, as I said, or when I have summers off to go away and work. From the student perspective it would be difficult to find a job that's as good as this and people who are going to be as patient to put up with my needs. (011B,M,22yrs,PT)

Many respondents reported that BigShop recognises that students and mothers of young children have other priorities and allow employees a degree of flexibility in the hours that they work. Security was also mentioned as part of the package.

> I might find a job with similar wages. I don't think the wages I get now, not quite as much, but I don't think I'd have the security I got now.
> (014B,F,46yrs,FT)

In contrast, those who thought that getting alternative employment would be 'quite' or 'very easy' cited the following reasons: experience and confidence in their own ability; qualifications and skills obtained from training/retraining received in their current or past job and their own flexibility. Two of the men said:

> I think it'd be very easy to get a shop job. Because I think a lot of people go for it. (008B,M,38yrs,FT)

> Yes. Because of the skills I've learnt in here. And I've got the experience to be able to do the job anyway. I don't think I want to go to another shop like this. (029B,M,25yrs,FT)

Several women also said they thought that they would find alternative employment relatively easily.

> Well, I don't think it would be too difficult because a lot of people seem to go from stores, you know, from [retail outlet] to [retail outlet], or whatever. So I think a lot of people seem to go from store to store.
> (006B,F,43yrs,PT)

These women were all relatively well qualified, many of them having GCSEs or 'O' levels, and perceived their skills as marketable. In addition, two of them were in management and their attitude towards potential re-employment seemed to have much in common with that of their male counterparts.

Most of those who thought they would find it difficult to get alternative employment shared the fact that they have other calls on their time, such as studying or childcare and family commitments and/or felt that they would face age-related discrimination in the labour market. Perceptions of the marketability of skills and skill levels also affected whether or not respondents felt that they would be able to find alternative employment.

Perceptions of job security

Thus far we have focused on a 'narrow' conception of job insecurity, exploring respondents' perceptions of their vulnerability to job loss and how easy it would be for them to find alternative jobs. Neither of these questions asked respondents to reflect on the security, or otherwise, of their jobs. A broader conception of job insecurity is invoked by the question about whether respondents thought their jobs were secure or insecure. This asks directly about perceptions of job security. In the sample as a whole a majority (83 per cent) thought their jobs were secure or very secure. There was a small gender difference with 78 per cent of men thinking their jobs were secure or very secure compared with 89 per cent of women. The distribution of responses in BigShop can be seen in Table 7.7.

As we can see, the majority of our respondents in BigShop felt their job was secure with only two feeling insecure. However responses to this question, and the others relating to insecurity, have to be seen in the context of the other interview material associated with job insecurity which paints a slightly different picture. In order to gauge the extent of job insecurity each case was classified on a three-point scale (high/medium/low) using as a basis for this an interpretation not only of responses to the three questions specifically on job insecurity but all the interview material. If this is done we find that none among men and 11 women scored high on one or more measure of insecurity while a further five men and six women scored medium. Thus the extent of insecurity, particularly labour market insecurity, is higher than suggested by responses to the questions discussed thus far. However, only six women and seven men (37 per cent of our respondents) scored medium or

Table 7.7 Job security or insecurity by gender

Would you say your job was secure or insecure?	Total employed	Male employed	Female employed
Insecure	2	1	1
	(5.7)	(5.9)	(5.6)
Quite secure	3	3	0
	(8.6)	(17.6)	
Secure	28	12	16
	(80.0)	(70.6)	(88.8)
Very secure	2	1	1
	(5.7)	(5.9)	(5.6)
Total	35	17	18
	(100)	(100)	(100)

Notes: '0' responses could reflect limited sample size. % Figures in brackets.

high on post or employer insecurity which is a measure of the levels of security most of them felt in their current employment.

High levels of security affected the way respondents felt about their jobs with both women and men linking motivation at work, commitment to their job and employer and their ability to do the job properly to levels of job security. Many respondents spoke of the way security at work reinforces commitment and of being prepared to do more if they feel secure. One of the older men said that because he felt secure in the job,

> I feel a loyalty towards the company. I feel that I want to learn, I've asked for more training for example, on the staff reception ... Yes, it does provide a certain motivation. A sense of wellbeing and belonging, which are healthy factors. (028B,M,57yrs,PT)

A few, however, considered that security might lead to complacency and, consequently, lack of motivation.

For some, high levels of insecurity on one or more measure was linked to difficulties in meeting the demands of the store for flexibility, both in terms of hours worked and function; those affected were men who had experienced ill health which meant that they could not be as flexible as their managers would have liked.

There is a gender difference in the way all three questions about job insecurity are discussed. Men's responses relate almost entirely to their current job and past experiences of work while women are much more likely to make reference to the experiences of co-workers and partners, their home life and childcare responsibilities. The inclusion of these issues in their responses appears to reflect the frame of reference they use to understand and locate their own experiences of work. One woman, when responding to the question about the possibilities of getting another job said:

> But I still feel the age would be against me now. If I went for another job. [Have you had an experience of other people telling you that, that that's actually happened to them?] No. It's just the way I think. And my husband has had experience of it when he's been looking for a job. [So he's looking for work?] He was. He's not now because he's a full-time househusband so I'm earning now. (003B,F,51yrs,FT)

Another woman talked about her own feelings of security in comparison to her partner's job.

> Much safer obviously. Safe ... I'm quite content really. ... my husband's job, for instance, is dreadful. He works for a small company, and he'll come home on a Friday, and say 'There's not much money in the company' and all this sort of thing. And I think, 'Oh! Off again'. So I'm

quite ... working for such a big company as BigShop, a good company to work for and he's working for a small company and gets the pitfalls. He gets three weeks holidays a year. On the floor now he should get four. That sort of thing. So he's quite envious of me. (004B,F,50yrs,FT)

And another woman discussed the insecurities that can arise when trying to juggle two jobs (hers and her partner's), both of which involve shift work, with childcare arrangements. She has a pre-school age child and is expecting her second but is constrained in the hours she can work by the availability of her child minder and her husband's shift patterns. Because of this she works part-time at a more senior level and feels that this makes her vulnerable.

I'll be back after my maternity leave but the only thing that is hovering over me is the fact that we're going to have a new store soon. And if it does go to the new store, my job won't be there. The ... job will be there, but not a part-time. They'll be loking for a full-time ... My other insecurity is the fact that I'm still worried about my hours ... If he [husband] didn't work shifts it wouldn't matter what hours I worked, I could work anything. (005B,F,32yrs,PT)

Later she says: 'If my childminder could look after my [child] a little bit longer in the afternoon I wouldn't have no fears. I would be OK.' For this woman, the fact that her hours of work are constrained by her husband's shift patterns, together with the availability of her childminder, creates insecurity in so far as she feels she may in future be required to work hours which she is unable to and that if this happened she would have no option but to hand in her notice. Her insecurity therefore stems from the way work and non-work-related factors come together.

These differences suggest that for women, perceptions of job insecurity are linked to the other dimensions of their lives and are not seen solely in terms of paid work as seems to be the case for most of the men we spoke to. Our evidence suggests that men tend to view paid work and consequently job insecurity as discrete and separable from the rest of their lives whereas for women the boundaries are less clearly defined. This could be related to the fact that only six of the men compared with 17 of the women were living with a partner and/or children at the time of interview. When asked directly, however, men readily discuss their home life and its relation to work: it is in relation to the questions specifically on job insecurity that it does not tend to feature in their responses as spontaneously as it does for women.

Changing gender boundaries?

In order to begin to explore whether or not our evidence supports the argument that globalisation and the proliferation of non-standard forms of employment are associated with a transformation in the TSOL, it is important to consider the impact of job insecurity on the distribution of paid employment and unpaid care work between our respondents and their partners. Twenty two of our respondents were living in a heterosexual relationship at the time of interviewing; 18 were living with a partner and children and four were living with a partner. One woman was a lone parent. The six men living with a partner and children defined themselves as the main provider for their family-household. Three of them were sole earners and were the only respondents to live in households which conformed strictly to the male breadwinner–female dependent model of the family. All but one of the men defining themselves as the main breadwinner had young children at home and their partners either worked part time or were not employed. Thus all six men in our sample who were married or cohabiting defined themselves as the main providers.

There was much more variation amongst the women, two of whom defined themselves as the main providers, seven defined their partners as the main providers and seven defined themselves and their partners as equal breadwinners. The two women defining themselves as the main provider were both living with their partner and children. One was the sole provider for her family-household. Three women, including the two who defined themselves as main breadwinners, had consciously adopted role reversal and their partners were either working part-time or not working at all and the fourth had a partner who was not in paid employment. All four of these women were *de facto* the main providers for their families. They were in full-time employment, had children who were either in their teens or had left home and partners whose paid employment was insecure or who had lost their jobs, sometimes through ill health. Thus job insecurity and job loss can lead to significant changes in the distribution of paid and unpaid work between spouses. Role reversal was understood as meaning that spouses took over childcare where needed and undertook more domestic labour.

The six men who were living with partners had been in full-time employment since leaving full-time education with some periods of unemployment, most often in their teens; two had experienced redundancy and one had returned to employment part time after this. And as we have seen, their partners were all either at home full time or in part-time employment. Almost all the women in this sample, including the two who defined themselves as main breadwinners, had taken time out of the workforce when their children were young, returning to part-time and some to full-time employment. Most of their partners had been in full-time employment throughout although three were now not in paid employment and a further four had insecure or casual employment. The only woman to have stayed in full-time employment throughout the period of family formation had become a lone parent soon after her child's birth. This suggests that, although most of our respondents do not live in family-households which rely solely on a male breadwinner, and some cannot rely on a male breadwinner due to insecure employment, to the possibility of unemployment or to low wages, the idea that providing and care work should be equally shared between differently gendered partners is by no means universal. It is rather a modified form of the male breadwinner family which seems to prevail where women move in and out of full- and part-time employment, perhaps taking some time out of the workforce when children are very young and if suitable childcare is not available, while men are expected to remain in full-time employment providing financially for their partners and children (see also Rubery *et al.*, 1996). This certainly seems to be the pattern amongst our retail sample. This can, however, change and men can take on care work in conditions of job insecurity, unemployment or ill health while women adopt the breadwinning role. There is also a suggestion, in our findings, that once the intensive phases of family formation are over, and children are older, there is a shift away from the male provider–female carer division of labour towards a more egalitarian division of labour, at least as far as participation in paid employment is concerned. This may only be the case, however, where men's wages are low and/or their jobs are insecure and women's wages are seen as essential for household survival. Thus although few of our respondents conformed to the male breadwinner–female dependent family, the connections between paid work and domestic and care work were still structured by gendered expectations about the provider and carer roles. And although the wages provided by BigShop cannot be seen as a family wage, several of our respondents, women and men, were relying on it in precisely this way.

Conclusions

The evidence we have presented here suggests that part-time employment, a form of non-standard employment, is not necessarily associated with job insecurity. Levels of security are relatively high amongst both the part-time and full-time workers we interviewed with women being slightly more likely than men to perceive their jobs as secure. Despite this there was a feeling that part-time hours were incompatible with promotion above a certain level and an inability to work full-time in some positions was associated with feelings of insecurity. Labour market insecurity is higher than other forms of insecurity with many of our older respondents linking this to age discrimination within the labour market. The older women in the least skilled jobs were the least confident about being able to find alternative employment, as were those who valued the flexibility provided by BigShop and the advantages of this for fitting in paid work around childcare and/or studying. There was some evidence that flexibility was associated with job insecurity in so far as those who were unable to meet employer demands for flexibility expressed high levels of job insecurity. For most, however, particularly those with child care responsiblities and students, flexibility worked in their favour; it was highly valued and associated with feelings of security. These findings suggest that there is no essential connection between flexibility, non-standard forms of employment (in this case part-time employment) and job insecurity and that much depends on employer policies. Furthermore, employer policies may vary between different categories of worker with those on full-time contracts being expected to be more flexible than those on part-time contracts.

The gender differences we have noted in the way job insecurity is discussed may reflect women's different positioning in social relations of class and gender and their (perhaps clearer) perceptions of the ways in which paid and unpaid work are interdependent. This interdependence is not peculiar to women (although they appear to be more aware of it) and is highlighted in the concept of Total Social Organisation of Labour. Thus despite claims that the male breadwinner is in terminal decline, our evidence shows that women and men continue to organise their labour differently at different stages of their lives and that the demands of paid work and unpaid care and domestic labour have gendered effects. Thus amongst this group of largely working-class respondents, men still expect to take on the provider role and be the main earner while women expect to adapt their paid work around their childcare responsibilities. Job insecurity can affect this gendered division of labour (but not necessarily the expectations) by leading to role reversal with women as the sole breadwinner, or to women claiming that they are the main or equal breadwinners. No men claimed to be equal or ancillary wage earners. The absence of a 'male breadwinner' wage at BigShop makes it difficult for those working there to be the sole providers for their families although some of our respondents were. The wages can rather be seen as suitable for main or ancillary rather than sole wage earners and most of our respondents, men as well as women, were indeed in this position. It seems then that there is some minimal support from this small sample of retail workers for the idea that increasing use of non-standard forms of employment and the decreasing availability of a family wage is associated with changes in the way care work and paid work are distributed between women and men within households in so far as the male breadwinner–female dependent model of the family is not widespread. This evidence is consistent with the argument that globalisation and non-standard forms of employment have modified the ways in which paid employment and, to a lesser extent, care work are distributed between women and men. However unpaid care work remains gendered female and a full-time breadwinner or provider wage gendered male; part-time or non-standard wages tend to be gendered female. There are indications of change in so far as some women take on the breadwinner role and some men earn ancillary wages (in our sample exclusively younger and older men). But these are still seen as exceptions which have not yet altered the normative gendered expectations surrounding different types of paid and unpaid work.

Acknowledgments

The research on which this paper is based was funded by the ESRC as part of its **Future of Work** programme, award number L212252012, and was carried out by Nickie Charles, Emma James and Paul Ransome at the University of Wales Swansea. We would like to thank Chris Harris for his valuable input into the project at critical moments and for his comments on earlier drafts. We also wish to thank all those at BigShop who took part in this research thereby making it possible.

Note

1. According to Glucksmann, this transformation consisted of a shift from 'male labour being allocated to the market and female labour' to both the market and domestic economies 'with a primary allocation to the household and a subsidiary allocation to the wage economy' to a situation where tasks which had previously taken place within the household were commoditised resulting in 'a long-term historical shift of labour out of the household economy and into the wage economy' (Glucksmann, 1995:71).

References

Brenner, J. and Laslett, B. (1991) 'Gender, social reproduction, and women's self-organisation: considering the U.S. welfare state'. *Gender and Society*, 5 (3): 311–33.

Burchell, B., Felstead, A. and Green, F. (1998) 'A growing sense of insecurity in Britain: reality or hype?' Conference paper presented at Work, Employment and Society Conference, University of Cambridge, 14–16 September 1998.

Charles, N. and James, E. (2003) 'The gender dimensions of job insecurity in a local labour market'. *Work, Employment and Society*, 17 (3): 531–552.

Cockburn, C. (1983) *Brothers: Male Domination and Technological Change*, London: Pluto.

Dex, S. and McCulloch, A. (1995) *Flexible employment in Britain: a statistical analysis*, Manchester: Equal Opportunities Commission.

Felstead, A. and Jewson, N. (1999) 'Flexible labour and non-standard employment: an agenda of issues', in Felstead, A. and Jewson, N. (eds) *Global trends in flexible labour*, Macmillan: Basingstoke.

Glucksmann, M. (1990) *Women Assemble: Women Workers and the New Industries in Inter-War Britain*, London: Routledge.

Glucksmann, M. (1995) 'Why "work"? Gender and the "Total social organization of labour"'. *Gender, Work and Organization*, 2 (2): 63–75.

Glucksmann, M. (1998) 'Retailing and shopworkers: filling the gap between production and consumption', paper presented to the WES conference, Cambridge, September.

Glucksmann, M. (2000) *Cottons and Casuals: the Gendered Organisation of Labour in Time and Space*, Durham: Sociologypress.

Hakim, C. (1995) 'Five feminist myths about women's employment'. *British Journal of Sociology*, 46 (3): 429–55.

Neathey, F. and Hurstfield, J. (1996) *Flexibility in Practice: Women's Employment and Pay in Retail and Finance*, Manchester: EOC.

Purcell, K. (2000) 'Gendered employment insecurity?' in Heery, E. and Salmon, J. (eds) *The Insecure Workforce*, 112–39, London: Routledge.

Rosenberg, R. and Lapidus, J. (1999) 'Contingent and non-standard work in the US: towards a more poorly compensated, insecure workfoce', Felstead, A. and Jewson, N. (eds) *Global Trends in Flexible Labour*, Basingstoke: Macmillan.

Rubery, J., Smith, M. and Turner, E. (1996) *Bulletin on Women and Employment in the European Union*, no. 9, Brussels: EOC.

Seccombe, W. (1993) *Weathering the Storm*, London: Verso.

Social Justice (Commission on Social Justice) (1994) *Social Justice: Strategies for National Renewal*, Report of the Commission on Social Justice, London: Vintage.

Walsh, J. (1999) 'Myths and counter-myths: an analysis of part-time employees and their orientations to work and working hours'. *Work, Employment and Society*, 13 (2): 179–203.

8
High Performance Work Systems, Labour Control and the Production Worker[1]

Andy Danford, Mike Richardson, Paul Stewart,
Stephanie Tailby and Martin Upchurch

Introduction

Discussion of partnership at work has given considerable emphasis to formal agreements between trade unions and employers and this also includes a developing assessment of union–management partnership agendas in terms of corporate governance (Oxenbridge and Brown, 2004; Deakin *et al.*, 2004). While our understanding of the importance of these hardly requires stating, and especially in light of the TUCs' well-rehearsed six principles, a significant lacuna is to be found in our understanding of partnership-as-labour-and-work-place process. This is inevitably more difficult to fathom since, in contrast to the scrutiny of formal agreements, analysis of the political economy and sociology of workplace relations requires a broad social and political compass capable of assessing the impact of developing partnership agendas on those actually affected by them. (For our assessments of partnership agendas, drawing on the relationship between formal and informal agreements in four organisations, see, Danford *et al.*, 2004, Tailby *et al.*, 2004; Richardson *et al.*, 2004.) Beyond this there should be the expectation that researchers recognise that there is sociology and historiography to the partnership agendas – partnership agreements *and processes*, cannot be understood if we see them as somehow appearing fully formed as if advocates (and critics) are without historical and political experience. Our overriding intention then has been to give partnership a broader sociological context against which we will be better able to judge the prospects for institutional agreements in our two organisations – *Jetco and Airframes*. (See the section on Methodology.)

This chapter focuses specifically on the employee dimensions of the TUC's core 'win-win' partnership principle (TUC, 2001). That is, in return for improvement to business performance, firms developing partnership relationships are expected to offer their workers real joint decision-making and problem solving and through this greater control over their immediate working environment. This more systematic employee participation constitutes the core of what have come to be known as high performance work systems (HPWS) (Appelbaum *et al.*, 2000; TUC, 2003).

For many writers, the HPWS techniques of team working and problem-solving groups provide the basis for employees 'opportunity to participate' in work decisions (Wood, 1999; Appelbaum *et al.*, 2000; Watson and Rosborough, 2000; Bélanger, J. *et al.*, 2002; Edwards, P. *et al.*, 2002). There is nothing especially novel in the use of these techniques and they have, for some years now, featured in many of the critical labour process debates on 'post-Fordist' work design. What is new, however, is the emphasis that is placed on employee autonomy in the labour process and a more *systematic* mobilization of tacit knowledge and worker discretion. This emphasis has prompted the advocates of HPWS to make much bolder claims for worker empowerment than has been the case hitherto. For example, job design on the high performance factory floor is expected to provide a greater degree of employee autonomy over tasks and methods; employees should be able to share skills and solve problems by drawing on their own experience and that of technical specialists; team working should be self-directed to some extent; and team workers should be given greater responsibility for core processes by their involvement in continuous improvement groups (Cutcher-Gershenfeld *et al.*, 1998; Appelbaum *et al.*, 2000; Bélanger, J. *et al.*, 2002; Buchanan, 2002).

Alternative critical assessments of the impact of teamworking on employees' quality of working life have questioned this empowerment thesis. With a reliance upon primarily case study material this labour process critique has highlighted processes of labour subordination, task enlargement, work intensification and job insecurity (for example, Garrahan and Stewart, 1992; Graham, 1995; Stewart and Garrahan, 1995; Rinehart *et al.*, 1997; Danford, 1998; Delbridge, 1998). However, more recent secondary analysis of the WERS98 data has suggested that a degree of caution may be necessary here, finding that teamworking had very little effect on either patterns of employee discretion or work intensification (Harley, 2001). The same author has also argued that the differentiated experience of employee autonomy is more likely to be a function of the skewed distribution of power in organisational hierarchies (towards management) than the latest innovations in work design (Harley, 1999, 2001; see also Steijn, 2001; Bacon and Blyton, 2003). One reason for these contradictory conclusions may well be the problem of specificity. Many of the critical labour process studies have been based in the 'labour-driven' environments of lean, mass production (such as, auto-motives and consumer electronics). But it may well be the case, and the advocates of HPWS would support this, that teamworking will not necessarily have uniform effects irrespective of sector and product market conditions. Outcomes will be contingent upon a number of factors, such as, the nature of production technology, whether this is small batch or flowline production, the skills base, human resource policies, the nature of industrial relations, and so on (Marchington, 2000; Procter and Mueller, 2000; Geary, 2003). Whilst we would not fully embrace this contingency approach, since surface appearances and apparent endless variety can too easily obscure shared underlying dynamics and exploitative social relations, we would accept that certain workplace conditions might be expected to foster more favourable employee responses to teamworking. For this reason we chose the aerospace sector for our case study research with its core characteristics of low batch production, craft work autonomy and high concentration of skilled labour.

The debates concerning manual worker involvement in continuous improvement initiatives raise additional problems. Of all the techniques in the HPWS portfolio continuous improvement (or kaizen) bears most similarity with Japanese manufacturing practice. In emphasising the scope for enhanced discretion and self-fulfilment by worker involvement in quality improvement teams, and broader interaction with technical specialists, the leading HPWS writers in the US, such as Appelbaum *et al.* (2000) and Osterman (2000), are clearly following the path marked out a decade earlier by their compatriots in the 'Japanization' school. For example, Kenney and Florida (1993) conceptualised Japanese management practice as a form of 'innovation-mediated production', involving new participative practices that integrated the knowledge of design and production workers. In this formulation job enrichment and worker empowerment became the new bywords in an anticipated post-Taylorist factory organisation driven by joint problem-solving. Writing in a similar vein, Adler (1995) argued that blurring boundaries between the design and execution of production tasks through worker participation in kaizen groups raised the prospects for the emergence of a new 'democratic Taylorism' (1995). The incorporation of this participative continuous improvement agenda into the high performance work regime requires careful scrutiny, not least due to the large body of critical work that has questioned its claims. For instance, there is now a great deal of research that has focused on attempts by employers to implement total quality management techniques (TQM). Adopting a 'critical management' perspective many such analysts have defined group problem-solving techniques as the core employee dimension of TQM. They have consistently argued that managerial short-termism, incrementalism and resistance have undermined the potential for employee empowerment (for example, Dawson, 1994; Hill and Wilkinson, 1995). A more profound critique from a critical labour process perspective has contended that although workers might derive satisfaction from problem-solving activity its inevitable subjugation to managerial parameters and dictates is likely to result in worker alienation, and in some cases, work intensification and job instability (Garrahan and Stewart, 1992; Graham, 1993; Rinehart *et al.*, 1997).

This chapter assesses the validity of the optimistic claims of the HPWS writers and the broader implications for notions of partnership at work. We argue that this needs to take into account the structural conditions in which firms operate. Our contention is that the impact of high performance work systems cannot be abstracted from the emergence of what Ackroyd and Procter (1998) have termed the 'new flexible firm'. In this scenario many large British manufacturers are increasingly basing their capital accumulation strategies on new systems of financial control and adopting a financially driven style of management. Multi-tasked labour – rather than multi-skilled – is reorganised into accountable units or cells that both contribute to flexibility and facilitate the calculation of marginal costs. And in contrast to the inherent status divisions between the core and periphery of Atkinson's (1984) flexible firm model, core employees in the new flexible firm forego privileged status and job security as they compete with sub-contract labour and alternative suppliers in production operations that are treated as discrete, dispensable units. Such financial control regimes are able to monitor the performance of business units and indirectly control workers through the threat of rationalisation and downsizing (1998: 171, 176).

Taking each case study organisation in turn we consider different patterns in the organisation of the labour process and skill deployment and the extent to which these have been reconfigured by both teamworking and continuous improvement campaigns. We also assess the evidence for meaningful employee involvement through these techniques. The final section focuses on the politics of production and factors influencing employees' readiness to accept or resist work organisational change in the high performance workplace.

Case studies

The two case study organisations are large design and manufacturing factories operating in the British aerospace industry. Both organisations employed large numbers of skilled production workers along with high concentrations of graduate engineers and other technical workers.

The two case study organisations are given the pseudonyms '*Airframes*' and '*JetCo*'. *Airframes* was responsible for the design and assembly of a particular type of aircraft that can be used for both civil and military purposes. The factory employed 4000 workers comprising 600 managers and supervisors, 1500 production workers (90 per cent skilled) and 1900 graduate, technical and administrative staff. The *JetCo* factory was responsible for the design and production of aero-engines. It employed 4300 workers comprising 1800 production workers (80 per cent skilled) and 2500 managers, graduate engineers, technical and administrative staff. Like many other firms in the British aerospace sector the two factories had been subject to considerable restructuring, organisational downsizing and mass redundancies during the 1990s. These processes were still ongoing at the time of the research.

The data were collected between the spring of 2001 and early 2002. Although the research adopted both questionnaire survey and interview techniques for the collection of data from all occupational groups this chapter draws solely on the interview material with shop floor workers, union representatives and managers. Taped interviews were carried out with 28 senior and line managers, 24 union representatives and 41 production workers (nearly all of whom were skilled). These were divided more or less equally between the two factories. (See Danford *et al.*, 2005, for a detailed account.)

High performance work organisation on the shop floor

A longitudinal survey of UK aerospace companies found that the use of cellular manufacturing, just-in-time (JIT) and kaizen techniques had significantly increased between 1999 and 2002. Moreover, these practices were becoming widespread in the industry: nearly 60 per cent of firms had adopted cellular manufacturing, nearly 50 per cent used JIT production control and nearly 55 per cent used kaizen techniques (Thompson, 2002). It is one measure of the leading position taken by the two case study organisations that they had both adopted all three manufacturing practices. In this section we explore the different patterns of their impact on the labour process, its control and employee autonomy.

Cellular manufacturing: the case of *Airframes*

Apart from spares manufacture, the *Airframes* production areas were physically divided into three main aircraft products. We have given these the pseudonyms *Gannet, Skua* and *Wasp*. The *Gannet* and *Skua* areas adopted broadly similar methods of production control whereas the *Wasp* area was designed effectively as a separate 'greenfield' site within the main site. For ease of analysis we consider this latter production area separately.

Different variants of the *Skua* aircraft had been in production since the early 1970s and of the *Gannet* since the early 1990s. In both cases, the introduction of a form of cellular production was a recent development, just two years before our fieldwork research began in 2001. From the point of view of management, the previous system of production control was characterized by a pattern of 'creative chaos' that eventually delivered aircraft, occasionally on time, but rarely within budget. A typical aircraft went through five separate phases in the production process. Major structural subassemblies, such as the rear fuselage and the cockpit, were delivered to the assembly area by either internal or external suppliers. The first phase of production was to assemble these structures and create the basic shell of the aircraft. The shell then progressed through a systems fit (such as fuel and hydraulics) before moving into an electrical wiring phase. After this, the assembly was fitted with engine and transmission systems. It would also be fitted with external panels and doors before moving on to systems and flight testing. However, this progression was not always achieved via a simple sequential movement. Skilled labour was deployed across these different operations in accordance with the competing demands of contract managers, production superintendents and component availability. If components were scarce in one area, or if a particular external customer was suddenly prioritised then gangs of skilled workers could suddenly find themselves switched to a different aircraft or phase of production. These workers were therefore subject to a specific form of flexibility in that they could be expected to work on any phase of aircraft assembly. One production director summarised these problems in the following graphic terms:

> The work organisation was, which way was the moon? Because the tide went with the tide. If the panic was at the front end then the Ops Managers would shove every fucker up the front end. If it was at the back end of the process then everybody would go to the back end. As a result there was no learning to be had in the whole place because nobody did the same job twice.
>
> ... But I think the best way describing the shop floor world would be, 'everybody else was a wanker'. Tides in, tides out, run up and down the line, no numbers bloody matched, headless chickens all the time, rob from here, rob from there, never recording things, scrub them, I'll pay you to scrub all the asset histories. You had project managers who kept nicking bits as well and giving them to the customer free. And then all of a sudden it's, 'all the assets are gone, why have we never got paid for them?' (Interview, Operations Director, October 2001)

In this context, the introduction of cellular working and lean production control was aimed at securing a greater degree of predictability and cost transparency in the assembly process whilst also recomposing the existing patterns of labour flexibility. Teams of production engineers developed a computerised system of JIT component supply. This allowed both external suppliers and a downsized internal store system to feed parts directly to lineside bins when requested by production operators via a kanban card system. The practice of robbing parts from other production areas was restricted as a result. The tradition of flexible labour deployment was also significantly altered by reconfiguring the five different production phases of the aircraft into formal, discrete cells. Each production cell was responsible for just one phase. A typical cell would comprise a stage manager, a stage supervisor, teamleaders (top-grade fitters who were responsible for the progress of work within their cells as well as carrying out production tasks) and five teams of six skilled operators covering a specific set of assembly tasks across different production shifts. Although the new cell workers could rotate around the different tasks required to complete a phase they would rarely be deployed on alternative work outside of their cell. As a result this change had contradictory repercussions for labour flexibility. Across the complete production cycle, overall flexibility was reduced as the management control regime opted to forgo its right to deploy labour on any assembly task anywhere on the factory floor. However, management gained through the cost reductions associated with the rationalisation of the labour process itself as each production worker took responsibility for a fixed cycle of tasks within a stage. This was an example of the use of teamworking to reshape labour flexibility via a more functionally and spatially focused type of work organisation (Martinez Lucio *et al.*, 2000). The outcome for many production operators was a more *intensive* form of narrow task flexibility. One stage manager described this:

> Now the guys normally only work 3 ops. plus a back up operation. They're continually rotating. They do op.1, op.2, op.3 and then back to op.1 again. So that takes us down the learning curve a lot quicker keeping those guys within the cell. (Interview, *Gannet* Stage Manager, October 2001)

These types of changes did secure 'high performance' outcomes for the supervisors of the production process. For example, between 1999 and 2001, the total build hours required for completion of a *Gannet* aircraft was reduced from 17,000 to 10,000 (the equivalent of 425 operators building an aircraft in one week reduced to 250 operators). Other indicators included reduced hours per assembly stage, reduced lead time, improved labour utilisation and downtime (interview notes). The key question then becomes, to what extent did these changes also generate a mutual gain for the manual workforce in terms of increased participation?

It is important to recognise that most of these production workers emerged from a craft tradition of relative autonomy that historically characterised the labour process in the aerospace industry. The deployment of discretion and tacit knowledge was an integral part of their daily work routines. Indeed, most of the workers we interviewed felt that within the teams they were still able to maintain a degree of autonomy and ability to manage their work themselves. However, many workers also articulated a sense of frustration that both their formal and tacit skills were becoming diminished in the face of production rationalisation and the demands of economies of scale. For example, some complained that the company was devaluing the status of their work by increasingly employing the likes of 'car mechanics' and 'agricultural engineers'. It was felt that although these less skilled workers were quite able to complete the new narrow tasks cycles they were not trained as aircraft fitters and did not have the necessary experience to build a complete aircraft. One aircraft fitter of twenty years experience explained the contrast between the old and new way of working:

> The job's changed quite dramatically from when I first started here. When I first started here it was just coming to the end of the days where you put the aircraft together yourself. There was health and safety, and there were drawings, but there were no build standards as such that were adhered to as they are now ... So without specifications, you were given a bit more political licence. You were fitting in the true sense of the word. You built the aircraft and you got it to work. And one of the key skills of being a fitter was to know what was acceptable and wasn't acceptable. So you thought okay, there's a problem here and I know how to get round it and I'll fix it and I'll carry on, to the point where you'd say no, I'm going to have to see someone about this and get it looked at.
>
> Whereas the line we run now, you don't have any opportunity to do anything but bolting. Whereas previously if something was too short, you'd go up a length and that would be the end of it. But now you can't do that. So in a way your fitting skills have been taken away from you.
>
> (Interview, *Gannet* Aircraft Fitter, November 2001)

Many workers also complained of a lack of involvement in decisions that had a direct impact on the ease with which they could carry out their work tasks. The implementation of JIT production control was a case in point. The predominant view was that although JIT might make some sense in large-batch, standardized mass production environments, it was a mistake to adopt it in the more complex, small-batch production routines of the aerospace sector where the rectification of unforeseen snags and faults is a constant. And it was the accountants, and others who were obsessed with cost control, who were party to this decision – rather than the workers who had to manage its repercussions:

> They keep operating on this just-in-time principle don't they? Personally I don't think it works in the aircraft industry. It might work in the car industry where there's continual production, it might work there, but on an aircraft, not as heavily tooled as a car production line, there's going to be mistakes made and the bits have to scrapped. We're all human at the end of the day and that can cause them problems because they haven't got the bits, they haven't allowed for that bit maybe being scrapped. I don't think the just-in-time principle works. The accountants are running the firm now, so that's it. They decide what's what and we have to go along with it. Accountants obviously aren't human, are they?
>
> (Interview, *Skua* Aircraft Fitter, November 2001)

The third main production area in the *Airframes* factory was devoted to the assembly of a US-designed aircraft, the *Wasp*. The cultural environment in this area was quite different from the rest of the shop floor. The *Wasp* order arose from a licensed production agreement between the UK government, Boeing in the US, and *Airframes*. Between 1999 and 2004 Boeing would deliver nearly 70 partially assembled aircraft to the *Airframes* factory. Most production stages would be completed at this point, the *Airframes* production operators would be responsible for the final stages of power and transmission assembly and systems test. What had been created was, in effect, a 'screw-driver' final assembly operation since most of the skilled work routines had been accomplished in the earlier manufacturing phases in the US. The range of skills required to complete the aircraft assembly was much narrower compared to the *Gannet* and *Skua* areas. Some of the *Wasp* managers we spoke to highlighted the more 'enriching' form of teamworking they had adopted within small teams of, typically six, workers who were now responsible for completing operations on a whole aircraft rather than just for one production stage. However, this obscured the fact that very few production stages had been entrusted to the UK factory.

What was unusual about the *Wasp* area was its creation as a discrete 'greenfield' production site within the confines of the main site. Apart from the modern plant and equipment that were provided its most notable characteristic was that the spatial demarcation of production was also marked by distinctive approach to the control of labour. That is, when management invested in new production facilities it was also seeking 'greenfield' labour and non-industrial worker attitudes. The overall labour requirement was just over sixty operators per shift. The first thirty to be selected were regarded as 'leading operators' who would train the remainder. Management refrained from recruiting from the existing workforce because it required individuals who did not carry the political baggage of union-mediated flexibility and demarcation. Instead, it employed operators who had recently completed military service in aircraft maintenance trades. A *Wasp* manager explained:

> For recruitment I had to go outside which meant I could start with a clean sheet. So whatever I decided to do then was pretty much what I wanted to do. I could forget all the bad traits which you get in any industry, things that have been going for years because it's custom and practice. I think people are like that because it's just an easy way of just following on. So I reviewed the things I didn't like and which way I wanted to go forward. And at the same time we did a roadshow at a large local RAF and naval base where we recruited ex-servicemen ... By this means we had a totally different organisation with a different view. People who didn't come with any baggage from industry, they came from the services with a totally open mind ... It sounds silly but what we actually put in place was a team. The skills were taken for granted because of the cvs, what we looked for was team players.
>
> (Interview, *Wasp* Operations Manager, October 2001)

This ex-military labour, recruited both for its positive attitudes to flexibility and acquiescence to managerial demands, was then sent to the Boeing factory in the US to become further inculcated with the methods of lean manufacturing and empowerment. When these workers returned to the UK they came to embody a new 'micro-corporate culture' that marked out an assumed attitudinal superiority to other more 'backward' production areas in the plant. One visible status marker adopted for this purpose was the requirement for all *Wasp* production operators to wear black overalls (in contrast to the green versions worn by the rest of the manual workforce). The *Wasp* operators came to be known as the 'men in black' much to the annoyance of many other workers in the plant:

> Not only did we make a team but we actually suggested to them that we accepted something which made them stand out, you know to mark them out as a team. So we reviewed all different issues and in the end it was a choice of overalls. We gave them a choice of overalls and they decided black and within days they were known as 'Men in Black'. And now they're known throughout the Board of Directors, outside in the Ministry as well, as the 'Men in Black'. Even in Boeing it's 'Men in Black'. So that give us a truly different team. It somewhat upset a lot of the other players in the factory. (Interview, *Wasp* Operations Manager, October 2001)

Our interviews with some of these ex-military personnel did confirm significantly more positive attitudes to lean manufacturing and teamworking. They also highlighted a willingness to 'go beyond the norm', to cross the skill boundaries between mechanical and electrical fitting work, for example, even though fellow workers in other production areas might object to this. But it was exactly that attitude, encapsulated in the following comment, that management sought to foster, and indeed, use as a catalyst for similar attitudinal change elsewhere on the shop floor:

> The way I look at it, for 29 years in the navy I signed a contract that I would serve my Queen and country. And part of that to work on an aircraft, keep that aircraft serviceable and get two guys to go out and fly it and take it away and make sure they come back again. But the big difference was I had to be flexible because I was paid in the navy over a 24 hour period. Now at any time they could come and get me out of my bed and they could say you've got to go and help. I was brought up over those 29 years never to question that, that was my job. And so as I got older it just became the norm. Unfortunately when you try and do that in a system which has got a trade union involved you cannot do it because you could be over stepping a boundary which actually goes into someone else's trade description if you like. I found it really hard to rein back on the flexibility side of things. And some workers within the company

tended to feel that we were doing jobs that we shouldn't be doing. We were going out on a limb whereas some of these guys were saying well I'm not going out on that limb because I'm not paid to go out any further than here. (Interview, *Wasp* Aircraft Fitter, November 2001).

Management's use of ex-military labour in this case provides a unique example of more general patterns in employers' exploitation of lean production settings and insecure market environments to create artificial fault lines and divisions within the working class (Yates, 1998). In this case, ex-military 'team players' were cynically inserted into a milieu of civil 'deviants'. The extent to which this strategy of management control succeeded is explored in the section on worker resistance below.

Cellular manufacturing: the case of *JetCo*

The pattern of labour process change at *JetCo* was quite complex, a function of the different technologies and work routines required to build an aero-engine. The underlying dynamic was management's determination to introduce lean manufacturing. In 1996, the company invited a firm of Japanese management consultants to audit existing practice and develop plans to secure time efficiencies in the organisation of plant and labour. This was in the aftermath of a series of major shop floor redundancies. Three years later, significant changes began to take hold. A business matrix was implemented involving the creation of a number of spatially partitioned production-oriented units. Large, function-based manufacturing departments, such as different machine shops, were broken up into different product and process-focused business units. At the same time, production flow and labour utilisation were both increased by the strategic reorganisation of machinery and processes to reduce so-called 'non-value-added' activity. Management referred to this as 'value stream mapping', one of a number of continuous improvement activities.

The company was also developing a computerised system of just-in-time production control. In some production areas more visible JIT techniques, such as kanban, had been introduced. These new methods provided a systemic interface between customer-order processes and engine assembly enabling tighter production planning and a reduction of stores, buffers and waiting time on the shop floor. One senior manager explained:

We have seen an increase in efficiency, through the working methods, through the implementation of technology as well, through driving waste out, getting flow into the shops. And the measures we're really looking at now are on inventory and stock turn, how much inventory we've got lined up in the business. Are we satisfying the customer? what's our delivery performance like? So it's the measures of schedule adherence, are we achieving our costs? and within all that have we got the right levels of inventory? Rather than the older way of let's just put inventory into the business, just in case, and keep it high, keep the guys busy.

(Interview, Operations Director, June 2001)

The reorganisation of production into smaller, discrete units was aimed at providing a new infrastructure for controlling production costs. It also created greater transparency for identifying less profitable parts of the business, and indeed, for locating suitable units for outsourcing. These types of changes generated widespread feelings of job insecurity (see Danford *et al.*, 2005). Their impact on the organisation of the labour process itself was less uniform. Although the production managers in all departments we visited adopted the discourse of teamworking, in fact, authentic cellular working was implemented only in those areas where work routines were more rhythmic and where production operations could more easily be divided up amongst small teams of workers. Just over 50 per cent of the shop floor workforce were deployed in cellular production, the remainder worked in 'teams' that were really larger sections of 60 or 70 operators.

Prior to the reorganisation, groups of skilled fitters could, in theory, be expected to work anywhere in the factory on a variety of engine building projects wherever their skills were required. Workers who were permanently resident in large, single function shops, such as machinists, would tend to operate just a single machine but produce a wide variety of jobs for different engine projects. The new work organisation, whether in cells or sections, made employees responsible for specific groups of tasks for specific projects whilst their line managers were accountable for unit output and cost control targets. Just as we saw at *Airframes*, it did not introduce greater skill flexibility, it merely reshaped the existing pattern of labour flexibility into a more 'cost-effective', more easily controlled and more intensive form. For example, workers in the production cells took on a narrower range of skilled tasks required for a single manufacturing process. Typical component production cells in the engine turbine unit, for instance, would comprise groups of grinding, milling and laser machines. Flexibility within the cells would entail, theoretically, job rotation around the three machine groups in accordance with just-in-time schedule requirements and the advice of cell 'coaches' (who in practice were little different to old-style foremen).

In some respects, the impact of these changes on the labour process and existing relations of control was modest. For the same reasons that we saw at *Airframes*, the traditions of craft autonomy and specialised knowledge in small-batch, complex production routines remained a resilient characteristic of shop floor social relations. As one worker described, these relations were quite different to the close supervisory control associated with mass production systems:

[The supervision] appreciate that we're all, mostly, skilled guys with experience and we can work unsupervised. You don't have to have somebody standing over you, watching you. We're very much left to our own devices as to how we do the job. (Interview, Engine Fitter, June 2001)

Nevertheless, many workers faced a potential loss of job control and skill recomposition as a result of the rationalisation of labour deployment within the new sections and cells. Prior to these changes, a typical machinist might be working on bevel gears one week, gear cases the next, rotor blades the next. Cellular working involved a more intensive but narrow task flexibility as the same worker became responsible for completing different machining tasks on just one component, or one element of a component, week in week out. One typical view was:

> Since we've gone into the cell structure the work can be boring at times because you're doing the same repetitive job whereas before we had more variety. There's certain components that we used to do the whole job for, machine it, everything. But because you've got this cell up and running, which is set up to deal with that one job, that's been taken away from us.
> (Interview, Machinist, June 2001)

The substitution of job variety on single machines by multi-machine minding in cells also created tensions between workers who were willing to support the new management objectives and those who were more oppositional for job security reasons. Some of the younger, less experienced workers we interviewed tended to display more accommodating attitudes compared to colleagues with longer service records. The latter, who were well accustomed to the tradition of securing livelihoods by controlling jobs, tended to comply only under duress or when advised to by their shop stewards. One younger machinist commented:

> I find that, because I am expanding my skills under the new management at the moment, I suppose I am enjoying it more. The reason being that I am not stuck on one machine every day. Today, for instance, I've been operating four machines in the same day, two in the morning and two in the afternoon, which people who are stuck on one machine every day, frown upon. They say, I can't be handling other people's work, going round all these different machines every day.
> (Interview, Machinist, July 2001)

A more experienced worker:

> You must maintain the demarcation for self preservation. People are frightened to death that if they cross the trade barriers it will mean less people. It all goes back to security of employment. The problem is the type of multi-skilling that management are after. Ideally they want a small

group of people with every skill they need ... but if you do that then you are slicing the workforce down to the bare bones, you are putting yourself out of a job. (Interview, Engine Fitter, June 2001)

At both case studies, therefore, the overall impact of the core high performance practice of teamworking was not greater autonomy but an intensification of narrow skill flexibility within the confines of cells and other smaller units. Worker reactions to this tended to be negative although subjective experience, and indeed, practice, differed in accordance with their varied employment histories and 'collective memories'.

Continuous improvement

Management at both case study organisations had introduced different continuous improvement initiatives during the two years prior to our research. Many of these bore close resemblance to standard practice in Japanese manufacturing plants. For example, under the campaign banner of ROCC ('Raising Our Company's Competitiveness') the *Airframes* management had attempted to involve shop floor workers in various schemes aimed at improving the flow of work through the production plants, reducing 'non-value added' activities and waste and tidying up work areas. These were labelled with the now customary Japanese tidiness and waste reduction jargon such as compliance with the '5Ss' and '7Ws' (very few workers or managers we interviewed could define these!). At *JetCo*, exactly the same lean manufacturing outcomes were sought from an even greater array of initiatives. Amongst these were '5S' campaigns, 'Total Productive Maintenance', 'Operational Equipment Effectiveness', 'Value-Stream Mapping' and 'Kaizen Scrums' (the latter denoting the idea of getting heads together to 'brainstorm' continuous improvements). At the time of the research, the *JetCo* management was also devoting considerable resources to giving workers time-off to participate in a new '40-day engine' campaign. The objective here was to reduce the lead time for engine manufacture from a current span of between 70 and 200 days (depending on engine type) to just 40 days by systematically rationalising the flow of work and non-production activity.

Our questionnaire survey results showed that just over 50 per cent of shop floor workers at both organisations had participated in at least one of these continuous improvement initiatives. The different interviews with these participants suggested that if the principles and practice of continuous improvement could somehow be abstracted from the demands of capital accumulation then many workers might enthusiastically embrace participation in discussions governing substantive engineering problems in production. As it was, the notion of 'pride in the job' constituted an important facet of their craft identities and most had no objections to the more mundane improvement activities, such as the '5S' clean up campaigns. However, it was once 'continuous improvement' metamorphosed into the more euphemistic 'business improvement' that worker participation became more problematic. 'Business improvement' came to be regarded by some workers in both organisations as a cipher for management control, staff reduction and job insecurity. For example, one ROCC participant at *Airframes* described how colleagues in his team had refused to give up information on how they carried out their work. They feared that management would use this to make job times more visible as a precursor to rationalising team organisation and labour (interview notes, November 2001). Another worker at *JetCo* voiced similar concerns:

Value stream mapping, kaizen scrums, 5S's and all that? Well the attitude of some people is, 'I'll go on it, it's easier to go on it than say no.' But once they've got them on it, of course they can drag it out of them, that's management philosophy isn't it? They're not daft, I'm not saying that management are daft, far from it. That's psychology. I mean, while I'm sat here with you Andy, you drag things out of me that I'd never thought of saying, I mean that's the profession isn't it? There are trained people in these teams to do that, to drag out stuff on improving productivity. There's been a marked improvement in productivity but we haven't gained anything from it, that's the only problem.

(Interview, Sheetmetal Worker and Shop Steward, June 2001)

As a result, it was perhaps inevitable that continuous improvement and joint problem solving did not generally result in the types of mutual gain outcomes suggested by the advocates of HPWS. Instead, many workers came to display a cynicism, and on occasions anger, at management's insistence on subordinating real worker concerns about their jobs and working environment to narrower managerial prerogatives. There were a number of sub-patterns to this. Some workers raised the superfluous logic of continuous improvement in the context of, from their own perspective, parsimonious company attitudes to investment in capital equipment. For example:

5S's? How the hell! Part of the 5S things that some of our chaps got involved in was brushing up around their machines and taking a photograph before and after. Don't get me wrong, we realise when you are doing high precision work you need the environment to work, there is no point in doing it in a shit-hole. But at the same time, it gets to a point where it goes beyond a joke. If the company is serious about quality then forget the 5S's, start giving manufacturing some investment. If a company is really serious it wouldn't ask blokes to make components for 2001 jet engines on machines that go back to the 1940's and 1950's.

(Interview, *JetCo* Mechanical Inspector, June 2001)

Others complained of a contradiction between the rhetoric and reality of employee participation. Although our management interviewees in both

organisations adopted much of the populist discourse of employee 'empowerment' and 'ownership' the common experience on the shop floor fell far
short of this. Many workers described situations involving a type of class
snobbery and a refusal by managers and white-collar engineers to entertain
the idea that manual workers might be their equals in work-related discussions. For example:

> I've got no influence. They will do what they want to do…you might
> have a designer down here with a jig and tool designer and a couple other
> more suit bods. All there with their shirts and ties on. And you'd be asked
> for a bit of input on your job, because something's going wrong. So you
> suggest something, a solution. Then they'll weigh it up and say, 'oh no
> no no, you can't do that'. Then, three, four, five years later, all of a sudden
> look! The drawing's changed to how we asked it to be done. They didn't
> want to admit that a person doing the job was as good or better than
> them for getting it done. So we get no credit or recognition…they don't
> like your input to tell them how to do it.
>
> (Interview, *Airframes* Aircraft Fitter, October 2001)

On the same themes of inequality and low trust, we uncovered many examples
of management's condescending attitudes to subordinates that, in some
respects, had the effect of reducing employee engagement with kaizen to the
teacher–pupil relationship of the junior school. For example, on the main
Gannet production line at *Airframes*, it was hoped that workers would come to
regard the idea of 'McDonaldization' at work as both genuine and literal. The
project's operations director described to us how, following the advice of a professional management consultant, teams of production workers would be
taken for an educational visit to a McDonalds fast food restaurant across the
road from the factory gates. In return for a bulk purchase of a 'Big Mac' and
chips workers would go behind the bar for half an hour to watch the just-
in-time production system in operation, no doubt in wonderment (interview
notes, October 2001). Similarly at *JetCo*, many workers described their demean-
ing participation in 40-day engine exercises that required them to do little
more than, 'put stickle bricks together like a bunch of school kids' as one
worker explained. Another described a typical kaizen team-building event:

> Yes, some of the blokes were totally cheesed off with this kaizen when
> they were stuck outside throwing a ball to each other. The idea is team-
> work and they had them all in a circle and they were throwing a ball to
> each other and all this sort of thing, to show them if they done it a cer-
> tain way, if they done it right, it is quicker. The blokes thought it was a
> load of bleeding rubbish. Everyone else around the site was just cracking
> up at it really. A load of blokes stood there throwing balls at each other.
>
> (Interview, Engine Fitter, July 2001)

Overall then, our examination of continuous improvement found plenty of evidence of multiple practice within the two organisations but little indication of enhanced worker discretion and influence. Employee responses ranged from lukewarm support for the more mundane activities to outright hostility to management agendas that either patronised or ignored independent worker interests.

Labour control and resistance

It is crucial to stress, however, that workers in these organisations were far from passive recipients of workplace change. For example, our analysis of worker responses to the companies' different continuous improvement campaigns highlighted how widespread cynicism, sometimes in the form of jokes, at other times more belligerent, can constitute a type of collective resistance, albeit a weak one (Graham, 1993). More powerful forms of organised counter-mobilisation were also present although these were mainly based at the *JetCo* factory. We complete this chapter by examining examples of resistance – the counterpoint to managerial notions of participation. We consider first, the factors that tended to militate against resistance at *Airframes* and second, the successful acts of mobilisation at *JetCo*.

Airframes: 'militarization' of labour control

It would be wrong to suggest that resistance and struggle were absent from the *Airframes* shop floor. During our discussions with different shop stewards and rank and file union members we found evidence that local collective controls still placed constraints against the free exercise of supervisory prerogatives. For instance, transparency and equal treatment in the distribution of overtime and shiftworking remained two key ethical principles for the manual workforce. Most shop stewards were effective monitors of local supervisory practice and ensured that if any one individual was offered the additional pay advantages of a few extra hours or shifts then all members of the section or workshop had to be offered the same. If this was not forthcoming then all workers would withdraw cooperation. One shop steward commented:

> If you've been offered Saturday morning and you'd love the overtime, then you won't be doing it unless I've been asked, that's quite clearly so ... If they offer some people Saturday morning overtime but not others then I will go in the bosses' office and say, 'well you know if you've offered it to one man then it should be offered to everyone.' And they will no doubt say, 'no we don't recognise that, sod off.' But then an hour later they will go out on the shop floor and find that everybody's happily busy because they're mowing the lawn Saturday morning, they've got

no-one who's prepared to do their overtime. That sort of thing can happen a lot. (Interview, Shop Steward, November 2001).

Nevertheless, the volume of shop floor resistance and conflict seemed to be much lower compared to *JetCo*. Two factors stood out in this respect. The first was the orientation to management of the manual union leadership within the *Airframes* plant. It was significant that the manual union convenor proactively supported partnership-based workplace relations and this did have an impact on the readiness of the rank and file to mobilise against some of the high performance management initiatives (see Danford *et al.*, 2005). The second was the unusual nature of labour control. We have already described how management attempted to create new fault lines on the shop floor by actively recruiting ex-military labour, a new type of 'team player' whose loyalty was more likely to reside with the supervisor than the shop steward or workmate. This process began with the recruitment of personnel for the 'greenfield' *Wasp* production area but by the time of the research a good number of new employees with recent armed services backgrounds were also working on the longer established production lines. These workers tended to ignore the instructions of shop stewards by, for example, breaking extant custom and practice governing skill demarcation, or agreeing to supervisory requests to work extra hours and shifts. This caused a good deal of resentment on the shop floor. For example, one worker on the *Gannet* line complained:

Well they work outside the shift system and work outside the overtime agreements. Unless you've got a five-hour overtime slot offered to everybody and it really is for everybody then we put a ban on overtime. But the ex-military lot tend to sneak in and do bloody extra work and undermine things for all of us. They're not the unionists that's the problem. They only join the union because they've got to.

(Interview, Aircraft Fitter, October 2001)

This division and conflict could be cynically manipulated by production managers to weaken any oppositional groups in their areas. One worker described how in some areas an atmosphere of fear and suspicion had developed since many of his peers believed that the ex-military employees had acted as management spies in union mass meetings and informal discussions on the shop floor. Another felt that these workers enjoyed discriminatory treatment when it came to career advancement:

I think if you look at the factory overall, they've become like a freemasons ... It's like a buddy system. See a job that comes up, it seems to be a forces guy who gets it. We have noticed that. They definitely do look after each other, it's a mutual help group. And it's caused resentment in the rest of us. (Interview, Aircraft Fitter, November 2001)

Whether or not these concerns were based on hard evidence the fact remains that management's strategic insertion of a new type of malleable worker into a traditional environment of craft-based job control engendered shop floor divisions and exacerbated feelings of insecurity. These conditions, coupled with a rank and file leadership that preferred partnership to conflict, tended to undermine the necessary worker confidence that is a prerequisite of effective collective resistance.

JetCo: instances of counter-mobilisation

The politics of production on the *JetCo* shop floor were marked by continual worker contestation of company attempts to fragment work organisation and group solidarities. The leading stewards at the plant adopted a hostile attitude to partnership, arguing that the protection of worker interests in capitalist firms will always require robust, independent trade union organisation. The collective base upon which this form of unionism depends came under constant threat from the organisational imperatives of decentralisation. For example, every one of the senior managers we interviewed spoke at some length of their desire to synchronise business unit employment costs with market conditions by devolving union negotiations to the level of the unit. The shop floor unions rejected this and insisted upon maintaining single site negotiations to secure equal employment rights and conditions for all members irrespective of their business unit attachment. This opposition was given organisational form by a strategic shift in member-activist relations. The tradition of shop steward accountability to the rank and file became subordinate to the gaze of a central, cross-business unit executive of senior stewards who monitored any local deviation from union agreements (see Danford *et al.*, 2002).

Our interviews with cell managers and other shop floor supervisors highlighted how, notwithstanding the widespread assumption that union control at the point of production is a relic of past British industrial relations, collective worker organisation and a culture of opposition maintained significant constraints over their perceived 'right to manage'. Although the incidence of strikes and other official industrial action had declined workers were still able to mount effective unofficial actions, such as overtime bans and go-slows, to defend their own independent sense of order and dignity at work. Supervisors, shop stewards and members provided different accounts of successful worker opposition to such issues as disciplinary actions, unequal overtime distribution, labour flexibility, unpopular continuous improvement activity, and in one case, an attempt to transfer work to another *JetCo* plant. One cell manager reflected wistfully on the collective constraint – or culture of opposition – that these forms of action embodied:

> If I talk to the workforce or you talk to the workforce as individuals, they say wonderful things and you think great you can do something here

with these people. But then suddenly, when they get together collectively, suddenly the collective view is quite different from the individual view ... I was looking out on the shop floor yesterday and watched one of our new recruits. He was quite a rarity, only 20 years old, and I was thinking that he could potentially be holding many fresh ideas and ways of thinking about problems. But he is going to come under tremendous pressure to conform. The men are set in their ways, there's tremendous trade union pressure to conform and I just knew that before too long this young lad would also be conditioned into conforming. If he was innovative and wanted to try new ideas then he would be shunned, ignored, his life would be made hell on the shop floor.

> (Interview, Cell Manager, June 2001).

The nature and form of this worker opposition sometimes varied in accordance with the different individuals involved and issues at stake. We were able to examine this in greater detail in one of the more militant areas of the plant where we gained interview access to a larger number of supervisors and shop stewards as well as manual workers. This area was engine test, a strategically important unit since it covered the final stage of engine manufacture and any dispute there would cause an immediate halt to factory gate output.

Prior to a reorganisation in 1995, the engine test area employed around 500 workers mainly in manual fitting trades and non-manual test and evaluation work. These workers were deployed in demarcated functional groups, such as, test engineering, maintenance, instrument fitting and engine fitting. The reorganisation involved a redundancy of 250 jobs. Remaining workers were redeployed into five main cells each of which were further subdivided into four or five teams. A typical team would comprise test fitters, maintenance fitters, electricians, tinsmiths and coppersmiths. Management's objective was to create a more 'efficient' test unit through lean techniques. That is, these different skilled workers were expected to maintain existing output levels by adopting multi-skilling, covering for each other when requested by the team managers. The engine test shop stewards were unable to halt the job losses but the experience of dealing with the distress and victimisation associated with compulsory redundancies led them into drawing a line in the sand when it came to further labour flexibility. In the interests of job stability, they developed a strategy of contestation of every management demand for multi-skilling within the cells. Their eventual success in limiting management's room for manouevre, helped by their members' relatively powerful position in the engine production cycle, created the paradox of a reduction of skill *and* task flexibility. The act of confining previously large groups of skilled workers into small, discrete cell units generated new demarcations both within and between cells.

Although the different teamworkers we interviewed had no objection to flexible working *per se*, it was because this was being proposed in an environment of continual job insecurity that they strongly endorsed the policy of their union. Multi-skilling was perceived as an inevitable path to job loss rather than job enrichment. And despite this insecurity, the union was highly effective in maintaining the tradition of job control. It did so by adopting a form of participative collective organisation that forced management to seek permission for workplace change rather than impose it on the workforce. The senior steward described this process:

> We have managed to keep hold of the shop stewards' organisation as the main body for communications in this plant. We hold sectional meetings to make decisions so everyone's involved and then if it goes beyond the section we have mass meetings throughout whenever the employer wants something. So we can sit in front of the employer and say, 'we are not in a position of authority to agree to that demand until we go back and discuss this with our members.' And they bloody hate it because a mass meeting is a strike without a ballot ... and we constantly, continually have meetings. And at the meetings we always bring in the *politics* of any managerial change, of why they want this change. It is not simply because of the 'business need' it is about this management ideology that underpins it. (Interview, Engine Test Senior Steward, July 2001)

The engine test supervisors spoke at length of their frustrations over the limits placed by the union on their ability to exploit cells to the full or to synchronise labour utilisation with the hours and shifts required by production scheduling. For instance, one somewhat abashed cell leader described the repercussion of his attempt to coax workers into giving up their bank holiday weekend without first going through the union channel:

> When you work with staff as individuals you have more flexibility as a manager to get things done because when you handle things at an individual level there's a lot less union involvement. And I've always been able to do something to get around bank holidays – a bit of time off in lieu or something. I tried to do that recently with the cell. Then, because I did not involve the works unions, after about two hours of informally sounding out the guys, I was hauled into my boss's office for a good kicking. And then the unions were called in and I was given a bit of a dressing down in front of the stewards for having 'gone outside my authority' so to speak. (Interview, Cell Leader, June 2001)

The sense of union control in this engine test area was quite palpable.*In this respect it stood out from the rest of the *JetCo* plant in terms of its more militant shop steward organisation and adroit exploitation of a powerful bargaining position. But it also serves as a conspicuous example of a broader pattern of shop floor struggle in the context of a deterioration of quality of working life, a deterioration that is inherent to the demands of capital accumulation in the high performance work regime. (See Danford *et al.*, forthcoming, 2005.)

Conclusion

On paper, the two case study organisations provided propitious conditions for the emergence of new workplace relations based on more systematic employee participation in job design. The traditions of labour control had always involved a good degree of 'responsible autonomy' on the shop floor (Friedman, 1977). The combination of complex and highly skilled manufacturing work with small-batch production meant that the typical craft worker was used to relatively relaxed forms of supervisory control. A considerable element of trust was therefore integral to management–employee relations. The introduction of HPWS in such an environment, involving managerial decentralisation, teamworking and multifarious problem-solving techniques, might be expected to foster employee autonomy and mobilise worker discretion for the benefit of the organisation and workforce alike. This would be the scenario expected by those writers who adopt a contingency approach to analysing organisational change; a pattern of mutual gain outcomes. The reality, however, was quite different. Although there were variations in degree, the underlying pattern was one of diminished employee autonomy (rather than enhanced discretion), more intense task flexibility (rather than job enrichment) and feelings that continuous improvement campaigns ignored independent worker agendas for improving the quality of working life.

The reasons for this were structural and linked to underlying political economy. If we consider first the impact of teamworking it became clear that its introduction into a high skill setting acted to demarcate potentially polyvalent craft workers into the confines of production cells responsible for a relatively narrow range of tasks. This was not an unintended outcome. The restrictions on autonomy and broad skill utilisation were a logical consequence of the system of financial control that provided the dynamic of organisational change. As Ackroyd and Procter (1998) argue (see also Harley, 2001), teams are usually managerially driven and designed to improve performance by allowing small unit transparency in the calculation of marginal costs and benefits. In this context it is almost inevitable that the supervisors of labour, subject to increasing accountability, will be more concerned with controlling staff costs and reasserting their prerogatives than 'empowering' their subordinates.

Similarly, although employee experiences of participation in the more mundane continuous improvement campaigns were not negative (or particularly enthusiastic) many workers became highly critical of management's determination to keep these campaigns firmly within the narrow parameters of improving efficiency and quality. That is, when employee participants attempted to interpose their own agendas, based on improving working conditions, or if they challenged the tenets of the various management initiatives then they were confronted by a wall of patronage, dismissal and resistance. Improving performance became the core concern of 'problem solving'.

It is a measure of the essentially managerialist nature of the mainstream accounts of HPWS that labour's position in the high performance work equation is reduced to one of recipient of participative measures and other incentives and provider of greater discretionary effort (for example, Wood, 1999; Appelbaum *et al.*, 2000). The problematic of worker resistance just does not feature in this objectified treatment of acquiescent labour. Our case studies provide an alternative picture. At both organisations, the introduction of HPWS created material conditions for employee discontent and potential counter-mobilisation. In the case of *Airframes*, the prospects for effective resistance were reduced, though not completely suppressed. Incidents of contestation and conflict tended to be more fragmentary due, *inter alia*, to an accommodationist union leadership and a management control strategy based partly on engendering schisms on the shop floor by externally recruiting a distinctive form of malleable labour. At *JetCo*, a more powerful and independent rank and file union organisation had greater success in constraining supervisory prerogatives and maintaining a form of job control. In some areas of the plant the sustained collective defence of a set of ethical practices and norms marked out an alternative 'employee autonomy' that exposed the superficial empowerment claims of partnership and high performance management.

Acknowledgement

This material is drawn from the ESRC Future of Work project, 'Patterns and Prospects for Partnership at Work in the UK' L212252096.

Note

1. This chapter draws from chapter 4 of our forthcoming book, *Partnership and the High Performance Workplace. Work and Employment Relations in the Aerospace Industry*. Palgrave Macmillan, 2005.

References

Ackroyd, S. and Procter, S. (1998) 'British manufacturing organisation and workplace industrial relations: some attributes of the new flexible firm'. *British Journal of Industrial Relations*, 36 (2): 163–83.

Adler, P. S. (1995) 'Democratic Taylorism': Re Toyota System at NUMMI, in Babson, S. (ed.) *Lean Work: Empowerment and exploitation in the Global Auto Industry*, 207–19. Detroit, WI: Wayne State.

Appelbaum, E., Bailey, T., Berg, P. and Kalleberg, A. L. (2000) *Manufacturing Advantage: Why High Performance Work Systems Pay Off*, Ithaca, NY: Cornell University Press.

Atkinson, J. (1984) Flexibility, Uncertainty and Manpower Management, Institute of Manpower Studies Report 89. Falmer University of Sussex.

Bacon, N. and Blyton, P. (2003) 'The impact of teamwork on skills: employee perceptions of who gains and who loses'. *Human Resource Management Journal*, 13 (2): 13–29.

Bélanger, J., Giles, A. and Murray, G. (2002) 'Towards a new production model: potentialities, tensions and contradictions', in Murray, G., Bélanger J., Giles, A. and Lapointe, P. A. (eds) *Work and Employment Relations in the High-Performance Workplace*, London and New York: Continuum.

Buchanan, D. (2000) 'An eager and enduring embrace: the ongoing rediscovery of teamworking as a management idea', in Procter, S. and Mueller, F. (eds) *Teamworking*, Basingstoke: Macmillan.

Cutcher-Gershenfeld, J., Nitta, M., Barrett, B., Belhedi, N., Sai-Chung Chow, S., Ishino, T., Lee, S., Lin, W., Moore, M., Mothersell, W., Palthe, J., Ramanand, S., Strolle, M. and Wheaton, A. (1998) *Knowledge-Driven Work: Unexpected Lessons from Japanese and United States Work Practices*, New York: Oxford Business Press.

Danford, A. (1998) 'Teamworking and labour regulation in the autocomponents industry', *Work, Employment and Society*, 12 (3): 409–31.

Danford, A., Richardson, M. and Upchurch, M. (2002) 'Trade union strategy and renewal: The restructuring of work and work relations in the UK Aerospace Industry', *Work, Employment and Society*, 16 (2): 305–27.

Danford, A., Richardson, M., Stewart, P., Tailby, S. and Upchurch, M. (2004) 'High performance work systems and workplace partnership: a case study of aerospace workers'. *New Technology, Work and Employment*, 19 (1): 14–29.

Danford, A., Richardson, M., Stewart, P., Tailby, S. and Upchurch, M. (2005) *Partnership and the High Performance Workplace. Work and Employment Relations in the Aerospace Industry*, Basingstoke: Palgrave Macmillan.

Deakin, S., Hobbs, R., Konzelmann, S. J. and Wilkinson, F. (2004) 'Working corporations: corporate governance and innovation in labour–management partnerships in Britain', in Stuart, M. and Martinez Lucio, M. (eds) *Partnership and the Modernisation of Employment Relations*, London: Routledge.

Delbridge, R. (1998) *Life on the Line in Contemporary Manufacturing*, Oxford: Oxford University Press.

Edwards, P., Geary, J. and Sisson, K. (2002) 'New forms of work organisation in the workplace: transformative, exploitative, or limited and controlled?', in Murray, G., Bélanger, J., Giles, A. and Lapointe, P. A. (eds), *Work and Employment Relations in the High-Performance Workplace*, London and New York: Continuum.

Friedman, A. (1977) *Industry and Labour. Class Struggle at Work and Monopoly Capitalism*, London: Macmillan.

Garrahan, P. and Stewart, P. (1992) *The Nissan Enigma: Flexibility at Work in a Local Economy*, London: Mansell.

Geary, J. (2003) 'New forms of work organisation: still limited, still controlled, but still welcome?', in Edward, P. (ed.) *Industrial Relations. Theory and Practice*, Oxford, Blackwell.

Graham, L. (1993) 'Inside a Japanese transplant. a critical perspective'. *Work and Occupations*, 20 (2): 147–73.

Graham, L. (1995) *On the Line at Subaru-Isuzu: The Japanese Model and the American Worker*, Ithaca, NY: ILR Press.

Harley, B. (1999) 'The myth of empowerment: work organisation, hierarchy and employee autonomy in contemporary Australian workplaces'. *Work, Employment and Society*, 13 (1): 41–66.

Harley, B. (2001) 'Team membership and the experience of work in Britain: an analysis of the WERS98 Data'. *Work, Employment and Society*, 14 (4): 721–42.

Kenney, M. and Florida, R. (1993) *Beyond Mass Production: The Japanese System and its Transfers to the US*. New York: Oxford University Press.

Marchington, M. (2000) 'Teamworking and employee involvement: terminology, evaluation and context', in Procter, S. and Mueller, F. (eds) *Teamworking*, Basingstoke: Macmillan.

Martinez Lucio, M., Jenkins, S. and Noon, M. (2000) 'Management strategy, union identity and oppositionalism: teamwork in the Royal Mail', in Procter, S. and Mueller, F. (eds) *Teamworking*, Basingstoke: Macmillan.

Osterman, P. (2000) 'Work reorganization in an era of restructuring: trends in diffusion and effects on employee Welfare', *Industrial and Labor Relations Review*, 53 (2): 179–197.

Oxenbridge, S. and Brown, W. (2004) 'Developing partnership relationships: a case of leveraging power', in Stuart, M. and Martinez Lucio, M.

Procter, S. and Mueller, F. (2000) 'Teamworking: strategy, structure, systems and culture', in Procter, S. and Mueller, F. (eds) *Teamworking*, Basingstoke: Macmillan.

Richardson, M., Stewart, P., Danford, A., Tailby, S. and Upchurch, M. (2004) 'Employees' experience of workplace partnership', in Stuart, M. and Martinez Lucio, M. (eds) *Partnership and Modernisation in Employee Relations*, Basingstoke: Palgrave Macmillan.

Rinehart, J., Huxley, C. and Robertson, D. (1997) *Just Another Car Factory? Lean Production and its Discontents*, Ithaca and London: ILR Press.

Steijn, B. (2001) 'Work systems, quality of working life and attitudes of workers: an empirical study towards the effects of team and non-teamwork'. *New Technology, Work and Employment*, 16 (3): 191–203.

Stewart, P. and Garrahan, P. (1995) 'Employee responses to new management techniques in the auto industry'. *Work, Employment and Society*, 9 (13): 517–36.

Tailby, S., Richardson, M., Stewart, P., Danford, A. and Upchurch, M. (2004), 'Partnership at work and worker participation: an NHS case study'. *Industrial Relations Journal*, 35 (5).

Thompson, M. (2002) *High Performance Work Organisation in UK Aerospace. The SBAC Human Capital Audit 2002*. Report compiled for the Society of British Aerospace Companies, London and Oxford: SBAC and Templeton College, University of Oxford.

TUC (2001) *Partnership In Depth*, TUC Partnership Institute, www.tuc.org.uk/pi/partnership.ht.

TUC (2003) *High Performance Workplaces*, Report, ttp://www.tuc.org.uk/economy/tuc-6995-f0.cfm.

Watson, T. and Rosborough, J. (2000) 'Teamworking and the management of flexibility: local and social – structural tensions in high performance work design initiatives', in Procter, S. and Mueller, F. (eds) *Teamworking*, Basingstoke: Macmillan.

Wood, S. (1999) 'Getting the Measure of the transformed high-performance organisation'. *British Journal of Industrial Relations*, 37 (3): 391–417.

Yates, C. (1998), 'Defining the fault lines: new divisions in the working class'. *Capital and Class*, 66, Autumn 1998.

9

Suspicious Minds? Partnership, Trade Union Strategy and the Politics of Contemporary Employment Relations

Miguel Martínez Lucio and Mark Stuart

Introduction

The emergence of partnership has been a central feature of current discussions regarding the renewal and regeneration of industrial relations institutions, in particular trade unions. To a certain extent this coincides with the changing political context, which has seen a sustained period of anti-union regulation, superseded in 1997 by the election of a New Labour government that brought a renewed interest in the positive role unions could play in economic and institutional terms through a closer collaboration with employers.[1] The trade union movement itself, however, has also been calling for a more co-operative, partnership-based approach to employment relations, based around a 'new agenda', since the late 1980s. The key point of departure in this discourse of partnership and the modernisation of employment relations is the perceived need to transcend adversarial employment relations; as such an approach is considered untenable in the global economic system of the twenty-first Century. Instead, a more trust-based approach to management–employee relations, it is argued, is required (see Giddens, 1998; Leadbeater, 1999). This chapter examines this critical departure in employment relations, which represents a central element in the discourse of the future of work, through an investigation of the strategic development of partnership within the leading technical and white-collar union, the Manufacturing, Science and Finance Union (MSF).[2]

The central objective of the chapter is to challenge what we refer to as the *binary* nature of recent debates, particularly the argument that trade unions have clear strategic choices facing them in terms of 'moderation' or 'militancy' (see Ackers, 2002; Kelly, 1996, 1998; Bacon and Storey, 1996). Instead, we will explore the complex way in which union choices are made and politically constructed through a discussion of the MSF's decision to embark on a strategy of partnership. The chapter will map the way MSF engaged with partnership in the late 1990s and how it was furthered, understood and acted upon within its membership structures, in particular its workplace representatives. Such strategic ventures, we argue, should be evaluated and understood in relation to the politics of employment relations *and* the realities of strategic calculations within trade unions, as organisations with a variety of organisational levels and spheres of decision-making. The chapter outlines the substantive and varied debates and concerns amongst trade unionists with regards to the viability of a partnership model of employment relations, noting how it has become a site of struggle which does not easily equate to notions of moderation and militancy within union strategy and practice.

We argue that the constitution of partnership by trade unions in the UK emerges from the way in which trade unionists perceive the actions, intentions and trajectories of management and employers. This is noticeable in the way even 'supportive' views amongst trade unionists of partnership are paralleled by very strong sets of concerns in terms of the risk of institutional engagement and the nature of management commitment. This lack of faith in the nature and attitude of British management makes the formation of policies regarding partnership problematic, even if the concerns vary across the different levels and arenas of union action. The data in this chapter reveal a critical and strategic approach to partnership, which was difficult to locate within any a priori formulation of ideology. Support for the critical positions that emerged within union conferences appeared to be underpinned by a general unease with the *context* and *deliverables* of partnership but not, ironically, the perceived *processes of partnership*.

The chapter begins by engaging with the main tenets of the partnership debate, focusing on issues of union renewal, such as strategic choices in contrast to more militant approaches. We then advance a three-level framework of analysis for the study of the politics of partnership within trade unions. The first level examines the genealogy of the concept of partnership within the MSF union, noting the way in which its meaning is contested (we call this the *intra-union dimension*). The second level presents selective survey findings on some of the basic attitudes and experiences of MSF workplace representatives vis-à-vis partnership, noting how the concept is understood and evaluated within the reality of contemporary workplace relations and management behaviour (we call this the *management–union dimension*). The third level focuses on the workplace, briefly reporting the qualitative findings of two cases studies of 'partnership building', paying particular attention to the dynamics of workplace representation (we call this the *inter-union dimension*). This three-fold framework allows us to show how concerns with trust – which are vital to partnership building – manifest themselves at different levels and in different ways, thus allowing an appreciation of the complex landscape of worker interests. It also allows us to appreciate that relations of trust have to be understood not solely in terms of management–union relations but in terms of the three dimensions outlined above. In conclusion, we argue that the regulatory and managerial legacies of employment relations continue to frame the concerns of trade unionists, and that such concerns are varied and not clearly mapped in ideological terms.

Partnership in the context of trade union renewal and politics

The concept of partnership has become the defining feature of the 'new' industrial relations settlement for the millennium. Championed at the European level and at the level of the nation state, partnership sets the foundations for modern unionism in, and beyond, the workplace. For its proponents, 'partnership means employers and trade unions working together to achieve common goals such as fairness and competitiveness' (TUC, 1999). By relinquishing the self interested agenda of adversarial industrial relations, for a new agenda based on consensual, occupational interests, such as training, reskilling and participation, workplace relations will supposedly flourish in a climate of cooperation, mutual trust and, most important of all, mutual gains. Thus, it has been suggested that trade union innovation, and ultimately their future position at the workplace, is dependent upon the development of such 'occupational interests' (Leisink, 1993). Against this backdrop, Ackers and Payne (1998) argue that unions should *use* the language of partnership, playing it back at employers, to construct a new, dominant employee relations project with unions at the centre. They follow Kochan and Osterman (1994) in viewing partnership as a positive development that may contribute to a revitalised role for trade unions, both politically and institutionally. The leaders of most British trade unions broadly supported these sentiments during the 1990s, yet the extent to which partnership represents a coherent and sustainable strategy of engagement remains unexamined. Others are less sanguine about the opportunities of partnership, noting that trade unions face significant difficulties, and even dangers, in adopting the partnership approach (Kelly, 1996; Taylor and Ramsey, 1998; Kelly, 2001; Danford *et al.*, 2002). For example, in the process of engaging with partnership trade unions may end up legitimating workplace change programmes, thus compromising their independence.

In order to understand the politics, strategy and implementation of partnership it is important to consider both the internal (organisational) and external (socio-economic and political) context (Martinez Lucio and Stuart, 2004). This remains one of the main weaknesses of the academic debate on partnership. Analysis tends to focus on the impact of partnership on working conditions and industrial relations structures, with less discussion of its ideological and political construction and development. There is also a tendency to regard such developments as part of a simple move to the 'Right' within the labour movement, fixing analysis on the customary axis of leadership–activist relations with the former engaging in this shift. The problem with such a line of argument is that it posits an unproblematic definition of partnership – whether critical or supportive. Partnership is often contrasted with alternative projects, such as the 'organising model' (Carter, 2000). Following this line of analysis, trade unions are seen to be facing a series of choices and policy models. Organising, for example, is viewed as a strategy focused on emphasising membership and workplace based patterns of recruitment and union activity. Such an approach aims to recruit and build membership organisation from the bottom upwards through workplace and local recruitment teams (Heery, 1996; Macdonald, 1996). This strategy, it is argued, sits uncomfortably, or at least ambivalently, with partnership-oriented approaches to employee relations which privilege moderate approaches to relations with management. In this respect, partnership is understood not in terms of its internal complexities and realities, but more in negative terms – that is, as an opposite to more 'direct', 'workplace' forms of trade unionism.

It could be argued, however, that the binary character of much contemporary debate – leadership 'accommodation' versus rank and file 'renewal' or trade union proximity to employers (e.g. partnership) versus workplace activism (e.g. organising) – is problematic. First, there is a need to reconstitute the partnership debate in such a manner that the broader political constructions of it, as a feature of employment relations, are comprehended. Thus, when discussing the political processes of union strategy and renewal there is a need to map the way alliances and interests are forged in a complex and, at times, even contradictory manner (Gall, 1998, 2001). Key concepts at the heart of contemporary debates about work need to be analysed in terms of their genealogy and competing meanings, so that emergent political calculations can be exposed (Stuart, 1996; Martinez Lucio *et al.*, 2000). Second, the 'choices' confronting unions are not reducible to a mere question of whether they approximate themselves to capital ('partnership') or labour ('organising'). It is important that discussion on concrete developments is sensitive to the interpretation advanced and use made of these 'choices' within the workplace and trade union organisational processes including the creation of union identity and internal politics. Outcomes will inevitably be hybrids of political positions and competing identities.

In an important contribution, Kelly (1996) argues that when analysing union strategies it is important to recognise that they are by no means coherently and consistently developed and ranged around the binary of, 'militancy – moderation', due to a range of contingencies and imperatives. Reviewing the literature on union responses to human resource management, in many respects the progenitor of the current partnership debate, Kelly asserts that union responses cannot be clearly mapped along any predetermined typology. He notes that whilst unions are caught between militancy and moderation – a continuing reference to the binary perspective outlined above – this occurs across various dimensions: *goal definition* (ambitious versus moderate demands), *reliance on constituencies* (membership or employers/state), *institutional resources* (bargaining versus non-bargaining arrangements),[3] *methods* (frequent versus infrequent use of collective bargaining), and *ideology* (belief in either competing or unitary interests vis-à-vis management). The key point here is that unions may find themselves militant in terms of one dimension (such as 'ideology') but moderate in terms of others (such as 'methods'). A militant union may expound an ideology that criticises employer agendas and interests, but it may also find itself in certain circumstances having to accommodate to these employer needs due to economic and industrial contingencies. Hence, union strategies are a combination of distinct, and contradictory, positions. This does not mean, following Kelly, that the union is not strategically oriented, rather, that trade unionists have to deal with a range of institutional and ideological relations that may not always cohere due to structural and political factors.

The relevance of Kelly's contribution is that it conceptualises union strategy and choices in a way that allows for complex political calculations. There is no one simple set of positions available to trade unionists on the question of partnership, because partnership necessitates a set of ideological, institutional, social and regulatory developments which may not be coherently related within and beyond the union. In fact, the very understanding of partnership may vary due to the way militancy and moderation is tied together across the five dimensions. This is an important point of departure for any discussion of partnership and union choice.[4]

We argue here that trade union strategies towards partnership must be studied at three levels, without succumbing to the false polarity of the union renewal debate. First, the actual discourse of partnership at the level of national and organisational decision-making must be evaluated. How are national strategies formulated – or not – and what significance should be attributed to the context in which decision-making and political calculations are made? In this respect we need to frame partnership in political terms – what we call the *intra-union interface*. Second, how are the concepts *and* strategies of partnership understood amongst union activists and workplace representatives? How do they perceive partnership and related strategies in the context of their working environment and relations with management? Strategy needs to be understood within the context of those who implement it – what we call the *union–management interface*. Third, having outlined the general predispositions of workplace representatives with regards to partnership, the chapter will address the construction of strategies towards partnership within the representational politics of the workplace, what we might term the *inter-union interface* and how management is seen to exploit this in certain cases. There is a problem, however, with the way Kelly constructs the key divide between militancy and moderation. Thus, we should be better placed to observe how issues of trust – which are vital to the 'game' of partnership – manifest themselves at different levels and in different ways, making the question of union choice as much political as it is strategic.

Partnership and union decision-making

At the time of the research the Manufacturing, Science and Finance Union was one of UK's largest trade unions, with over 425,000 members. Whilst mainly representing skilled and professional workers (typically technical and scientific), it covered a wide range of industries and services in the public and private sectors and had a reputation for developing innovative trade union strategies (for example, around training and development and organising). A number of high-profile partnership agreements were signed by the union in the late 1990s (for example, at Legal and General), but, despite this, the leadership 'displayed a generally cautious and pragmatic approach to the question of partnership' (Upchurch and Danford, 2001: 102). This cautious and pragmatic approach can be understood in terms of the different levels of union engagement and politics which we discuss below.

Strategic choices union politics: the intra-union interface

Typically characterised in the 1990s as a 'moderate' union, and close to the New Labour administration, the MSF was formed through a merger of two unions in 1987, one of which was known for its radical leadership (TASS – Technical and Supervisory Staff) and the other for its innovative union approaches (ASTMS – Association of Scientific Technical and Management Staffs) (Carter, 1991, 1997). Whilst the consolidation of a new type of leadership style altered some of the apparently militant features of the new union, the MSF was regarded as a relatively innovative union engaging with new types of union strategies and methods. It was one of the first unions in the UK, for example, to adopt the 'organising model' as a way of reinvigorating its shop floor representatives in the face of ongoing criticism of the leadership's 'managerial' approach to change (Carter, 1997, 2000) – although its implementation internally, as in most cases, has been uneven (Carter and Poynter, 1999). Indeed, the adoption of such a model was the subject of intense political debate and internal discussions.

During the 1990s the MSF began to evaluate the furtherance of partnership as a possible model of industrial relations practice, although like the organising debate this was not a clear and coherent development that merely contrasted with more activist approaches. Pre-empting the election of a Labour government, key circles within the union leadership saw in the new language of partnership a model for re-establishing a dynamic role within collective bargaining and reinvigorating relations with management generally. Partnership was visualised as a way of expanding union influence within the firm along a range of new issues, such as training, health and safety and equal opportunities. It was also seen as a way of marketing the union to employers in a context where union recognition and membership expansion would come to the fore due to proposed regulatory changes.

Whilst already beginning to sign high-profile partnership agreements, there had been no systematic outline by the leadership of the meaning and objective of partnership. Partnership was seen as an extension of the overarching project to 'modernise' the union and create a new form of relationship with employers and government based on an acceptance of the exigencies of the new economy and a widening of trade union influence within the firm into both social and business related matters. However, in 1999, the MSF leadership confronted a motion from key branches within its annual conference. The conference witnessed a debate on partnership that saw the overwhelming majority of delegates vote for a counter-motion that emphasised the importance of 'mutual respect' with employers and guarantees of union independence. The concern was that without such guarantees partnership would be 'unequal and compromising for unions'. This was underpinned by a belief that social actors within industrial relations would become indistinguishable. This motion would also allow, it was argued, for independent and radical campaigning to be prioritised. Carter and Poynter (1999) point to this emerging tension in terms of the contradiction between the organising and partnership dimensions of the MSF's activities.

The leadership responded by outlining a strategy that was, in theory, sensitive to these concerns. The argument forwarded was that partnership would be developed 'within a framework of independent, campaigning trade unionism' (MSF, 1999: 7).[5] However, whilst effective collective bargaining would be a central feature of partnership its character would vary from company to company depending on the industrial relations tradition (MSF, 1999). The issue here was that partnership would still constitute an extension of union remits and roles but this would be contingent on the nature of union involvement. What is more, partnership continued to be a part of both the MSF's modernising discourse and its attempt to create a more 'moderate' – in this case New Labour oriented – union.

At the annual conference in 2000 the issue of guarantees and activist concerns re-emerged (despite the publication of a series of national MSF guidelines and documents in the interim). The issue of union independence and alternative strategies, along with the perception that 'good' partnership agreements were few and far between, resurrected a number of motions and amendments that carried favour amongst the conference delegates and which, whilst not undermining the strategic shift towards partnership, did argue for its rethinking as a central plank of policy making and union action. It was asserted, for example, 'that such policies confuse and disarm trade unionists and help them to maintain the existing system which gives resolute power to employers, whose sole purpose is to satisfy shareholders' interests …' (MSF, 2000: 5). Although this debate did not significantly shift the leadership's position, it did force key players to try and formulate a critical tone to the approach to partnership.

Such developments, whilst located at the institutional and policy level of the union, illustrate the instability of the meaning of partnership and its varied forms. A large constituency saw the partnership concept as an extension of earlier discussions on the union's role vis-à-vis new management practices. The concern was that the union risked having its independence undermined by a close relation with management in the implementation of such projects. In other words, partnership was seen to be an issue that had consequences for union purpose and identity. The instability in the term was also related to the way it was used as part of a broader political project and shift in union identity. Hence, the policy debates focused on defining *guarantees* and establishing common understandings of '*good' industrial relations practice*. These internal political processes within unions, and how elements of employment relations or management strategy become complex objects of union discourse and engagement, cannot be easily structured around the binary, militancy–moderation (Martinez Lucio *et al.*, 2000), as we illustrate below.

Management–union interface: the attitudes and experiences of workplace representatives

Moving from the level of policy making, we now turn to an evaluation of the meanings and understandings of partnership at the level of the workplace. Having detected an ambiguity in the term, we need to locate this in the way partnership was viewed by those at the forefront of the implementation process. It is always difficult to evaluate the effect of formal, organisational discussions within a union on a specific topic within its broad membership, particularly when materials handled by workplace representatives regarding the subject are rarely linked to union conference processes. Nonetheless, with this caveat in mind, we draw here selectively from a large-scale survey of MSF workplace representatives' perceptions and experiences of partnership, conducted during April and May 2000. In total, 2084 questionnaires were distributed, generating 317 unable responses (a response rate of 15 per cent).[6] In broad terms, the survey sought to assess trade unionists' experiences of contemporary employment relations and the management of change, including their attitudes towards the principles and practices of partnership. Our aim was to map the changing nature and forms of employment relations across MSF's key sectors, and to assess the extent to which partnership-type arrangements were taking root. The distribution of questionnaires was not, therefore, restricted to those organisations with partnership agreements.

Just under a third of the MSF representatives surveyed responded that that they had a clear understanding of the union's policy towards partnership. Perhaps unsurprisingly, the level of understanding was found to be much higher in those 17 per cent of cases where a partnership agreement had been signed. Nonetheless, given the relatively low levels of awareness amongst workplace representatives of official MSF policy towards partnership, it is worthwhile examining the extent to which respondents held positive or negative attitudes towards the principles of partnership, as this provides an indicator of the degree of receptivity to the furtherance and implementation of partnership strategies at the workplace level.

Table 9.1 presents data on attitudes towards the principles of partnership. The findings reveal a generally pluralistic approach to industrial relations. Approximately six out of every ten MSF representatives reported that management at their workplace recognised that at certain times there might be legitimate differences in the interests of the employer and employee.This is an important building block for the development of partnership and mutuality at the workplace, in contrast to the more unitarist approaches as exemplified in so called 'sweet-heart' deals that deny differences of interest and hence compromise the position of unions.

The findings also suggest that MSF representatives were engaging with concerns relating to the management of change. Forty per cent of representatives responded that employment security should be dependent upon the development of greater flexibility, with just under a quarter of respondents disagreeing with this statement. In addition, just under half of the sample reported that training and development were regarded as non-conflictual issues between unions and management at their organisation, with just 27 per cent of respondents stating that this was not the case. So, in theory, the possibility of facilitating a deeper role for unions in the development of skills and qualifications was likely to be supported. At a more practical level, low levels of involvement were visible in relation to the development of business issues. Respondents were more likely to agree (46 per cent) than disagree (29 per cent) that the business goals of their organisation were clearly explained to the union and its members. Similarly, 55 per cent of respondents claimed that the union was afforded the opportunity to express their members' views on key business issues, compared to 30 per cent who felt that this was not the case. The flow of information from management to union could however affect the traditional methods of communication between the union and its membership. Sixty six per cent of MSF representatives agreed with the statement that 'unions may have to accept conditions of confidentiality on certain issues and manage their membership communications in new ways'.

Whilst these findings provide some tentative support for the development of a closer and, stronger consultative, relationship with management, the evidence on the conditions underpinning partnership was less positive. Thus, even though MSF members have, according to their representatives,

Table 9.1 MSF representatives' attitudes to the principles of partnership (valid percentage)

	Agree	Neutral	Disagree
Effective industrial relations are based on a shared understanding of the business goals of the organisation	84	9	7
The business goals of this organisation are clearly explained to the union and its members	46	26	29
Management has become more willing to share, and develop jointly, the future business goals of this organisation	34	25	41
Management recognises that at certain times there might be legitimate differences in the interests of the employer and employee	57	20	24
There is a high degree of mutual trust between management and unions at this organisation	19	25	56
Employment security should be dependent upon the development of greater flexibility	40	37	24
Management has become more committed to employment security	23	35	42
Measures to improve the employability of staff have become an increasing priority	25	34	41
There has been an increased investment by the organisation in the quality of members' working lives	11	29	61
Training and development are regarded as non-conflictual issues between unions and management at this organisation	46	28	27
Opportunities for non-vocational training exist at this workplace	28	20	53
Management shares information, and discusses openly, the future plans of the business	33	21	47
Unions have the opportunity to express their members' views on key business issues	55	16	30
Unions may have to accept conditions of confidentiality on certain issues and manage their membership communications in new ways	66	21	13
Employee commitment is dependent upon non-adversarial industrial relations	57	24	19
The future role of the union at this organisation should be dependent upon its success in contributing to performance improvements.	29	27	45

Note: The data is presented by reducing a 5 point likert scale to 3. Due to rounding the totals per item may not always add to 100.

had some input and exposure to the development of organisational goals, it was clear that information sharing was rather limited and one directional. MSF representatives were far more likely to disagree (47 per cent) than agree (33 per cent) with the statement that 'management shares information, and discusses openly, the future plans of the business'. Similarly, respondents were generally less (41 per cent) rather than more likely (34 per cent) to have had the opportunity to jointly develop the business goals of the organisation with management.

The supports for partnership were least apparent with regard to working conditions and investments in human capital. Less than a quarter of respondents noted that management at their organisation had become more committed to employment security, compared to over four out of ten who reported that this was not the case. In addition, measures to improve the employability of staff had become an increasing priority in just 25 per cent of cases, and opportunities for the furtherance of non-vocational training were limited to just over a quarter of the sample. It is unsurprising, therefore, that approximately six out of every ten MSF representatives disagreed with the statement that 'there has been an increased investment by the organisation in the quality of members' working lives'.

The limited nature of involvement with regard to business decisions and the lack of investment in human capital can clearly influence 'mutual-trust' at the workplace and 'hold-back' the development of genuine partnership relations. Less than a fifth of MSF representatives claimed that there was a high degree of mutual trust between management and unions at their organisation, compared to 56 per cent of respondents who reported that this was not the case. Perhaps as a consequence, MSF representatives were more likely to disagree (45 per cent) than agree (29 per cent) with the statement that 'the future role of the union at this organisation should be dependent upon its success in contributing to performance improvements'.

In summary, the findings suggest that MSF representatives were sensitive to the changing context and needs of contemporary organisations. In this regard, they were open to the challenge of workplace change and were realistic about management constraints. Yet as far as involvement, information sharing and the working environment were concerned MSF representatives were much more ambivalent as to whether there had been any significant change.This is vital for understanding the development of partnership and the prospects for change at the British workplace. According to the survey findings that addressed investment around what we called the three pillars of partnership – involvement, quality of the working environment, and training – the extent of investment in change was minimal (Martinez Lucio and Stuart, 2001).

What emerges, therefore, is ambivalence. Whilst at one level the respondents were open to the aspirations of partnership, they recognised that the process of 'building' partnership was contradictory, uneven and not central to managerial and employer agendas. Thus, support for the critical positions that emerged within union conferences appeared underpinned by a general unease with the *context* and *deliverables* of partnership and not necessarily the *process*. This is suggestive of critical understandings and positions within what are ostensibly 'moderate' views of relations with management. In other words, there was not just a problem of partnership in terms of its content and definition there was also a problem in terms of the perceived context within which it was to develop. In this respect, partnership was being read by trade union representatives in relation to other contextual factors: the institutional environment, the character and legacies of management, and the changing experiences of work. The more supportive view of partnership as a new agenda of employment relations served as a basis of the leadership's position, yet the reality of relations with management tended to undermine any attempt to create a clear consensus on the issue. Within the union's branches, the basis for strategic ventures such as partnership was undermined by the legacy of uncertainty and the lack of trust generated within the workplace.

Workplace politics and the issues of representation and trust: inter-union interface

Having discussed partnership as an object of political engagement, both within the union and in the *perceived* relations between union representatives and management, we now focus on how partnership is defined and utilised within the political relations that exist at the level of the workplace. We draw here from two qualitative case studies designed to track the evolution of partnership. The cases are based upon interviews and the observation of joint management and union meetings related to partnership in a medium-sized food ingredients manufacturer (employing approximately 300 people) and a large hospital Trust (that employs over 10,000 people). In both cases a concerted effort had been made over a number of years to move towards a partnership-based approach to employment relations. In the case of the food ingredients manufacturer, this was driven by the desire of a new human resource manager to move away from an employment relations tradition typically characterised by the set piece negotiations of the annual pay round, which tended to be prolonged and adversarial. The basis for partnership was laid over a two-year period via a 'working together' management–union forum, and advice and guidance from the Arbitration, Conciliation and Advisory Service (ACAS). The motivation for partnership in the NHS trust was centrally driven (see Stuart and Martinez Lucio, 2000), but again was advanced via a joint management–union forum – in this case specialising on improving employee involvement – and was assisted by the Involvement and Participation Association (IPA). In both cases, despite a strong initial interest and commitment from management and union constituencies, the transition to partnership did not materialise. In the case of the food ingredients manufacturer, partnership was eventually derailed by the poor financial performance of its parent company and its eventual takeover by an (anti-union) American multinational, although as we document below the process of partnership-building had reached an impasse well before this. In the case of the NHS trust, the process of building partnership stalled due to broader contextual factors, such as commercialisation.

From these two cases it is possible to extrapolate three related themes which explain some of the instability in the politics and practice of partnership relations: the fragility and unevenness of voice mechanisms; the significant impact of inter-union relations; and the subsequent problem of low-trust due to the manner in which management are seen to exploit the fragmented nature of union representation and exclude specific unions from broader involvement.

In both cases, a similar pattern emerged which confirmed some of the characteristics of partnership in the UK and the problem of *voice mechanisms*. The joint management–union forums developed in both cases for discussing the issue of partnership became hamstrung with debates on the meaning of partnership. The lack of clarity in management intentions, in terms of the partnership agenda, was seen to exacerbate this problem. Certain union representatives – in particular those of the MSF – were concerned that partnership appeared to be an extension of the management's ongoing concern to develop new forms of work organisation based on direct involvement and individualised employee relations. The more critical trade unionists, when not distrustful of management intentions, accepted partnership when presented to them as a deepening of traditional consultative roles and forms of joint regulation, which was not necessarily obvious as far as the management rhetoric was concerned. In this respect, partnership was viewed as a possible extension of the contemporary trade union agenda of enhancing the democratic role and thematic influence of labour. This contrasted in both cases with a management approach that viewed partnership as central to 'cultural transformation'. From management's point of view, changes at such a level, through the development of new line management structures and individual forms of employee communication and involvement, would, it was believed, be facilitated by union support through partnership structures. This perspective further exacerbated the concerns of key trade unionists in both cases that viewed partnership as representing a by-passing of collective forms of communication.

In this respect, the problem was one of emphasis in terms of the way the meanings of partnership were tied to distinct organisational readings of participation and involvement, which were further compounded by the lack of national regulatory supports for 'voice' mechanisms at the workplace especially in the private sector (Towers, 1997; Smith and Morton, 2001). This was a particular problem in the food manufacturing plant where the concern with derecognition was prevalent amongst the two unions present. In effect, there was a view that the risk to unions of engaging in new forms of partnership could undermine their long-term prospects due to the way individual voice mechanisms would be legitimated and due to the way such culture changes could be used to privilege one union over another. This issue of risk is central to the development of partnership structures.

This lack of trust, and the associated risk of engagement, was also influenced by the nature of *inter-union relations*. In the case of the food manufacturing plant it was felt that USDAW (the Union of Shop workers, Distributive and Allied Workers) – a union renowned for its political commitment to partnership – was less likely to be derecognised, according to the MSF branch of the plant. Whether issues of derecognition were ever on the management agenda was another matter, but concerns for this issue were apparent in the strategic calculations and behaviour of both unions. Matters came to head in a management-union workshop designed to ratify the defined approach of partnership in the organization. In the case of USDAW, full time officials were observed to force a partnership agreement onto the shop stewards during workshop 'breakouts'. This differed from the way the MSF branch was allowed to develop a more critical line around one representative, with the support of his members and officials. These inter-union tensions had a profound effect on the strategy, and political will, of management to further the partnership agenda. In essence, the line advanced by the MSF on partnership served to expose the previously ill-defined intentions of management, based around a more business and culturally driven understanding of partnership. Hence, the process of building partnership was, in effect, derailed and management chose to pursue its re-evaluation of employment relations more closely with USDAW, to the gradual isolation of MSF.

In the case of the health trust, where derecognition was less likely, there was a comparable problem of how 'agreements' could be struck within an environment of multi-unionism. Here, the problem was less one of derecognition and more one of how different unions were privileged, or marginalised, by management once participation was extended beyond the remit of traditional consultation and bargaining. For example, during the research the use of informal and secretive communication between certain unions and management was found to reinforce the problem of a lack of regularity and transparency in systems of worker representation. The process of achieving partnership appeared to necessitate a selective approach to matters of communication. This led to concerns that weaved themselves into the tapestry of union decision-making with regards to how partnership represented a more fragmented approach to worker representation. The lack of guarantees regarding representation and communication reinforced the general concerns of MSF trade unionists with regards to management's intentions towards partnership building.

Third, these inter-union dynamics were also shaped by the way in which trust relationships were strained by further developments related to organisational change. In the case of the health trust there were ongoing discussions within management and NHS structures regarding the neo-privatisation process surrounding the Private Finance Initiative that did not include trade unions in any formal manner. This made the reference to transparency within the discussions on partnership somewhat shallow as far as key trade unionists were concerned. Hence discussions on workplace change were not tied into any broader discussion of strategic issues of change. In the case of the Food Manufacturer, the demerger of the company that owned the plant did not involve any consultations or discussions with the trade union branches. Officers of the unions were not systematically and evenly involved in any informal discussions. The changing personnel within senior management and the failure to involve local representatives in key developments regarding ownership intensified the fragility of the partnership process. This led to a greater reliance on informal information and hearsay and undermined consistent relations between unions.

Of relevance to this chapter is the fact that the development and definition of partnership was conditional and dependent on negative perceptions of the regulatory environment and the context of management intentions, the impact of unstable systems of union representation and the poor legacies of *involvement*. These factors were creating a politics of partnership that were not emerging from any a priori political or ideological discourses related to moderation and militancy – although there is no doubting that in some cases such conscious discourses and educational processes did play a role. The question appears to be the way concerns about union *voice* and union *roles* had been defined within the workplace historically and were then woven into the current institutional dynamic of employment relations.

Conclusion: union strategy and context

Strategy and choice within employment relations is currently an object of discussion and evaluation as substantial changes occur within the world of work and employment. This chapter has attempted to contribute to the discussion by being sensitive to the politics of partnership at three levels of employment relations: the intra-union, the management-union, and the inter-union interfaces. Choices in terms of partnership are made in the context of political processes that influence the way such concepts evolve, not just as strategic 'ventures' but as sites of struggle in their own right.

First, within the macro-politics of the union we saw an intriguing set of engagements as the union's leadership and various constituencies of activists tried to forge meanings of partnership around questions of union identity. In this case, the issue was the nature of the relationship with employers and management in terms of the union's independence and role. The concern within the annual conference related less to the process of partnership than with the 'cost' that partnership would have on the purpose and scope of union action. These concerns led to a series of accommodations and reconfigurations in the meaning of partnership within the politics of the MSF. However, these accommodations could not stifle the concerns that constantly re-emerged within the annual conference and at the level of the workplace.

Second, at the level of workplace representatives, the issue of union independence remained important but was underpinned by a broader set of concerns about management. Our analysis reveals that support for partnership as a form of involvement and information-sharing was seriously undermined even within the 'moderate' approaches. The issue at this level was the perception that partnership was not just an ideological problem but also a practical one due to the nature of employment relations and poor management predispositions. Support for the critical positions that had emerged within union conferences appeared underpinned within the workplace by a general unease with the *context* and *deliverables* of partnership, but not necessarily the *process*.

Finally, the chapter noted that these concerns over the purpose and practicalities of partnership were exacerbated by the complex relations between unions within the workplace and worries about management manipulation during the development of partnership agreements and structures. The failure to crystallise and develop systematic voice mechanisms within industrial relations is a salient feature of partnership in Britain (Stuart and Martinez Lucio, 2002). Hence, it is difficult for observers to evaluate partnership and its meaning when the relations of trust and the clarity of roles it is contingent upon are unclear. In this respect, the analysis of political processes remains central to the evolution of partnership and new forms of employment relations.

The chapter points, therefore, to the complex and multi-layered construction of partnership as a strategic venture within the UK. The meaning of partnership is fragile in part due to 'unsupportive' external political, regulatory and economic factors (see Martinez Lucio and Stuart, 2004), but also due to the political dimension of industrial relations in the UK. We have argued for an analysis that moves beyond simply framing partnership in terms of union militancy and moderation, as the dynamics of contemporary employment relations and the development of trust-based relations need to be conceptualised in a distinctly different register. First, trade union action does not necessarily cohere around easily definable ideological cleavages. Second, future research on partnership must be sensitive to the multi-layered mechanisms by which trust-based relations are furthered, constrained and, in many cases, undermined.

Acknowledgements

This chapter draws from research funded by the Manufacturing, Science and Finance Union. We wish to thank MSF for its financial assistance, and particularly Peter Carter and Ciaran Naidoo for their encouragement and support. The views expressed are, of course, our own.

Notes

1. This is not to suggest, of course, that New Labour has backed up its call for partnership in employment relations with more supportive collective regulation (see Smith and Morton, 2001).
2. MSF merged with the Amalgamated Engineering and Electrician's Union (AEEU) to form AMICUS in 2001. Whilst our work with the MSF section is ongoing, the current chapter explores the period immediately prior to the merger.
3. Curiously, collective bargaining for Kelly is seen as being potentially complementary with militant strategies.
4. There is a problem, however, with the way Kelly constructs the key divide between militancy and moderation. Whilst there are complex combinations across the dimensions outlined above, they still rest on under-developed notions of militancy and moderation (which may fail to capture the internal variety in either). Ironically, this is apparent in his own critique of partnership which leaves little room for such complexity, as suggested in his work on militancy.
5. This being a common outcome of union conferences that deal with management-led change (Martinez Lucio and Weston, 1992).
6. For a more detailed account of the survey methodology see Martinez Lucio and Stuart (2001).

References

Ackers, P. (2002) 'Reframing employment relations: the case for neo-pluralism.' *Industrial Relations Journal*, 33 (1): 2–19.
Ackers, P. and Payne, J. (1998) 'British trade unions and social partnership: rhetoric, reality and strategy' *International Journal of Human Resource Management*, 9 (3): 529–50.
Bacon, N. and Storey, J. (1996) 'Individualism and collectivism and the changing role of trade unionism', in Ackers, P., Smith, C. and Smith, P. (eds), *The New Workplace and Trade Unionism*: 41–76, London: Routledge.
Carter, B. (1991) 'The making of MSF: politics and process in the making of the Manufacturing, Science and Finance Union (MSF)'. *Capital and Class*, 45: 35–72.
Carter, B. (1997) 'Adversity and opportunity: towards union renewal in Manufacturing, Science and Finance'. *Capital and Class*, 61: 8–18.
Carter, B. and Poynter, G. (1999) 'Unions in a changing climate: MSF and Unison in the new public sector'. *Industrial Relations Journal*, 30 (5): 499–513.
Carter, B. (2000) 'Adoption of the organising model in British trade unions: some evidence from Manufacturing, Science and Finance'. *Work, Employment and Society*, 14 (1): 117–36.
Danford, A., Richardson, M. and Upchurch, M. (2002) ' "New Unionism", organising and partnership: a comparative analysis of union renewal strategies in the public sector', *Capital and Class*, 76: 1–27.
Gall, G. (1998) 'The prospects for workplace trade unionism: Evaluating Fairbrother's union renewal thesis'. *Capital and Class*, 61: 149–57.

Gall, G. (2001) 'The organisation of organised discontent: the case of the postal workers in Britain'. *British Journal of Industrial Relations*, 39 (2): 393–410.

Giddens, A. (1998) *The Third Way*, Oxford: Polity Press.

Heery, E. (1996) 'The new new unionism', in Beardwell, I. (ed.) *Contemporary Industrial Relations*, Oxford: Oxford University Press.

Kelly, J. (1996) 'Union militancy and social partnership' in Ackers, P. Smith, C. and Smith. P. (eds) *The New Workplace and Trade Unionism*: 77–109, London: Routledge.

Kelly, J. (1998) *Rethinking Industrial Relations: Mobilization, Collectivism and Long Waves*, London: Routledge.

Kelly, J. (2001) Social partnership agreements in Britain: union revitalisation or employer-counter-mobilization?, in Martinez Lucio, M. and Stuart, M. (eds) *Assessing Partnership: The Prospects for and Challenges of 'Modernisation'*, Leeds: Leeds University Business School.

Kochan, T. A. and Osterman (1994) *The Mutual Gains Enterprise: Forging a Winning Partnership among Labour, Management and Government*, Boston, MA: Harvard University Press.

Leadbeater, C. (1999) *Living on Thin Air: The New Economy*, London: Penguin Books.

Leisink, P. (1993) 'Is Innovation a Management Prerogative? Changing Employment Relationships, Innovative Unions', Leverhulme Public Lecture, University of Warwick.

Macdonald, D. (1996) 'Revitalising trade unionism: confusion, contradictions and continuities', Centre for Industrial Policy and Performance, *Occasional paper in Labour Markets and Industrial Relations. No.4*, University of Leeds.

Martinez Lucio, M. and Weston, S. (1992) 'Trade union responses to human resource management: bringing the politics of the workplace back into the debate', in Blyton, P. and Turnbull, P. (eds) *Reassessing Human Resource Management*: 215–232, London: Sage.

Martinez Lucio, M., Jenkins, S. and Noon, M. (2000) 'The question of teamwork and union identity in the Royal Mail: beyond negotiation?' in Mueller, F. and Procter, S. (eds) *Teamworking*, London: Macmillan.

Martinez Lucio, M. and Stuart, M. (2001) *In Search of Partnership: Experiences of Changing Employment Relations*, London: Manufacturing, Science and Finance Union.

Martinez Lucio, M. and Stuart, M. (2004) 'Swimming against the tide: social partnership, mutual gains and the revival of "tired" HRM'. *International Journal of Human Resource Management*, Forthcoming.

MSF. (1999) *Annual Conference Documentation*, London: MSF.

MSF. (2000) *Partnership*, London: MSF.

Smith, P. and Morton, G. (2001) 'New Labour's reform of Britain's employment law: the devil is not only in the detail but in the values and policy too'. *British Journal of Industrial Relations* 39 (1): 119–38.

Stuart, M. (1996) 'The industrial relations of training: a reconsideration of training arrangements'. *Industrial Relations Journal*, 27 (3): 253–66.

Stuart, M. and Martinez Lucio, M. (2000) 'Renewing the model employer: changing employment relations and 'partnership' in the health and private sectors'. *Journal of Management in Medicine*, 15 (5/6): 310–25.

Stuart, M. and Martinez Lucio, M. (2002) 'Social partnership and the mutual gains organisation: remaking involvement and trust at the British workplace.' *Economic and Industrial Democracy*, 23 (2): 177–200.

Taylor, P. and Ramsay, H. (1998) 'Unions, partnership and HRM: sleeping with the enemy?' *International Journal of Employment Studies*, 6 (2): 115–43.

Towers, B. (1997) *The Representation Gap: Change and Reform in the British and American Workplace*, Oxford: Oxford University Press.

Trades Union Congress (TUC) (1999) *Partners for Progress*, London: TUC.

Upchurch, M. and Danford, A. (2001) 'Industrial restructuring, "globalisation" and the trade union response: a study of MSF in the south-west of England.' *New Technology, Work and Employment*, 16 (2): 100–17.

10
Strategy, Contracts and Control in Government IT Work

Steven Vincent and Irena Grugulis

Introduction

This chapter develops and applies a heuristic framework to analyse the structure of contractual forms of organising and the ways that these condition work. The framework is informed by sociological, economic, institutional and labour process theories about work. From a sociological perspective, social structures are understood in terms of the balance of power existing between different social groups. Jessop (1996) outlines a 'strategic-relational' approach, in which the location of groups affects the strategies that they may adopt in pursuit of sectional interests. From this perspective the reproduction of social processes is affected by the 'structural constraints' operating within specific localities. For the purposes of this chapter institutional, labour process and economic theories are used to inform our understanding of the structural constraints that affect the strategies groups may pursue (also see Hyman, 1987; Ackroyd, 2002). This is not to deny the reflexivity of the agents involved, or that they can and do transform their social structures through their actions, but that action is contingent on location. Archer (1995) draws a useful distinction between 'corporate' agents and 'primary' agents. The former group find themselves in a structural location where they are able to pursue collective interests and the latter, whilst an identifiable group, are relatively powerless. To a greater extent all those involved in productive organisations are corporate agents (Ackroyd, 2002), whether managers, employees, shareholders or governmental policy makers.

This orientation is used in our analysis of the impact of a ten-year contract, signed in the mid 1990s by FutureTech.[1] FutureTech is one of a handful of computing specialists that oligopolise the market for managing large IT contracts. The contract was for the delivery of IT services to Govco, a government department that outsourced its Information Technology Office (ITO). FutureTech, a US-based multinational, had expanded rapidly over the previous decade by taking over computer work from large firms and government departments. This particular contract specified a 50 per cent reduction in the unit cost for IT systems development over the first five years, which was achieved and hailed as a success. However, this evidence identifies significant problems with both the accountability of managerial employees at the centre of the governance structure and in the employment policies and practices adopted before and after the signing of the contract. There was evidence of poorly performing new IT systems, increased tightness in the control of IT workers at various levels and a question mark over the organisation's ability to reproduce its skill base. This chapter argues that these problems were, in large part, attributable to the way that contracts were drawn-up and regulated.

The chapter is divided into several sections. First, we delve further into economic, institutional and labour process theories to consider the particular, capitalist structures that affect the agencies involved in contractual forms of organising, as well as the nature of government contracting. The second section goes on to explore the case study itself. The contractual arrangements between Govco and FutureTech are compared to earlier inhouse IT operations and consideration is given to the way that this contract was managed and the forces that influenced managers' choices. The chapter also considers the effect that outsourcing had on the organisation's ability to produce and reproduce knowledge.

Inter-organisational governance and the control of work

From the perspective of transaction cost economics (Williamson, 1975, 1985) the more complex and uncertain the thing to be contracted for, and IT services are highly complex and uncertain, the less the purchaser can control the outcome. Exact contractual specification is impossible. This means that the purchaser can be vulnerable to opportunistic behaviour, as managers may be tempted to cut costs and make profits at the expense of quality in the service delivered. It is prudent, therefore, to contract for goods and services where outcomes can be easily specified in advance, typically low-skilled and peripheral work. Opportunistic behaviour is likely to stop short of compromising the viability of the other organisation in the relationship, as this will not be to its economic advantage (Krepps, 1990; Dore, 1996). It is possible for non-optimal and monopsonistic economic structures to exist, provided that dominant actors are happy for events to continue. Also, whilst there may be the potential for opportunistic behaviour on one side of a relationship, it cannot be assumed that such behaviour will occur. The purchaser may either regulate the supplier, at extra cost, or trust that the supplier is acting in their interests.

In this regard, institutional theorists lead us to consider the forms of regulation and trust that exist where any transaction is embedded. Sako (1992) distinguishes between arms-length contractual relations (ACR), such as that associated with low-skilled outsourcing, and obligational contractual relations

(OCR), where inter-organisational managers share information to coordinate the delivery of more complex services. She suggests that Britain's relatively weak regulatory context pushes relations towards the ACR type as there are few structures encouraging cooperative forms of inter-firm behaviour. Likewise, Lane and Bachmann (1997) compare the institutional context of Germany and Britain and suggest that strong forms of regulation through, *inter-alia*, trade associations, vocational training policies and industrial relations procedures encourage 'systems trust' and more cooperative forms of behaviour in Germany as outcomes are more predictable. This is the central conundrum of contracting in the UK, that while it may be more 'economic' to contract for certain goods and services, it is also more difficult for the most efficient outcome to be achieved. Trust cannot be assumed and needs to be developed through local management relations between organisations (Bachmann, 1999). The general point is that trust is context specific and where regulations exist, such as in the chemicals industry of the UK, OCR type relationships are more likely to be effective (Marchington and Vincent, 2001). The question is whether or not the forms of regulation that exist in government contracting are appropriate for the development of long-term, trusting inter-organisational relations of the OCR type.

The rise of 'government by contract' (Carnaghan and Bracewell-Milnes, 1993) or the 'contract state' (Kirkpatrick and Martinez Lucio, 1996) has altered public services provision so that many are delivered through contractual relations rather than hierarchical authority structures (Deakin and Walsh, 1996). This shift was originally inspired by the neo-liberal ideology of the Conservative government (1979–97) that saw markets as the most effective distributors of goods and services. The logic being that, since different markets will enjoy different advantages it should be possible (given appropriately specified contracts) to harness these for the benefit of the public. The Labour administration that has been in place since 1997 has done little to switch emphasis. Under the Conservatives various interventions, including the Local Government Act (1988) and the 'Competing for Quality' White Paper ensured that many activities previously undertaken by the public sector were transferred to private sector firms. Labour interventions, such as Private Finance Initiatives, have sought to secure private sector investment in public infrastructure; effectively transferring the responsibility for short-term costs which are often politically sensitive. This process has transferred many 'peripheral services' to private sector contractors (see Grimshaw *et al.*, 2002) and continues, despite research questioning the cost effectiveness of government contracts (Boyne, 1998). It may be that political expediency, coupled with blind faith in the efficiency of market provision (Gamble, 1994) is rather more influential in decisions to outsource infrastructure developments and services than policymakers would like us to believe.

Most government outsourcing is of low skilled work (Boyne, 1998; Rainbird and Munro, 2003). In these contracts, outsourcing often makes cost savings through the deterioration of staff terms and condition, as in McIntosh and Broderick's (1996) account of refuse collectors. Attempts to mitigate this through TUPE (Transfer for Undertaking Protection of Employment) have had a limited effect (Cooke *et al.*, 2001). More generally, the fact that many savings are the result of deteriorating terms and conditions rather than private sector 'expertise' is a cause for concern.

While unskilled work may be measured in terms of cost, the legitimation for outsourcing skilled work is more nuanced with calls for a shift from hierarchical structures to 'quasi' market control mechanisms (Bartlett and Le Grand, 1993; Bartlett *et al.*, 1994; Challiss *et al.*, 1994). Some suggest that it is possible to create a new hybrid sector, incorporating the public values of quality service and accountability with private sector efficiencies (Brereton and Temple, 1999). However, mixed forms may erode the public service ethos (Corby and White, 1999); lack transparency and accountability, particularly where difficulties in verifying 'quality' are apparent (Grimshaw *et al.*, 2001); and may introduce rigidity in the form of contractual (mis) specifications and repetitions double counting, due to the increased need to demonstrate efficiency (Grimshaw *et al.*, 2002; Grugulis *et al.*, 2003).

As suggested in the introduction, a focus on the employment relationships of those that work in and control these organisational forms would seem a useful starting point for an analysis of outcomes. Transaction cost economics (Williamson, 1975, 1985; Krepps, 1990) and more institutional perspectives (Sako, 1992; Bachmann, 1999) suggest that behaviour is contingent on the nature of the economic context within which it is situated. For example, for Williamson the comparatively most efficient or transaction cost minimising form of behaviour will always prevail. Institutionalists, on the other hand, study the ways that specific social and political contexts shape behaviour towards predictable outcomes. Both may be accused of neglecting the capacity for agency (see Ackroyd, 2002).

Social scientists from a range of traditions including managerial strategists (Boxall, 1996; Boxall and Purcell, 2000), labour process (Braverman, 1974; Thompson and Smith 2001; Thompson and McHugh, 2002) and critical social theorists (Friedman, 1977; Edwards, 1979; Ackroyd and Thompson, 1999) tend to concentrate on how the control of work is driven by managers and employees acting and reacting to specific organisational contexts. In these accounts agency and management actions cannot be simply 'read off' from either organisational structure or market conditions. Managers make policy choices as to how best to deploy the resources available to them and as these choices may conflict with the wishes of other groups, organisations are political and contested arenas.

Here, the way that organisations control employees is central to understanding organisational choices and strategies. Friedman (1977) captures these tensions in his distinction between *direct control*, in which work is strictly prescribed by managers, and *responsible autonomy*, in which the employee is afforded control within a given jurisdiction. For Friedman, peripheral groups tend to be controlled directly and treated on the basis of their skills. Here, 'centre–periphery' relationships, (such as outsourcing), are not unproblematic but arise 'out of struggle, out of a *combination* of differential workers and managerial strategies' (pp. 116–17, own emphasis).

These tensions apply equally to inter-organisational arrangements. Most accounts of collaboration focus on relative forms of advantage. Given, for example, the competition for key knowledge workers that occurs in particular sectors, even well-funded organisations may not be able to afford to finance expensive specialist employees indefinitely. Particularly Boxall and Steeneveld's (1999) study of engineering consultancies suggests that a critical mass of personnel, or 'table stakes', is required to function as an effective organisational unit. Organisations that cannot (or do not wish to) meet these table stakes may think that the potential costs and rigidities of transacting in the (external) product market outweigh the costs and rigidities of transacting in the (internal) labour market.

In order to analyse the governance of inter-organisational relations and employment outcomes it may be helpful to combine the notions of direct control and responsible autonomy with ACR/OCR (see Figure 10.1). Here, contractual specifications and the control of work provide four categories: output control, procedural control, normative control and technical control (see also Lepak and Snell, 1999). Such a device is, inevitably, a simplification. In reality, jobs may have autonomy in some areas but be subjected to control in others, and different groups of workers may have their work controlled differently under the same contract. Likewise, obligational and transactional elements can coexist (Sayer and Walker, 1992; Rubery *et al.*, 2003). However, this framework may provide a useful starting point for a strategic-relational

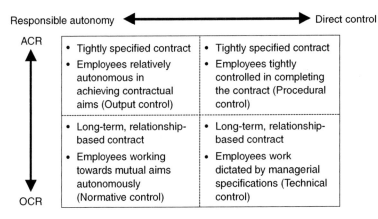

Figure 10.1 Contractual relations and employee control

analysis into the effect of different contractual structures on employment relationship outcomes.

Introducing the case study: IT work at Govco

The research presented here is taken from a wider project on *Changing Organisational Forms and Organisational Performance*, funded by the ESRC as part of their Future of Work programme. Work was conducted in eight case study companies between 1999 and 2002. One case study, 'FutureTech', is taken from the wider project and explored in detail here. In total, 14 interviews were conducted with senior managers involved with contract management in FutureTech and Govco (the department that outsourced its IT provision) as well as 33 with line managers and programmers in FutureTech. The data was collected over two years, and was combined with access to a large collection of government reports, internal documents and observations of the way that specific contracts for computing services operated. In addition, employees were also asked to describe and reflect on their work histories and experiences, providing an elementary longitudinal profile.

Previously all IT work had been undertaken in-house and the ITO, which employed over 2250 staff, had an annual budget of £250 m and considered itself to be in the vanguard of governmental IT systems development. However, the task of servicing 30 Govco divisions, which often competed for resources when few outside the ITO possessed expertise in computing, was fraught. One senior manager Colin, who still worked in IT management for Govco, explained that:

> Users with the most vague idea about what they wanted would come along to the [ITO] and we'd sit down with them, and we wouldn't charge for the service, and we would understand what their objectives were, and we would take that to programming, and we would test it for them, and we would roll it out and hold their hands for the first few months. So, they didn't really understand what was involved in developing the product.

The lack of specialist knowledge outside the ITO was reflected in the lack of control structures imposed on it. There was no comprehensive audit of systems and capabilities. Nor was the overall performance of the ITO systematically measured. Control of resources was left to local project managers and technical experts who used their own judgement as to the relative price and effectiveness of the technologies available. As David, one FutureTech senior technical expert said:

> in the old ITO it was almost a techies bunch. Managing direct relationships with vendors was 'Okay, what's the latest hot stuff? We'll have some

of that, oh don't worry about that', and the business was done. There was a certain interplay of value for money there. I mean, people weren't stupid.

Strategy was driven by the technologies available and local knowledge about how they might be applied. This kept the control of IT development in the hands of the ITO, leading to widespread resentment from other divisional managers and accusations of poor accountability, with many projects not held to timescale or budget. According to two independent consultants' reports the ITO was 25 per cent less efficient than equivalent private sector organisations and could operate with up to 880 fewer staff. Such claims should be treated with caution, as the development of unique IT systems is notoriously difficult to price. Despite years of negotiations Govco and FutureTech could not agree on a valid reference point for benchmarking the performance and relative value of the work done. However, reports were highly influential and, coupled with the 'Competing for Quality' White Paper, it was these that persuaded Govco to outsource its IT services. Following a tendering process, the contract was awarded to FutureTech and a new contractual discipline brought in to control the work of managers.

The new organisational structure was intended to be both more transparent and more accountable and, to a certain extent, it succeeded. In order to manage the new inter-firm relationship, as well as the 1700 staff who had transferred across from Govco, an elaborate 'partnership' arrangement was devised. The structure included around 200 managers from the Govco side, organised within its Business Operations Division, and an equivalent number of managers from FutureTech, organised within a newly formed Govco Contract Division. The Govco side of the partnership was answerable to the Govco board, and other governmental institutions, such as the National Audit Office, which regularly reviewed the accounts. The FutureTech side was accountable to Govco and the Board of FutureTech and the respective heads of each organisation met every year to discuss the performance of the contract. As part of the transfer, FutureTech was also required to recognise a trade union for bargaining purposes. This was agreed, but FutureTech management did not extend bargaining privileges to employees hired after the initial transfer and the union could claim little involvement with the day-to-day running of the contract:

> You are not obliged to talk to the unions about your business plan. They used to put it on the agenda and I used to refuse to talk about it. He couldn't understand why. I told him in private that I wasn't prepared to talk about strategic direction of the business, to be blunt, in front of people who were only interested in tea breaks and goodness knows what.
>
> (Frank, Senior Manager: FutureTech)

In practice, the senior managers, who liased between FutureTech and Govco, enjoyed a great deal of influence in ensuring the success of the relationship.

A contractual specification was needed for each piece of work and the managers at the centre of the 'partnership' were responsible for coordinating, defining, pricing and monitoring these. Contracts were priced on the basis of a complex system of the number of 'function points' (an industry standard measurement of computer code) that needed to be developed. This was then used by FutureTech to assess the 'man hours' (their term) required to do a particular job. In practice specifications often had a considerable amount of latitude; timescales were almost always set, but the exact requirements for completing a contract might not be known in advance. Nor were all function points equal in terms of cost and this was acknowledged and allowed for in the system. When FutureTech delivered function points cheaply they were expected, retrospectively, to accept a lower price. When scarce skills were required, these had to be purchased separately at a price that reflected their 'market' value.

Many of the contractual mechanisms that existed to assist the smooth running of the 'partnership' acknowledged the fallibility of the function point system and were designed, not to improve the system, but to make efficiency improvements mutually beneficial. These included: open access to FutureTech accounts, a practice rare in outsourcing which also made it possible to negotiate prices after contracts had started; a profit-sharing arrangement, should FutureTech make more than a given amount in any financial year resources would be given back to the Business Services Division (typically to be invested in research); and financial disincentives to failure, such as reduced bonus payments for FutureTech in the event of an overspend and increased financial costs for Govco when contracts were poorly specified. Liaison took the form of a hierarchy of meetings between the two organisations, with problems that could not be resolved locally referred up the line. Contracts that were likely to fail were to be referred to the most senior management, although this was said to be rare. Since contractual specifications needed to be both flexible and precise and since prices could be negotiated retrospectively negotiations were often complex with both sides engaged in 'horse trading'.

One of the main strengths of the 'partnership' was not the system of governance but the similarities between the senior management from both organisations and their shared interest in making the project a success. Both sides were dominated by middle-aged, white men, all driven by the same set of efficiency-related goals. Colin also said with pride:

> I pull [FutureTech] into meetings with me to other customers and they cannot tell the difference. They can't say 'well you're the [FutureTech] bloke and you're the [Govco] bloke'. We talk the same language, we say the same things, we are motivated by the same goals, we both want to be successful.

Both sides stood to benefit from profit sharing. When this occurred, the Govco Account Division could show the FutureTech board that they had achieved a reasonable profit and the Business Services Division could show the Govco board that they were delivering results. Such a 'partnership' structure may drive the demonstration of competence and efficiency over and above that which is really present (see also Grimshaw *et al.*, 2001). The scope provided in contractual specifications could, as one senior industry respondent conceded, lead to both sides colluding in order to demonstrate shared achievements.

With a few notable exceptions, such as the Internet technologies, the vast majority of contracts have been delivered within timescale and budget, and a profit share has been returned to the Business Services Division on every year of the contract. These achievements were presented as marks of success, suggesting that the partnership has more successfully controlled both the work of the programmers and the deployment of resources. But it is also possible that generous specifications made contracts easier to deliver and much of the 50 per cent increase in efficiency may be attributable to more general advancements in the 'tools' used to do the job, technologically it is possible to do more with less. One FutureTech manager described the organisation's 'core competence' as 'the ability to predict the future price of developing computer code'.

Contractual structures and employment relationships

Outsourcing had significant implications for the way that programmers' work was controlled. As noted above, when work was undertaken internally programmers had a considerable amount of autonomy. Once the department had been contracted out the programmers became subject to 'scopes of work', which specified the times allocated to projects. Managers too were more constrained, in the sense that their careers depended to a greater extent on their ability to demonstrate that money being spent had been accounted for. David said:

> I think that what happened when [FutureTech] took over we became more technically constrained because we had to start taking notice of the fact that this cost money, therefore we had to justify it. We became more commercially competent but we didn't become more technologically aware because in the past we ran our own evaluations without interference. When [FutureTech] came on board there was another angle of evaluation to be taken. It almost seemed as though another echelon of management activities had to be gone through to manage those types of evaluation and relationship things (Technical Manager: FutureTech)

Despite these changes in governance, there were broad continuities in working practices that were conditioned by the relationship between the IT systems and the organisation. IT systems were, and remain, central to Govco's organisational performance and its cost reduction strategy. Govco's work is to administrate high volumes of unique and interrelated transactions. A task that is complicated by regular government policy changes that had to be catered for when designing IT systems. This means that the IT systems are highly complex, idiosyncratic and interconnected. When new functions are developed, they must be integrated to existing systems (that are often written in different computer languages) to ensure that the system works as a whole. This requires the combination of a variety of different types of knowledge: knowledge of new technologies; knowledge of existing IT systems (so that new technologies could be adapted to them); specific knowledge of the wider Govco operation and its relationship with central government; and, knowledge of the administrative structure of IT delivery. Work was organised on a project or programme basis with large pieces of development often running simultaneously, so that existing systems were maintained and enhanced and new IT functions developed. Some consistency in practices was retained after the transfer of undertakings as the project management structure of the work was dictated by a predictable bi-annual flow of government policy changes.

Under the ITO programmers had been in a comparatively favourable position. Terms and conditions were subject to collective bargaining and there was a complex status-based pay grading arrangement related to both hierarchical position and length of service, with additional increments awarded individually on the basis of performance appraisal. There was also a flexi-time arrangement and overtime pay. Within the ITO these arrangements were complicated by recruitment difficulties and the labour market power IT workers could exercise. In practice this meant that promotion was rapid since it was the only means of raising pay, a practice resented by managers elsewhere in the organisation.

The ITO tended to recruit internally when they could. This ensured that employees already had a great deal of local knowledge of Govco practices and systems before being trained in the technology. Despite this, there were significant skill shortages and these were compounded by financial austerities, which included a general embargo on recruitment. Since contractors were not classed as 'employees' in the accounts the cutbacks resulted in increasing numbers of costly consultancy workers, occasionally in preference to updating employees' skills and promoting them (see also Harvey and Kanwal, 2000). Some workers, with highly specialised skills, were purchased for short periods to develop new technologies. Others were ex-Govco employees who had resigned to sell their work back to Govco at a higher price. The cost of contracted labour was reported as four times the price of equivalent internal supply. Unsurprisingly perhaps some contractors, who bragged about their pay, were described as having poor people-management skills and a 'cavalier attitude'. Outsourcing the ITO was first considered in 1991, after expenditure on contractors quadrupled from around £2 m to over £8 m during the 1980s.

After the transfer, FutureTech was able to end the relationships with these consultancy workers, either by offering them permanent employment contracts or waiting for the existing agreements to expire. While this ended the relative financial autonomy and freedom from local constraints that these workers enjoyed, it may have alleviated some of the ITO's problems. As Geoff, one transferred manager said:

> People liked being managed by [FutureTech] people, [they] tended to be more professional … everyone was treated with respect for the work they did.

However, the removal of contractors did not signal a more general stabilising of employment relationships. There were changes in personnel with most new staff having individualised employment contracts; inter-organisational contracts were used to drive projects and performance-monitoring practices were introduced. These had significant implications for the way that the programmers experienced work. While the ITO had had few hard measures of performance, in the new organisational structure over 400 measures of contractual efficiency were used to guide decision-making.

Under FutureTech each request for work required a business case and an analysis of the resources that would be needed. Contractual specifications were written and awarded, after discussions with programmers and technical experts and these acted as planning tools, allowing resources to be allocated over a pre-set timescale. The degree to which individuals felt constrained by this structure varied depending upon the type of skills they had, the employment contract that they held with FutureTech and the type of contract for services they worked on. For a minority of the skilled IT developers and managers there were opportunities on other FutureTech contracts to obtain promotion and develop new skills. In theory, these transfers could benefit Govco since it would no longer have to pay the costs associated with retraining or terminating an employment contract when an individual's services were no longer required. In reality Govco managers argued that much of their best talent was transferred from Govco work, leaving their business to be run by a 'B-team'. FutureTech management, however, maintained that Govco only purchased the work to be done, not the specific people who did it and would only accept Govco intervention in the event of a failure to deliver work to contract. Given the position of FutureTech and flexibility in the contracts awarded Govco intervention was unlikely in all but extreme cases, although there were examples of managers on failing projects being 'moved sideways' after a 'quiet word' from senior managers. As a result of Govco's concerns an assessment of skill needs was undertaken. This identified significant skill gaps, particularly in the area of Internet technologies, which FutureTech was taking steps to remedy. In some areas FutureTech itself started to hire external contractors.

The transfer was also designed to make cost savings through a voluntary redundancy programme, financed by Govco, in which some 200 personnel (of the 800 that applied) left the organisation. Yet over the first five years of the contract the amount of work to be completed doubled and several hundred university graduates were recruited. A smaller number of people were hired from the wider labour market, typically at more senior levels. The graduates were cheaper than the workers they replaced, but, while many had technical skills, none enjoyed the in-depth knowledge of Govco's existing systems and work practices, and their role was variously and insultingly described as: 'warm bodies', 'bums on seats' and 'cheap labour'. Supervisors, also working to meet contractual deadlines, rarely had the time to develop their subordinates in a systematic way. Employees also thought that the removal of experienced personnel meant that the remainder had to work harder. Peter, one graduate employed as a supervisor, said:

> The redundancy programme and stuff ... certainly reduced the amount of, not just business but the technical knowledge as well because a lot of them they have a mass of business knowledge, but also a technical experience as well and it's certainly limiting the amount we've got at the moment ... I think it might just mean you need to work a little harder the time you're here, I think. But essentially yes, it may be that you have to work a bit longer ... It's such a challenge though when they lose these people what they do to replace them, because it's almost impossible.
>
> (Graduate: FutureTech)

According to one ex-Govco programmer, the internal systems were so complex that, after working on one of Govco's larger system for two years 'you can only scratch the surface of being useful to the team because of the business knowledge'.

The new graduates were both much younger than their ex-Govco colleagues (because of the freeze on recruitment) and employed under very different terms and conditions. Over 1500 ex-Govco personnel worked for FutureTech in administrating, managing and doing programming work, with a handful, who had considerable technical knowledge, acting as internal consultants. All ex-Govco staff had their terms and conditions protected by TUPE and, although they could transfer onto a 'Standard' FutureTech contract, none of the staff questioned said that they had done so. Their working time arrangements were protected and the union continued to conduct collective bargaining. There was little that FutureTech managers could do to compel this group to stay late to meet a deadline, and, when they did overtime they could claim this back through flexi-time arrangement or extra pay.

Despite these benefits, transferred staff in the lower grades suspected that they were underpaid. As Alex, one programmer argued:

> There are three of us on the team who've got the same sort of money and we are all in the lowest quartile of the range. There are people on the team

who, within the next two or three years, will pass my salary. They've been here for four years and can do the code as good as I can. They might be quicker than I am. They are more conversant with PCs if they are younger, but they haven't got the business knowledge to realise the impact of changing the system. And that does cause a bit of resentment, but if I was driven purely financially then I could probably go to my boss and say I want to go on the standard package...but I don't want to do that...I'm married with kids. I'm 46 years old so I'm well down the line. There's always the chance that when I reach 50 I might be able to get out by early retirement and we've got a fairly good early retirement that they do offer.

In marked contrast to the ex-Govco employees, no graduate interviewed was over thirty. They were recruited directly from universities and typically occupied more junior jobs in programming and contract management. Two in supervisory roles were interviewed and three others, with scarce technical skills, had already reached higher status technical roles in the new online services group, but graduates were not found at senior levels elsewhere in the structure.

All of these new hires had the 'Standard' package, with individualised terms and conditions and annual pay and performance reviews. None were paid overtime. For those on the Standard package promotion and taking on more responsibilities did not lead directly to increases in pay. Pay was determined by annual performance reviews. In these career and pay recommendations were linked to a systems of peer-group and supervisory performance appraisals. Raises could also be on an *ad hoc* basis for effort above the norm. In addition to this there was a series of 'morale boosting' minor rewards, generally given to those who worked through the weekend to solve a problem or meet a deadline. This could be anything from lunch at McDonald's to 'a night out with the girlfriend or boyfriend'. Ultimately the team leaders made recommendations for bonuses and pay and the local managers decided whether or not to award these. Many of those interviewed complained that the bonuses offered by FutureTech for completing contracts did not match their expectations but the lack of skills development (with its implications for career trajectories) was a more serious source of grievance. In some cases graduates were asked to do repetitive tasks for long periods. Managers confessed that careers were often constrained by the demands of the contract. According to two employees:

I talked to other Standard package people who work on projects, they work so many extra hours a week consistently and they don't get paid for that ...You're paid this much a year to finish a job and although they don't use those words that's the way it is. (Rob, graduate programmer)

At the end of the day it boils down to what business needs dictate so at the end of the day whatever you want comes second place to what

[FutureTech] want, which is perhaps fair enough because they pay your wages. (Peter, graduate supervisor)

It seems that, while the new structure succeeded in introducing a mechanism for controlling the work undertaken by IT programmers it was less effective at reproducing and developing the requisite skills. For new recruits getting on in the organisation often meant working long hours whilst completing repetitive tasks and contractual pressures often limited their opportunities to develop a broader base of skills. In this context it is unsurprising that those who were career-minded considered moving away from the Govco contract. For Govco, FutureTech could provide a repository of expertise but its other work meant that skilled staff might be transferred to other posts, new hires had little of the local knowledge that was necessary and some work was still undertaken by contractors.

Synthesising accounts: governance, employment and technology development

Programmers who were employed adapting existing IT systems were very tightly controlled. Here, since managers on both sides had a considerable amount of local knowledge, contracts could be very tightly specified and, since most effort was put into delivery, the success rate was almost 100 per cent. The same could not be said of the development of new systems. FutureTech was given the task of introducing Internet technologies, as part of a government commitment to providing online services. Interestingly, despite its expertise in other areas of computing, FutureTech had little experience of the Internet. It did however employ so many ex-Govco IT staff, that it would have been extremely difficult to develop and incorporate any new IT systems without large amounts of work going to FutureTech. Govco was effectively 'locked in' to development work with FutureTech for the duration of the contract. Furthermore, it is likely, given the knowledge of Govco systems that FutureTech managers held, that they would continue to depend on FutureTech expertise after the existing contract expired (also see Grimshaw *et al.*, 2002).

Graduates, who were more likely to have developed the required technical skills at university (though some were retrained after recruitment), dominated the online services group. As in other areas, hiring graduates was less expensive than retraining existing or ex-Govco staff. Various FutureTech and ex-Govco managers were deployed to the group to advise on developing the systems. Here though, the nature of the task not only gave employees more autonomy, it also meant that there was less scope for generous contractual specifications. FutureTech failed to meet its deadlines and Govco purchased 'off the shelf' packages from a third party. David, a FutureTech technical expert, said

> I couldn't say I'm proud of the quality of the stuff that we've done because the engineering discipline wasn't in the teams. However, if you talk to the customer [about the project] quality, they don't care about quality … so they are happy to accept functional degradation, they are happy to accept performance degradation. We don't deliver all the functionality, it doesn't run as fast as you might like.

Failure had implications for the managers involved:

> The natural consequence of it all is that you tend to think of what are the implications of everything you do. If this is scrutinised and it all goes wrong, which it may do because there are risks associated with everything, what would happen? And you tend to get, particularly in the user community and in [FutureTech] to some degree, is a risk aversion driven, not by risk analysis as a business would do it but in terms of what would be the effect of someone blaming me for this thing if it goes wrong.
> (Roger, senior business development manager: FutureTech)

FutureTech management preferred to implement proven IT solutions rather than 'risky' new technologies. And, given tight government budgeting, FutureTech could and did repackage technologies deployed elsewhere, whether or not these were suitable, because they were cheap and easy to implement:

> [FutureTech] puts its own slant on the partnership, its technology set-up, its pacts of technology, and basically, tries to leverage those to the customer's advantage, but sometimes it might not work to the best of the customer's advantage. (David, senior technical expert: FutureTech)

Given the age structure of the workforce the pool of ex-Govco personnel is likely to shrink dramatically in the medium-term. Under the new organisational structure, specific knowledge of Govco is more difficult to reproduce. The alignment of internal recruitment and business knowledge that existed under the ITO is gone. It may be that future changes to the service will be dictated by what FutureTech can provide, rather than the uncertainties of a broadly specified and obligational contract. And, given the centrality of IT to Govco's wider business objectives, the technological tail may well start wagging the governmental dog.

Discussion and conclusions

This case study provides a dramatic illustration of the way that agency impacts on social structures. The partnership with FutureTech was intended to provide private sector business practices and a repository of computing expertise for Govco. FutureTech's resources would enable it to cope with rapidly changing technologies and skill requirements and the agreement between the two organisations would ensure that technological innovations did not result in profiteering. In practice, Govco was so concerned at the possibility of failure that success was a political expediency. This might have been expected. Management is a political, rather than a neutral process, and managerial actions will be influenced by expectations of performance (Jackall, 1988). Indeed, a key element of sociological and labour process writings is the impact of control systems on outcomes (see, for example, Braverman, 1974; Thompson and McHugh, 2002). Actors 'reflect[ing] on their identities and interests, are able to learn from their experiences and, by acting in contexts that involve strategically selective constraints and opportunities, can and do transform social structures' (Jessop, 1996, p. 125).

Managers were charged both to reduce costs by 50 per cent and to define and complete the contractual schedule by which this would be achieved. This in turn provided a set of rules through which managers' acted to demonstrate their control over work. In the case study managers were observed removing expensive skills from the organisation to reduce costs despite an increase in workload, yet contracts were still almost inevitably completed to schedule. Ultimately, the managers were accountable to government auditors, not other IT experts who might judge the standards that they set themselves. The contractual process that managers used to demonstrate their control of the costs affected how expertise was produced and reproduced. Within the new organisational form employees often had reduced career prospects and individualised terms and conditions encouraged unrewarded increases in the effort bargain.

This reading of the evidence has direct implications for the way that (particularly externally sourced) work is controlled and the types of work that might be suitable for outsourcing. In the 'partnership' there was an uneasy tension between the need to tightly specify the work (that existed amongst managers due to the financial controls in place) and the fact that new work could not be controlled through direct contractual structures.This, in turn, created a requirement for managers to negotiate the outcomes. As a result of this contractual auditing, the discretion individual workers and managers could exercise sharply reduced (Grugulis *et al.*, 2003) with negative consequences for the learning potential of the organisation over the long-term.

Much of the existing evidence suggests contractual governance structures are not the best way to manage complex IT developments. For example, Willcocks *et al.* (1995) case study evidence suggest that problems are likely where, as at Govco, organisational strategy and performance is highly contingent on effective IT systems. Also, Lacity and Hirschman (1993) suggest that IT contractors almost invariably perform relatively poorly as corners are cut and information withheld in order to secure greater profits. It would seem that 'opportunism' is endemic within this field. This evidence suggests that 'opportunism' is conditioned by the strategies and identities of those involved in organisational practices. These are in turn influenced by the structure of markets and institutions that constrain and enable strategic choices. As Hyman notes, 'changes in the external environment of corporate activity which in one sense narrow the range of strategic options may compel internal restructuring which facilitates strategy within the area of choice which remains' (1987: 49).

In the case of the Govco–FutureTech 'partnership' managers may be accused of behaving opportunistically to demonstrate their successes. The accountancy and 'partnership' structure provided a tool to (re)shape the labour process of IT workers, and managers used this tool to control the work of programmers more directly. However, it is questionable whether or not the managers of the 'partnership' were truly accountable for the standards that they set themselves. It appeared that the 'partnership' set its own standards and the accountancy structure created a risk adverse climate within which innovation was stifled by the desire to demonstrate successes. Ackroyd (2002) suggests that the emergence of inter-organisational relations in contemporary Britain is associated with decline in the corporate agency of other stakeholders relative to that of managers. This evidence suggests, in the absence of significant countervailing forces that challenge the standards managers set, managerial control comes at the expense of innovation in contractual relationships.

Acknowledgements

The three-year research project associated with this paper is funded by the UK Economic and Social Research Council Future of Work Programme, grant number L212252038. The project is investigating 'changing organisational forms and the reshaping of work'. It involves a number of in-depth case studies of a variety of organisational forms, including franchises, employment agencies, Private Finance Initiatives, partnerships, supply chain relationships, and outsourcing. The full research team is Mick Marchington, Jill Rubery, Hugh Willmott, Jill Earnshaw, Damian Grimshaw, Irena Grugulis, John Hassard, Marilyn Carroll, Fang Lee Cooke, Gail Hebson and Steven Vincent.

Note

1. As far as possible the names of organisations, job titles and personnel have been made anonymous.

References

Ackroyd, S. (2002) *The Organisation of Business: Applying Organisational Theory to Contemporary Change*, Oxford: Oxford University Press.
Ackroyd, S. and Thompson, P. (1999) *Organizational Misbehaviour*, London: Sage.
Archer, M. (1995) *Realist Social Theory: The Morphogenic Approach*, Cambridge: Cambridge University Press.

Bachmann, R. (1999) *Trust, Power and Culture in Trans-Organisational Relations*, ESRC Centre for Business Research, Working Paper Series 129.

Bartlett, W. and Le Grand, J. (1993) 'The theory of quasi-markets', in Le Grand and Bartlett (eds) *Quasi Markets and Social Policy*, London: Palgrave Macmillan.

Bartlett, W., Propper, C., Wilson, D. and Le Grand, J. (eds) (1994) *Quasi-Markets in the Welfare State: the Emerging Findings*, Bristol: SAUS Publications.

Boxall, P. (1996) 'The strategic HRM debate and the resource-based view of the firm'. *Human Resource Management Journal*, 6 (3): 59–75.

Boxall, P. and Purcell, J. (2000) 'Strategic human resource management: where have we come from and where should we be going?'. *International Journal of Management Reviews*, 2 (2): 183–203.

Boxall, P. and Steeneveld, M. (1999) 'Human resource strategy and competitive advantage: a longitudinal study of engineering consultancies'. *Journal of Management Studies*, 36 (4): 443–63.

Boyne, G. A. (1998) 'Competitive tendering in local government: a review of theory and evidence'. *Public Administration*, 76 (4): 695–712.

Braverman, H. (1974) *Labor and Monopoly Capital: The Degradation of Work in the Twentieth Century*, London: Monthly Review Press.

Brereton, M. and Temple, M. (1999) 'The new public *service* ethos: an ethical environment for governance'. *Public Administration*, 77 (3): 455–74.

Carnaghan R. and Bracewell-Milnes, B. (1993) *Testing the Market: Competitive Tendering for Government Services in Britain and Abroad*, London: Institute of Economic Affairs.

Challiss, L., Day, P., Klein, R. and Scrivens, E. (1994) 'Managing quasi-markets: institutions of regulation', in Bartlett, W., Propper, C., Wilson, D. and Le Grand, J. (eds) *Quasi-Markets in the Welfare State: the Emerging Findings*, Bristol: SAUS Publications.

Cooke, F. L., Earnshaw, J., Marchington, M. and Rubery, J. (2001) *For Better and for Worse: Transfer of Undertakings and the Reshaping of Employment Relations*, International Journal of Human Resource Management, 15 (2): 270–88.

Corby, S. and White, G. (eds) (1999) *Employee relations in the public services: themes and issues*, New York: Routledge.

Deakin, N. and Walsh, K. (1995) 'The enabling state: the role of markets and contracts'. *Public Administration*, 74 (1): 33–48.

Dore, R. (1996) 'Goodwill and market capitalism', in Buckley, P. J. and Michie, J. (eds) *Firms, Organisations and Contracts: A Reader in Industrial Organisation*, Oxford: Oxford University Press.

Edwards, R. (1979) *Contested Terrain*, London: Heinemann.

Friedman, A. (1977) *Industry and Labor*, London: MacMillan.

Gamble, A. (1994) *The Free Economy and the Strong State*, London: Macmillan.

Grimshaw, D., Vincent, S. and Willmott, H. (2001) 'New control modes and emergent organisational forms: private-public contracting in public administration and health service provision'. *Administrative Theory and Praxis*, 23 (2): 407–30.

Grimshaw, D., Vincent, S. and Willmott, H. (2002) 'Going privately: partnership and outsourcing in UK public services'. *Public Administration*, 80 (3): 475–502.

Grugulis, I. Vincent, S. and Hebson, G. (2003) 'The rise of the 'network organisation' and the decline of discretion'. *Human Resource Management Journal*, 13 (2): 44–58.

Harvey, C. and Kanwal, S. (2000) 'Self-employed IT knowledge workers and the experience of flexibility: evidence from the United Kingdom', in Purcell, K. (ed.) *Changing Boundaries in Employment*, Bristol: Bristol Academic Press.

Hyman, R. (1987) 'Strategy or structure? capital, labour and control'. *Work, Employment and Society*, 1 (1): 25–55.

Jackall, R. (1988) *Moral Mazes*, Oxford: Oxford University Press.

Jessop, B. (1996) 'Interpretive sociology and the dialectic of structure and agency'. *Theory, Culture and Society*, 13 (1): 119–28.

Kirkpartick, I. and Martínez Lucio, M. (1996) 'Introduction: the contract state and the future of public management'. *Public Administration*, 74 (1): 1–8.

Krepps, D. M. (1990) 'Corporate culture and economic theory', in Alt, J. E. and Shepsle, K. A. (eds) *Perspectives on Positive Political Economy*, Cambridge: Cambridge University Press.

Lacity, M. C. and Hirschman, R. (1993) 'The Information systems outsourcing bandwagon'. *Sloan Management Review*, 35 (1): 73–86.

Lane, C. and Bachmann, R. (1997) 'Cooperation in inter-firm relations in Britain and Germany: the role of social institutions'. *British Journal of Sociology*, 48 (2): 226–54.

Lepak, D. P. and Snell, S. A. (1999) 'The human resource architecture: towards a theory of human capital allocation and management'. *Academy of Management Review*, 24 (1): 31–8.

McIntosch, I. and Broderick, J. (1996) 'Neither one thing nor the other: compulsory competitive tendering and southburgh cleansing services'. *Work, Employment and Society*, 10 (3): 413–30.

Marchington, M. and Vincent, S. (2001) *The Role of Institutional Forces, Employer Choice and Boundary Spanning Agents in the Formation and maintenance of Inter-organisational Relations*, ESRC Future of Work Programme, Working Paper No. 18.

Rainbird, H. and Munro, A. (2003) 'Locating workplace learning in the employment relationship: an exploration of research evidence from the public sector'. *Human Resource Management Journal*, 13 (2): 30–44.

Rubery, J., Cooke, F. L., Earnshaw, J. and Marchington, M. (2003) 'Inter-organisational relations and employment in a multi-employer environment'. *British Journal of Industrial Relations*, 41 (2): 265–89.

Sako, M. (1992) *Prices, Quality and Trust: Inter-firm relations in Britain and Japan*, Cambridge: Cambridge University Press.

Sayer, A. and Walker, R. (1992) *The Social Economy: Reworking The Division of Labor*, Oxford: Blackwell.

Thompson, P. and McHugh, D. (2002) *Work Organisations: A Critical Introduction*, Basingstoke: Palgrave.

Thompson, P. and Smith, C. (2001) 'Follow the red brick road: reflections on pathways in and out of the labour process debate'. *International Studies of Management & Organization*, 30 (4): 40–67.

Willcocks, L., Fitzgerald, G. and Feeny, D. (1995) 'Outsourcing: The Strategic Implications'. *Long Range Planning*, 28 (5): 59–70.

Williamson, O. E. (1975) *Markets and Hierarchies: Analysis and Antitrust Implications*, New York: Free Press.

Williamson, O. E. (1985) *The Economic Institutions of Capitalism*, New York: Free Press.

11

Career Perceptions and Career Pursuit in the UK, 1986–2002

Michael Rose

Introduction

The term 'career' has become more widely used in the last 20 or so years, both by employment professionals and by employees themselves. In the UK, the job-title 'careers adviser' or some equivalent is now used invariably in educational organisations, including schools in areas characterised by high local unemployment and the limited career opportunities of those jobs which are available. In the various government employment services, in private employment agencies, and in job opportunity advertisements, 'career' sometimes appears to be displacing the term 'job' itself. The best evidence of changing practice comes from statements by people who are themselves current employees: survey evidence to be cited shortly shows a significant growth among employees in more routine occupations of the *perception* of having a career.

On the face of it, therefore, important social change seems to be taking place. However, exactly why such an alteration in perspectives is occurring, and might be significant in terms of existing theories of career holding, requires extensive clarification. Publications referring to the term *career* may be very numerous, but most of these contributions show little agreement at the theoretical level and have an empirical underpinning that is fragmented and disparate.

Theoretical context

The standard reference work on career as a social science concept (Arthur, Hall and Lawrence, 1989), running to well over 500 pages of closely printed text written by over 50 experts on career research, leaves three main impressions: first, of the disparity of approaches to career between disciplines; second, of the absence of an agreed core problematic; and third, of the considerably lesser achievement of sociology, beside psychology, in applying the concept empirically.

This sociological weakness is surprising. Everett C. Hughes (1958) and his sociological collaborators at Chicago pioneered the study of career as a process by adopting the term 'as a heuristic applicable to a much wider range of situations' (Barley, 1989: 45), for example by placing the status passages of medical practitioners or executives directly alongside those of marijuana users. Brilliantly instructive for such a purpose of processual generalisation, such inclusive usage seems to justify Harold Wilensky's comment (1960: 554):

> Just as the concept of 'profession' loses its precision when we speak of the 'professionalization' of auto-workers in Detroit, so the concept of 'career' loses utility when we speak about the 'career of a ditch-digger'. In dealing with the organization of work, it is better to take a more restricted view of career.

A tighter definition of career will be used here. Barley's own suggestions for a sociological development of the career concept hinge on an application of Giddens structuration theory, as outlined in *Central Problems of Social Theory* (1979). Barley perceives them as making a fortuitous conjunction with the Chicago tradition. Maybe Barley intended to write 'fortunate', and given Anthony Giddens' wide knowledge of such literature, his implied development of the Chicago work is most unlikely to have been fortuitous. Giddens has certainly deployed the term career often in his work; it provides a good example of the problematic relation between everyday conceptualisation and formalised concepts in social science, that is to say of the *double hermeneutic* (Giddens, 1976).

Career has acted as a second major empirical reference-point in sociology, quite distinct from that established by the Hughes legacy. This is in relation to the study of social mobility in relation to the occupational structure. In practice, at an early point, the term *work-history* or some close equivalent came to be preferred by sociologists of work, with the term *career* reserved for those patterns of job holding, exhibited most clearly in managerial and professional levels, characterised by success in achieving a number of significant promotions, either in an organisational hierarchy or in a series of well-judged moves between employers. The most evident reason for this limitation of the term was that the great majority even of white-collar workers held jobs with uncertain security, relatively few promotion prospects, and almost no continuing in-post training; while in blue-collar work, 'advancement' very rarely consisted of anything better than opportunist moves to jobs that were better-paid, more secure, less dangerous, cleaner, or, as Blackburn and Mann (1978) once pointed out, simply indoors rather than outdoors in the wind and the rain.

This practice is now institutionalised, at least implicitly, in the UK and the northern countries of Western Europe, where the Erikson–Goldthorpe or CASMIN class schema (Erikson and Goldthorpe, 1992; Goldthorpe,

2000: chapter 11 especially) dominates theories of social stratification and mobility. In CASMIN, the fundamental principle of class allocation for employees is the modal employment contract in a given unit occupation, and more specifically upon the approximation of such employment contracts either to a *labour only* or to a *service relationship* pattern. The ideal typical employment contract characteristic of a service relationship applies to a relatively secure post with many non-financial or other *prospective* advantages – permanent tenure, regular salary increments, training opportunities, an adequate retirement pension, and not least a promotion ladder with clearly stated universalistic selection criteria.

Even for the service class groups, the CASMIN schema points to a particular pattern of career – that within a single employing organisation – when wide variations occur empirically. Alvin Gouldner (1957–58), in his classic distinction between *locals* and *cosmopolitans* in organisations, set up a series of contrasts that have remained helpful: the distinction, in a somewhat repackaged form, seems implicit in current discussion of 'boundaryless careers' (Arthur and Rousseau, 1996). For Gouldner, *locals* are those employees who consciously choose to pursue ambitions for promotion within one particular organisation large enough to provide good career progression, focusing their energy on developing the localised tacit knowledge, particularised commitment (loyalty), and in-house contacts; *cosmopolitans* regard membership of any given organisation as strictly provisional, valuable as a context for developing experience but a temporary arrangement to be followed by a switch to another employer, for which fundamental qualifications and industry-wide contacts will count most.

Such patterns may be most commonly found in management and professional level occupations, but the possibility that they may also affect large minorities of more routine employees, notably in public administration, the police, the armed forces, or the emergency services, is well worth exploring.

Both the local and cosmopolitan patterns seem to warrant the term 'career' in so far as they result from purposive action resulting from long-term prospective planning by more ambitious employees. Showing that there has occurred a substantial democratisation of career as an organising logic in employment contracts no doubt requires more evidence than is currently available. However, a spread in career outlook – which some researchers (Li *et al.*, 2002) regard as a longstanding pattern among British blue-collar workers – and a career-building set of employment priorities would form a necessary step in such a process. The present treatment has a contribution to make at this point, by examining a variety of recent datasets for the UK which enable further development of career problematics. It embodies an operationalisation of the career concept with three elements.

1. *Self-concept.* The employee considers himself or herself to be actively following a career, rather than simply occupying a given work, role or a

succession of such roles, as a result merely of adventitious or opportunist development of a work-history; even if such control is achieved in practice only partly, or not at all, some intention of wishing to achieve it should be involved and demonstrated by research.

2. *Prospective rationale.* The employee possesses a rationale of paid work as a whole which places career development either at its core or very close to it, implying continuity in employment objectives over the longer term; such objectives may at times be specific in terms of given posts, or material rewards, but will include aims that are qualitative as well as quantitative (e.g. to fully utilise certain skills or abilities).

3. *Constructive action.* Albeit sometimes in only a rudimentary way, a rational long-term calculus guides job selection, tenure, and switching between jobs; a given post will therefore be assessed in some measure for its capacity to supply work experience in a core role, and the opportunity to observe accomplished exponents of skills viewed as valuable for some future role; formal training, or encouragement and support from the employer in seeking it, will be considered important. In a minority of cases, these characteristics are combined and highly evident.

UK survey data on careers

Until quite recently, there has been a general lack of data with adequate comparability, especially longitudinal data, on trends in career holding and career orientation in the UK. The most valuable data-sets are the Work Histories and Attitudes survey (1985–86) from the ESRC Social Change and Economic Life (SCELI) programme; the PSI-Nuffield College Employment in Britain survey (EBS) of 1992 (Gallie *et al.*); the employee data in the British Household Panel survey (BHPS) wave 1 (1991) and wave 9 (1999); and the Working in Britain (WIB) survey of 2000.

Examination by the writer of the career data they offer began as part of the writer's contribution to ESRC Future of Work research programme in 1999 (Rose, 2000a), Changes in the wording of questions about career following, or in methods of putting the same question, limit the comparability of some of these findings. A follow-up study (Rose, 2003) set out to assess the degree of comparability in more detail, and to suggest methods of reconciling the findings of these previous studies. The Office for National Statistics Omnibus survey was used in early 2001 to produce a further specialised data-set (ONS) to assist in this process. The data sources used for the following analysis are shown in the Appendix.

Career perception trends

The *perception* of having a career unquestionably expanded sharply between the mid-1980s and early 2000s. Table 11.1 shows proportions of people

Table 11.1   Having a career, 1986 and 2001

	SCELI (1986) %	ONS (2001) %
All current employees	49	62
Full-time	57	67
Part-time	22	37
Sex		
Men	59	69
Women	39	54
Age group		
20–24	56	69
25–29	59	75
30–34	59	67
35–39	50	69
40–44	44	63
45–49	40	59
50–54	40	54
55–60	27	44
Monthly pay level		
Level 1 (low)	14	34
Level 2	32	42
Level 3	39	50
Level 4	51	63
Level 5	58	72
Level 6	66	84
Level 7 (high)	84	83
Highest qualification		
Nil	23	36
GCSE lower/CSE 2–5	30	50
O level/GCSE higher	40	56
ONC/OND/BTEC	73	67
A level/Higher	61	67
Non-degree higher	82	80
Degree/degree equiv.	86	88

Sources: Work Histories and Attitudes Survey (SCELI), 1985; Omnibus Surveys, Office for National Statistics, 2001.

classified by reference to five core variables: sex; hours worked; age group, pay level, and highest qualification. Overall, the proportion of employees of all kinds saying they saw themselves as having a career rose from just under half to over three out of five.

Already in 1986 (SCELI), a clear majority of men considered they had a career; by 2001 (ONS) seven out of ten males thought so. In fact, in proportionate terms, the increase among women from 39 per cent to 54 per cent was over twice as large. Only one part-time worker in five said they had a career in 1986; by 2001 this rose to 37 per cent, making it proportionately the second biggest rise of all in the data-set out in Table 11.1. Younger people in both years were rather more likely to say they had a career – in 1986, a majority of the under-40s were already doing so. In 2001, around two-thirds of under-30s were saying they had a career. At the same time, many more older employees were saying they had a career in 2001 than in 1986, with only the oldest employees now failing to offer a majority of career perceivers.

The association of career perception with pay was particularly clear and steeply sloped for the SCELI sample in 1986. In the ONS samples, the gradient still remained steep; however, the proportion for the top band remained the same as in 1986, while that for the second-highest band now equalled it. But the most striking change of all was that for the lowest pay-band, with the proportion declaring a career perception increasing no less than two and one-half times, from 14 per cent to 34 per cent.

A similar pattern is apparent for association with highest educational qualification. While the qualification banding pattern remained broadly similar – though it should be remembered that change in examination structures renders full comparison difficult – the greatest proportional jump, to 36 per cent from 23 per cent, affected those people who reported *no* qualifications at all. Thus it would be incorrect to conclude that the readiness to say one has a career simply reflects the spread of formal educational qualifications in the 15 years separating the two enquiries. One in three people lacking any such qualifications were now saying they think of themselves as having a career.

Career perception and occupation

Evidently, there is likely to be a social class distribution to career perception. Unfortunately, however, it is not possible to hold social class constant for the two enquiries. The rather unsatisfactory Registrar General's social class scheme, while available in the SCELI data-set, was altered with the introduction of SOC, 2000 (Rose and O'Reilly, 1998); thus although the ONS Omnibus survey does offer the new classification, it is quite different from its less-well-theorised predecessor. The Omnibus does not at present offer the Goldthorpe–Erikson schema; in any case, the latter classification has undergone revision since SCELI, again making comparison difficult.

To add to frustration, the Standard Occupational Classification (SOC) also changed in 1990, rendering much of the earlier occupational coding used in SCELI completely non-comparable with any data coded for SOC, 90. However, SOC, 90 did not introduce a complete break with the earlier scheme. Thus about two-thirds of SCELI employee cases *can* be imputed with a SOC, 90 occupational code that either approximates the earlier group very closely or completely matches it. As noted, a difficulty is that ONS introduced SOC, 2000 coding between the first two and the final Omnibus samples in 2001 which produced the Career and Transitions data-set. Thus the comparison involves samples reduced in each case by one-third. To make comparison valid it is necessary to exclude many otherwise comparable occupational groups

Table 11.2   Career in occupations, 1986 and 2001 (simplified SOC, 90 labels)

	SCELI (1986)	ONS (2001)
Production managers	79	74
Sales managers	81	85
Personnel managers	78	78
Computer systems managers	86	100
School teachers	91	87
Social workers/probation officers	64	64
Computer analyst/programmers	83	76
Nurses/nursing auxiliaries	78	74
Cashiers/counter clerks	44	43
Warehousemen/women	32	20
Police officers (sergeant and below)	100	100
Chefs/cooks	42	60
Sales assistants	20	29
Check-out/retail cash desk operators	24	30
Assemblers/lineworkers	8	23
Packers	22	38
Drivers, road goods vehicles	26	26
Drivers, bus and coach	18	56
Postal workers/mail sorters	35	0
Counterhands, catering assistants	5	13
Cleaning staff	8	18

Sources: Work Histories and Attitudes Survey (SCELI), 1985; Omnibus Surveys, Office for National Statistics, 2001.

because they lack sufficient numbers of cases in one or other, or in both, employee samples. It is especially frustrating that not a single unit occupation from SOC, 90 major group 5 (craft-skilled occupations) could be compared.

Otherwise, however, 21 unit occupations could be compared satisfactorily. Table 11.2 again shows the proportions of respondents in each occupation reporting that they see themselves as having a career. Table 11.2 has been left in descending order in terms of the nine SOC major occupational groups (i.e. *managers, professionals, associate professional and technical, clerical and sec-retarial, craft skilled, personal and protective services, sales, plant and machine operators, other unskilled*). It should be remembered at this point that while the central principle of classification in the Goldthorpe–Erikson scheme is the nature of the employment contract (Goldthorpe, 2000), for SOC, 90 (and its successor SOC, 2000) the classificatory principle is that of *skill*, first in the sense of broad skill level, and second in that of skill specialisation (Elias and McKnight, 2001).

Skill required in jobs of course does correlate – though far from as neatly as predicted by theories of industrialism – with level of skill possessed by persons, as indicated by educational or other qualifications normally required for the work (Rose, 1994). It is no surprise that the skill hierarchy implied by SOC, 90 leaves a strong mark on career perception in both surveys, falling from over four-fifths among professional/managerial occupations to less than one in five at the table bottom. It is notable that the only group showing a full hundred per cent for career perception in both surveys is *police officers* (sergeants and below): like the armed forces, the Police service offers secure employment, clear prospects of promotion in accordance with bureaucratic criteria, regular increments in salary, and enviable retirement provisions; moreover, recruits are expected to display high long-term commitment, and broadly 'canteen culture' appears to support this high involvement. It should be noted that the fire service seems traditionally to have had a similar high level of blue-collar career perception, but insufficient cases were available to document this adequately in the two data-sets under consideration.

The next highest concentration of career perception is registered by school-teachers and computer managers. (As primary and secondary school teachers were not distinguished before 1990, the categories are merged for this analysis.) Eight other groups – *production managers, sales managers, personnel managers, social workers, computer programmers, nurses, cashiers, goods vehicle drivers* – show virtually identical or closely comparable proportions for career perception in the two enquiries. Except for the cashiers and goods drivers, the unit occupations with little change in the frequency of career perception belong in the top half of the table. The dramatic changes in career perception, then, are those occurring in the lower half of the occupational structure.

True enough, Table 11.2 provides two instances – *warehouse staff* and *postal workers* – of a decline among the bottom-half occupations. That for the warehouse staff is substantial; if broadly correct, it is not easy to explain, and, as it is based on 50 cases in SCELI and 35 in ONS, a fall on the scale indicated might just result from an rather unusual statistical event. The case of the postal staff is quite different. Here the decline is massive, indeed catastrophic, and though based on just under 20 cases in each survey it is statistically significant. The virtual disappearance of the 'career postman' surely reflects changes in organisation, market position, and ethos in this industry. The postal service has also suffered a drastic erosion of job satisfaction since the 1980s; not just because of changes in working practices and self-image, but because the job itself is currently, contractually speaking, much less attractive in a long-term perspective. The British mail service in the last two decades should provide an instructive subject for case-study research on career: in occupational terms, it provides a potentially instructive deviant case, with employee career perception almost completely disappearing.

Eight of the 21 occupations show clear or substantial increases in career perception. In three cases, the bus/coach drivers, assembly-line workers, and packers – the ONS sub-samples barely reach double figures, and should therefore be treated with extreme caution. In particular, the leap from 18 per cent to 56 per cent among bus/coach drivers is surprising, and no specific reason for it can be suggested here. Possibly some privatised service providers have been making efforts to retain staff by creating career-type benefits and a longer-term job planning horizon among staff: there is now a specialist trade magazine (*Bus and Coach Professional*) committed to this project; yet a trebling of career perception seems unlikely. However, though all three results may well over-estimate the *degree* of change, it is unlikely that they misrepresent the *direction* of change. The scale of the other five increases are far more secure from a statistical viewpoint.

Career perception and orientation to work

Perception of having a career should be associated with other attitudes regarding paid employment and the jobs market, because these attitudes may affect career perception, because career perception encourages adoption of other attitudes, or because other factors create both career perception and the other work attitudes in question. The concept of orientation towards work, although sometimes criticised for lack of clarity, is useful here, at least in so far it as it can be provided with a clearly stated content. Orientation will be operationalised here in terms of two related aspects of work attitudes, preferences and values. The first is the broad rationale of paid work held by the employee, as indicated in employee surveys by answers to the standard question 'what do you see as the most important reason for having paid work?' (A list of possible choices is offered, and a second main reason may be sought.) The second concerns the more specific priorities people have when weighing up the advantages of particular jobs, for example when considering a move to another job: the most common priorities mentioned spontaneously, and often listed as options in employee surveys are: total pay, promotion opportunities, good relations with manager/supervisor, hours of work, the work itself, chances to use initiative and security of the job.

Certain kinds of work orientation might be expected to be more widely spread among people possessing a career perspective to work, especially in those regions of the occupational structure where it has not formed a traditional part of expectations. As noted, career outlook embodies *prospectivity*, that is the willingness to accept a longer-term outlook on employment, with tolerance of some present inconvenience, and acceptance of deferred gratification in terms of leisure activities, because in the longer term such behaviour will pay off in terms of promotion or readily transferable work experience. A related underlying element should be greater commitment to paid work as a whole.

Non-financial work commitment ('work ethic')

Numerous surveys show that quite large majorities of employees as a whole subscribe to some sort of non-financial commitment to work. This commitment is registered in answers to the so-called Lottery Question, in which interviewees are asked whether they would continue to have paid work (though not necessarily their present job) even if they had enough money to live comfortably without doing so. Saying that one would go on working is viewed as a good indicator of whether people may have a work ethic, in the sense of a moral obligation to be gainfully occupied. However, there are other, less admirable reasons for wanting to continue – for example, the macho belief that having a job demonstrates that one is a 'real man', or simply from fear of boredom. Thus such inferences must be made with caution (Rose, 1994).

In SCELI, Table 11.3 shows, just under two-thirds (65 per cent) of current employees said they would carry on with paid work even if their financial circumstances changed so as to allow them to stop if they wished to do so. Readiness to continue working varied somewhat with sex and hours worked, with 67 per cent of male full-time workers but only 59 per cent of female part-time workers saying they would continue to work. The SCELI question about non-financial commitment was repeated with the 830 employees in the first sample of ONS. The ONS data shows an overall slightly less strong degree of non-financial commitment, which may reflect sampling error. Similar differences related to sex and hours worked are apparent. However, these differences disappeared completely in both surveys once career perception was controlled: among those employees saying they had a career, the proportions saying they would continue to work were not only significantly different from those lacking career perception, but virtually identical for the three key activity groups (all males, female full-time, female part-time), as shown in Table 11.3. (The high proportion for the women part-timers in 2001 is especially striking.)

Table 11.3   Having a career and commitment to paid work (those, saying they would continue to have paid work in %)

	SCELI (1986)	ONS (2001)
All employees	65	60
Has a career		
Male employees	72	64
Women employees (full-time)	73	63
Women employees (part-time)	71	75
No career, but would like to have one		
Male employees	—	63
Female employees	—	68

Sources: Work Histories and Attitudes Survey (SCELI), 1985; Omnibus Surveys, Office for National Statistics, 2001.

Main rationale of paid work

It was widely forecast in the 1970s and 1980s that the onset of a post-industrial society, entailing a growth in qualifications, training and a general need for more theoretical knowledge in the workforce, would have a profound impact on economic values. There would occur a switch from more economistic rationales of work towards expressive rationales giving prominence to using personal creativity in work-roles with greater inherent meaning, resulting in a greater sense of personal fulfilment (*self-actualisation*). It can be said with some confidence that such a change has not occurred in the UK. What was earlier taken to be a trend towards post-industrial values may even have been reversed.

In the first ONS sample, the questions asked in SSCELI about main and secondary rationales of work were repeated. Again, the smaller ONS sample *might* have produced the results shown in Table 11.4, where choice of the self-expressive reasons for having a job (*use abilities to the full, enjoy working,* and *do something worthwhile*) among career perceivers is shown as totalling 20 per cent rather than the 27 per cent of SCELI; at the same time instrumental reasons for working (*money for essentials, money for extras*) were chosen more often. Data from the far larger employee samples in BHPS, for 1991 and 1999, though using slightly different question-forms, shows a closely comparable picture. Overall, instrumental rationales, together with the partly fatalistic, partly macho *working is normal*, now lie at the heart of paid work rationales of up to three-quarters of British employees. True enough, those people who see themselves as having a career remain more likely to have self-expressive rationales, just as they did in the 1980s. But the survey shows a sharp decline in readiness of career perceivers to cite such reasons, when the proportion might have been expected to increase.

A more explicit aspect of work orientation relates to the priorities people cite as most important to them when considering the advantages of a job.

Table 11.4   Having a career and main reason for job, ONS (2001)

	No career	Has career
Working is normal	4 (5)	6 (5)
Need money for essentials	57 (50)	61 (53)
Earn money to buy extras	14 (20)	9 (7)
Company of other people	4 (1)	1 (1)
Enjoy working	6 (7)	10 (12)
Use my abilities to the full	1 (2)	5 (8)
To do something worthwhile	2 (4)	5 (7)
To give me a sense of independence	9 (8)	3 (7)
To get out of the house	2 (3)	0 (1)

Note: SCELI percentages in parentheses.

Sources: Work Histories and Attitudes Survey (SCELI), 1985; Omnibus Surveys, Office for National Statistics, 2001.

Table 11.5 Having a career and job facet priorities ONS (2001) (sample 1)

	Does not see self as having career (%)	Sees self as having career (%)
Promotion prospects	2	4
The total pay	27	27
Good relations with supervisor/manager	6	3
Your job security	23	25
Being able to use your own initiative	11	10
The actual work itself	18	26
The hours you work	11	2
Other	3	2
n	309	504

Note: Question 'Here are *aspects* of a job that people say are important. I'd like you to look at this card and say which is the most important to you about a job'.

Source: Omnibus Surveys, Office for National Statistics, 2001.

BHPS periodically asks about such priorities, but unfortunately does not ask whether people look on work as a career. Table 11.5 shows results for the ONS survey module of 2001 designed by the author, which allows job facet priorities for career perceivers to be set beside those of non-perceivers, first for priorities cited as most important. While smaller numbers of cases make findings non-significant, the table suggests that career perceivers are likely to put much more stress on promotion opportunities and the actual work itself, and rather less on good relations with a supervisor. Very clearly indeed, they place a far lower rating on the hours they work. Second-choice priorities, which are not shown, broadly duplicate these patterns.

People who have longer-term aims for their own employment are more likely to look forward to, and seek promotion. Stressing the importance of the 'work itself' may imply concern to have work tasks supplying qualitative rewards and experiences. However, it can also be seen as concern with having work that builds upon previous experience in a particular occupational role, or provides new work experience of a particular kind, in both instances adding to the employee's stock of human capital. More ambitious people may be more likely to accept conflict in general, including strains in their relations with immediate supervisors. They certainly seem more likely to expect to work harder in the sense of how many hours they work. (Evidence is given below.) There is, then, a thematic harmony of prioritisation of job facets with longer-term planning of employment development and priorities; clearly, though, it is not very pronounced.

Career pursuit

The analysis thus far makes it clear that *perception* of having a career has to an important extent been 'democratised' since the 1980s. But does this amount

Table 11.6   Career perception and career pursuit

	No career	Has career
Working is the normal thing to do	4	5
To pay for essentials	60	54
To earn money to buy extras	11	7
To earn money of my own	11	9
For the company of other people	3	1
Enjoy working	9	14
To follow my/their career	—*	9
Other reason	—	1
n	577	976

Note: * 2 cases were recorded as citing 'follow my career' as their main reason for working although they were not recorded as saying they had a career.

Source: Omnibus Surveys, Office for National Statistics, 2001.

to anything very much more than a discursive change? Has the perception also been accompanied by a growth in *pursuit* of career aims? After all, the ONS data show that less than one in ten of career perceivers gave *following a career* as their most important reason for having paid work (see Table 11.6). However, around 15 per cent of the ONS career perceivers gave *following career* as their second most important reason for working. Thus, career pursuit appears to have some importance for between 20 and 25 per cent of all employees with career perception.

How far career perception by itself may underlie differences in behaviour is not a very productive question, as the two categories (career perceivers, non career perceivers) are too broad. However, differences in the intensity of career pursuit itself *can* be examined. Some extremely valuable longitudinal data – that is, information gained from adding to the work-histories of individuals in the annual interviews which BHPS seeks with its panel members – is available for mapping the association between intensity of career pursuit as a work attitude and subsequent work careers. In the first wave of BHPS (1991–92) employees were able to cite 'following my career' as their first or second most important reason for working. BHPS also asked about promotion opportunities as a job facet priority. As promotion opportunities have a logical connection with career development, while those people who say they prioritise such opportunities are much more likely to say they have a career, a score of 0–4 for career pursuit can easily be created simply by scoring the priority given to seeking promotion opportunities as a job facet, and to following career as a reason for working, in an appropriate way (first choice 2 points, second choice 1 point, neither chosen 0 points). Though a somewhat rough and ready measure, this provides an effective means of defining quite marked differences in work history. These patterns are explored elsewhere (Rose, 2004) in some detail but summarised below.

1. Around 10 per cent of employees in BHPS wave 1 had a weak or mild commitment to career following, a further 10 per cent had a moderate or strong commitment, but only 2 per cent had very strong commitment. The careers pursuers were still concentrated among white-collar workers, managers and professionals (the Service Class). Women are only slightly less likely than men to prioritise career pursuit.

2. Strength of career pursuit is positively associated with wishing for a better job with the same employer or a new employer, and for work-related training. It is negatively associated with the wish to give up paid work altogether. Those people who are more career ambitious were more likely to say they would like to start their own business.

3. In the 9–10 years after 1991, both men and women defined as career pursuers in the base year (1991–02) changed employers up to twice as often as other employees, obtained 'disproportionate' increases in pay, and enjoyed very high upward job mobility: excluding people already in a managerial or professional job in 1991–92, 54 per cent of non-pursuers remained at the same occupational level in 2000–01, but only 12 per cent of very strong career pursuers did so – and were over twice as likely to achieve very high upward mobility.

4. Career pursuers work significantly longer hours than non-pursuers, about five per week on average, and over twice that if they are women. Surprisingly, despite their more 'workaholic' temporal profile, the male pursuers did not report significantly more stress feelings, but women pursuers did; however, both men and women pursuers reported *fewer* stress symptoms such as sleeplessness, panic attacks, digestive problems, migraine, or abuse of illegal substances. (However, intensity of career pursuit was associated with readiness to admit to smoking cigarettes.) Women pursuers reported much less satisfaction, and men pursuers rather less, with any domestic partner; and both sexes seem to have had more trouble in creating stable relationships in the first place, than did non-pursuers of either sex. The 'no one to play with' problem (Jenkins and Osburg, 2003) is a real one for people who work longer hours from choice.

5. The career pursuers of both sexes were, despite small numbers for the most highly career committed, significantly more likely to say they were satisfied with the way their lives were moving. Career pursuers seek higher income, status, and organisational power: as career pursuers are much more likely to achieve such advantages, this comes as no surprise. The social and other disutilities of go-getting seem often to have been 'priced into' their expectations.

Career pursuit in the 1990s – decline?

The survey results described earlier point to a rather sharp increase since the 1980s in the proportion of British employees who say they see themselves as having a career. It is known that the readiness to see work as a career is closely associated with higher educational attainments. So too is the readiness to choose 'follow my career' as a reason for having paid work. As the level of educational attainment, in terms of highest qualification obtained, rose sharply during the same years, it might be supposed that the proportion of British employees making 'follow my career' their main reason for having paid work would also have grown sharply. Surprisingly, perhaps, the data fail to show such an expansion of career building rationale: if anything, they show the reverse.

The proportion of employees giving 'follow my career' as first reason for working *fell* from well over 8 per cent in BHPS wave 1 (1991–92) to rather less than 7 per cent in wave 9 (1999–2000). Though the fall in per centage points might seem insignificant statistically, given the very large samples of employees at each wave it is in fact highly significant ($p < 0.001$). Endorsement of 'follow my career' as second most important reason for working also fell from 10.4 per cent in wave 1 to exactly 10 per cent in wave 9. True enough, two recent specific employee surveys suggest a small growth in those picking 'follow career' as main reason for working, with Employment in Britain (Gallie *et al.*, 1998) in 1992 giving 5.6 per cent, and Working in Britain (ESRC Future of Work, 2001) showing 7.2 per cent. However, the difference is just short of significant at the 95 per cent level, thanks to two much smaller samples; in any case, the question was not put in a strictly comparable way in these two surveys.

It is at first hard to accept that rising educational qualifications have not changed the proportion of people for whom career pursuit is highly important. The association of career pursuit with level of educational attainment remains as clear among the wave 9 employee sample of BHPS as among that at wave 1; however, Table 11.7 shows that this association had altered in two main ways. At BHPS wave 1, even having a CSE pass resulted in a sharp

Table 11.7 'Follow career' chosen as main reason for working (as percentage of level of highest educational qualification)

	BHPS 1991–92	BHPS 1999–2000
No qualification	1.8	1.7
CSE	6.6	4.1
O level	6.7	4.9
A level	14.2	7.6
Professional below degree	16.2	8.5
Degree/higher degree	19.4	16.8
'Follow career' main reason for working among all employees at wave	8.4*	6.7**

Notes:
* $CI_{99} = \pm 0.010$, n = 4,974.
** $CI_{99} = \pm 0.007$, n = 7,386.

Source: British Household Panel Survey, Waves 1 (1991–92) and 11 (2000–01).

increase in the likelihood of having a career pursuit rationale of work; there was an even greater jump between having O level and having A level (or their equivalents). Yet at wave 9 the proportion even of degree holders citing career pursuit fell to 16.8 per cent from the 19.4 per cent of wave 1, and the proportionate fall is rather significant in statistical terms ($p < 0.01$). What is equally striking is the scaling down of the proportions among employees with any other qualifications who gave following a career as their main reason for working.

The most obvious interpretation is that merely possessing a degree, still less a professional qualification below degree level, does not of itself generate aspirations for upward job mobility. Indeed, the situation is such as to support the view that the proportion of employees with career aspirations remains a more or less fixed proportion of the working population; thus when an expansion of opportunities to attain higher educational qualifications occurs, many aspiring employees who would previously have attained moderately high qualifications (in particular, A level) now attain higher qualifications, while those people who now attain moderate qualifications instead of low qualifications do not develop career aspirations so often.

Gender differences in educational attainment perhaps cannot provide an adequate explanation of the stability of overall career pursuit aspirations. Yet consideration of them may be required to produce such an explanation. At wave 1 of BHPS, there was little difference in career pursuit aspirations between men and women first degree holders; in each case around 18 per cent gave 'follow career' as their main reason for working. At wave 9, only 13 per cent of men degree holders did so, against 17 per cent of women first degree holders. Moreover, only 14 per cent (wave 1 = 30 per cent) of male higher degree holders cited career following at wave 9, against 24 per cent (wave 1 = 39 per cent) of women higher degree holders. On the face of things, higher educated men have trimmed their expectations of building careers, or their wish to do so, while more women have been developing them. However, closer analysis of existing material, further targeted surveys, and case-studies are required to elucidate these changes.

There is one further complication: an apparent contraction in the availability of career opportunities of the traditional kind in large organisations, with greater effect on female workers in white-collar jobs as a whole. Table 11.8 shows proportions of employees in each of the Major Occupational Groups of the SOC, 90 scheme who reported that their current posts had a recognised career or promotion ladder, in the 1992 Employment in Britain survey and the 2001 Working in Britain survey. The reported contraction of such career opportunities in terms of per centage points is most evident for professional, technical, clerical and service occupations; in proportionate terms, craft workers also suffered severely though the difference is not so clear-cut in statistical terms as it is for the professionals, the technical specialists, and – above all – routine white-collar workers.

Table 11.8   Current job is a step in a recognised career ladder or promotion ladder

	Employment in Britain (1992) %	Working in Britain (2001) %	Change %
Managers/administrators	67	64	−5
Professional occupations	87	68**	−22
Associate professional/ technical occupations	80	65**	−19
Clerical/secretarial occupations	61	43**	−30
Craft and related occupations	41	30*	−22
Personal/protective service occupations	54	40*	−26
Sales occupations	50	48	−4
Plant/machine operatives	32	33	−3
Other occupations	31	26	−16
Total	58	47**	−16
n	3,445	2,125	

Notes:
* Difference significant with CI_{95} (one-tail).
** Difference significant with CI_{99} (two-tail).
Source: Employment in Britain Survey, 1992; Working in Britain Survey 2001.

That managers themselves remained relatively little affected by such a loss of such career ladders will be noted. In a cynical view of these things, the relative immunity of managers from the organisational redesign which they often prescribed for others might seem predictable. Yet this is not quite how managers themselves saw things. The data for job satisfaction in the two surveys shows a perception of fewer – or perhaps less attractive – promotion opportunities among managers too. There was a sharp fall among managers in very high satisfaction with promotion opportunities to lower (but still positive) levels of satisfaction, and this fall among managers was the highest of all the major groups in terms of a mean score.

To be sure, a very clear majority of people (2 out of 3) in the professional and technical occupations, just like those in management occupations, still reported that they had career opportunities in 2001; however, prospects for career progression were becoming far less certain in a number of occupations where formerly they would have been regarded as reasonably good. In particular, in the clerical and craft skilled occupations, formerly modest career opportunities had now become rather indifferent ones. Women's opportunities generally contracted only slightly more than men's, and in the associate professional and technical occupations they actually contracted less than men's; but among clerical/secretarial employees, the proportionate decline for women (35 per cent) beside that for men (9 per cent) was close to catastrophic.

Conclusion

Further research and analysis is needed to fully confirm these declines in opportunity, and to specify the occupations most affected. However, the aggregate figures provided here are sufficient to tarnish key sections of HRM discourse, notably those promising steady progression as a return for developing new organisation specific skills. The findings examined above are somewhat paradoxical: a strong increase during the 1990s in the perception of having a career, yet no growth or even a slight fall in readiness to make pursuit of a career a personal priority, fewer or less clear career ladders in the work organisation or occupation, and a drop in the level of satisfaction with the job facet 'promotion opportunities'.

Whether observers choose to characterise such a situation as one of inconsistency between personal goals on the one hand, and, on the other, organisational and labour market realities, as a novel form of contradiction in contemporary capitalism, or as some other process, depends on the analytical categories which the observers favour. If the findings examined point to trends which later research confirms and shows to be sustained or growing, a further set of questions will arise: above all, how far will employees find it possible to accommodate to, and to rationalise, their experience of disappointed aspirations. A career problematic therefore promises to be of gowing interest to students of employment relations, organisational behaviour, and the sociology of work.

Appendix

Table 11.9 summarises the somewhat complicated position with regard to comparability between relevant data-sets. The essential feature is that each of the three Omnibus samples for 2001 provides a separate link with each of the larger surveys. The ONS conducts Omnibus fieldwork about once a month, drawing a new sample, generating about 1800 adult cases, of which approximately half are current employees. The SCELI form of the main question ('Do you think of yourself as having a career?') was asked of each sample, producing a total sample of employees with size sample (around 2600 cases) fully adequate for most comparisons attempted. However, in the first sample, the SCELI question forms about work rationale were repeated, in the second the BHPS question forms were adopted, and in the third the EBS question forms. For each of these samples, there are over 800 cases each.

A more practical difficulty for the present study was the decision of ONS to switch from the 1990 to the 2000 version of the UK Standard Occupational Classification (SOC) in early 2001, introducing a new source of non-comparability at the occupational level for the third sample (one-third of employee cases). However, ONS agreed to code cases for all samples for the International Standard Classification (ISCO) for occupations, permitting full comparability with the key BHPS surveys, albeit on a somewhat obsolescent schema. Some additional work attitude questions were asked in the first Omnibus sample, dealing with wish for a career among those people who said they did not see themselves as having a career, the work ethic in the sense of non-financial commitment to work using the 'lottery question' (Warr, 1982), and to women working.

Table 11.9 Data-sets relevant to career analysis

Survey	Main field-work	Current employees, weighted cases	Do you think of yourself as having a career?	Does your job have a career or promotion ladder?	'Follow my career' could be chosen, as one or more from a list of 7 specified reasons, plus an option for another but un-listed reason for wanting a job; it could then be selected as the main reason	'Follow my career' could be chosen as the main reason for wanting a job from a list of 7, plus an un-listed additional reason; 'follow my career' could be chosen as a second reason for wanting a job from an identical list
SCELI	1985	3,649	Yes			
BHPS wave 1	1991	4,974				Yes
EBS	1992	3,458		Yes	Yes	
BHPS wave 9	1999	7,669				Yes
ONS Omnibus Sample 1	2001	816	Yes			
ONS Omnibus Sample 2	2001	837	Yes			Yes
ONS Omnibus Sample 3	2001	882	Yes		Yes	
Working in Britain	2001	2,132		Yes	Yes	

Source: End of Award Report ESRC Grant R000223499 'Labour Market Trajectories and Rationales of Work'.

Acknowledgement

The findings reported develop analysis undertaken for ESRC project R000223499 *Labour Market Trajectories and Rationales of Work* and ESRC-FOW *Work Centrality, Work Careers, and Household* L21230200251.

References

Arthur, M. B. and Rousseau, D. M. (1996) *The Boundaryless Career: A New Employment Principle for a New Organizational Era*, Oxford University Press.
Arthur, M. B., Hall, D. T., Lawrence, B. S. (eds.) (1989) *Handbook of Career Theory*, Cambridge University Press.
Barley, S. R. (1989) 'Career, identities, and institutions: the legacy of the Chicago School of Sociology', in Arthur, M. B., Hall, D. T., and Lawrence, B. S. (eds) *Handbook of Career Theory*, Cambridge University Press.
Blackburn, R. and Mann, M. (1979) *The Working Class in the Labour Market*, Macmillan.
Elias, P. and McKnight, A. (2001) 'Skill measurement in official statistics: recent development in the UK and the rest of Europe'. *Oxford Economic Papers*, 3: 508–40.
Erikson, R. and Goldthorpe, J. H. (1992) *The Constant Flux: A Study of Class Mobility in Industrial Societies*, Oxford: Clarendon Press.
Gallie, D., White, M., Cheng, Y. and Tomlinson, M. (1998) *Restructuring the Employment Relationship*, Oxford University Press.
Giddens, A. (1976) *New Rules of Sociological Method*, Hutchinson.
Giddens, A. (1979) *Central Problems in Social Theory*, Berkeley: University of California Press.
Goldthope, J. H. (2000) *On Sociology: Numbers, Narratives, and the Integration of Research and Theory*, Oxford University Press.
Gouldner, A. W. (1957–58) 'Cosmopolitans and locals: toward an analysis of latent social roles', parts I and II. *Administrative Science Quarterly*, 2: 281–306, 444–80.
Hughes, E. C. (1958) *Men and their Work*, Glencoe, Il: Free Press.
Jenkins, S. and Osburg, L. (2003) 'Nobody to play with? The implications of leisure coordination', Colchester, Essex: Institute of Social and Economic Research, Working Paper.
Li, Y., Bechhofer, F., Stewart, R., McCrone, D., Anderson, M. and Jamieson, L. (2002) 'A divided working class? planning and career perception in the service and working classes'. *Work, Employment, and Society*, 16 (4): 599–616.
Rose, D. and O'Reilly, K. (eds) (1998) *Final Report of the ESRC Review of Government Social Classifications*, Swindon: ESRC.
Rose, M. (2004) 'The cost of a career in minutes', in Housten, D. (ed.) *Work–Life Balance*, Palgrave Macmillan.
Rose, M. (2003) *Labour Market Trajectories and Rationales of Work: End-of-Award Report*, ESRC award no. R000223499.
Rose, M. (2000) *Work Centrality, Work Careers, and Household: End-of-Award Report*, for ESRC award no. L21230200251.
Rose, M. (1994) 'Skill and Samuel Smiles: Changing the British work ethic', in Penn, R., Rose, M. and Rubery, J. (eds), *Skill and Occupational Changes*, Oxford University Press.
Warr, P. B. (1982) 'A national study of non-financial employment commitment'. *Journal of Occupational Psychology*, 55: 11–121.
Wilensky, H. L. (1960) 'Career, life-styles, and social integration'. *International Social Science Journal*, 12: 553–58.

Data-sets used

Gallie, D. (1991) Social Change and Economic Life Initiative Surveys, 1986–87 [computer file]. Colchester, Essex: The Data Archive [distributor], 28 June 1991. SN: 2798.

Economic and Social Research Council Research Centre on Micro-Social Change. British Household Panel Survey (computer file) (2003). Colchester, Essex: The Data Archive (distributor), SN: 4340.

White, M., Hill, S., McGovern, P. and Mills, C. (2003) *Changing Employment Relationships, Employment Contracts and the Future of Work*, 2000 [computer file]. Colchester, Essex: UK Data Archive [distributor], 4 April 2003. SN: 4641. (WIB2000)

Office for National Statistics, Omnibus Surveys, January, March, and April 2001. Colchester, Essex: The Data Archive (distributor), 2003; SN4533, SN4534, SN4535.

Gallie, D., Employment in Britain Survey, 1991–92. Oxford: Nuffield College, OX1 INF.

12
Young Adults' Experience of Work in the 'New' Economy: Initial Themes from an Explorative Project[1]

Harriet Bradley, Ranji Devadason, Steve Fenton, Will Guy and Jackie West

Introduction

Research on young people and employment in the post-war period has focused very much on the 'transition from school to work'. The age group under study was characteristically 16–24 and research tended to stop at the point when transitions were deemed completed, an assumption being then that the future trajectories were fairly predictable (Ashton and Field, 1976).[2] But recent research, drawing attention to the protracted and multiple nature of youth transitions since the spread of mass youth unemployment in the 1980s (see, for example, Jones, 1995; Roberts, 1995; Furlong and Cartmel, 1997; Wallace and Kovatcheva, 1998) has signalled the need to study the subsequent labour market experiences of young employees. Coles (2000) calls for extending research to explore the slightly older age group (25+). It has also been recognised that youth research has tended to focus on school-leavers entering directly into 'the world of work' with relative neglect of the graduate labour market (Ashton and Lowe, 1994).[3]

This chapter reports some initial findings from a research project based in Bristol which is exploring young adults' employment trajectories, defining young adults (YAs) as aged 20–34. The context for the study is the package of significant economic and social changes which has characterised the past two decades: an increasingly globalised economy: the switch from manufacturing to services in western societies; the search by employers for flexibility; the rise and rise of information technology and 'e' commerce; the feminisation of employment; the rise of dual-earner families; the increase in government training provision for the unemployed; and the increased proportion of young people entering higher education. This package of changes has been variously conceptualised as part of 'postindustrialism', 'postmodernity', or the coming of the 'knowledge society', 'the information society' or the 'new economy'.

While retaining some scepticism about these macro-sociological concepts, we work with the assumption that transitions into employment stability and adult independence are indeed now more complex and problematic for young people and may take a considerable period to achieve. Indeed, we accept that some people may never 'settle down' into a stable career or a 'job for life' although we believe that this remains the aspiration and expectation of many young adults. As other recent research has noted (Allatt and Dixon, 2001; McDowell, 2002), the conventional desires for 'a nice home and a car', 'family and kids' and 'a good job' are still strongly evident, especially among young people for manual working-class backgrounds. We also work with the assumption that the economic changes listed above have created new cohorts of 'winners and losers' within evolving labour markets – and of course others who might be categorised as being 'in between'. However, it is important to stress that in using this popularly espoused terminology we are not suggesting that people have inherent properties or characteristics that make them succeed and fail; rather that 'winning' and 'losing' is a product of social and economic forces which help shape the destiny of individuals.

Thus, a key aim of our research is to explore the processes by which labour market successes and failures are produced; a further key issue is the way in which young adults' labour market choices and activities are interwoven with their family circumstances and domestic commitments. Finally in attempting to trace out such patterns of 'winning and losing' we are concerned to show how existing inequalities related to class, gender and ethnicity are either being confirmed or eroded.

Research design and progress

The research is based within Bristol, as a case-study of a globalising urban labour market. It is based on four zones of the city with contrasting socio-demographic profiles. Bristol exemplifies many of the economic changes listed above. It is a thriving city with a strong concentration of financial and other service organisations. Over 75 per cent of employment is in services. Service employment has grown particularly in two areas: the city centre (for example, a large new development for financial sector offices, Temple Way, near the railway station) and on the perimeter of North Bristol (for example, Cribbs Causeway, a regional retail centre, or Aztec West, a business park). There has been considerable loss in manufacturing and manual employment (the tobacco industry, central docks), although some elite companies hold strong (British Areospace, Rolls Royce). Recent employment growth has been in the typical areas of the 'New Economy' (call centres, leisure and catering, retail, media and communications, computing and telecommunications): the region in which Bristol is located (UKK1: Avon, Gloucestershire, Wiltshire and North Somerset) has the seventh highest proportion in Europe of total employment in the IT sector (2.9 per cent) (Jagger and Huws, 2001).

Women slightly outnumber men within the Bristol labour force. In 2000 the overall unemployment rate for Bristol was 4.5 per cent (6 per cent for men and 2.6 per cent for women) but in two of the wards covered by our survey male unemployment stood at 17.9 per cent and 10.8 per cent.

Like many 'globalizing cities' (Marcuse and van Kempen, 2000) Bristol is highly segmented. We were therefore able to choose four contrasting zones for our research which would provide a demographic cross-section and which we hypothesised would contain cohorts of 'winners and losers' – and of those in between. Marcuse and van Kempen state

> Ask any resident where the most impoverished ethnic or 'racial' minority live in any globalizing city … and they will tell you; likewise, they will tell you where the very rich and powerful live and work. (2000: 52)

In Bristol Zone A represents the former, Zone D the latter. Zones B and C were chosen to cover contrasting intermediate populations: Zone B houses 'traditional' white working-class and lower middle-class groupings, along with some young professionals buying into the highly inflated Bristol housing market, while Zone C is home to more deprived white working-class communities in newer forms of employment.

The research involved three phases:

1. Loosely ethnographic research (primary interviews) comprising visits and interviews with employers, agencies and young adults. This was carried out largely in the four zones, but not exclusively as we wanted to get some feel of the broader Bristol/Avon labour market.
2. A household-based survey of 1100 young adults in the four zones.
3. Follow-up in-depth interviews with a sub-sample of 80 young adults from the survey.

The research was completed in the autumn of 2002 and analysis of the survey and follow-up interviews is still under way. In this chapter we draw on the findings from Phase 1 to set out some aspects of the experience of the young adult workers we interviewed.

Phase 1 findings

This chapter deals with three key aspects of the Phase 1 research. First we discuss the nature of the specific local labour market in which our young adults were placed and highlight the importance of locality. Second, we look at the attitudes to work displayed by the 50 young adults we interviewed as part of the Phase 1 exploration. Finally, we look briefly at the typical patterns of entry to the labour market as displayed by the interviewees and subsequently confirmed by Phases 2 and 3 of the research. The discussion draws on the interviews with employers and the 50 young adults. These were contacted partly through the agencies and employers whom we spoke to, while others we met through our own networks of contacts within the city and through a snowballing process. It is important to stress that this in no way constitutes a representative sample of young Bristol adults, though we managed to interview a good mix in terms of gender, ethnicity, employment status and educational background.

Mapping the labour market

Interviews were held with employers in a range of employment sectors (retail, finance, catering, manufacturing, employment services) and with individuals and agencies dealing with employment and training (e.g. Learning Partnership West, WESTEC, Bristol City Council, Employment Service, locally-based projects and career-teachers). These interviews highlighted *the importance of locality* in determining opportunities.

It is suggested that the 'Bristol labour market' is better conceptualised as three interlocking sets of labour markets with different spatial configurations:

1. locally based labour markets offering mainly unskilled or semi-skilled work advertised through organisations or local job centres.
2. a city-wide labour market for skilled manual work and service-work typically requiring lower-level qualifications.
3. a nationally based graduate and professional labour market.

Movement between these labour markets is possible but limited. In particular, those with minimal assets or qualifications tend to get trapped within their localities. This may be partly a matter of discrimination (if people come from stigmatised 'post-code' areas such as St Pauls, an inner-city area of ethnic diversity with an established Afro-Caribbbean community, or Southmead or Hartcliffe, areas of white working-class deprivation) but is quite largely a matter of choice. Both employers and agencies report the reluctance of people in the south half of Bristol to cross the city to take the many jobs in retail on offer in Cribbs Causeway in flourishing North Bristol. People prefer to look for employment close to where they live, in view of the cost, effort and time involved in travel to work.

Given the reluctance of organisations to locate themselves in 'problem' areas, this has key consequences for some of the young adults resident in Zones A and C who find it hard to break out of the trap of unemployment or dead-end, insecure jobs. For example, Steve grew up and was educated in a very deprived area. He truanted from school, started taking drugs including heroin 'just to be part of a group', lived in a squat and was drawn into criminal activities, culminating in a spell in jail. At 30 he still lives with his parents in the same area. Since leaving school with 3 CSEs at 16 he has drifted between training schemes (building, driving), labouring and driving jobs, redundancies and unemployment. Steve blames the corrosive drug culture which has developed in this area on the lack of activities for young people. It is significant that while he wants to get his own housing, he wishes to continue to live in the locality.

Marcuse and van Kempen characterise such spatial traps as 'walls' within which

> Life can be lived in its totality: places of residence, of work, of recreation, of socialization are increasingly available within the walls themselves, whether it be the citadel, the edge city or the excluded ghetto. The quarters of the city become *totalized*. Everyday life can reasonably be conducted within the quarter itself. (2000: 250)

The interviews with young adults confirm the importance of locality in their lives and the survey was designed to explore this further.

Another key theme from employer and agency interviews is *the mystique of skill*. Agencies in particular, and employers to a lesser extent impute unemployment and employment failure to individuals' lack of necessary skills. The role of trainers and government-sponsored programmes such as the New Deal is, in part at least, to impart these 'necessary' skills. When asked what skills they sought in their employees, recruiters were likely to mention IT skills and customer service skills. But as far as was discernible these 'skills' were quite vaguely defined and low-level. For example one agency spoke of the need to equip people with the skills for retail work – handling relations with people, dealing with customers, working in a team. It is hard to escape the conclusion that these vaunted skills are more to do with 'social acceptability' than with technical expertise of any kind. Indeed, the kind of skills repeatedly mentioned were interpersonal skills, customer service skills, personnel management and presentation rather than vocational or academic qualifications. One agency representative put it concisely: 'Employers are far more interested in attitudes and aspirations than in qualifications.' Interviews with the young adults in Phase 3 suggest that many of them share this concern with 'people skills', team-work and motivation. 'Getting on with people' is seen by many as crucial for success in the 'new economy'.

We suggest that to work successfully in the service economy, young men and women from manual backgrounds must learn to act at home within a middle-class *habitus*. However, some of our young people looked with some scepticism on the mystique of these rather ambiguously definable skills:

> In the kind of world we are living in they are always asking you to be more broadly skilled, yet you have to be specialized in something otherwise you've got nothing to offer. (Tim, 20, engineering apprentice)

I ended up in this YTS thing right and like, it was like a local skills centre
and what it was was just basically somewhere for like adolescent kids just
to hang around all day and not do anything like, you know what I mean.

(Jack, 31, call centre)

Jack was something of a veteran of courses and schemes, which he views
with scepticism as basically being there to 'massage the jobless figures':

I remember one, one time, there was like older fellas there that had been
like made redundant and they had like you know, actually had trades, and
like electricians and bricklayers and shit like that and there was a really
patronising girl, she was going 'Right I want you all to market an imagi-
nary product.' So we had to sit there with pens – have you seen 'The
League of Gentlemen?' Pauline, she goes 'have you got any pens!' ... it
was a bit like that 'Morning, job seekers'! ... It's not even marketing or
whatever, it's just like an exercise, it's like the equivalent of, you know, in
prisons they used to say 'could you shift that load of rocks from this part
of the room over to that part of the room'.

This is confirmed by the stress on discipline which emerged from some of
the employer interviews. One employer described his ideal employee as
'somebody who will get on and do what I tell them'. This is seen by some
recruiters as a problem in the employment of young adults, especially the
younger age group. The ideal employee, presentable, disciplined, good at
charming customers is seen to be in conflict with *hedonistic youth cultures*.
Employers typically stated that younger workers were better in respect of IT
skills, team work and problem solving. A problem however was the rowdy
drinking 'work-hard, play-hard' culture typical of young people especially
those working in call centres, computing and financial organisations. A personnel manager from a building society spoke of the appeal of her organisation's location in the city centre, as the young call-centre workers could go
straight out after work to Bristol's thriving bar and club culture. Indeed,
there is evidence that some well-qualified YAs from middle-class backgrounds are happy to spend some time in unskilled employment to earn
money to participate in 'party culture' or to go travelling around the globe.
Matthew (23), a wine-buyer and website manager who works very hard and
is ambitious describes himself as having 'matured massively' since leaving
school but adds 'although if you'd seen my antics on Sunday night you
might not agree'. Friends and friendship cultures were certainly very important to many of our interviewees, while some looking back on the earlier
phase of their life regretted that partying had consumed too much of their
energy at school or university:

I would have liked to have gone to uni, I'd like to have studied something
really specific and been really good at it. I would liked to have done tourism,

travel and tourism. I wouldn't have danced on the table and made a fool of myself so many times, you know, stupid things like that.

(Diane, 26, shop assistant)

Young adults and the experience of work

However, while there was some evidence of this trend a strong theme to emerge from our primary YA interviews is the inverse. Many YAs expressed a high level of career-orientation. There was little sign of a diminished work ethic, as suggested by Bauman (1998). Most of these YAs remained remarkably work-centred with many suggesting that getting their careers established was currently the most important thing in their life:

From the age of 13 I've always focused on my career 'cos I believe that's a strong area for me and especially being brought up in the hairdressing industry I really want to dedicate my life to that. (Dan, 22, hairdresser)

Basically since I started back to work, my life has just gone up since then. From just doing temporary part-time jobs, I've not been able to do anything full-time, but now it's just looking up – it's just great at the moment to be honest with you. Yes, it's really good. … If I lost my job I don't know what I'd do. (Karen, 28, single-parent, administrative assistant)

Well my work's quite important to me at the moment, not just for the work aspect of it but erm I've got quite a good social life at (store). I'm in the softball team – so we had 'Oscars Night' last night, down the pub where we had nominations and awards ceremony so that was really good … I hope to be with (store) for quite a considerable amount of years and hopefully climbing the ladder … Work is my only main priority.

(Diane, 26, shop assistant)

As the last quotations show, ambition as well as work commitment is marked among many YAs, even those who are not in high-status professional occupations. Some had managerial or entrepreneurial aspirations:

I would love to be my own boss, have my own company, doing something. (Karen, admin assistant)

I'd quite like to run my own company when I'm a bit older. So I guess what I thought was this – in my 30s I'd get as much experience as I could together working with other people and then in my 40s I'd think about setting up my own business. I think the teaching has made me realise I can't work for other people, long-term, I'm too bolshy and especially management, you know I can't, I find it really hard to be told what to do and when to do it. So I think if I ran my own company although it would be hard work and all sorts of risks involved then I'd have that control. And I am a bit of a control freak anyway. These are all inherited things from my father. So I guess that's my life plan.

(Jayne, 31, MA student, ex-teacher)

At the moment it's my degree (in Business Studies) and then following that it's my erm job or career if you like it ... I don't know definitely what I am going to try and do but I'm aiming for some kind of management role, probably in training or education – along the lines of that. But something that's challenging and not repetitive and comes with a lot of responsibility and new things to deal with. 'Cos the thought of like doing the same thing. ... I haven't got any main worries about anything else, just kind of building up useful contacts and such. (Annie, 26, trainer)

Annie is Indian and typifies a number of young South Asian women we have interviewed who are determined to develop a career and achieve independence, rejecting what is seen as the more desirable life trajectory of early marriage and family formation within their communities.

Even those who were drifting through unemployment or whose work histories had suffered from drug use seemed to have an aim of sorting themselves out and eventually finding stable employment. Thus Steve, whose disrupted employment history and delayed transition into independence was described above, is currently on a Community Development scheme learning plastering and has aspirations to drive an articulated lorry.

The major exceptions to this high priority given to jobs and career were expressed by young mothers. Jessie 30, has a degree and her parents are professionals, but she has never settled into any kind of career and her current priority is her two-year-old daughter. She describes herself and her partner 'as not very ambitious':

At the moment (daughter) is the most important thing, we've just finished doing up the house ... You know, I think me and (partner) feel that work is something you do just because. ... I more think about the pleasure side of life when I think about the future. I do think about work when I think about the challenges and the different things with different people I'll be meeting and stuff, but I think at the moment because it's just me and (partner) and (daughter) and the friends that I've got, it's hard for me to visualise it at the moment.

From a very different background, Tahira, a 23-year-old Pakistani, whose father was a market trader and mother a housewife states her current priority as:

My child and then my new child that's going to come, erm that is the main thing at the moment, I'm just basically living round that really. Work is important also obviously because the money comes in but I can't work full time because of my baby and then I'm having another baby. Most probably I won't be working after I have my second baby, but as I only work on Sunday anyway I don't think that would affect, you know, me bringing up the children, so that's the main thing for me.

Yet Jessie, who describes herself as being a 'family mother' and the 'pivot' in her family of origin and who seems happy with a domestic role, nevertheless displays an element of apology for her lack of work-orientation, as the above excerpt shows. And Tahira, who has trained as a beautician and hairdresser, anticipates working when the children are grown because her husband's earnings as a post office worker are not very large:

> After the bills have been paid, the rent and everything, there's not a lot left – and that's the main reason I think I would work – but I don't want to work somewhere like just for the money, it has to be where you enjoy or like doing the work as well.

While family circumstances alter and with them priorities (see Procter and Padfield, 1998), there is little evidence among our respondents of any general diminished attachment to career development, jobs or earning. Rather, we discern an intelligent endeavour to secure a reasonable 'work–life balance' with attention given to career development, and to family establishments and to a 'good' leisure life of friendship and fun. And as has always been the case, a mix of financial considerations and self-fulfilment are displayed in the YAs' discourse on working. Indeed, it may be possible to argue that in a climate that emphasises individualistic achievement work will become more not less important as a source of self-identity (see Bradley, 1999). Lavalette (1998) links this to a bourgeois ideological stress on work which he argues has led to an increase in schoolchildren engaging in part-time work, even among those from affluent backgrounds. Parents see this as equipping their children for successful labour market futures and there is certainly evidence of this in our interviewees' narratives.

This also highlights the *crucial influence of parents* on their children's employment aspirations, choices and behaviours. We asked our YA interviewees who had been the strongest influences in their lives: mothers and fathers were by far the commonly mentioned followed by other family members (siblings, grandparents, uncles). Asked who had been particularly important as an example or role model, 15 per cent of our 1100 survey respondents named mother or father, again the most popular choice. This confirms the findings of Metcalf (1997) that parents are the main influence on young people's career choices.

The influences of family are not necessarily benign. Some YAs described how their schooling and adolescence had been adversely affected by family breakup, divorce and so on and a few had 'run away from home' in their late teens because of conflict with parents. For most, however, the family influences were positive. Family members, especially parents are central in equipping YAs with various forms of economic, cultural and social capital. For example, Jez is a young dot.com entrepreneur. At 25 he designs and manages websites. He describes the crucial influence of his father:

> My dad worked for a bank, senior bank manager in the city, affluent housing, big houses and stuff ... So I've always had a strong business back-ing, or almost the knowledge I get from my father to be able to help me out in certain business situations. Because even though the internet, web business place is brand new, a lot of the old business stuff still exists – you've still got to manage your cash flow, deal with employees correctly and that background helps you know, without a doubt ... My dad's good, he can always check over a proposal, he's always been a strong supporter of that.

Jez's father now owns a hotel where Jez has use of a room – and feels that the good schooling he had has been also crucial in developing a network of clients and influences in the city.

Karen also has received family help and assistance of various types . She comes from a business family – both her parents are property-owners – and described herself as having 'gone off the rails slightly' when her parents split up in her mid teens. A single parent, she held a variety of temporary and part-time jobs before the New Deal scheme helped her into her present employment. Among these were jobs provided by her family – cleaning her mother's large house, looking after her mother's foster-child for six months when her mother was hospitalised, doing administrative work for her father and for her grandfather (an accountant). When she had her son, her mother helped with childcare and she had also spent some time living back at home before finding her current flat. Now she is working full-time, her son goes to stay with his father's mother every weekend and if a special demand on her time comes up her mother helps look after him. Her brother is also a single parent and they spend a lot of time jointly with their two children, while her stepfather has given her help and advice with the part-time BTEC she is doing. So Karen is embedded in a complex network of family support.

Similarly Jayne's father has helped her to buy a house and car and provides regular financial aid, while her mother works for a retailer 'so she's always buying us little bits and pieces for the house and things like that, through her job, which is nice'.

Clearly the support of parents embraces values and aspirations, as well as financial help and backing. Dan was helped into his hairdressing career by his father who owned a salon and employed him there as a teenager:

> He's been a major part of my life, I socialised a lot with him. We had the same kind of interests, we played pool together, snooker together. He was

a person not only my father but I looked up at as like 'that's who I want to be' – kind of idolised him really, want to follow his footsteps ... He was the major, major person to back me and influence me and to take me there and he did financially back me as well – cos who else was there?

As we saw earlier, Jayne believed she had inherited from her father the traits she saw as shaping her work history.

Changing trajectories

Some of the examples discussed so far should give an indication of how 'the long transition' (Hollands, 1990) has affected youth transitions. The discussion has indicated how important work and career were to many of the YAs as part of a trajectory of self-development. Yet few of the 50 had actually achieved settlement into what looked like a 'career for life'. One exception was Joe (22) who works for a coffee-house chain and is now manager of his branch, with aspirations to climb up the management hierarchy: it is perhaps instructive that Joe, who is of mixed ethnic origin but who identifies as Afro-Caribbean, was brought up in care and has no family support whatsoever. But in the majority of cases the young adults, whether doing relatively well or badly, seemed a long way off reaching any final employment destination.

Broadly speaking we can divide our YAs into two groups of fairly equal size: *shifters* and *stickers*. *Shifters* have characteristically moved between many jobs and employers, often of very different types, and quite often they have included spells abroad, either working or travelling. *Stickers* have found a job which suits them and have worked within it fairly steadily. However, some stickers do not see the occupation they are currently in as where they will ultimately end up and some may consider an abrupt change, as in the case of Jayne abandoning her teaching career to train for media work, or Anita, a 29-year-old Gujarati woman, who has risen rapidly as a management consultant but felt the time had come to make a switch into academic work. Thus there is a smaller group whom we label *switchers*. Conversely, some who have started out as shifters may make a decision that the time has come to settle down. Two such are Diane and Karen, whose cases were discussed above. Perhaps some 15 per cent of young adults in our study fall into this fourth group of *settlers*.

To the extent that few of the YAs have reached that moment of 'settling down' it is predictable that many of them remain at least partially dependent on their parents, for financial or other support, especially at times of movement between jobs. In this way it seems likely that, despite the constant talk of the break-down or 'end' of the family (for example, Beck, 1992, Pakulski and Waters, 1996), recent processes of economic change may actually serve to strengthen family ties and interdependence – and that this occurs at all levels of the class hierarchy.

Conclusion

Our initial findings, then, point to a complex picture of young adults' adaptations to labour market change. Young people's aspirations and hopes are not perhaps markedly different from previous generations (good job, marriage, nice house and car) but they may have to be mobile and flexible to achieve them. There is no convincing evidence of decreased work-orientation: many young people are ambitious and employ a range of tactics and assets to find their way into opportunities. Patterns of shifting, sticking, switching or settling were evident in the Phase 1 interviews and were con-firmed by the survey and follow-up interviews.

The research supports the notion that lengthened transitions will mean a delay in the transition to adult independence. But even more crucially, it highlights the extreme importance of parental support and family transmis-sion of economic, cultural and social capital. In 1987, Metcalf reported that 8 per cent of young people from semi-skilled and unskilled families and 16 per cent of those from skilled manual and junior non-manual went into HE as opposed to 39 per cent from managerial and professional families. It appears highly unlikely that this will have changed. The implication of this is that existing class divisions are likely to be strengthened, rather than eroded: class relations are closely linked to locality and our data from all three phases strongly confirm the important impact of locality on young people's lifestyles.

Notes

1. ESRC Grant no R000238215. Research team: Steve Fenton, Harriet Bradley, Jackie West, Will Guy and Ranji Devadason. Additional Phase 1 interviewing by Matthew Cole, Judy Kidger and Hugh Ortega Breton.
2. The one exception was the study of long-term employment (e.g. Coffield *et al.*, 1986, Hutson and Jenkins, 1989). A recent counter-example is the very interesting work on young adult women by Procter and Padfield (1998).
3. Recent work on the graduate labour market by Kate Purcell at the University of the West of England is rectifying this trend.

References

Allatt, P. and Dixon, C. (2001) ' "Learning to labour": how 17-year old A-level students manage part-time jobs, full-time study and other forms of work in times of rapid social change'. ESRC Youth Citizenship and Social Change, Newsletter 4.

Ashton, D. and Lowe, G. (1994) *Making their Way*, Milton Keynes: Open University Press.

Ashton, D. and Field, D. (1976) *Young Workers*, London: Hutchinson.

Bradley, H. (1999) *Gender and Power in the Workplace*, London: Macmillan.

Bauman, Z. (1998) *Work, Consumerism and the New Poor*, Milton Keynes: Open University Press.

Beck, U. (1992) *Risk Society*, London: Sage.

Coffield, F., Borrill, C. and Marshall, S. (1986) *Living at the Margins*, Milton Keynes: Open University Press.

Coles, R. (2000) Paper presented at Youth Research 2000 conference, Keele University, September 2000.

Furlong, A. and Cartmel, F. (1997) *Young People and Social Change*, Milton Keynes: Open University Press.

Hollands, R. (1990) *The Long Transition*, London: Macmillan.

Hutson, S. and Jenkins, R. (1989) *Taking the Strain*, Milton Keynes: Open University Press.

Jagger, N. and Huws, U. (2001) *Where the Butterfly Alights: the Global Location of E work*, London: IES.

Jones, G. (1995) *Leaving Home*, Buckingham: Open University Press.

Lavalette, M. (1998) 'Child labour: historical, legislative and policy context', in B. Pettitt (ed.) *Children and Work in the UK*, London: Child Poverty Action Group.

McDowell, L. (2002) 'Young men leaving school: White working class masculinity', York: Joseph Rowndnee Foundation/National Youth Agency.

Marcuse, P. and van Kempen, R. (2000) *Globalizing Cities: A New Spatial Order*, Oxford: Blackwell.

Metcalf, H. (1997) *Class and Higher Education: The Participation of Young People from Lower Social Classes*, London: PSI.

Pakulski, J. and Waters, M. (1996) *The Death of Class*, London: Sage.

Procter, I. and Padfield, M. (1998) *Young Adult Women, Work and the Family*, London: Mansell.

Roberts, K. (1995) *Youth and Employment in Modern Britain*, Oxford: Oxford University Press.

Wallace, C. and Kovatcheva, S. (1998) *Youth in Society*, London: Macmillan.

Index